Patricians and Emperors

Patricians and Emperors

The Last Rulers of the Western Roman Empire

Ian Hughes

Pen & Sword
MILITARY

First published in Great Britain in 2015 by
Pen & Sword Military
an imprint of
Pen & Sword Books Ltd
47 Church Street
Barnsley
South Yorkshire
S70 2AS

ISBN 978 1 84884 412 4

Typeset in Ehrhardt by
Mac Style Ltd, Bridlington, East Yorkshire
Printed and bound in the UK by CPI Group (UK) Ltd,
Croydon, CRO 4YY

Pen & Sword Books Ltd incorporates the imprints of Pen & Sword
Archaeology, Atlas, Aviation, Battleground, Discovery, Family History,
History, Maritime, Military, Naval, Politics, Railways, Select, Transport,
True Crime, and Fiction, Frontline Books, Leo Cooper, Praetorian Press,
Seaforth Publishing and Wharncliffe.

For a complete list of Pen & Sword titles please contact

PEN & SWORD BOOKS LIMITED
47 Church Street, Barnsley, South Yorkshire, S70 2AS, England
E-mail: enquiries@pen-and-sword.co.uk
Website: www.pen-and-sword.co.uk

Contents

Dedication   vii
Acknowledgements   viii
List of Maps   x
List of Plates   xi
Introduction   xiii

Part One: Prelude   1

Chapter 1   The Roman Empire, 395–455   3

Chapter 2   The Western Army, 454   14

Part Two: Ricimer   37

Chapter 3   A Brief Prelude: Petronius Maximus – 17 March 455–22/31
                   May 455   39

Chapter 4   Eparchius Avitus – 9 July/5 August 455–October 456/
                   February 457   49

Chapter 5   Majorian – 1 April 457–August 461   65

Chapter 6   Majorian: Apotheosis – 458   73

Chapter 7   Majorian: The Fall   85

Chapter 8   Libius Severus – 19 November 461–15 August/post 25
                   September 465   97

Chapter 9   Anthemius: Hope Renewed – 12 April 467–11 July 472   116

Chapter 10   The African Campaign   125

Chapter 11   Anthemius: Disintegration And Civil War   138

Chapter 12   Olybrius – April/May 472–22 October/2 November 472   154

Part Three: Dissolution of the Empire – Gundobad and Orestes   163

Chapter 13   Glycerius – 3 March 473–June 474   165

Chapter 14   Julius Nepos – June 474–28 August 475   174

Chapter 15   Romulus Augustulus – 31 October 475–4 September 476   187

Part Four: The End – Odovacer, Julius Nepos And Syagrius   195

Chapter 16   Odovacer, Julius Nepos and Syagrius   197

Chapter 17   Conclusion   218

Outline Chronology   229
Notes and References   235
Bibliography   263
Index   271

Dedication

Firstly, to all of the family and friends who have supported me through a very difficult time in my life. The phrase cannot do full justice to my feelings, but all I can say is 'Thank you all very much'.

Secondly, but by no means least, I would like to thank the dedicated and hardworking staff at Barnsley General Hospital under the urologist Dr Kate Lynton, and at Sheffield Hallamshire Teaching Hospital under the consultant urological surgeon, Mr David Yates. Without their care and attention it is likely that this would have been my last book – if it had been finished.

It is interesting to note that during my stay in hospital a nurse by the name of Grace stated that with my glasses on I "looked intelligent". Thankfully, she didn't tell me what I looked like with them off.

Acknowledgements*

For the fifth time (but not the last!), I must express my gratitude to Philip Sidnell for keeping faith with a relatively unknown author. Hopefully, the fact that this is my fifth book means that I am no longer as unknown as I was. As usual, I would like to thank Adrian Goldsworthy and Philip Matyszak for reading excerpted chapters from the book, despite the subject being outside their comfort zone. Finally, as with *Aetius*, I would like to express my extreme gratitude to Perry Gray for not only agreeing to read large sections of the manuscript but for taking the time to discuss significant points throughout the process. As usual, the comments, criticisms and corrections of the above have been a valuable asset in the writing process. However, it should not be taken for granted that they agree with all that is written here, and for any mistakes which remain I am solely responsible.

For helping me to secure otherwise impossible-to-acquire books, I would once again like to thank the staff at Thurnscoe Branch Library, Barnsley, and especially Andrea World of the Inter-Library Loans Department of Barnsley Libraries. I am also extremely grateful to Jason Sivertsen for his help in finding some of the more obscure references in the book. Without their help this book would have been far shorter and not as comprehensive.

I would very much like to thank the following people for kindly allowing me to use their photographs in the plates: Beast Coins (www.beastcoins.com), CNG coins (www.cngcoins.com), and Wildwinds Coins (www.wildwinds.com/coins). Given that for the period in question there is a limited amount of evidence that can be used in the plates section – hence the overwhelming reliance on surviving coinage – their generosity is very, very much appreciated.

For their patience and for permission to use photographs from their extensive and valuable libraries I would like to thank Professor Manfred Clauss of ILS and http://www.manfredclauss.de/, and Dr Andreas Faßbender and Professor Manfred G. Schmidt of CIL.

As with my first four books, this tome would not have been the same without the contribution of the members of both www.romanarmytalk.com/rat and www.unrv.com.forum. They have yet again been exceptionally patient, especially with regards to questions about the availability of photographs.

It goes without saying that my utmost gratitude goes to the individuals and institutions that have made available the ever-growing corpus of source material

---

* Please also see the 'Dedication' at the front of the book.

available on the internet. As with my previous books, I will refrain from mentioning individuals by name, since a look at the bibliography will show that it would need a separate book to list all of the people involved, so to single individuals out for special praise would be unfair. To all of these people, once again, my heartfelt thanks.

At the top of my list are still the two people who have made me smile and kept my feet on the ground and my nose to the grindstone – even through recent health scares: Joanna and Owen. Joanna remains in need of praise for her endurance and patience in reading through another book, this time about 'yet more blokes from ancient Rome'. For her endless patience and understanding, I remain forever in her debt.

To my son, Owen: thank you for your patience, my friend. Thankfully, I'm balancing the work/play aspects of my life much better now. However, you've had your revenge for the past few years by choosing to support Rotherham United rather than Burnley. How will I cope with the embarrassment?

List of Maps

Map 1   The Roman Empire on the Death of Theodosius, AD 395   xiii
Map 2   The West c. 455   7
Map 3   The Western Army according to the *Notitia Dignitatum* c. 420
          (after Jones)   21
Map 4   The Vandal Settlements   26
Map 5   The Balkans   30
Map 6   The *fabricae* as attested in the *Notitia Dignitatum*, c. 454   35
Map 7   The West during the reign of Avitus   50
Map 8   The West during the early reign of Majorian   66
Map 9   Assumed Barbarian expansion during the early reign of Majorian   74
Map 10   Majorian's recovery of the West   79
Map 11   The Vandalic War, including the campaign of Marcellinus   86
Map 12   Vandal expansion in Africa and the fall of Majorian   92
Map 13   The division of the West   98
Map 14   The deaths of Aegidius and Severus   112
Map 15   The early reign of Anthemius, including Marcellinus' possible
          proposed campaign   117
Map 16   The African Campaign of 468   126
Map 17   The Civil War and Barbarian expansion   139
Map 18   The reign of Glycerius   166
Map 19   The reign of Julius Nepos and Gothic expansion   175
Map 20   The Empire in 475   182
Map 21   The Empire after the reign of Romulus Augustulus   189
Map 22   Odovacer's Empire at its greatest extent (c. 486)   206
Map 23   The Evacuation of Noricum   209
Map 24   The East   210
Map 25   Theoderic's invasion of Italy   213

List of Plates

Plate 01   Coin of Petronius Maximus, © CNG

Plate 02   Tremissis of Avitus, © CNG

Plate 03   Coin of Majorian, © CNG

Plate 04   Tremissis of Majorian, © Wildwind coins

Plate 05   Coin of Libius Severus, © CNG

Plate 06   Gothic coin of Libius Severus. This clearly shows that Severus' reign was accepted by the Goths, © CNG

Plate 07   Tremissis of Anthemius, © CNG

Plate 08   Coin of Olybrius, © CNG

Plate 09   Coin of Glycerius, © CNG

Plate 10   Coin of Julius Nepos minted during his reign in Italy, © www.romancoins.com

Plate 11   Coin of Julius Nepos minted by Odovacar in Ravenna after Nepos' exile to Dalmatia. Such evidence proves that Odovacer was a consummate politician, © www.romancoins

Plate 12   Coin of Romulus Augustus, © www.romancoins

Plate 13   Coin of Romulus Augustus, © CNG

Plate 14   Coin of Leo II (Public Domain)

Plate 15   Coin of Ricimer showing disputed inscription (Public Domain)

Plate 16   Solidus minted by Odovacar depicting Zeno. The coin dates to after the death of Nepos, © CNG

Plate 17   A rare coin possibly depicting Ricimer, not an emperor (Public Domain)

Plate 18   Coin of Zeno (Public Domain)

Plate 19   Coin of Euric. The coin clearly demonstrates the influence the Empire had on the 'successor' states, © CNG

Plate 20   Coin of Gaiseric. Such coins are the only depiction of Gaiseric on record, © CNG

Plate 21   The 'Ricimer Plaque', © Professor Manfred Clauss, Epigraphische Datenbank Clauss–Slaby (http://www.manfredclauss.de/)

Plate 22   Bust of the Eastern Emperor Leo I, now in the Louvre (Public Domain)

Plate 23   The Mausoleum of Majorian, Rectory of the Church of San Matteo, Tortona

Plate 24   The Castel dell'Ovo, alleged retirement place of Romulus Augustus

Plate 25   A detail of the Missorium of Aspar, depicting Aspar and his elder son Ardabur

Plate 26   The Tomb of Clovis I in the Basilica of St Denis, Saint Denis, France (Public Domain)

Plate 27   Signet ring of Childeric I. Inscription reads CHILDIRICI REGIS ('belonging to Childeric the king'). Found in his tomb at Tournai, now in the Monnaie de Paris (Public Domain)

Plate 28   Golden Bees with Garnet inserts, found in Childerics tomb at Tournai, now in the Monnaie de Paris (Public Domain)

Plate 29   Statue of Euric at the Plaza de Oriente in Madrid, sculpted in white stone by Juan Porcel

Plate 30   Romulus Augustulus Surrenders to Odovacer, William Zimmerman c. 1890

Introduction

Over the past half-century publications concerning the Fall of the Western Roman Empire have blossomed, with many major historians emerging. Some of these have been connected with the growth of interest in the barbarian kingdoms that emerged after the Fall, but those focusing on the Empire itself have almost all either analysed the processes of the Fall, with the concomitant 'overview' of the period necessary to such studies, or have proposed a new or supported a pre-existing theory concerning the nature of the Fall, often concerned with whether the Fall was due to internal weakness or external invasion.

This book takes a slightly different approach. Rather than being thematic and tracing a variety of different topics in parallel with each other, the attempt has been made to write a coherent chronological narrative of events, in most cases leaving the reader to judge for themselves what the major causes of the collapse were. Only in the Conclusion at the end of the book is there an attempt to analyse the causes of the Fall.

The book covers the period from the death of the *magister militum* (Master of the Troops) Aetius in 454 to the death of Odovacer, the man ruling Italy when the Ostrogoths under Theoderic invaded, in 493. Although only covering a period of around forty years, the contrast between the start and the end of the period could hardly be greater. When Aetius was assassinated by Valentinian III the only territory definitively lost to the Empire was 'Africa', the area surrounding the city of Carthage, surrendered to the Vandals as a result of the Treaty of 442.[1] Given the collapse of the Hunnic Empire in 454, it is possible that Aetius may have considered the possibility of a campaign to regain the lost province of Africa prior to 460 – although this is obviously speculation.

Apart from the loss of Africa, there were several groups of barbarians settled within the Empire under different treaties, although the necessity of providing troops for the Roman army was almost certainly a prerequisite for all but one of these proto-kingdoms. The exception was the Gothic kingdom in Gaul, based around the settlements granted much earlier in the century. The Goths remained largely autonomous and the fact that Aetius had been forced to seek their help, rather than expecting it as a matter of course, when Gaul was invaded by Attila the Hun in 451 implies that the relationship had transformed into one where the Goths saw themselves as the equal of the *magister militum* in Italy, if not of the emperor himself.

In 493, less than forty years later, the situation had changed dramatically. The Goths were fully independent and in control of the whole of South Gaul and a large

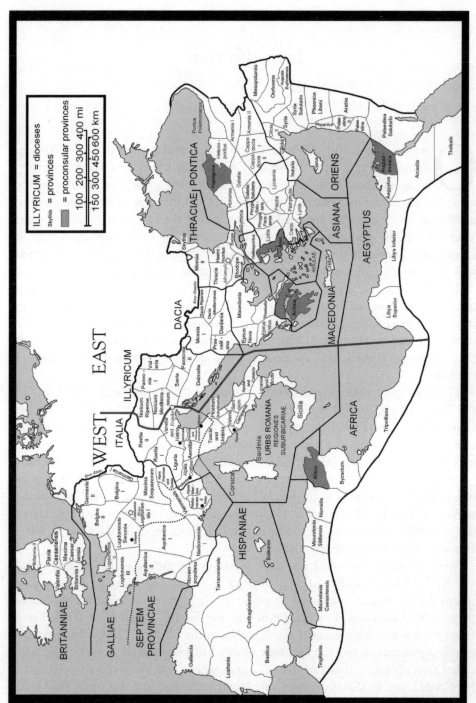

Map 1: The Roman Empire on the Death of Theodosius, AD 395.

part of the Iberian Peninsula; the Vandals ruled all of the North African provinces from Tripolitana to the Straits of Gibraltar, as well as the Balearic Islands, the islands of Sardinia and Corsica, and the western part of Sicily; the Franks were in control of most of northern Gaul; and the Burgundians had set up an independent kingdom between the Franks, the Goths and Italy. The only parts of the West that could in any way be classed as 'imperial' were Italy and Dalmatia, yet even here a barbarian king ruled in the name of the Eastern Emperor. In effect, the Western Empire had disappeared.

This book is, therefore, an attempt to chronicle these events and to clearly describe how the West was transformed in such a short period of time from a viable, seemingly never-ending political entity into an entry in the history books. Many methods of writing the book were considered before that of using the 'loose biographical' approach here adopted, where the reign of each emperor is described in as much detail as possible within sections composed around the leading *magister militum*. This includes an attempt to track events throughout the West, so the reader can assess the condition of the Empire as the years pass.

There are many factors behind this decision. One is that it allowed for a detailed analysis – or as much as is possible – of each emperor's reign without the recourse of having Ricimer, Gundobad or Orestes as the over-riding character. In this way it was hoped that the stereotype of 'Kingmaker' applied to these men would be avoided and that where possible the emperors would emerge from their shadows. It was also hoped that by using a different approach it would be possible for a new analysis of the Last Days of the West. It is up to the reader to decide whether this has been successful.

It should be noted, however, that previous attempts at a similar approach have come in for a little criticism: '*The problem is, biography is an inherently dangerous genre when one doesn't, and indeed can't, know much if anything about one's subjects … if this is the case, how can … anyone write a history of the end of the Roman Empire?*'[2] The question is valid: but only from a modern context. It is obvious that a modern biography, focusing upon the everyday lives and detailed political actions of the people in the book, is impossible. However, to a large degree this is true of any of the individuals who lived in the Ancient World. Even where this is deemed possible, such as with the lives of illustrious individuals such as Alexander the Great or Julius Caesar, it is sometimes overlooked that we are reliant on 'official' or 'unofficial' ancient '(auto-) biographies' that tend to be heavily biased – especially in the case of Caesar – and whose veracity has to be assumed rather than proven.

The truth is that it is indeed impossible to write the definitive biography of any of the last Roman Emperors: the sources are far too meagre and in the majority of cases there is no indication of the personality or manner of rule of the shadowy figures occupying the throne. What has been possible, however, is to describe the events in each emperor's reign in order and so bring a little more detailed context to the manner of their rule. In this way, it has been hoped, re-analysis of their reigns has been made possible, though obviously within strict limits.

A further benefit of this approach is that it has been possible to narrate in great detail the rapid contraction of the Empire and the expansion of its two major opponents – the Goths in Gaul and the Vandals in Africa. In addition, it has also allowed a greater analysis of the deeds of the barbarian kings (or, in the case of the Vandals, one long-lived king), and describe how the main protagonists interacted at any given time.

Given the fragmentary nature of the sources it is easy to believe that such an undertaking is fruitless: after all, much of the evidence is inaccurate, or at least confused – especially with regards to dates – so that accuracy can be seen as all but impossible. However, detailed examination has shown that the dates given rarely clash to any great degree, and even where dates are unspecified it has usually been possible to assign an arbitrary chronology to events based upon actions before and after the event described. In addition, when only a handful of incidents are described for each emperor, it has been found that, surprisingly, chronological exactness has not been a major issue. When only one event is described over a period of three years, most of the time it has not been necessary to worry too much over to which exact year it belongs: it is the context that has mattered rather than the precise date.

The Sources

Histories

The major problem with the surviving evidence is its brevity. Although some histories were written at the time, especially in the East, these only survive in excerpts, which are copies of earlier works, which themselves are epitomes of the original. For example, the 'fragments' of Priscus are taken from many later works. The question then remains as to whether the later writer has used Priscus word for word or whether he has abbreviated, miscopied, or misunderstood his source.

The major Eastern histories that have been used include the fragments of Priscus, Malchus, Eunapius, and Olympiodorus. As noted above, these can be used, but their fragmentary nature, plus the fact that the snippets that survive are obviously out of context, means that they need to be used with care. Unfortunately, many of these fragments cover events that are nowhere else recorded in detail so there is little choice but to use them, whilst all the time remaining wary of their contents.

Another major source is the *Wars* of Procopius. Unlike the others, these books exist almost in their entirety. However, Procopius was a later writer, writing in the mid-sixth century, and his sources for events in the West in the previous century are not always accurate. Furthermore, his political agenda and his focus on the wars against the Ostrogoths in Italy results in his work being very heavily biased and even inaccurate at times. As a result he needs to be used with caution.

In the West the major full-length works of Jordanes, the *Getica* (History of the Goths) and the *Romana* (History of the Romans), cover much of the period. Writing in the mid-sixth century, Jordanes used the (lost) *Gothic History* of Cassiodorus as the foundation for the *Getica*. Sadly, his bias towards the Goths and his desire to distort events to fit with his theme of Gothic superiority, plus the fact that his work contains many errors, means that Jordanes needs to be carefully analysed before being used.

The same is true of the works of Isidore of Seville. His *Historia de regibus Gothorum, Vandalorum et Suevorum* (History of the Kings of the Goths, Vandals and Sueves) and the *Chronica Maiora* (Great Chronicle) are major works, but again the author's bias towards the Goths, effectively asserting that they are the inheritors of the Jews and Romans of the title 'Chosen People of God', results in many major falsehoods, or at least an interpretation of events in a manner that would support his theme. As a consequence, his works – although useful in some ways – need to be approached with extreme care.

Serving under Theoderic I, the first Ostrogothic king of Italy, the Roman Cassiodorus wrote a variety of works. Most of these are either lost, or exist only in fragments. For example, and as noted above, his *Gothic History* survives only in the works of Jordanes, and his *Laudes* (panegyrics) only survive in very fragmentary form. However, his *Chronicle*, which covers the period under analysis, does survive, as does his *Variae Epistolae* or Letters, usually abbreviated simply to *Variae*. These works contain some valuable information, but again care needs to be taken, as they were written during the reign of the Ostrogothic king, Theoderic, and therefore can be biased towards the Goths.

Also worth mention is Paul the Deacon. Writing in the eighth century he composed his *Historia Romana* (History of Rome), a continuation of the *Breviarium* of Eutropius, plus the *Historia Langobardum* (History of the Lombards). Both of these works, as with all of those written for later rulers, have serious flaws, but if used with caution they may help to either fill gaps or corroborate evidence from other sources.

Chronicles

In the West, and unsurprisingly given the context of the collapse of the Empire, our main source of evidence is the many surviving chronicles. Usually Christian in nature, these purport to assign a year to the brief record of the events contained. Sadly, the dates given can easily become confused. For example, it is clear that the Chronicler Hydatius, writing in Spain in the middle of the fifth century, either had to guess at the date of events or simply ascribe them to the year in which he learned of them, as news of events in Italy and the East obviously arrived in Spain at a later date. In addition, the Chronicle, our major source for events in Spain, finishes in 468, leaving us to grasp at the fragments of other sources for a hint of what was passing in the peninsula after this date.

A further problem is the fact that all too often the sources do not overlap, which results both in there being neither corroborative nor contradictory data with which to judge the evidence, but also the appearance of *lacunae*, gaps in our knowledge which are not covered. In these cases it has been necessary to either simply accept the evidence at face value, or, if possible, to adopt a judgemental method based upon perceived chronological factors, confirming whether an event could or could not have happened in the timescale presented.

To add to the confusion, many times where the sources do record the same event they give conflicting evidence, especially with regard to the date. In most of these cases both sources have been recorded and where necessary an analysis is made to decide upon which date is preferable. However, more often than not this is impossible and both dates are simply recorded. Although in many ways an unsatisfactory approach, in those reigns where few sources survive – especially during the reigns of the later emperors – it has made little difference to the overall text and thus has been deemed the only usable method.

The Western Chronicle tradition is mirrored in the East, for example in the works of John Malalas and John of Antioch. The *Chronographia* (Chronicle) of John Malalas, written in the mid-late fifth century, survives in a later abridgement, although a few fragments also survive. Although now seen as of little value, due to the inaccuracies present in parts of the text, it is likely that there are some facts present within the text and so it can be used as a secondary validation for information found elsewhere.

The work of John of Antioch, the *Historia Chronike*, was written in the early-mid sixth century, but has again been lost and now exists only in fragments. As with most of these works its value is unclear, as it has little context in which to place events and so a chronology including the information has to be pieced together by comparison with other, more reliable sources. As a result, and as with the Chronicle of John Malalas, its primary use is as a secondary validation for information found elsewhere. On the other hand, the fragments that remain contain detail not found in other sources, so where possible these have been used in order to build a potentially more detailed picture.

Letters

Another source of information, especially with regards to events in Gaul, is the many letters produced by the ruling classes of the West, including several Popes. As noted above, a selection of those written by Cassiodorus have survived, however the major author of letters in this period is undoubtedly Sidonius Apollinaris. Many of his letters cover events in Gaul during the final days of the West, and act as a vital insight into the minds of the Gallic aristocracy during the withdrawal of the Empire from Gaul. However, as usual care needs to be taken. Sidonius adopts different tones at different times to different people, acting as a 'wind-vane' of the ebb and flow of the Empire in Gaul, as well as demonstrating the intense pressure placed on the Gallic aristocracy in their struggle to adapt to the change in political masters. Therefore it is necessary to analyse each letter in context to provide a framework in which to use the information.

Hagiographies

Apart from a tendency to prefer writing chronicles rather than lengthy Histories, a further change due to the conversion of the Empire to Christianity was the proliferation of Hagiographies: biographies of the lives of Saints, usually following a standard formula in which the subject is attributed many miraculous deeds. Needless to say, some of these stories are a little far-fetched, their purpose being to laud the Saint rather than to write objective history. Nevertheless, they can prove useful to the historian by giving details about the background conditions during which the Saint lived. For example, the *Vita Severinus* (Life of Saint Severinus), written by Eugippius, provides a clue as to the conditions in Noricum in the mid-late fifth century with respect to the dwindling power of the Empire and the emergence of barbarian leaders.

Another major hagiography from the period is the *Vita Epiphanius / Epifanius* (Life of Saint Epiphanius, Bishop of Pavia) composed by Ennodius. Epiphanius was used by emperors as an envoy to barbarian kings, and also appears to have played a major part during the civil war between Ricimer and Anthemius. Yet even here there are problems: in an attempt to establish the importance of his subject, Ennodius inflates the role played by Epiphanius, a factor discussed at the appropriate place in the text. The inherent bias of all of the hagiographies towards their subjects results in all of their narratives being open to at least a modicum of doubt, and as a result, and as usual, these works need to be used with extreme care.

The *Notitia Dignitatum*

When assessing the military capabilities of the Late Empire it is common for ancient historians to refer to the *Notitia Dignitatum* (List of Officials), a list ostensibly giving the name and location of military units throughout the West. Whilst it is true that the document is important for the information it gives, its shortcomings are often glossed over to allow it to be used. With reference to the last decades of the West, the most important of these revolves around the date of its compilation.

The Western section dates to around 420, the Eastern to around 395, but both contain data from before these dates, resulting in the duplication of entries. Alongside this is the fact that no attempt was made in the document to give muster strengths for any of the units listed. As a result, the strengths of the units listed is completely unknown and must be estimated from other evidence, usually archaeological excavation of Late-Roman forts, but whether the forts excavated were typical of those built throughout the Empire is again open to question.

What effect these issues have for the accuracy of the *Notitia* is unknown. Furthermore, the fact that the Western list was compiled so early results in its value for the period from 455 onwards being extremely dubious. By the later date Britain had been lost, large parts of Gaul were under the control of the Goths, and, most importantly, Africa had been lost to the Vandals. The loss of the vital revenues from Africa resulted in the Empire becoming bankrupt, doubtless with a major effect on the recruitment and equipping of the army. As a result, by the death of Aetius in 455 it is certain that the information contained in the *Notitia* is long out of date and therefore of very dubious value. However, due to the fact that there is no comparable source for the late-fifth century, where completely necessary it has been used to give some idea of what resources *may* have been available to the Empire. Obviously, these figures cannot be accepted at face value.

Conclusion

Although the above may give the reader the impression that nothing is certain about the Last Days of the West, this is actually far from the case. The sheer number of sources for events between 454 and 493 (as demonstrated by the Abbreviations listed below) results in the major events being confirmed by a number of independent sources, with only some specific dates being under question. As a result, although there are many inconsistencies and gaps in our knowledge what remains is still enough to fashion a fairly comprehensive chronology and hence to allow for a description of events which is more detailed than most students of the period realize. Whether there is enough evidence and certainty for the account which follows is left to the reader to determine.

Finally, a note should be made concerning one piece of terminology being used. Throughout the text the word 'barbarian' is used to describe several of the tribes that invaded the Empire in the fifth century. The term has fallen out of use in recent times due to the assumed pejorative nature of the word: a quick check in a Thesaurus gives alternatives such as 'uncivilized', 'uncultured' and 'aggressive'. Sadly, no suitable replacement has gained acceptance and so 'barbarian' has been retained. However, it should be noted that it is here used simply as a generic word to describe the various peoples of non-Roman origin inhabiting the Empire but owing little or no loyalty to the emperor. It is always necessary to bear in mind that it is not used in a negative manner, simply as a 'catch-all' when no other word is available.

Abbreviations to the source used in the text

Addit. Ad. Prosp. Haun.	*Additamenta ad Chronicon Prosperi Hauniensis*
Ann. Rav.	*Annals of Ravenna*
Anon. Cusp	*Anonymus Cuspiani*
Anon. Val.	*Anonymus Valesianus*
Auct. Prosp. Haun. ordo prior.	*Auctarium Prosperi Hauniensis ordo Priori*
Auct. Prosp. Haun. ordo post.	*Auctarium Prosperi Hauniensis ordo Posterior*
Auct. Haun. ordo post. marg.	*Auctarium Prosperi Hauniensis ordo Posterior Marginialia*
Aust. Lett.	*Austrasian Letters*
Cand.	Candidus
Cass. *Chron*	Cassiodorus, *Chronicle*
Cass. *Variae*	Cassiodorus, *Variae*
Cedr.	Cedrenus (Kedrenus), *Historiarum Compendium*
Chron. Caes.	*Chronicon Caesaraugusta (The Chronicle of Saragossa)*
Chron. Gall. 511	*Chronica Gallica a. DXI*
Chron. Pasch.	*Chronicon Paschale*
CIL	*Corpus Inscriptionem Latinarum*
CJ/Cod. Iust.	*Codex Iustinianus*
Cod. Th.	*Codex Theodosianus*

Cons. Const.	*Consularia Constantinopolitana*
Cons. Ital	*Consularia Italica*
Corrip.	Corripus
Dam. *Epit. Phot.*	Damascius, *Epitome Photiana* (see Dam. *V. Isid.*)
Dam. *fr.*	Damascius, *fragments*
Dam. *V. Isi.*	Damascius, *Vita Isidori*
Ennod. *Epist.*	Ennodius, *Epistulae*
Ennod. *Pan.*	Ennodius, *Panegyricus Theoderici*
Ennod. *Vit. Epiph.*	Ennodius, *Vita Epiphanius (Epifanius)*
Eugipp. *Vita Sev.*	Eugippius, *Vita Severini*
Eugipp. *Ep. ad Pasc.*	Eugippius, *Epistle ad Paschasius*
Evag./Evag, Schol	Evagrius Scholasticus
Exc. Val.	*Excerpta Valesiana*
Fast. Vind. Prior.	*Fasti Vindobonenses Priores*
Fred. *Chron*	Fredegar scholasticus, *Chronica*
Gel.	Pope Gelasius I, *Epistulae*
Greg. Tur, *de Mir. S. Mart.*	Gregory of Tours, *de Miraculis S. Martini*
Greg. Tur. *HF.*	Gregory of Tours, *Historia Francorum*
Greg. Rom.	Gregory of Rome
Hilarus, *Ep.*	Pope Hilarus, *Epistulae*
Hyd.	Hydatius Lemicensis, *Chronicon*
ILS	*Inscriptiones Latinae Selectae*
Isid. *Hist. Goth.*	Isidore of Seville, *Historia Gothorum*
Joh. Ant. *fr.*	John of Antioch, *fragments*
Joh. Nik.	John of Nikiu, *The Chronicle of John of Nikiu*
Joh. Ruf.	John Rufus, *Plerophories*
Jord. *Get.*	Jordanes, *Getica*
Jord. *Rom.*	Jordanes, *Romana*
Land. Sag.	Landolfus Sagax, *Historia Romana*
Laterc. Imp. ad Iust.	*Laterculus Imperator ad Iustiniani*
Lib. Hist. Franc.	*Liber Historiae Francorum*
Lib. Pont.	*Liber Pontificalis*
Lup. Troy.	*Life of Lupus of Troyes*
Mal. *Chron.*	John Malalas, *Chronographia*
Mar. Av.	Marius Aventicensis, *Chronicle*
Marc. *com.*	Marcellinus *comes*, *Chronicle*
Mich. Syr.	Michael the Syrian, *Chronicle*
Nest. *Baz. Her.*	Nestorius, *The Bazaar of Heracleides*
Nic. Call.	Nicephorus Callistus Xanthopulus, *Historia Ecclesiastica*
Not. Dig.	*Notitia Dignitatum*
Nov. Anth.	Anthemius, *Novellae*
Nov. Maj.	Majorian, *Novellae*
Nov. Sev.	Severus, *Novellae*

Nov. Val.	Valentinian III, *Novellae*
Olymp.	Olympiodorus
Patr. Const.	*Patria Constantinopolitana*
Paul. Diac. *Rom.*	Paulus Diaconis (Paul the Deacon), *Historia Romana*
Paul. Diac. *De Gest. Lang.*	Paulus Diaconis (Paul the Deacon), *Historia Langobardorum*
Paul. Petric.	Paulinus Petricord (Paulinus of Perigueux), *Vita San Martini*
Phot. *Bibl.*	Photius, *Bibliotheca*
PLRE 2	*Prosopography of the Later Roman Empire, Volume 2*
Pol. Silv.	Polemius Silvius, *Laterculus Principum Romanorum*
Prisc.	Priscus, *Fragments*
Proc.	Procopius, *de Bello Gothico*
Prosp. Tiro	Prosper Tiro, *Chronicle*
Pseud. Zach. Rhet.	Pseudo Zacharias Rhetor, *Historia Ecclesiastica*
Sid. Ap. *Carm.*	Sidonius Apollinaris, *Carmina*
Sid Ap. *Ep.*	Sidonius Apollinaris, *Epistulae*
Suid.	Suidas, *Lexicon*
Theod. Lect.	Theodorus Lector, *Epitome Historiae Ecclesiasticae*
Theoph. AM.	Theophanes, *Chronographia* (dates 'Anno Mundi')
Fl. Val. Th.	*Fl. Valila qui et Theodovius*
Veg. *Epit. Rei Mil.*	Publius Flavius Vegetius Renatus, *Epitoma rei militaris*
Vict. Tonn.	Victor Tonnennensis, *Chronicle*
Vict. Vit.	Victor Vitensis, *Historia Persecutionis Africanae Provinciae*
Vit. S. Dan. Styl.	*Vita Daniel Stylites*
Vit. S. Gen.	*Vita Sancta Genovefa*
V. S. Marcelli	*Vita et Conversatio S. Marcelli archimandritae monasterii Acoemetorum*
V. Lup.	*Vita Lupicini*
Zach. *HE.*	Zachariah, *Historia Ecclesiastica*
Zintzen, *Damascii*	Zintzen, *Damascii vitae Isidori reliquiae* (see Bibliography)
Zon.	Zonaras, *Extracts of History*
Zos.	Zosimus, *Historia Nova*

Part One

PRELUDE

Chapter One

The Roman Empire, 395–455[1]

Historical Overview

In 378 the Roman Emperor Valens was defeated and killed by a Gothic army at the Battle of Adrianople. The devastating loss was one of the worst defeats ever suffered by the Roman Empire, with many thousands of troops being killed alongside the emperor. Although the battle has sometimes been seen as having drastic repercussions, including being a major factor in the Fall of the West, many of these interpretations are now seen as exaggerations and so have long since been amended. Valens' replacement, Theodosius I, only concluded a treaty with the Goths in 382, after a campaign lasting several years. Yet in one way it was the Roman 'victory' in the Gothic war of 376–382 that was to have major consequences: although technically defeated, in contrast to the fates of other 'barbarian' tribes 'defeated' by the Empire, the Goths were allowed to settle in the Empire en masse, rather than being divided and scattered across Europe and the Middle East. Furthermore, unlike previous settlements, the Goths were allowed to keep their political leaders, a decision which resulted in the Goths retaining their cohesion as a single entity. As time passed they quickly became a major alien force within the Empire, intent on maintaining their identity and resisting assimilation into the Empire. The consequences for the Empire would be dramatic.

Unlike the defeat at Adrianople, the revolt of Magnus Maximus in 383 and his subsequent defeat and death at the hands of Theodosius in 388 is sometimes overlooked, but the war resulted in a major loss of troops for the West. When combined with the Civil War of 394, during which Theodosius was again forced to invade the Western Empire to defeat Arbogast and Eugenius at the Battle of the Frigidus, it is clear that in the 380s and 390s the Western Empire suffered severe losses in manpower.

Following the death of Theodosius in 395 Honorius, Theodosius' younger son – still a minor – was made Emperor of the West. Stilicho, the husband of Theodosius' adopted daughter Serena, became Honorius' *magister militum* and regent. At the same time Alaric, the leader of a group of Goths in the Balkans, revolted – probably due to the way the Gothic ally troops had been employed by Theodosius during the Battle of the Frigidus in the previous year, during which many Goths had been killed at the first encounter.

In 395 Stilicho campaigned against the rebellious Alaric in Illyricum but political interference from Constantinople resulted in the campaign being a failure. A second campaign in 397, by which time Alaric was in Greece, also ended in failure. Shortly afterwards the army commander in Africa, a man named Gildo, revolted against Stilicho's rule but he was defeated in a very quick campaign.

Whilst this was happening in the West, in the East Alaric accepted an official military position in Illyricum with the Eastern Empire. However, due to internal politics in the East, in 401 Alaric invaded Italy. Fortunately in April 402 he was defeated at the Battle of Pollentia and in June of the same year at the Battle of Verona. Forced out of Italy Alaric appears to have accepted a relatively minor position in Illyricum under the command of Stilicho.

In 405 a large army of Goths under the command of Radagaisus invaded Italy. After the defeat of Radagaisus in 406, Stilicho made the momentous decision to invade those parts of Illyricum held by the East. These were important recruiting grounds for the West and their loss had severely hindered Stilicho's policies. His plans were ruined by the invasion of Gaul by a mixed force of Vandals, Sueves and Alans. Stilicho was forced to abandon the Illyrian campaign. The combination of the failed campaign into Illyricum and the invasion of Gaul was enough to secure Stilicho's downfall. In 408 he was killed by order of the Emperor Honorius.

Stilicho's execution marked the beginning of a period of confusion and revolt, during which in 410 Alaric and his Goths sacked Rome. Fortunately for Honorius, shortly afterwards Alaric died from an unknown illness. At the same time as these events in Italy, the Vandals, Alans, and Sueves took control of large parts of Hispania. The West appeared to be on the point of disintegration. However salvation was at hand. In 411 a man named Constantius was made *magister militum*. Constantius reconquered Gaul and in 418/19 settled the Goths in Aquitaine, but only after they had attacked and decimated the Vandals in Hispania, so restoring large parts of the Iberian Peninsula to Roman rule.

Although often seen as a grave error of judgement, the settlement of the Goths had many precedents: the practice of absorbing 'new human resources from marginal areas was ingrained' from the earliest period of Roman history.[2] The only difference from earlier practice was that in this case the Goths were again allowed to keep their leaders, rather than being dispersed and absorbed into the local population from the start. Constantius will have had no way of knowing the consequences of his actions. At the time, it appeared that Constantius would be able to restore the fortunes of the Western Empire, and, possibly in recognition of his ability, in 421 he was made co-Emperor to Honorius as Constantius III. Sadly for the Empire, he died shortly after his elevation.

In 423 Honorius also died. When Theodosius II, the Emperor in Constantinople, failed to nominate a new emperor for the West, a man named John was proclaimed. He sent a follower called Aetius to the Huns to ask for support. Unfortunately for John, in 425, before Aetius and the Huns could return, John was killed by forces acting on behalf of Valentinian III, the son of Constantius III and the candidate nominated by Theodosius as Western emperor – and yet another minor. When Aetius arrived in Italy with a Hunnic army he quickly came to an agreement with Valentinian and was given the post of *magister militum per Gallias*.

For the next four years Aetius campaigned in Gaul until in 429 he was made *magister equitum praesentalis*. In the same year the Vandals under their King Gaiseric, previously devastated by the Goths, crossed from Hispania to Africa before beginning the long journey towards Carthage. The Roman commander in Africa, a man named Boniface, was at war with Valentinian and so failed to stop their advance. Yet again internal politics had interfered with the smooth running of the Empire. Although Boniface and Valentinian quickly patched up their differences, Boniface was beaten by Gaiseric. Sadly, and despite the fact that a major enemy force was loose in one of the most important areas of the Empire, the West was once more riven by Civil War. In 432 Boniface left Africa and at the Battle of Rimini, in Italy, Boniface defeated Aetius. A short time after, Boniface died of wounds received in the battle and his son-in-law Sebastian took control of Rome. At this point Aetius fled to the Huns, returning in 433 to oust Sebastian and take his place as *magister militum*. From 433 until his death in 454 Aetius retained control of the Western Roman Empire.

The period of Aetius' rule was one of great difficulty for the Empire. For example, the Goths in Gaul 'rebelled' in 436 and constant campaigns were needed to subdue them, as well as the Burgundians, the Franks, the Sueves, and the incessant *bacaudic* revolts in Gaul and Hispania.[3]

Yet the greatest disaster for the West took place in 439. In 435 constant pressure from all quarters had forced Aetius to allow the Vandals to settle in the western areas of North Africa. It was in 439 that Gaiseric broke the treaty and captured Carthage. The loss of the most productive region of the West, both in terms of agriculture and of revenue, was a blow from which the West would never recover. From this point on the West was to teeter on the brink of insolvency, with a detrimental effect on its ability to maintain an effective army and so wage war – as will be seen below.

Despite these major setbacks Aetius was seen at the time – and is still seen – as the last Roman commander who made a serious attempt to maintain the integrity of the Western Empire. Sadly, his efforts would be futile. His downfall began with the accession of Attila as King of the Huns, probably in 439.[4] When Attila had his brother Bleda assassinated in 444 and assumed sole rule, it allowed Attila to increase the pressure on both East and West. At first his attention was focused on the East, which gave Aetius time to continue the necessary campaigns to maintain the unity of the West.

Events in 449/450 changed this. Honoria, sister of Valentinian, was caught having an affair. In desperation, Honoria appealed to Attila for support. At the same time, in August 450 a man named Marcian was crowned as the new Emperor of the East. He immediately renounced all the treaties with the Huns. Attila could now choose whether to attack the East in retribution or accede to Honoria's appeal for help. He chose to confront Aetius in the West.[5] In 451 Attila invaded Gaul, reaching as far as Orleans. Confronted by an alliance coordinated by Aetius, Attila retreated before being defeated at the Battle of the Catalaunian Plains.

Baulked in Gaul, in 452 Attila invaded Italy, where, despite initial success, he was forced to retreat. In the following year he was preparing to attack the East when, after drinking too much at a wedding feast to celebrate another marriage,

Attila died. Ironically the removal of the Empire's greatest foe spelled the doom of Aetius. Believing that Aetius was no longer necessary, in 454 he was assassinated by Valentinian III. In the following year Valentinian was himself killed. The death of Valentinian III was to prove a major watershed for the Western Empire.

The Condition of the Empire

When the Emperor Theodosius died in 395 the Empire still resembled in outline the Empire of earlier centuries.[6] However by the time of Aetius' death in 454 things had changed. Although the East retained some of its vigour and managed to guard the frontiers against attack, the Western Empire was in terminal decline. In Gaul, the Franks had expanded their control far beyond the previous boundaries of the Empire; the Goths were now a settled and separate entity in Aquitaine; there were two allied settlements of Alans, one in the North and one in the South; and the Burgundians had been settled in the area now known as Savoy. In Hispania, although the Vandals had left and gone to Africa, the Sueves had remained and expanded their area of dominance. Furthermore, both Hispania and Gaul were victim to sporadic outbreaks of *bacaudic* revolts (on the nature of these 'revolts', see below).

All of these losses in land resulted in a concomitant fall in revenue, as well as the loss of recruiting grounds and prestige. But the losses in Gaul and Hispania were dwarfed by the loss of Africa. The province of Africa had supplied the city of Rome with its grain since Constantine the Great had ordered the building of Constantinople in the fourth century. The loss of this great source of food to the Vandals was detrimental to the Empire for obvious reasons. Just as importantly, many senators had lost a large proportion of the massive estates that had been the foundation of their wealth and power. Furthermore, the affluence and trade of Africa had also been the source of a large proportion of the tax income for the Western Empire. As a result, the Emperor was under constant pressure to re-establish control of the area by destroying the Vandals with a major military campaign.

A further consequence of the loss of Africa to the Vandals was the fact that in capturing Carthage the Vandals also appeared to have taken control of the Roman fleet. There is some confusion amongst modern historians concerning the nature of this 'fleet', and it is most likely that the majority of the ships stationed at Carthage were merchant ships, although there may have been a few warships in Carthage as a precautionary measure against attack, and as encouragement to traders to maintain their belief in Roman domination of the Mediterranean.[7] With this fleet Gaiseric began to raid neighbouring islands such as Sicily and Sardinia, as well as the mainland of Italy itself. These actions helped disrupt the economic base of the West and further undermined the Emperor's financial situation.

Another aspect sometimes overlooked is the fact that with the Western Mediterranean perceived as being overrun with hostile Vandal ships, the threat of attack meant that many traders would have been unwilling to risk sailing through the troubled waters. As a result, the Emperor lost yet another source of much-needed income in the form of taxes levied on the buying and selling of goods, especially

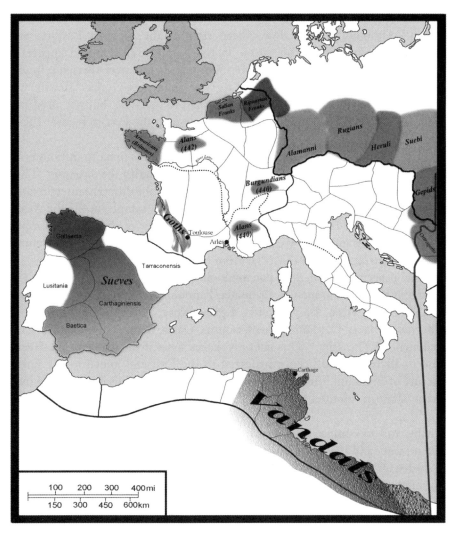

Map 2: The West c.455. Note that all the settlements of the Alans and the Burgundians in Gaul were on Roman terms, and that the locations of the 'barbarians' beyond the frontier are approximate.

the luxury goods imported from the Eastern Empire which could no longer reach Rome without severe danger of attack.

With the loss of Africa and the disruption of local trade routes the Empire quickly found itself economically bankrupt. In fact, in July 444 the Emperor Valentinian III was forced to accept that the Treasury was empty.[8] Despite the imposition of new taxes, for the remainder of its existence the Empire was to remain on the verge of bankruptcy. (For more on the military results of the financial collapse, see Chapter Two.)

For modern historians, allied to these difficulties is the confused status of Illyricum.[9] Although it had always been part of the Western Empire, when Theodosius I had assumed the throne in the East in 379 it would appear that Gratian, the Western Emperor, had given him jurisdiction over Illyricum in order to have a single commander in charge of the war against the Goths. After the war's conclusion part of the diocese had been returned to the West, but not all of it. As a result, Stilicho had been prepared to go to war with the East to recover the lost provinces.[10]

From this point onwards the legal status of Illyricum is open to question, with many different interpretations being put forward to clarify the situation. This is largely due to the confusion in the ancient sources, plus the different interpretations of the actions of the Eastern and Western emperors. For example, in 437 the Western Emperor Valentinian III had married Eudoxia, daughter of the Eastern Emperor Theodosius. At this point the Western diocese of Illyricum may have been returned to Western control, although this is far from certain.[11]

On the other hand, in 448 Polemius Silvius, a Western writer, listed the provinces in Illyricum to include Dalmatia, Pannonia Superior, Pannonia Inferior, Valeria, Prevalis, Misia, Epirus Vetus, Epirus Nova, Noricus Ripensis, Noricus Mediterranea, Savia, Dardania, Haemimontus, Dacia, Scitia, Creta Insula, Achaia, Macedonia and Thessalia.[12] This list only makes sense if the whole of the Western diocese of Illyricum had been transferred to the East and joined to the Eastern Prefecture of Illyricum.[13] In some respects the latter hypothesis is reinforced by the fact that Marcian 'granted lands in Pannonia to Gepids, Huns, Goths, and other tribes.[14]

Finally, and to confuse matters further, in 467 Sidonius Apollinaris lists only Noricum, Gaul and Italy as belonging to the West.[15] Yet this would be impossible if, as in the list above, Noricum had been transferred to the East.

Although certainty is impossible and many different interpretations are available, the most likely reason for the confusion is that the region was extremely important for the defence of both the Eastern and Western Empire: an enemy crossing into the provinces adjacent to the 'Noricums' could easily invade either West or East. As a result, it would appear that the two Empires were in constant communication concerning ownership of these regions and that different accommodations were reached by different emperors at different times, depending upon circumstances. Consequently, the status of Illyricum in general and individual provinces in particular will be analysed in detail whenever such clarity is necessary.

Social Problems

A further difficulty faced by the Empire, and one not usually addressed by historians, is that the limited evidence we have points to the conclusion that around the peripheries of the Empire, especially in the West, many provinces and regions were no longer loyal to the Emperor. In many of these regions local loyalties had asserted themselves, especially as in this period 'leading members of the Roman elite, especially the Senate, developed internal political factions ... and ... more regional solidarities emerged'.[16] In some cases the local political elites were in the process of transforming themselves into Christian bishops who then relied upon their local contacts for the growth of their religious and political status, a development further enhancing the picture of a fragmenting Empire. For these individuals the Church offered a; 'career path: a sphere of responsible and constructive action denied them in the civil service or army' and also a 'chance of promotion in a democratic form'.[17] To many, this was more appealing than serving the emperor, whose loyalties were to his close friends. Furthermore, as time passed the local bishops came to wield ever-increasing power, coordinating the defence of their cities against attack or acting as envoys to barbarian kings, sometimes even being able to influence the actions of these kings to the benefit of their own pastoral flock.[18] Other individuals sought to avoid such earthly distractions by turning to monasticism: during the fifth century there was to be a growth in monasticism, with individuals of both sexes taking vows of chastity and becoming monks or nuns.

Although the division of the Empire can sometimes be overplayed, especially in the first half of the fifth century, it forms a permanent and increasingly important backdrop upon which events were to play themselves out. The only exception to this pattern can be found in Southern Gaul and Italy, where the Roman Senate and the 'Council of the Seven Gauls' were 'gatherings of rich, interrelated, and politically powerful landowners', not 'forums through which genuinely regional views were expressed'.[19] The connections between the senates of Italy and Southern Gaul would have grave political ramifications later in the Empire.[20]

Yet it should be noted that even from the earliest times the Empire itself had fostered a focus on local events: technically, each city was 'an autonomous republic sheltered beneath the vast umbrella of the Roman Empire'.[21] Once the Empire began to fail in its duty to protect these areas, local loyalties once again came to the fore. Possibly the greatest evidence for such parochialism is the fact that during the fifth century the so-called *bacaudic* revolts became almost endemic in Hispania and Gaul. Although sometimes interpreted as local banditry, it is possibly more realistic to see the uprisings as local areas abandoning their loyalty to Rome and taking up arms to defend themselves, both against imperial control and barbarian attack. This would explain why Aetius had to spend so much time organizing campaigns, especially against the peoples of Armorica in Gaul and Tarraconensis in Hispania (see Map 2).

There may have been at least two major factors – not including religion (see below) – that led to such high levels of social unrest. One of these is that the outlying regions of the Empire were becoming more and more open to attack by larger numbers of barbarians. Wracked by internal problems and with the court and the military commanders focusing more on defeating internal rivals than repelling barbarian raids, the army remained largely stationary in Italy, so there was a consequent loss of security for the other inhabitants of the Empire. The need to provide for their own defence would have led many indigenous peoples to dismiss the Empire as irrelevant, and so refuse to pay their taxes to the Emperor. Obviously, this led to intervention from central government, with commanders being sent on a regular basis to put down these 'rebellions'.

A second cause may have been the attitude of the Roman aristocracy to the defence of the Empire. The refusal of wealthy and influential landowners to pay the necessary taxes to fund the army, as well as refusing to supply men as recruits, will almost certainly have left many men from the lower classes wondering why they should fight to serve the interests of men who could not be bothered to help the Empire themselves.[22] In fact, the refusal of the aristocracy to either supply men for the army or to put aside their right not to pay taxes was to be a major factor in the last days of the West.

The 'Barbarians'

The slow division of the West into parochial regions was to help the new settlers on Imperial lands, especially the Goths, Burgundians and Vandals. Due to the fact that the Empire was now having to deal with a large number of 'semi-autonomous' regions, it was easy for the three main barbarian groups to become just another of the large number of factions with which the emperor had to deal. After 453 the Goths and Burgundians became increasingly heavily involved in Roman politics and as early as 455 the Goths would have a hand to play in the crowning of a Roman Emperor.[23] The political involvement of these groups in the last days of the West would have a strong influence in how these peoples came to see themselves, and their absorption of Roman customs and laws would blur the distinction between conquest and peaceful takeover.

Christianity[24]

One of the many assumptions concerning the later Roman Empire is that by the turn of the fifth century the entire Empire was a monolithic Christian structure under the rule of Christian emperors. This is not true. During the period under review both East and West were home to a diverse number of religious groups all proclaiming their own version of Christianity, as well as the last remnants of the so-called pagan religions, including traditional Roman beliefs as well as imports such as Mithraism.

The belief that Christianity was one of the dominant forces in the later Empire is probably correct. Yet even at this early date it was fragmented and bitter rivalries existed between these divisions.[25] In the West the major internal schism was between the Catholics and the Donatists in Africa. The dispute was caused by events during the reign of Diocletian (284–305). Diocletian had instigated a series of persecutions of the Christians, and this was carried out with a special zeal in Africa. Many Christian leaders in Africa opted to 'hand over' religious texts to be destroyed, and some even denounced their own supporters to the authorities: hence the name *Donatists* (those who hand over). After the persecution had finished many Christians in Africa believed that these leaders were no longer suitable to act as bishops or to consecrate others into important Christian posts. The Emperor held a series of inquests into the subject and it was decided that these men remained eligible to serve as bishops. However many Christians continued to oppose the ruling and so the Donatist movement was born. Despite increasingly vindictive attempts by the Emperors to crush the movement it remained strong, and the 'persecution' of Donatists only increased their sense of alienation from Rome. Indeed, one of the major factors that allowed the Vandals to settle in Africa with so little opposition may have been the intense religious rivalry between the Donatists and the Emperor. As a result the Donatists may have initially welcomed the Vandals who, as Arians, were also religiously opposed to the Christianity practised at Rome.

In this period the majority of the barbarians who had become Christian had chosen Arianism as opposed to the Western Empire's 'Catholicism'. In contrast to the Donatists, Arians believed in a relationship between God and Jesus that was different from that of the Catholic Church. As a result Arians were considered to be heretics and their belief was to act as a major dividing force between the settling Germanic kingdoms and the native Roman population. Although Arianism had been strong in the East, supported by no less a person than the Emperor Valens, in the West it had received little support. Unfortunately, many of the barbarian tribes that had invaded the Empire in the late fourth and early fifth centuries had either been converted to Arianism during the reign of Valens or had followed the model of their fellow non-Romans. Their religious isolation was to be a factor in them retaining a strong sense of identity in opposition to their imperial Catholic subjects.

Finally, it should be noted that, although the histories and other sources that survive are dominated by Christian belief, there were large areas of the Western Empire that even at this late date may have remained loyal to the old gods of Rome or to local pagan deities. The religious rifts between Catholic and pagan, Catholic and Donatist, and Catholic and Arian, may only have exacerbated the feeling of disunity and disloyalty towards the Empire felt by many in the West.

The New 'Barbarian Kingdoms'

One of the greatest difficulties facing modern historians is the interpretation of relations between the Empire and the so-called barbarian kingdoms. It is commonly asserted that when these so-called kingdoms were first founded, especially the Goths in 418 and the Vandals in 439, they were instantly autonomous regions ruled under their own kings owing little or no loyalty to Rome. Furthermore, their foundation is seen as being instantly detrimental to the existence of the Western Empire.

Yet a close analysis of the new kingdoms and of the Roman response to their existence implies a much more complicated series of relations. Although it is certain that the barbarian kings were intent upon expanding their influence and power, it should be noted that for most of this period they continued to act largely within the established imperial political and military network. For example, it is almost certain that the early rulers of the Goths in Aquitaine were not intent upon establishing an independent kingdom free of all restraint from Rome, but appear to have focused upon expanding their own power base and were hopeful of gaining acceptance and a military position within the Roman hierarchy. This implies that although the Goths were not yet fully independent, nor were they fully under control.

The two settlements of Alans and the main settlement of Burgundians within the boundaries of Gaul during the lifetime of Aetius provide a completely different scenario. The Alans had served Aetius for a long period of time and their settlement within Gaul can be interpreted as having two separate functions. One is that they were settled in areas which were sparsely populated, so the Alans could repopulate the depopulated areas. They were also settled where unrest was endemic to act as a police force to quell any incipient *bacaudic* revolts in neighbouring regions before they could get out of control.

In the case of the Burgundians, it is clear that, shortly after they had been decimated by the Huns, Aetius settled them within the Empire in the traditional manner that had been applied to defeated barbarians for centuries. As a consequence, neither the Alans nor the Burgundians can be seen as being barbarian invaders settling within the Empire on their own terms. Previous attempts to make this hypothesis work have ignored the context of their settlement, and instead the evidence has been manipulated to reinforce the erroneous belief that the Roman Empire was overwhelmed by hordes of invading barbarians.

There is one major exception to the cases given above, which may be the model used as a template by historians working towards the 'barbarian invasion' theory: Gaiseric, King of the Vandals. Attempts to interpret his actions are complicated by the fact that there are no surviving Vandal sources which give any indication of his motives and plans – if indeed he had any long-term plans at all. In fact, it is impossible to determine whether Gaiseric was proactive or reactive in his dealings with the Empire. It is possible that Gaiseric too desired an official high-ranking position within the Roman hierarchy, but it is just as likely that Gaiseric was the exception to the rule and that he wanted to expand the sphere of his power as far as possible in opposition to Roman rule.

As a result of the uncertainty, it is possible to hypothesize that in many cases Gaiseric responded simply to local opportunity, a theory which would explain the disjointed policies of the Vandal king between 435 and the death of Aetius in 454. It would also explain many of his actions following the death of Valentinian III in 455, as will be seen below. Unfortunately any interpretations derived from analysis of the existing evidence mostly remain conjecture thanks to the paucity of the sources. As a result there are a large number of explanations possible for his actions, a fact which should be remembered when reading what follows.

The Domination of the Military

Alongside the aforementioned difficulties there is one other factor which needs to be highlighted. When Theodosius I died in 395 both of his sons were minors. In the East direct rule devolved upon the bureaucratic arm of government. In the

West the appointment of Stilicho as *magister militum* and guardian to the young Emperor Honorius set a trend that would never be broken: military commanders would henceforth dominate the West.

After the execution of Stilicho Honorius found himself unable to act on his own. After a hiatus of three years he appointed Constantius as the new *magister militum* (see above). After the deaths of Constantius and Honorius, the coronation of the young Valentinian III meant that once again a minor was the Emperor of the West. A relatively short period of infighting between the various military commanders was followed by the imposition of the rule of Aetius, who came to dominate the West more completely than any of his predecessors.

It is likely that the main motive for Valentinian's execution of Aetius was an attempt to establish himself as the sole ruler in the West without the domination of a *magister militum*.[26] In the event, he was killed before he could be put to the test. As a result, and due to a large number of unforeseen factors, the 'rules' of Stilicho, Constantius, and Aetius had merely set a precedent whereby a dominant *magister militum* would be in a position to control the West, even countermanding orders by the ruling emperor if they felt it to be necessary or desired.

Conclusion

The dominance of Stilicho, Constantius III, and Aetius had served to marginalize the civilian bureaucracy and establish the leading military commander as the de facto leader of the West. Yet the military necessities of the period resulted in high taxation and constant legislation demanding conscription – on which see Chapter Two – in an attempt to bolster the defences of the West. When coupled with constant warfare and the invasions of roving bands of barbarians the net result was a loss of loyalty to the Emperor, a loyalty which was transferred to any local leaders willing to take command – or, in more Romanized areas, to local bishops.

The long rule of Aetius had simply covered the fragility of the Empire. Many of the problems faced by Stilicho and Constantius III had not gone away, they had merely been masked by Aetius' ability as a commander and the hard work put in by his able subordinates. The fact that even during the rule of such a gifted organizer large parts of Gaul, Hispania, and Africa had been lost clearly demonstrates that even if he had continued to live Aetius would have been unable to maintain the unity of the Empire. The financial crisis initiated by the Vandal capture of Africa and the loss of loyalty to Rome in large parts of the West was to come to full fruition only during the rule of Aetius' successors.

Chapter Two

The Western Army, 454

Introduction

T he Late Roman army has recently been the subject of much investigation. Earlier opinions that the Roman army of this period was poor in equipment, training and discipline when compared to its earlier counterparts have been overturned – or at least heavily revised.[1] Yet there does remain one problem. Most analyses are based around Ammianus Marcellinus, the *Notitia Dignitatum*, and Maurice's *Strategikon*.

The *Roman History* of Ammianus is obviously too early to be certain of its application to the mid-fifth century, and although the dating of the *Notitia Dignitatum* has been extended to the 420s, most historians have baulked at the idea of using it to inform their concepts about the armies used either by Aetius or his successors. In a similar manner, the later *Strategikon* has been used to postulate about the armies of the mid-sixth century and in the East, but rarely, if ever, earlier and usually not in the West.

This is understandable. After 420 the armies of the West were poorly documented and were the subject of disruption, attrition and reorganization. By 454 the loss of Britain, of large areas of Gaul, of the majority of Hispania, and of Africa to the Vandals, means that the army as listed in the *Notitia Dignitatum* no longer existed. Furthermore, the substantial differences in the composition of the armies of the fourth century and the armies of the sixth century means that it is impossible to use the *Strategikon* for the fifth century: the date of the changes between the two is unknown and therefore liable to interpretation. To fill the gaps in our knowledge, large amounts of speculation are required.

Yet it is difficult to analyse events from 454 to 480 without an analysis of why the Roman army failed to deal with the barbarian incursions, and it is hard for students of the earlier Empire to understand why the citizens of Italy, who had earlier conquered such a vast Empire, were unable even to hold on to one half of their previous conquests. Yet in reality the seeds for the 'Fall of the West' were sown in the second century BC. Even at this early date the citizens of Rome were becoming unhappy at the prospect of serving in the army. Two of the *Leges Porciae* (Porcian Laws), probably dating to 197 BC and 184 BC, protected Roman citizens serving in the army from 'abuses' and as a result it is clear that Rome was happy for the burden of war to fall on the other Italian peoples.[2] As the Empire expanded the extension of citizen rights to the whole of Italy resulted in the burden of war passing to those peoples nearer the frontier. By the fifth century AD the peoples of Italy had been relieved of the burden of fighting for so many centuries that in many respects they were no longer suited to war.

Army Strength

AHM Jones in his magisterial *The Later Roman Empire, 284–602: A Social, Economic and Administrative Survey* analysed the *Notitia Dignitatum* and arrived at a series of figures for the strength of the Western army c. 420 (Map 3). It is clear that, given the numerical superiority the Romans had over invaders, the West should easily have been able to defeat the barbarians. Yet they failed. What follows is an attempt to piece together from fragmented or non-existent evidence the fate of the armies of the West and of the people that manned them. However it should be noted that attempts to analyse the composition and size of the army and its individual units are hypotheses and should not be taken as fact.

The manpower of the units within the Roman Army is not known. The figure calculated by Jones in the mid-twentieth century has since been heavily revised. For the sake of comprehension both Jones' and later figures are given here:

According to Jones (and Nicasie):

Troop Type	Number of men
Guard units (*scholae* etc.)	500
auxilia palatinae	800
legions (*comitatenses*)	1000
legions (*limitanei*)	3000
limitanei / riparienses	300
cavalry (*limitanei*)	350

According to more recent suggestions:[3]

CAVALRY	Comitatenses (inc. Palatinae)	Limitanei
Scholae	500	
Vexillationes	400–600	
Ala		120–500
Cuneus		200–300
Equites		80–300
INFANTRY		
Auxilium	400–1,200	
Cohors		160–500
Legio	800–1,200	500–1,000
Milites		200–300
Numerus		200–300

These are estimates and modern scholars are continuously revising the figures, based, for example, on the results of archaeological excavations of Late Roman forts.[4] As a result, these numbers should not be accepted as fact but as guidelines. Furthermore, the units' strengths will have been greatly affected by the campaigns fought in the different regions of the Western Empire in the first half of the fifth century. For a greater analysis of these campaigns and their possible effects on the army, see below.

One interesting aspect of the above figures is that Jones' specific numbers have now been adjusted to figures within, in some cases, quite wide boundaries. This implies that unit strengths in different regions of the Empire may have differed from each other. For example, in Gaul the expectation of major campaigns may have resulted in recruits being supplied on a regular basis in order to maintain a viable fighting force, as against Egypt, where troop numbers may have remained low as the army was simply fulfilling policing duties and so did not need regular drafts of recruits.

The army was now separated into several different types. The troops on the frontiers were labelled either *limitanei* (border defence, land) or *riparienses* (border defence, river) troops (both classed as *limitanei* in the tables).[5] These troops had three main functions: to police the borders, to gather intelligence, and to stop small-scale raids.[6] In the interior of the Empire were stationed troops known as *comitatenses* (companions) whose purpose was to deal with intruders who broke through the outer defences, to discourage usurpers from attempts to take the throne, and to act as an internal police force against banditry.

As time passed there grew an intermediate group known as *pseudocomitatenses*, formed from border troops who were promoted to the ranks of the *comitatenses* in order to fill gaps or take part in specific campaigns.[7]

Above these, and theoretically with the emperor himself, was a further tier known as the *palatinae* (palace troops), with their own mini hierarchy.[8] At the top were the elite bodyguard to the emperor, the *scholae palatinae* (schools of the palace); these units acted as informal training bodies for many of the army's senior officers, and below them were the *palatinae* (of the palace), who supplied the emperor's army with the majority of its troops, with the *auxilia palatina* (allied palace troops) ranking above the *legiones palatina* (legionary palace troops).

Finally, there were units whose status is either unclear or whose rank could differ between individual units, such as the *foederati*, *gentiles*, *dediticii*, *tributarii*, and the *laeti*. However, the actual status of the troops at the lower end of the scale is vague. This is mainly because the sources use a wide range of terminology which is applied almost indiscriminately to a variety of units, usually of barbarian origin, and the application of titles need not necessarily follow a set pattern.[9]

The *gentiles* appear to have been composed of tribesmen, either recently settled within the Empire or recruited from tribes still living beyond the frontiers: with the sources available it is impossible to say for certain which of these was more prevalent.[10] Their exact status is unclear but *gentiles* are later listed amongst the *scholae* of Diocletian, and in the *Notitia Dignitatum* they are found in the *scholae* attached to both the Eastern and the Western *magister officiorum*.[11] Units of Sarmatian *gentiles* (*Sarmatarum gentilium*) are also attested as being stationed in Italy.[12] Due to the context, it is possible that they were settled as farmers throughout these regions with individuals then being enrolled in regular units.[13]

The *laeti* may have been different to the *gentiles*. They were formed from barbarians settled within the Empire who were obliged to provide troops for the army in exchange for land. The settlements were not self-governing, being administered either by a Roman military official or by the council of a local city.[14] However, there were units combining the two titles, such as the *laetorum gentilium* stationed in Belgica Secunda, which suggests that any differences between the two may be coincidental and more of a reflection of modern prejudices than of ancient custom or title.

Tributarii and *dediticii* appear to have been obtained from external sources. As their names suggest, it is possible that they were supplied as part of a treaty by tribes who had been defeated by the Romans.[15] However, it is impossible to be certain whether this format applied to all troops with the name, as sometimes this may be a hangover from when a unit was formed rather than later recruiting practice.

The *foederati* cause the greatest confusion to historians. This may be because the same title was given to troops recruited in several different ways. As with the Goths, the name may be given to non-Roman troops serving the emperor as part of a treaty but who were not a part of the regular Roman army and did not serve under Roman officers. However, it may also refer to barbarian troops recruited directly into the army to either fill the ranks of normal Roman units, or instead to form their own, distinct, tribal units within the framework of the army. Furthermore, the name was given to barbarian troops of different tribes who were attracted to serve under one leader, either Roman or barbarian, who was part of the Roman hierarchy. Due to the indeterminate nature of the *foederati* it is impossible to be clear on their nature and their status. As a result, each unit so designated has to be assessed solely using its own history.

There is also the problem of the emergence of the *bucellarii*. These men may have started as *foederati* serving as bodyguards to one specific commander, however they are generally accepted to have begun as troops serving under local magnates rather than under military commanders. Only slowly were they accepted as part of the military hierarchy, serving as bodyguards to Roman generals. In fact, it is possible that Stilicho (395–408) was the first Roman general to have had *bucellarii* serving as a bodyguard.[16] They would become increasingly important during the course of the fifth and sixth centuries.

Command Hierarchy

After Aetius assumed sole control of the army in 433 the command hierarchy of the West becomes a little confusing, in part because modern historians are only familiar with modern, logical, strictly linear military ranks. This was not the case during the Roman era. During Aetius' regime many men were given the title of *magister militum*, and this has been used by some authorities as evidence of political infighting within the top ranks of the army, due to modern conceptions of how military ranking should work. However, it is more likely that Aetius retained personal control of all of the army and gave his supporters the title of *magister militum* in order both to establish their military authority in their respective areas and to reward them with a high political rank within the Empire as a whole.[17]

Below the *magistri* were the *comes* and *duces*. As with the *magistri*, the two titles were not wholly distinct, with one serving above the other. It seems likely that the designations *comes* and *dux* had been given by different emperors depending upon the circumstances surrounding individual appointments. Their use by Aetius and his successors probably followed the early Imperial trends but this cannot be proven.

The above shows that, contrary to the expectations of modern authorities whose experience is dominated by rigid hierarchies and naming conventions, neither troop designation nor the titles of commanders were linked to specific methods of recruitment or use and appear to have been dependent upon the needs or whim of the individual emperor or his *magister*. As a consequence, the changes must be seen as 'organic and progressive, not wholesale or ordered' and any attempt to impose a rigid structure that lasts throughout the course of the later Empire is doomed to failure.[18] Furthermore, it is obvious from a close reading of Ammianus Marcellinus that the higher ranks owed their loyalty solely to the person that appointed them: it should not be taken for granted that a *magister*, *comes* or *dux* would be able to give orders to other commanders theoretically below them in rank. His area of command would need to be specified when he was first appointed.

Recruitment

There were three methods of recruitment in the later Empire: enrolment of volunteers, conscription, and levies from 'barbarians' settled either as prisoners of war or as normal 'Roman' farmers with a duty to provide troops for the army when a levy was demanded.[19]

Earlier laws demonstrate that in the past the Empire had only wanted to recruit troops suitable for service in the army. Anyone found to be below these standards was not allowed to join. By the mid-fifth century it is likely that the majority of these laws had been waived. Military leaders could no longer afford to be picky about the quality of men that they enrolled. Sadly, by this time a career in the army was almost certainly unpopular. One of the main difficulties was that in the extremely uncertain times of the fifth century joining the army could mean a recruit being posted to a province far from his home.[20] This could leave his family unprotected and so many men may have preferred to stay and defend their own homes. Furthermore, there is some evidence for citizens being disillusioned with the government and its heavy taxation, and angry at the behaviour of troops, who may by now have been billeted in citizens' homes in cities. There is even evidence of them siding with invaders in the expectation of better treatment and booty.[21]

In earlier times conscription would be needed to fill the gaps in the ranks only in times of war, but in times of peace emperors had different agendas. When the need for men was not urgent, provinces were allowed to pay a tax – the *aurem tironicum* (gold for recruits) – instead of supplying men. It is possible that as resources dwindled and emperors often found themselves to be short of money, they were tempted to pass a decree calling for conscription simply in order to commute this to the *aurem tironicum* to boost the treasury.[22] In the meantime, they could spend some of the money to hire 'barbarian' mercenaries, who did not need to be trained or equipped by the state, so maintaining the army at a functioning level with less cost.

Whether new troops were conscripts, volunteers or mercenaries, the *duces* were responsible for recruitment and for the assigning of individuals to units.[23] Unfortunately we are not given any details as to how this took place. All that can be accepted is that the system appears to have worked up until the early fifth century.

Training

According to Zosimus, the training and discipline of the army was not as it had been in earlier centuries, and the years of almost constant warfare in many provinces of the West must have ensured that the training of recruits was kept to a minimum in order to ensure their arrival in the front line.[24] Although the poor quality of troops in the Later Empire has long been accepted as fact, analysis of battles – especially those of Argentoratum (Strasbourg) and Adrianople – has resulted in a reappraisal. It is now accepted that, to a large degree, Roman training methods continued into the fourth century: indeed, Ammianus affirms the esprit de corps and the survival of old skills in the *comitatenses*, such as the building of marching camps and permanent forts.[25] When properly led, and when training was combined with strict discipline, the Roman army was still a formidable fighting force.

Supply

At the time of Valentinian I (364–375) the *limitanei* still received the supplies needed for nine months of the year straight from the government. However, for the remaining three months they were paid in gold and had to locate and purchase the supplies themselves.[26] Over the ensuing decades the system of 'self supply' had been extended until by 406 it included virtually all military personnel.[27] In such a situation, it would be easy for the troops to begin taking more than their money was worth. It is hard for military men to pay full price for goods from people they are protecting: instead, they are likely to have expected a discount for any goods bought.

Barbarian Settlements

One final aspect of the fifth century is rarely analysed in detail, largely because historians writing after the event have the benefit of hindsight and realize that the Empire would fall. The Romans did not know this. It is certain that barbarian groups allowed into the Empire were not seen as the threat that they later became. This is due in part to Roman arrogance. In the preceding centuries all of the tribes and political entities that had been conquered by Rome had seen the benefits of inclusion and became members of the Empire: there was no reason why tribes such as the Goths or Franks should be any different. Allowed to settle and have the benefits of Roman rule they would lose their identity amongst the common Roman citizenry. This theory helps to explain why so many German leaders were accepted into service in the army. By serving the Empire they would gradually absorb the benefits and mentality of citizens – as had happened to the Gauls, the Britons and many other belligerent tribes.

Once the above theory has been evaluated it is necessary to trace events between 395 and 454 in order to determine how the financial and military losses suffered by the Empire prior to the assassination of Aetius affected the condition of the army in the different parts of the Empire. In some respects this section repeats information found in Chapter One. This is felt to be necessary in order to avoid having the reader constantly referring back to the previous chapter in order to establish the full nature of events. If necessary, this section should also be read in conjunction with the Chronology.

Britain

The popular image of the nineteenth and most of the twentieth century of tearful relatives saying goodbye to the Roman legions as they left the island for good in AD 408 has long been acknowledged as being in error. Although many troops did indeed cross the Channel to Gaul to support the usurper Constantine III, the majority of the army appears to have remained in situ in the island. The troops who had left for the continent appear to have been either disbanded or, more probably, enrolled in the continental armies to replace losses they had themselves caused.

As military links with the continent diminished, the army changed. Although some historians and archaeologists have been using archaeology in an attempt to establish a specific date for the abandonment of Roman forts in Britain and hence the end of the Romano-British army, this is probably a mistake. Rather than units simply disbanding of their own volition, it is probably better to see them as being slowly transformed from Roman regular troops into local militias as the quality of their training and equipment became degraded. In these circumstances, being billeted in forts makes little sense and it is likely that the forts were abandoned before the army units finally disappeared. Whatever happened, these troops take no further part in the history of the Roman Empire in the West.

Hispania[28]

The case of Hispania can act as a standard model for events elsewhere on the peripheries of the Empire. Events in Hispania are nearly as confused as those in Britain. Although the departure of the Vandals for Africa theoretically left a vacuum which the Romans could easily have filled with spare troops, this does not seem to have happened. Instead the vacuum was filled by the Sueves, who in the sources are shown continually expanding their dominions despite numerous protestations from the Roman government and the odd campaign to push them back into their original territories. What is completely ignored by the sources and hence by most historians is the fate of the army. Although again this is understandable, a brief outline of the campaigns fought in the fifty years prior to the death of Aetius gives clues to the problems faced by the army in Hispania.

Map 3 shows that, in theory, the Spanish army may have contained 10,500 *comitatenses* and 5,500 *limitanei*. On paper these were more than enough to defeat any barbarian army that evaded the forces in Gaul and crossed into Hispania.[29] However there are difficulties with these numbers. Firstly, they are theoretical figures based on modern assumptions concerning the strength of the units involved (see above). Secondly, these figures are the paper-strength of the army. Even if they are an accurate estimation of the full-strength army, it is extremely unlikely that the army in the peninsula was maintained at these levels. It is far more likely that troop numbers were lower, with half- to two-thirds being the maximum.

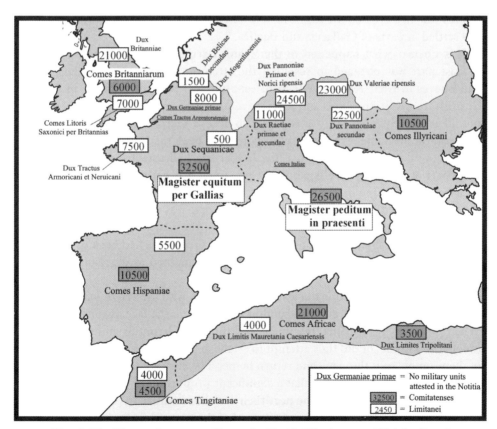

Map 3: The Western Army according to the Notitia Dignitatum c.420 (after Jones)

The reason for this is simple: there was very little for the army in Hispania to do apart from deal with internal security, with the exception of the odd piratical raid from elsewhere in the Mediterranean – especially Mauretania. The net result was probably that the army in Hispania was poorly equipped to deal with invasion: the peaceful conditions will have resulted in equipment made in imperial *fabricae* being retained for more threatened parts of the West. It is almost certain that the Spanish army had less equipment when compared, for example, to the army of Gaul. In a cash-strapped Empire, any means of saving money would be utilized.

Finally, none of the Spanish army, not even the *comitatenses*, would have been kept as a single centralized force in Hispania. They would be scattered in garrisons throughout the peninsula, especially on the southern coasts (to guard against raids) and in important towns in the interior. Given that it appears common for the Romans to garrison towns with pairs of units, and that most units would in theory number c. 500 men, then the theoretical 16,000 men of the Spanish army would be spread around 16 towns, resulting in a fairly widespread distribution. Their dispersion would cause serious difficulties when faced with major external or internal threats.

The problems for Hispania began in 409 when the usurper Constantine III's general in Hispania, a man named Gerontius, rebelled. In order to expand his army and enforce his will in the peninsula Gerontius enlisted the Vandals, Alans and Sueves who had crossed the Rhine in 406. These forces crossed the Pyrenees and in 409 settled in parts of Gallaecia and Baetica.[30]

It is unclear what happened to the Spanish army, but according to Hydatius at least part was engaged in resisting the attempts to settle the Vandals, Alans and Sueves in their respective territories: after two years of fighting, in 411 the Spanish troops 'in the cities and forts surrendered themselves'.[31] It is certain that not all of the Spanish army was happy to accept Gerontius' claim to rule and opposed the settlement. There are likely to have been many casualties during the two years of ensuing strife. Once the barbarians had established themselves, a large part of the army of Hispania that remained was gathered by Gerontius for an attack into Gaul to defeat his benefactor, Constantine III. Although victorious, the army suffered losses in the campaign, but worse was to come. Shortly after his victory Gerontius was attacked by Constantius, the new *magister militum* in the West. Gerontius' Spanish troops 'deserted' and Gerontius fled back to Hispania, where almost immediately the troops who had remained as garrisons mutinied and Gerontius was killed.[32]

What exactly happened is unclear: did the troops who 'deserted' leave the army and go home, or did they simply abandon Gerontius in the face of superior forces? When the army in Hispania 'mutinied', did they kill Gerontius and then all await orders from Rome, or did they attempt to establish their independence, or did some of them simply quit the army and return home? The answers are impossible to find, but it is reasonable to assume that a significant proportion of the troops deserted and returned home, if only to be near their families in order to protect them from the barbarian settlers, whose reaction now that their erstwhile benefactor had died would be worrying to say the least.

There is little information concerning Hispania for the following years until in 416 the Goths under Wallia were induced by the Empire to attack the Siling Vandals in Baetica. Due to the brevity of the few remaining sources the behaviour of the army is unknown: they may have sided with the Goths against the Vandals, in which case they almost certainly suffered casualties, or they may have stood aside and awaited developments. What is known is that the Siling Vandals were decimated and the remnant joined the Asding Vandals, before in 419 the now united Vandals attacked the Sueves, possibly in an attempt to force the Sueves to become subservient allies against further imperial and/or Gothic attacks.

At this point we hear at last of the Spanish army. The Emperor Honorius and his *magister militum* Constantius appointed a man named Astyrius as *comes Hispaniae* and sent him to Hispania to face the Vandals. The Vandals abandoned their attack on the Sueves and instead in 420 they attacked the Roman town of Bracara, with attendant losses to the Spanish army.[33] Obviously, the remaining Spanish forces were unequal to the task of defeating the Vandals unaided.

Consequently, in 421/422, possibly following the death of Constantius, an expeditionary force was sent to Baetica under the new *magister militum* Castinus.[34] At first Castinus was successful but he was then defeated and forced to flee to Tarraco. This information is interesting in several ways. Firstly, the fact that Castinus was given troops in Italy suggests that by this time the Spanish army had been much reduced in strength and needed reinforcements in order to assure victory. The second is that despite these the Romans eventually lost, with the normal casualties attendant upon such a defeat. The third is that, despite their earlier defeat at the hands of the Goths and their flight to Gallaecia, the combined Vandal army had been able to reassert control of Baetica.

In the turmoil surrounding the death of Honorius and the usurpation of John (423–425), the Vandals took full advantage of Roman weakness. With the court preoccupied with the civil wars and political machinations of Aetius, Felix and Boniface, the Vandals were left virtually unopposed in Hispania.[35] In 425–426 the Vandals captured Carthago Spartaria (Cartagena) and sacked Hispalis (Seville). They also used the ships captured at Cartagena to raid the Balearics and Mauretania.[36]

However the Empire managed to maintain some pressure on the Vandals and their King Gaiseric decided that as long as they remained in Hispania they would be vulnerable to attack, especially from the Goths in Aquitaine. There also appears to have been a substantial number of imperial troops still in the peninsula. In 429 Gaiseric led most of his people across the Straits of Gibraltar and into Africa. In theory this should have allowed the Romans a respite and given them a chance to recover lost territory in Hispania. This did not happen: instead, it was the Sueves who expanded to fill the vacuum left by the Vandal migration. In 430 they attacked towns in central Gallaecia from their settlements in the north and west of the province, whilst the people (*plebem*) in the area retreated to and defended local forts.[37] Interestingly, there is no mention of local troops.

What is completely unknown at this time is the fate of Lusitania. Thanks to the lack of opposition the Sueves maintained an expansionist policy, attacking at will and rarely opposed by the imperial army. It is possible that Lusitania was also coming under the control of the Sueves, but it is more likely that the Sueves were concentrating their efforts in a more easterly direction. These were areas which the Empire could easily reach and the Sueves may have been working to establish a buffer zone against any Imperial counter-attack. If that was the case, then the Lusitanians may have reverted to self-control, in much the same way as the British had earlier in the century. Unfortunately, unless some new and unexpected information comes to light, the truth about the Lusitanians will never be known.

In those parts of the peninsula where we do have information, the situation was becoming increasingly ominous. On the odd occasions when the court decided to send an expedition the Sueves could still be defeated, yet their expansion was steady, if unspectacular. In 439 they captured Emerita, in 440 Martylis (Mertola), and in 441 Hispalis (Seville).[38]

As the Sueves were expanding their control, the Empire, now firmly in the hands of Aetius, had other things on their minds: in 441 and 443 campaigns were launched against the *bacaudae* of Tarraconensis.[39] These campaigns were necessary: the Empire needed a secure base from which to attempt any 'reconquest' of Hispania, and Tarraconensis had to be secured before any major campaigns against the Sueves could begin. Once the *bacaudae* had been crushed, in 446 the Empire launched an attempt to regain lost territory. A man named Vitus was appointed *magister militum* and sent to Hispania with an army. Despite Vitus' best efforts he was eventually defeated. Carthaginiensis and Baetica remained firmly under the control of the Sueves.[40]

The fact that Vitus had to take an army with him to attack the Sueves leaves open the question of what had happened to the last remnants of the Spanish army. They may have disintegrated completely, or been reduced to just a handful of units desperately defending the few towns left under Roman control, or they may have joined the *bacaudae* in attempting to create a new autonomous state for the defence of Tarraconensis, the last area under Roman control. The answer is unknown, but with the value of hindsight it is likely that the answer is to be found in a combination of the last two suggestions. Those troops still loyal to Rome will have been defending their posts against Suevic expansion, whilst it is possible that a few troops saw no help coming from the Empire and so decided to defend themselves. It is also credible that some of the troops in Tarraconensis were part of the later *bacaudic* revolt of 449 (see below) and came to an agreement with the Sueves, or even simply joined the Sueves in order to ensure their own survival, although this is conjecture.[41] Whatever the case, it would have appeared to the citizens of Hispania that the contemporary comment that 'Gaul and Hispania were demolished and utterly destroyed by the barbarian nations of the Vandals, Sueves and Alans' was a simple statement of the truth.[42]

The lack of a successful defence of the peninsula resulted in rebellious elements in Hispania coming to the fore. So much so that in 449 a man named Basilius assumed control of some *bacaudae* and attacked the church of Tyriasso (Tarazona). Later that same year Basilius joined with the Sueves in an attack on Caesaraugusta and captured Ilerda.[43] After many centuries of peace, Imperial control of Hispania appeared to be on the point of collapse.

In the emergency surrounding the war with Attila it appears that little was done to rectify affairs in Hispania. However, with the Huns defeated at the Battle of the Catalaunian Plains and their assault on Italy neutralized, Aetius had agreed to appoint the Gothic King Theoderic II's brother Frederic as *magister militum*: partly as a means of thanking the Goths for their support, but mainly as a means of 'hiring' a large force of Goths to help in the recovery of Hispania.

When news arrived that Attila had died, in 453/454 Aetius responded by sending Frederic to Hispania.[44] The composition of this army is unknown, but it is likely that the vast majority was composed of Gothic troops. Once in Hispania, Frederic attacked the *bacaudae* of Tarraconensis, slaughtering them in large numbers.[45] With a secure base established, the recovery of Hispania could now begin.

Overall, the above implies that by the mid-420s the Spanish army had lost large amounts of manpower through warfare and desertion, as well as the more usual retirement and disease. It also suggests that by the 450s the Hispanic army had virtually ceased to exist as a loyal Roman force. There may have been garrisons stationed in those towns still loyal to the Empire, but from later events it would appear that many towns – especially in the south – asserted their independence.[46] It can be assumed that throughout the early fifth century the confused situation in the Peninsula was having a negative effect on army recruitment: citizens in Gallaecia and Baetica especially would not want to join an army stationed elsewhere, leaving their loved ones undefended and at the mercy of barbarian tribes who were usually in open conflict with the Empire.

Yet even the unsuccessful Roman campaigns had one minor benefit for the Empire: prior to the death of Aetius the Sueves would always be wary of an imperial attack.[47] As a result they could sometimes be cajoled into relinquishing recent gains and halting their raids and assaults, as happened in 453 when Mansuetus, the *comes Hispaniae*, and another *comes* named Fronto, were sent to negotiate a peace.[48] Despite these diplomatic 'victories', it was clear that Roman control of the Iberian Peninsula was in danger of collapse.

Africa

In a similar vein to the story of Hispania, that of Africa is one of barbarian invasion – although in this case it was only one 'group' of barbarians and a remarkably rapid collapse of Roman control. As with Gaul and the barbarian intruders following the crossing of the Rhine in 406, the Vandal invasion of Africa was helped by the fact that a Roman civil war was being played out in the area, although in the case of Africa the war was ongoing even before the Vandals arrived.[49]

By 417 a man named Boniface was commanding the troops in Africa. In 422 he argued with the *magister militum* Castinus prior to the latter's doomed attack on the Vandals in Hispania (see above). Following the death of Honorius in 423, Boniface refused to accept the usurper John as the new emperor, in 424 defeating John's forces as they attempted to invade Africa. As a reward for his services, when Valentinian III became the new emperor Boniface was promoted to *comes domesticorum et Africae*.[50]

Unfortunately, imperial politics now played a vital role in events. In 427 Boniface was accused of wanting to create his own Empire in Africa.[51] Valentinian – or rather his mother: Valentinian was still only 8-years-old – responded by sending an army to Africa, so beginning a civil war. Boniface overcame this army and further Imperial forces were sent, the ensuing war dragging on for the following two years.

As the civil war continued into 429, the Vandals under Gaiseric crossed to Africa and began their long march across the northern stretches of the continent. Fortunately the civil war now ended and Boniface was allowed to face Gaiseric in pitched battle somewhere to the west of Hippo Regius. Gaiseric was victorious and so began the year-long siege of Hippo (May/June 430 – July/August 431).[52]

Shortly after the Vandals raised the siege of Hippo, the Eastern general Aspar arrived with reinforcements and in 432 the Romans again faced the Vandals in battle. Once more the Vandals were victorious and this time as the Romans retreated the city of Hippo was sacked. With organized resistance temporarily removed the Vandals went on to attack the whole of the Prefecture.

In this they were helped by developments within the Empire. Boniface was recalled to Italy and, taking a large number of troops from Africa, he faced Aetius at the Battle of Rimini. In the meantime, Aspar was left with the remaining troops to conduct a campaign of containment against the Vandals in Africa. He appears to have been a superior general to Boniface, as despite the earlier defeats he was so successful that in 435 a treaty was signed in which the Vandals were given territory in Mauretania Sitifensis and Numidia in return for peace (see Map 4), after which

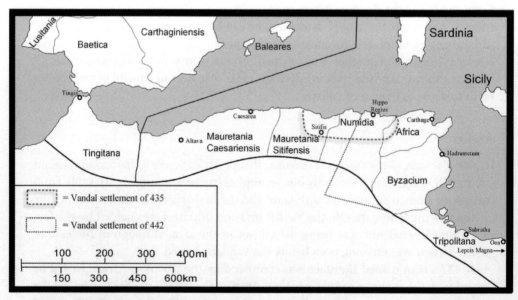

Map 4: The Vandal Settlements. Note that the exact boundaries are unclear, especially the amount of territory taken by the Vandals in Tripolitana after 442.

Aspar returned to the East.[53] Interestingly, there is no evidence suggesting that Aetius replaced Boniface with a new *comes* in Africa. In some ways this explains what happened next.

In a surprise attack, in 439 Gaiseric captured Carthage. The loss of the provinces of Africa, especially of Africa Proconsularis, resulted in panic in Italy. Italy relied upon supplies of grain from Africa to feed its people, especially the citizens of Rome. Without these supplies Italy faced famine. Although an attempt was made to reclaim Africa with a combined army of troops from both East and West, the campaign foundered when the Eastern troops were recalled to face the Huns. Bowing to the inevitable, in 442 Aetius signed a treaty allowing the Vandals to retain their conquests. In return, Gaiseric restored to the Empire the territories the Vandals had been given earlier and agreed to the resumption of the grain supply. In the following years Gaiseric concentrated on internal security and the organization of his new kingdom and so peace was restored between Vandals and Romans from 442 until 454.[54]

The effects of these repeated wars on the armies of North Africa are unknown. The fact that the area had not suffered from any major conflicts for the previous centuries may have meant that prior to the Vandals' arrival units were kept at well below paper strength. In this context it is understandable that the *comes Tingitaniae* would be unwilling with his army of far less than 10,000 men to face the full might of the Vandals as they crossed the Straits of Gibraltar. Furthermore, it is unlikely that any fighting took place in the area as the Vandals were intent upon crossing into richer and more productive regions of Africa than the coast opposite Hispania, so quickly moved east.

Likewise, the army of the *comes Africae* was almost certainly well below the calculated number of 21,000 men even before the civil war began. The losses in the civil war, in the Siege of Hippo, in the two defeats against the Vandals, and following the withdrawal of troops by Boniface to face Aetius in Italy, will all have severely reduced the number of troops available in North Africa. As a result, it is likely that following the Treaty of 442 the Romans withdrew the remaining troops to Italy to help reinforce the main army there, leaving only a skeleton force in those areas still under Roman control. The rest of the army would either have been disbanded or, possibly more likely, refused to leave the area, deserting to rejoin their families in the face of expected Vandal aggression. Any remaining armed forces in Africa would have existed on paper, but in reality would only have had a small core of troops at best.

Italy

In comparison to Hispania and Africa, Italy had suffered little from the invasions of the early fifth century. The invasion of Radagaisus in 405 had been easily defeated, and although the Goths had sacked Rome in 410 in reality the army had suffered very few casualties as the Goths had been unopposed. Losses during the civil war between John and Valentinian III were almost certainly light, and at the Battle of Rimini in 432, fought between Aetius and Boniface, casualties may have been high, but these were probably replaced by the retention of the troops brought from Africa by Boniface.

The main casualties suffered by the Italian army in this period would doubtless be caused by four major campaigns: in 430 against the Iuthungi in Raetia, in 431 against the Nori in Noricum, and obviously Aetius' campaign against Attila culminating in the Battle of the Catalaunian Fields in 451 (on the latter, see below). Finally, many men were lost at the siege of Aquileia and during the sack of Milan when Attila invaded Italy in 452. Alongside these operations, Aetius often campaigned in Gaul with the *praesental* (in the presence of the emperor) army (see below), but there is no means of estimating the Italian forces used in these campaigns or their losses.

Thanks to the presence of the emperor, the chances are that the majority of new recruits were enrolled in the army of Italy. As a result, the *praesental* army in Italy would have been maintained as close to full strength as possible, but given the dire financial straits of the Empire other areas may have seen numbers dwindle as the supply of recruits dried up. Moreover, the hiring of mercenaries was almost certainly largely restricted to the *praesental* army: although it is in this period that the use of *bucellarii* (see above) became ever more widespread, the majority of mercenaries would have been tightly controlled by the emperor and/or his representatives.

Gaul*

Having given a relatively detailed account of the fate of the army in Hispania and Italy, it is unnecessary to go into the same level of detail with the army in Gaul. All that is needed is a list of the campaigns fought in Gaul in the first half of the fifth century. The fact that the army of Gaul remained a viable entity is evidence that, despite the focus of the Emperors and their military commanders on maintaining the integrity of Italy, Gaul came a close second. The reason for this is clear: members of the Senate maintained large estates in the south of Gaul and will have put political pressure on the Emperor and his representatives to safeguard their investment. This would be even more the case after the loss of their estates in Africa following the Vandal seizure of Carthage in 439.

What follows is a list of campaigns in Gaul between 406 and 454. It should be noted that this does not aim to be a comprehensive list, only a representative sample to demonstrate the large number of battles fought by the Gallic field army, sometimes aided by Italian forces, during the period in question:

406	crossing of the Rhine by the Vandals, Alans and Sueves
407	civil war against Constantine III
409–11	extension of civil war to include Gaudentius
	battles between Constantine III and Gaudentius, and campaign of Constantius III
	expansion of Franks
413	campaign of Constantius III against Goths in Gaul

---

* For all places named in this section, see Maps 1 and 2.

426	war against the Goths
428	war against the Franks
430	war against the Goths
431–2	war against the Franks
432	(Civil War between Aetius and Boniface: the Battle of Rimini. This will have included troops taken from Gaul.)
435	war against the Burgundians
435–7	wars against the *Bacaudae*
436–7	war against the Burgundians
436–9	war against the Goths
*437	war against the Franks
445	war against the Franks
448	war against the *Bacaudae*
450–51	war against the Huns; many cities sacked; Battle of the Catalaunian Plains

With Attila defeated in battle, Aetius needed to withdraw troops to Italy to counter any further incursions by the Huns. Unfortunately for Aetius, the Goths were intent on taking advantage of the chaos brought about by the invasion. In 453 King Thorismund attacked and defeated the Alans north of the Loire.[55] Although there are several possible explanations for the attack, the likelihood is that Thorismund was responding to internal politics and was intent on demonstrating his independence to his fellow tribesmen, as well as expanding his sphere of influence in the West.[56]

Taken by surprise, Aetius led a relief force north from Italy.[57] In response, Thorismund laid siege to Arles, a siege Aetius failed to break.[58] Fortunately Ferreolus, the Praetorian Prefect of Gaul, now invited Thorismund to a banquet at which he convinced Thorismund to accept a treaty and raise the siege.[59] As part of the treaty Frederic was made *magister militum* and appointed to command the troops sent against the *bacaudae* in Taraconnensis (see Hispania, above).

Sadly for Thorismund, his brothers were unhappy with this train of events. Late in 453 Thorismund quarrelled with his brothers Theoderic and Frederic, and he was defeated and garrotted.[60] Theoderic became the new king, now known as Theoderic II, but he renewed the treaty with Aetius and Frederic kept his position as a member of the Roman military elite.

It is clear that in the majority of the campaigns listed above the army of Gaul was reinforced by large numbers of troops from Italy. Despite repeated battles, the army remained in existence as a viable fighting force, testament to the desire of the Emperor and the Senate to defend their large estates in the south of Gaul.

Illyricum[61]

The exact state of affairs in Illyricum is unknown. After the catastrophic defeat at the Battle of Adrianople in 378 the Emperor Gratian had ceded Illyricum to the new Emperor of the East, Theodosius. At the end of the fourth century Stilicho had received the Diocese of Pannonia (Pannonias I and II, Noricum Ripenses and

Noricum Mediterraneum, Savia, Valeria, and Dalmatia) back from the East, and this later became known as 'Illyricum'. However, Stilicho had been ready to go to war to regain the rest of Illyricum, both to ensure the safety of Italy and to maintain an area that was a rich source of recruits for the West. After the death of Stilicho tensions had receded and 'Illyricum' was kept by the West, with the rest of the Balkan peninsula being retained by the East.

In many ways this made sense. For the full defence of Italy the present arrangement was satisfactory. The long curve of the Balkan Mountains and the bulk of the Rhodope Mountains ensured that nearly all barbarian attacks into the Balkans focused on the Valley of the Maritsa River and further east towards Constantinople (See Map 5.) As long as the Succi Pass (Trajan's Gate) was secure, attacks on the Eastern Empire attempting to put pressure on Constantinople made no impression on the West.

The history of Dalmatia emphasizes its isolation from the rest of the Empire. The worst event in living memory was probably the rebellion of the Goths under

Map 5: The Balkans.

Alaric in 395, which had seen some Dalmatian cities 'sacked' and the Goths may even have reached the shores of the Adriatic. However, the scale of this devastation is exaggerated in the ancient records.[62] The only Roman campaign in the area attested in the sources is when Aetius defeated the rebellious 'Nori' (probably settled Vandals) in Noricum in 431.[63] Unfortunately one side effect of the 'peace' in the region appears to be that the *Claustra Alpium Iuliarum* (the military defences in the Julian Alps – see Map 5) were abandoned at some time early in the fifth century.[64]

Difficulty of access also played its part. By the fifth century Dalmatia in particular was easily accessible only by sea (see below). As a result, many parts of Illyricum, especially Dalmatia, became increasingly isolated.

The concept of the marginalization of Illyricum is reinforced by the unknown political status of the area. Before Aetius' death the political situation with regards to Illyricum/Pannonia becomes confused and debate has raged over the status of the region.[65] The whole question is based upon a possible marital agreement of 437 between Valentinian III and Licinia Eudoxia, daughter of the Eastern Emperor Theodosius II. Both Cassiodorus and Jordanes state that as part of the marriage ceremonies Galla Placidia (mother of Eudoxia) 'shamefully' gave Illyricum to the East.[66] Only the late, eastern source of Procopius implies that Illyricum remained part of the Western Empire.[67]

As a result of the confused sources, modern opinion is divided as to whether the Diocese was Eastern or Western. The majority view is that the East had suzerainty, whilst acknowledging that Dalmatia itself attained effective independence after Aetius' death.[68]

What has not been discussed in many of these deliberations are the actions of Aetius in 443, six years after the marriage, when he ceded territory in Pannonia to Attila.[69] For Aetius to do this it is obvious that the whole of Illyricum could not have been transferred to the East, but remained under Western control. Yet there were problems with the West's control of Pannonia. Enemies crossing the border in these provinces largely avoided the mountains to the south and west and so tended to attack Thrace. The West's continued focus on affairs in Gaul, Hispania and Africa, plus the lack of invasion from Pannonia, resulted in Pannonia being neglected. Obviously, the East would be unhappy with this state of affairs and would want to take action.

Yet the majority of Illyricum was not strategically important to the East except for maintaining links with the West, resulting in Theodosius not wanting to take responsibility for the whole diocese: the main strategic focus in the area for the East remained Pannonia.[70] In this context it is possible to propose that the agreement of 437 only ceded *parts* of Illyricum to the East: in 448 the Eastern Emperor Theodosius granted territory in Pannonia to the Huns.[71] The easiest way to resolve this difficulty is to assume that Pannonia I was kept by the West and that the East assumed responsibility for Pannonia II. Sharing responsibility in this way would reduce tensions between the East and West concerning the origins of invaders from this area.[72]

The hypothesis would also explain the confusion in the sources. Those in the West, unhappy with the loss of territory, would exploit the agreement for their own purposes to the full: hence the comments by Cassiodorus and Jordanes. As far as the East was concerned, the 'whole' of Illyricum would remain affiliated to the West, hence Procopius' acceptance of Western control. Although unsatisfactory in many respects, this is the most likely solution to the vexed question of Illyricum.

Surprisingly, despite his fearsome reputation and the close proximity of the Hunnic Empire to Illyricum, Attila appears to have completely ignored the area prior to his invasion of Italy in 452. Defeated at the Battle of the Catalaunian Plains in 451, in 452 Attila passed through Illyricum – according to Prosper, more specifically Pannonia[73] – on his way to invade Italy. Due to the speed of the invasion it is unlikely that Attila faced any opposition in Illyricum. Although it is probable that several of the cities he passed had a garrison, his desire to invade Italy itself in order to defeat Aetius and avenge his defeat in 451 almost certainly resulted in him bypassing defended cities and heading straight for Italy itself. As a result few losses will have been incurred by the army of Illyricum.

After the collapse of the Hunnic Empire (454), the Eastern Emperor Marcian stabilized the Danubian frontier by granting territory to many barbarian tribes who had been settled in the region during the height of Hunnic power: it would appear that the territory lost to the Huns had actually been settled by tribes who were subjects of the Huns, not by the Huns themselves. Accordingly, Marcian gave land to the various barbarians who had settled 'within' the Empire in return for a *foedus*, a treaty in which it was common for the barbarians to serve in the Roman army.[74] The 'Ostrogoths' received Pannonia, including Sirmium, and some Sarmatians, Cemandri and Huns were given Castra Martis in Illyricum.[75] Although the latter may have been in territory theoretically controlled by the West, this land may have been previously occupied by these tribes and Marcian will have known that the West was militarily incapable of evicting them. In that case, agreeing a treaty was making the best of a bad situation. In this way Marcian was able to re-establish many of the defences in the Balkans. As the East appears to have retained control of the eastern part of Pannonia Secunda, it would appear that the River Sava became the new border.[76]

Unsurprisingly, the rest of Illyricum, and especially Dalmatia, were ignored by all. Yet the confusion and uncertainty had its effect: although there are no recorded attacks on Dalmatia, it would appear that around this time some of the upper classes from the area moved to Italy, while refugees from both Pannonia and inland Dalmatia took shelter in the coastal cities.[77] As no appointee was forthcoming from the Western court, what was needed was a man of political and military competence to fill the political and military vacuum. The man would almost certainly need to be a native of Dalmatia.

Marcellinus

Eventually, a local grandee, a man named Marcellinus, slowly emerged as a leading political and military leader in the area, putting down local revolts when they arose.

Marcellinus' origin is unknown, but he appears to have been a pagan and it is likely that his main residence was at Split, Diocletian's 'Imperial Palace' – a fact which explains the lack of Christian symbols in the area until relatively late in the century.[78]

Although Marcellinus is sometimes called a friend of Aetius, their relationship is unknown. It is probable, though unprovable, that Marcellinus rose to prominence in the region and was then introduced to Aetius, the two men establishing a mutual understanding towards affairs in Illyricum. Whether this 'mutual understanding' became close friendship is unknown, although it has been suggested that Marcellinus was given the official appointment by Aetius of *comes rei militaris* in Illyricum, and his namesake Marcellinus *comes* states that Marcellinus was *patricius*, although this may be an anachronism referring to later events.[79]

The confusion concerning Marcellinus' position is demonstrated by an extract of one modern historian:

> Henceforth, he was militarily secure in his control of the province of Dalmatia which became virtually autonomous. The *comes rei militaris Dalmatiae* had a substantial fleet which was based at Salona. Hunnic federates formed the core of his army which he supplemented with the important sources of manpower and military resources from the Dalmatian hinterland which was within his sphere of influence. The contemporaneous break up of the Hunnic Empire in 454 meant that the *comes* could draw upon significant supplies of manpower from north of the Sava and from the traditional sources of sturdy Illyrian peasants of interior Dalmatia. Marcellinus also had within his region the Imperial arms factory and naval arsenal at Salona and access to the mining resources of the interior at Domavia (lead) and the Sava Valley (iron). Because the fleet at Salona gave him virtual control of the Adriatic and the geography of Dalmatia deterred approach by land, his position in Dalmatia was virtually unassailable. Entrenched on the eastern coast of the Adriatic, Marcellinus played an opportunistic and ambitious role in the affairs of the western part of the Empire.
>
> *Wozniack, 1981, 357.*

More recent historians have challenged some of these conclusions. For example, there is no historical evidence for the existence of a fleet at Salona, so Marcellinus is unlikely to have been as secure in his position as indicated: indeed, part of the reason for his later involvement in Western affairs may have been due to the vulnerability of the coastline to Vandal attacks. However, it is likely that his army was almost all raised by Marcellinus in person and comprised a main force of barbarian – Hunnic – mercenaries, possibly supplementing a small core of Roman *limitanei*, although the exact nature and balance of these forces are unknown.[80] The only thing stated by the sources is that he had a bodyguard of Huns and that his army was 'distinguished for the preparedness of its equipment'.[81] Whatever the status of Illyricum, the fact that Marcellinus acted as a Western military commander suggests that at least the majority of the area still remained outside Eastern political control.[82]

As a result of the above deliberations, the idea that the whole area from the borders of Italy to the gates of Constantinople was devastated continuously by barbarian invasions is a misconception: the attackers rarely, if ever, crossed the mountains into Illyricum. In reality, the army of Illyricum was relatively untouched by the events of the late fourth and early to mid-fifth centuries. It is also possible that Marcellinus or his predecessors kept the army of Illyricum at nearer to full strength than some of the other areas in the West, thanks to their access to the Illyrian recruiting grounds. Further, there is no record of troops being withdrawn to strengthen the armies of Italy or Gaul. As a result, with a core of seasoned troops, after the death of Aetius Illyricum would come to play a large part in the unfolding of events.

Conclusion

The never-ending wars fought throughout the West between 404 and 454 killed or disabled large numbers of Roman troops. It is likely that none of the units still remaining in existence numbered anywhere near the paper strengths described earlier in the chapter. The vast majority of the armies of Hispania and Africa will have been greatly under strength. The only areas where the Western emperors and their commanders will have attempted to maintain units at anywhere near to their full complement will have been Italy, Gaul, and possibly Illyricum, yet there is a possibility that even here there were times when the units of the *comitatenses* were one-third under strength.[83]

The Changing Army

As has been seen, events outside the control of the Western court caused drastic changes in the Western army in the last years of its existence. Unfortunately, these changes are nowhere clearly documented and there are no indications of numbers, percentages of different troop types, nor any other information concerning the nature of the Western army after 420.

Despite the loss of territory to barbarian incomers and the deficit in revenue this entailed, many senators, including some of the richest individuals of the Empire, looked back to the old days of the imperial legions and demanded that the army remain composed of Roman troops. Yet ironically, the same senators clung to their tax exemptions, so denying the Emperor the money with which to train and equip new recruits, whilst at the same time not allowing the recruitment of men from their own vast estates, so denying the Emperor the manpower necessary to build the legions into an efficient aggressive fighting force.[84] Claims that the Late Roman Army did not have recruiting problems apply only to the army of the late fourth and early fifth centuries.[85]

As army numbers dwindled, army commanders had little choice but to rely even more on the hiring of barbarian mercenaries to make up for the shortfall in numbers. The result was that the army became more and more 'Barbarized' as time

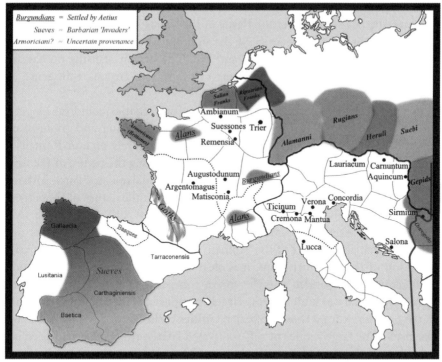

Map 6: The *fabricae* as attested in the Notitia Dignitatum, c.454.

The arsenals mentioned below:

In Illyricum:
- of shields, saddle-cloths and weapons, at Sirmium,
- of shields, at Acincuin (Aquincum),
- of shields, at Carnuntum,
- of shields, at Lauriacum,
- of weapons, at Salona.

In Italy:
- of arrows, at Concordia,
- of shields and weapons, at Verona,
- of leather corselets, at Mantua,
- of shields, at Cremona,
- of bows, at Ticinum,
- of broadswords, at Luca.

In the Gauls:
- of all weapons, at Argenton (Argentomacus),
- of arrows, at Macon (Matisconia),
- of leather corselets, ballistae, and mail, at Autun,
- of shields, at Autun (Augustodunum),
- of shield, ballistae (artillery), and armour, at Soissons (Suessiones),
- of broadswords, at Rheims (Remensia),
- of shields, at Trier,
- of ballistae, at Trier,
- of broadswords and shields, at Amiens (Ambianum).

passed. Interestingly, the higher echelons of the Roman military command began to use increasing numbers of *bucellarii* as personal bodyguards, as evidenced by the bodyguards of Aetius, Marcellinus and Litorius.[86] Over time these would become the core around which Roman armies were built.

If financial difficulties were causing problems within the army prior to 439, then after the loss of Africa to the Vandals the situation became critical. Following Valentinian III's declaration that the Empire was bankrupt, the chances are that most of the expenditure on the army, and especially on the *fabricae* that supplied the army with equipment, was withdrawn. Although some of the *fabricae* in Italy and Gaul may have been kept working, it is likely that the majority – especially those threatened by barbarian expansion – were at this point closed (see Map 6). From now on the army would have to rely on a much smaller supply of new equipment once the weapons and armour stored in imperial armouries had been used up. This would especially be the case after the Battle of the Catalaunian Fields in 451, when, even though victorious, the severity of the fighting would have resulted in large amounts of equipment being damaged and lost. The benefit of using mercenaries was that the Empire would not be expected to supply the troops with arms, and especially with armour.

Furthermore, the low cost of hiring barbarian mercenaries could no longer be ignored: when compared to the cost of recruiting, equipping and training new recruits the bankrupt Empire now had little choice but to rely on non-Romans for defence. This is nowhere more evident than when analysing the nature of the forces employed against Attila the Hun at the Battle of the Catalaunian Plains. Although Aetius commanded a body of Roman troops at the battle the nature of these troops is unclear. It is likely that the majority of the Allied troops at the battle consisted of the Goths and the Alans, with smaller contingents from all the tribal groups allied to Rome, and that at least part of the 'Roman' force was composed of mercenaries.

As a result of these deliberations, it is clear that Roman generals of the mid to late fifth century commanded polyglot forces consisting of a small core of Roman troops around which was built an army largely composed of mercenaries from either across the frontier or from those barbarian entities earlier settled within the Roman Empire itself. The large armies of self-motivated citizen troops that had been seen from the days of the Republic were long gone. The large majority of battles fought by the Empire in its last years were fought on a small scale with large numbers of mercenary troops and this should be remembered when reading the following description of the events that led to the Fall of the West.

Part Two

RICIMER

Chapter Three

A Brief Prelude: Petronius Maximus

17 March 455–22/31 May 455

In 451 Aetius had been the undisputed *magister militum* for eighteen years. A generation had grown to adulthood knowing of no other military commander. In that year Aetius crowned his efforts with the defeat of Attila at the Battle of the Catalaunian Plains. In the following year Attila had invaded Italy itself but, despite several successes, including the capture of both Aquileia and Milan, had failed to defeat the Roman army and due to disease and famine had finally been forced to withdraw. In 453 Attila had unexpectedly died and the Empire of the Huns had dissolved into civil war, rebellion and anarchy. At the Battle of the River Nedao (Nedava) in 454 the sons of Attila met their rebellious subjects in battle and were defeated: the Empire of the Huns collapsed, never to be reborn. Aetius' position seemed unassailable.

Yet the removal of the Hunnic threat convinced some of the courtiers that Aetius was no longer needed. The main difficulty would be in gauging the reaction of a coup on the emperor, Valentinian III. Born 2 July 419, Valentinian had become emperor on 23 October 425 at the age of 6. Understandably, power had at first rested with his mother, the authoritative and dominating Galla Placidia, half-sister of the Western Emperor Honorius (d.423) and wife of the (short-lived) Emperor Constantius III (d.421). Following the protracted political turmoil of 430–433 (see Chapters One and Two) the influence of Placidia appears to have diminished, being replaced by that of Aetius, the *magister utriusque militiae* (Master of all the Troops). By 454, and now aged 35, Valentinian had spent 20 years in Aetius' shadow and as a result was an unknown factor.

Around the time of Attila's death Aetius' opponents' luck changed. At some point prior to 454 – the date is unknown – Eudoxia, the wife of Valentinian, decided that her daughter Placidia should marry a man named Majorian, an up-and-coming military man, possibly of Egyptian origin, whose star was rising and who had earlier fought alongside Aetius, and whose father was the 'paymaster' for Aetius' troops.[1] Valentinian had two daughters, Eudocia and Placidia. In 442, as part of the peace treaty with the Vandals (see Chapter Two), Eudocia had been betrothed to Huneric, son of Gaiseric, King of the Vandals. Due to the betrothal agreements she had been eliminated from the succession: the concept that Huneric could one day inherit the Empire was unthinkable. This meant that any man who married Placidia would have a strong claim to be emperor when Valentinian died.

Given the context it is possible that the proposed betrothal was part of a series of complex political manoeuvres aimed at reducing Aetius' influence at court, although this is nowhere explicitly stated in the sources.[2] Aetius – or possibly his wife, Pelagia – blocked the marriage and Majorian retired from active service.[3] Valentinian was forced to agree to Placidia's betrothal to Aetius' son Gaudentius.[4] In theory, Gaudentius would now be heir to the Empire. Valentinian was doubtless angry that Aetius, a servant of the emperor, was in a position to deny the emperor's wishes.

Petronius Maximus[5]

Of more import, the idea that Aetius' son would continue his father's dominance appears to have been the last straw for a man named Petronius Maximus. Maximus was born at some time around 396–7. Sadly, the names of his family are not recorded by surviving contemporary sources, only by much later writers. These texts, including Procopius, Nicephorus Callistus, Georgius Cedrenus and Theophanes, all claim that he was a descendant of Magnus Maximus (emperor/usurper 383–388), but a combination of their late authorship and the fact that the claim appears to be based on the shared name 'Maximus' – which is relatively common – suggests that this may be unlikely: on the other hand, recent research has attempted to re-establish the claim.[6]

Other historians, however, may have begun to shed light on Maximus' origins. It has been suggested that he was a member of the Anicii, a distinguished and powerful family with a long tradition of serving the Empire.[7] If this is true, and it is likely, it helps to explain how Maximus was able to embark on his illustrious career at such an early age.

Maximus' first official post appears to have been as a *praetor* around the year 411, when he was about 15-years-old. From here on his rise through the bureaucratic ranks was rapid. Around the year 415, almost certainly at the age of 18, he held the office of *tribunus et notarius*, and in the following years (c. 416–419) he served as *comes sacrarum largitionum* (Count of the Sacred Largesses, or chief treasurer). After this, and at some time between 419 and 438, he twice became *Praefectus urbi Romae* (Prefect of the City of Rome) and once *Praefectus praetorio Italiae* (Praetorian Prefect of Italy): sadly, the dates of these are unknown. In 433 he became consul for the first time, a considerable achievement for a man without ancestral family support. In 439 he became Praetorian Prefect of Italy again, and in 443 he was given the post of consul for the second time, 'an extremely distinguished honour'.[8] Finally, some time before 445 he gained the title of *patricius* (patrician), which, alongside his consulates, would almost certainly have made him the highest-ranking of all Roman senators.[9]

The majority of these posts had been gained under the 'guidance' of Aetius, and so Maximus must be seen as being a supporter of Aetius earlier in his career. Yet thanks to Gaudentius' betrothal it was now clear that Maximus would never gain any higher honours.

John of Antioch gives a further reason for Maximus' unhappiness, this time concerning Valentinian:

Valentinian, having fallen in love with the wife of Maximus … used to play at dice with him. When Maximus lost and was unable to pay, the emperor took his ring. Rising, he gave it to one of Maximus' friends so that the man showed it to Maximus' wife and, as though from her husband, ordered her to come to the palace to dine with him there. She came, thinking this the truth, and when it was announced to the emperor, he arose and without Maximus' knowledge seduced her. After the lovemaking the wife went to meet her husband as he came, wailing and reproaching him as her betrayer. When he learned the whole story, he nursed his anger at the emperor. Knowing that while Aetius was alive he could not exact vengeance, he laid plans through the emperor's eunuchs to destroy Aetius.

John of Antioch, fr. 200.1., *trans. Gordon, 51–52.*

It is hard to accept this claim. There are few, if any, independent sources claiming that Valentinian was inclined to play such games with his courtiers, and it seems most likely that John is repeating fabricated propaganda aimed at justifying Maximus' seizure of the throne: Maximus was simply one of those who were alarmed at the prospect of Gaudentius following in his father's footsteps.

Searching for potential allies, Maximus found a eunuch named Heraclius, at the time the *primicerius sacri cubiculi* (Officer of the Imperial Bedchamber), who was also unhappy with Aetius' power.[10] Entering into a conspiracy, together Maximus and Heraclius were able to convince Valentinian that Aetius was planning to overthrow Valentinian himself.[11]

Death of Aetius

Accordingly, Aetius was summoned to the palace on either 21 or 22 September 454 to discuss proposals to raise money.[12] During the meeting:

While Aetius was laying the matter of the revenues before him and was making a calculation of the total money collected from the taxes, Valentinian jumped up with a cry from his seat and said he would no longer stand being abused by such treacheries. He charged Aetius with being to blame for his troubles and indicated that Aetius desired the power of the Western … Empire. As Aetius stood amazed at the unexpectedness of his anger and tried to appease his unreasoning ire, the emperor drew his sword from its scabbard. He attacked with Heraclius, for this fellow was carrying a cleaver under his cloak (for he was a chamberlain …). Both of them together directed their blows against the head of Aetius and killed him – a man who had performed many brave deeds against both internal and foreign enemies.

John of Antioch, fr. 200.1., *trans. Gordon, 51–52.*

John of Antioch suggests that Valentinian himself was unsure of whether this had been a good act. Valentinian is alleged to have said to an unknown individual, 'was the death of Aetius not well accomplished?' The respondent replied, 'whether well or not. I do not know, but I do know that you have cut off your right hand with your left'.[13]

Immediately following Aetius' death a large number of his supporters were also killed.[14] The bodies of Aetius, Boethius and others were exposed in the forum as a warning to traitors. Valentinian then gave a speech to the Senate outlining his reasons for killing Aetius and word was dispatched across the Empire that Aetius had been executed.

Marcellinus

Although the responses of other military commanders to the news that their benefactor was dead are unknown, Marcellinus in Illyricum – or, more specifically, Dalmatia – immediately renounced his loyalty to the emperor and allegedly declared himself 'independent', although what specifically Procopius means by this is unclear.[15] From this date onwards the territory of Illyricum/Dalmatia was to remain theoretically independent from Rome, ensuring that the region was unavailable as either a source of taxes or as a recruiting ground for the Empire.

By the mid-fifth century the roads from the Adriatic to the East appear to have fallen into disuse, so the main links to Italy and Constantinople were by sea, which may also have been the case earlier as the main products of the region – iron, copper and gold from inland mines – would be easier to transport by sea than by land.[16] The increased importance of sea travel naturally had an effect on the importance of Salona, the main city on the coast, in the same manner as the rise of Ravenna, likewise a seaport on the Adriatic (see Map 5).[17] As a result of these developments Salona had now become a major strategic location on the east–west axis between Italy and Constantinople.[18] As a consequence, Marcellinus was able to achieve a political importance that would have been denied to a leader in a more peripheral area.

Despite the secession of Illyricum and the consequent loss of manpower and tax, with the death of Aetius Valentinian was in a position to set up his own rule. To do this he needed to establish good relations with his army. The major flaw in his plan was that Aetius' personal bodyguard of *bucellarii* comprised a large proportion of the Italian army.[19] In the hope of placating these men Valentinian recalled Majorian from 'retirement' and made him *comes domesticorum* (Count of the Household).[20] He also appears to have deployed the majority of the troops in the Po Valley, both to defend the passes into Italy and to remove them as a threat to his own person. At the same time Valentinian sent envoys to the Goths, Sueves, Alans, and Vandals.[21] Before these could return events in Rome changed the political circumstances of the Empire.

Maximus, having removed Aetius, attempted to fill his place. Unfortunately, having eliminated Aetius, the eunuch Heraclius appears to have switched his support from Maximus to Majorian.[22] Thwarted, Maximus summoned Optila and Thraustila, two of Valentinian's guards who had served in Aetius' *bucellarii* before being promoted. In their meeting Maximus placed blame for the death of Aetius squarely with Valentinian.[23]

Death of Valentinian III

In the meantime, Valentinian had been training with the troops in the hope of gaining their loyalty. On 16 March 455:

> Valentinian rode in the Field of Ares (the *Campus Martius*) with a few bodyguards and the followers of Optila and Thraustila. When he had dismounted from his horse and proceeded to archery, Optila and his friends attacked him. Optila struck Valentinian on his temple and when he turned around to see the striker he dealt him a second blow on the face and felled him, and Thraustila slew Heraclius. Taking the emperor's diadem and horse, they hastened to Maximus ....[24]
>
> *John of Antioch*, fr. 201.4–5., *trans. Gordon, 52–3.*

So died the last male of the Theodosian dynasty.

With the assassination of the emperor accomplished, Maximus needed to move quickly as there were other possible successors to the emperor, the two most prominent being Maximianus – previously a *domesticus* (bodyguard) to Aetius – and Majorian. In the context of the times securing the loyalty of the army was paramount. Maximus acted fast:

> The military forces were divided among themselves, some wishing Maximus to assume the royal power and some eager to give the throne to Maximianus … In addition, Eudoxia, the wife of Valentinian, strongly favoured Majorian. But Maximus gained control of the palace by distributing money and forced Eudoxia to marry him by threatening her with death, thinking that his position would be more secure. So Maximus came to the leadership of the Roman Empire.
>
> *John of Antioch*, fr. 201.6., *trans. Gordon, 53.*

John's claim that Maximus used wealth to secure the throne may be 'reflected in the relatively large amount of gold coinage that he struck at Rome for such a short reign'.[25]

The attempt to establish himself as successor to Valentinian by forcing the recently bereaved widow to marry him is in some respects understandable – his former wife had apparently died before 455.[26] It quickly became apparent that the manoeuvre had not gone as planned. The chronicles especially berate him both for failing to punish Optila and Thraustila for killing Valentinian, and for forbidding Eudoxia from grieving for her husband:[27]

After this parricide had been perpetrated, Maximus, a man with a double consulate and the patrician dignity, obtained the rule ... He not only did not punish the murderers of Valentinian, but he even received them in friendship, and after a few days he compelled Valentinian's wife [Eudoxia], who had been forbidden to grieve the loss of her husband, to marry him.

Prosper, 5.a. 455

The reasons behind his pardon of the two assassins is clear: Maximus wanted to guarantee the loyalty of the *bucellarii* and this would be lost if he punished two members of the guard for an act which he had himself encouraged.

Maximus' marriage to Eudoxia was not the only way in which he attempted to establish a 'new' dynasty to succeed the old. Maximus gave his son Palladius the title of Caesar and he married him to one of Valentinian's daughters, Eudocia or Placidia, although the sources do not specify which one. Maximus will certainly have wanted to gain the loyalty of those supporters of Aetius that had survived, but his actions in this regard are unrecorded.[28] As is usual, confusion surrounds these events as none of the sources are clear as to what occurred and when, but there is a way to amalgamate the few pieces of evidence into a coherent narrative.

According to the outstanding treaty with the Vandals, Valentinian's eldest daughter Eudocia was betrothed to Huneric, Gaiseric's son. To ensure the new dynasty, it was logical that this betrothal be cancelled and that Palladius, Maximus' son, marry her instead. Maximus may have decided that alienating the distant Vandals was worth the risk of having his son securely placed as heir to the throne. The marriage would go ahead.

There remained the problem of what to do with Valentinian's younger daughter, Placidia. Although some historians have suggested that it was she who married Palladius, not Eudocia, later events imply that this was not the case. Eudoxia, the girls' mother and wife of Valentinian, had earlier expressed a desire for Placidia to marry Majorian. There is no reason why plans for this marriage could not have resumed after the assassination of Aetius.[29] The most likely scenario is that there had simply not been time to arrange the marriage in the brief interval before Valentinian was also killed. Obviously, any marriage plans collapsed with Maximus' seizure of the crown.

Although uncorroborated by the few remaining sources, the most logical outcome is that early in his reign Maximus married Palladius to Eudocia and that he arranged for the marriage of Placidia and Olybrius, a member of the powerful Anicii family. In this way he may have hoped to secure the support of the Senate for his elevation, and if not the whole senate then at least that part owing allegiance to Olybrius' family. Once married, it seems that Olybrius was not allowed to remain at rest in Rome: the next time we hear of him he is in Constantinople.[30] The reason for the presence of a high-ranking Roman senator at the Eastern court is nowhere explained, but the likelihood is that he had been sent by Maximus as an envoy to secure Eastern support for the new regime in the West: it is hard to think of a better envoy than Olybrius, a Roman senator with a long, outstanding lineage.

Gaul

Although he was willing to anger the Vandals by effectively negating the Treaty of 442, Maximus knew that the Goths in Aquitaine, within striking distance of Italy, needed to be accommodated towards the new regime in Italy. At this point he managed to 'kill two birds with one stone': he appointed Eparchius Avitus, possibly his brother-in-law and one of Aetius' most loyal commanders, as *magister militum praesentalis* (Master of the Soldiers in Attendance) and sent him to Toulouse to secure the loyalty of the Goths.[31] Avitus had a long history of dealing with the Goths and had served Aetius in several capacities in Gaul during the previous twenty years.[32]

Theoretically, the confusion and turmoil of the passing of Valentinian should have been slowly easing. The Senate appeared to have accepted Maximus' elevation: after all, he was one of their own, had had a long political career, was a *patrician*, and furthermore, the 'people believed that he would be in every way beneficial to the endangered state'.[33] There appeared to be only one major failing in Maximus' political policies: he was not recognized by the East. Although at this early stage of little importance, there remained the danger that after a short period the East would support a rival claimant to the West with men and materiel, as had happened with Valentinian himself in 423. The problem would need addressing if at all possible.

Yet it was not external problems that would cause the greatest difficulty for Maximus:

> But when the supreme effort brought him to the yawning gulf of the imperial dignity, his head swam beneath the diadem at sight of that enormous power, and the man who once could not bear to have a master could not now endure to be one ... this man, once made emperor, and prisoned in the palace walls, was rueing his own success before the first evening fell. ... His rule of it was from the first tempestuous, with popular tumults, tumults of soldiery, tumults of allies. ... Fulgentius ... used to say that whenever the thrice-loathed burden of a crown set Maximus longing for his ancient ease, he would often hear him exclaim: 'Happy thou, O Damocles, whose royal duress did not outlast a single banquet!'
>
> *Sidonius Apollinaris*, Letter to Senarius, (*II, 13.3–5*).

It appears from the above that, having achieved power, Maximus could not cope with the burdens of State, issuing orders that made the citizens of Rome and the troops unhappy. (On the 'tumults of allies' see below.)

Gaiseric

According to Malchus, most of all it was Maximus' actions towards Eudoxia that made her willing to take any risk to rid herself of her new husband. Possibly following the example set by Honoria, sister of Valentinian (who had allegedly asked for help from Attila, King of the Huns), Eudoxia decided to ask for help from a different 'barbarian' king:[34]

> The empress Eudoxia, the widow of the emperor Valentinian and the daughter of the emperor Theodosius and Eudocia, remained unhappily at Rome and, enraged at the tyrant Maximus because of the murder of her spouse, she summoned the Vandal Gaiseric, king of Africa, against Maximus, who was ruling Rome.[35]
>
> *Malchus*, Chron. 366.

The veracity of this claim is unknown: even the contemporary chronicler Hydatius calls the suggestion a 'lying rumour'.[36] On the other hand, it is possible that the request for help is accurate: it is easy to forget that Eudoxia would have few options unless she accepted her position as the wife of Maximus, and that desperation can lead to wayward logic. In addition, Gaiseric was the prospective father-in-law of Eudocia and Eudoxia would have realized that Gaiseric was angry with the fact that Eudocia had been married to Palladius. Furthermore, Eudoxia could have convinced herself that Gaiseric would simply send troops to Italy to depose Maximus and support her in making the appointment of a replacement. On the other hand, previous experience spoke against such invitations: Eudoxia would have known the outcome of Honoria's (alleged) request for help to Attila, with Attila's invasion and devastation of Gaul, so this must remain a possibility rather than a probability.

Whether Eudoxia sent a message to Gaiseric or not is in fact immaterial. He apparently had his own sources of information:

> Gaiseric, the ruler of the Vandals, heard of the death of Aetius and Valentinian and concluded that the time was right for an attack on Italy, since the peace treaty had been dissolved by the deaths of those who had made it with him and the new emperor did not command an estimable force. They also say that Eudoxia, the wife of Valentinian, out of distress at the murder of her husband and her forced marriage, secretly summoned Gaiseric, who crossed from Africa to Rome with a large fleet and the people whom he led.
>
> *Priscus*, fr. 30 = *John of Antioch* fr. 201.

Gaiseric clearly had his own spies in Italy. They pointed out to him that the majority of the Roman army had remained posted away from Rome – doubtless to ensure that they could not revolt against Maximus – and also told Gaiseric that the new ruler was inept and was quickly losing support, both of the army and the population. In these circumstances a quick attack could reap numerous benefits, not least of which were taking Eudocia back to Africa in order to marry her to his son Huneric, as had been agreed in the Treaty of 442. It could also lead to the establishment of a new treaty that was even more favourable to the Vandals.

Yet there may have been further reasons for the attack. Possibly the most important was that Gaiseric constantly feared an invasion of Africa by the Empire, especially if the imperial army was helped by a sizeable number of Gothic allies. By this time it was clear to all that financially the Empire could not long survive without the return of its African tax base. The dispatch of Avitus by Maximus to negotiate with the Goths will have become known in Africa and Gaiseric may have concluded that an attack on his kingdom was imminent. An able strategist, Gaiseric will have acknowledged that the best way to impede military action by the Empire was to sack the capital and remove the imperial treasury: without funds, an attack by Rome was far less likely.[37] Although this theory is unsupported by the sources, it is feasible.

Finally, and possibly apocryphal, is the opinion in Africa that the death of Valentinian removed the last of the Theodosian house. In the *Liber Genealogus*, 'a book consisting mainly of biblical genealogies ... The fourth Donatist edition, published at Carthage in 455 ... contains two notices ... [which] make it clear that the Donatist editor regarded the death of Valentinian as the end of the Roman Empire'.[38] It is possible that Gaiseric agreed with this estimation and was simply determined to 'stake a claim' within the framework of the new political order.[39] Sadly, without corroborating evidence, all of these hypotheses must remain both feasible and open to doubt.

Whatever the case, without delay Gaiseric called for a gathering of the Vandal army – which would have been scattered throughout their own lands in Africa – before beginning the sea journey to Italy. The summons to a muster will have taken time, as will the sea journey to Italy: yet in spite of these difficulties his speed of action ensured almost total surprise.

Only a few weeks after the new emperor had been crowned in Rome and a few days after his marriage to Eudoxia, terrifying news spread through Italy: 'After another month, he [Maximus] got news of the arrival of Gaiseric from Africa, and many nobles and commoners fled the city.'[40] According to Priscus, Gaiseric's arrival was spectacular in its speed: 'Maximus learned that Gaiseric was encamped at Azestus (a place near Rome).'[41] If this was the first news received in Rome of Gaiseric's arrival, it is evidence that Gaiseric had acted with commendable speed and had taken Maximus completely by surprise.

With only a few days' notice before the arrival of Gaiseric at the walls of Rome, Maximus lost his nerve. Rather than organizing for the defence of the city walls by positioning the few guardsmen he had in strategic positions, by enrolling able members of the citizenry into a militia, and by sending messages around Italy to demand the support of the Italian army:

> He panicked, mounted a horse and fled. The imperial bodyguard and those free persons around him whom he particularly trusted deserted him, and those who saw him leaving abused him and reviled him for his cowardice.
>
> *Priscus* fr. 30 = *John of Antioch* fr. 201.

It has even been suggested that in fear for his life he attempted to abdicate, although this may be a mistranslation of an entry in *Hydatius*.[42]

There are conflicting accounts concerning what happened next.

When he himself also fearfully desired to depart, having given everyone the liberty to flee, he was butchered by the imperial slaves on his seventy-seventh day of rule [22 May 455]. His dismembered body was cast into the Tiber, and he did not have a tomb.

Prosper a. 455.

Sadly, the date as calculated from Prosper contradicts that given by the *Fasti Vindobonenses priores et posteriores* (*s.a.* 455), which gives the date of 31 May for Maximus' death. Furthermore, Priscus makes no mention of Imperial slaves:

As he was about to leave the city, someone threw a rock, hitting him on the temple and killing him. The crowd fell upon his body, tore it to pieces and with shouts of triumph paraded the limbs about on a pole.

Priscus fr. 30 = *John of Antioch* fr. 201.

Interestingly, Jordanes and Sidonius add details not included in the other sources. According to Jordanes, 'Maximus ... was killed by a certain Ursus, a Roman soldier', whereas Sidonius confusingly claims that 'the Burgundian, with his traitorous leadership, extorted the panic-fury that led to an emperor's slaughter', an entry that has resulted in confusion amongst modern historians.[43]

The most likely conclusion must be that in the period surrounding the death of Maximus, plus the chaos of the Vandal attack and its aftermath, events and dates became confused, the only remaining certainty being that Maximus' body was dismembered and paraded through the streets for a short period before being thrown in the Tiber. Nothing is heard of Maximus' son Palladius after Maximus' death. As he is not listed amongst those captured by the Vandals it must be assumed that he was killed at the same time as his father. Doubtless the dishonour to his son by the marriage of Huneric's betrothed to Palladius was one of the main reasons given by Gaiseric for his attack on Italy, so it is almost certain that Palladius was killed by the citizens in the hope of placating Gaiseric.

Conclusion

History has not been kind to Maximus. He is remembered solely as a usurper who masterminded the deaths of Aetius, the 'last hope of the West', and Valentinian, the last Emperor of the Theodosian Dynasty. The nature of his brief rule and the manner of his death reinforce Sidonius' claim that here was a man totally unsuited to rule. Yet his previous record under Aetius proves that Maximus was a capable individual who worked well in a subordinate role. Sadly, as with many rulers, he found the pressure of ultimate control and responsibility too much and failed as an emperor.

Chapter Four

Eparchius Avitus
9 July/5 August 455–October 456/February 457

The Sack of Rome

Prior to his death, Petronius Maximus had failed to send orders to the *praesental* army in Italy requesting that they assemble and march to the aid of Rome as the Vandals approached the city. Immediately upon Maximus' death messengers would have been sent throughout the Empire with the news of his end. In Rome, and left with only the guardsmen and possibly a few small contingents of troops to man the walls, the citizens panicked.[1]

In 452 Leo, the Bishop of Rome, had been sent as an envoy in order to secure the release of prisoners held by the Huns (the claim that he convinced Attila to leave Italy is mistaken).[2] That time he had almost certainly been acting on the orders, or at least had the consent of, Aetius, and by association of the emperor. With the emperor recently killed, it would appear that Leo either volunteered to meet Gaiseric, or was asked by the citizens to intervene on their behalf.

> Holy Bishop Leo (*sancto Leone Episcopo*) met him outside the gates and his supplication mollified him through the power of God to such an extent that, when everything was given into his hands, he was held back nevertheless from burning, killing, and torture.
>
> *Prosper* a. 455.

Despite the Vandals' fearsome reputation, it appears that Gaiseric acceded to Leo's request: as Gaiseric took up his temporary residence in the imperial palace, there was little in the way of the rape or killing common during the sack of a city.[3] Nevertheless, the Sack of Rome by the Vandals was a far more thorough affair than that of 410 by the Goths under Alaric. Several accounts of the Sack survive – for example:

> On the third day after Maximus was killed, Gaiseric, king of the Vandals, entered Rome and during fourteen whole days denuded the city of all its riches and took with him the daughters and wife of Valentinian and many thousands of captives. The intercession of Pope Leo restrained him from arson, torture, and murder.
>
> [Gaiseric] … captured the city, and … took everything from the palace, even the bronze statues. He even led away as captives surviving senators, accompanied

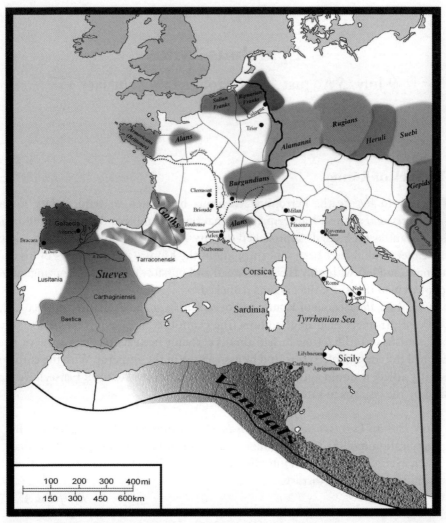

Map 7: The West during the reign of Avitus. Note that the extent of Gothic and Vandal expansion is unknown.

by their wives; along with them he also carried off to Carthage in Africa the empress Eudoxia, who had summoned him; her daughter Placidia, the wife of the patrician Olybrius,[4] who then was staying at Constantinople; and even the maiden Eudocia. After he had returned, Gaiseric gave the younger Eudocia, a maiden, the daughter of the empress Eudoxia, to his son Huneric in marriage, and he held them both, the mother and the daughter, in great honour.

Victor of Tonnena s.a. 455.

From Hydatius we learn that Gaiseric took; 'Valentinian's widow, his two daughters, and Gaudentius, son of Aetius'.[5] It is noteworthy that despite Aetius' murder and the death of Valentinian, Gaudentius had survived. He was obviously not seen as a threat to Maximus' regime. As noted above, however, there is no mention of Palladius and it must be assumed that at this point he was already dead. It is also worth noting that at no point is the senator Olybrius mentioned as a captive, despite some modern assertions that this was the case: on the contrary, Malalas states decisively that Olybrius was in Constantinople at the time of the Sack.[6] Although his abduction remains a possibility, the likelihood is that Olybrius was still acting as an envoy to the East on behalf of Maximus when Gaiseric attacked Rome.

Gaiseric had agreed not to kill or torture the inhabitants of Rome. On the other hand, due to the lack of any serious opposition, the city was sacked for a period of fourteen days.[7] The Vandals took everything of value that they could find, including all of the treasures from the Imperial Palace, churches, and anything of value from the poorer inhabitants. Included in the haul were the spoils taken from Jerusalem by Titus in AD73. (These were later recaptured by Belisarius when he conquered the Vandal kingdom in 433.) The only damage recorded to the city during the sack was that part of the roof of the Temple of Jupiter Capitolinus was stripped before the looters realized that it was simply gold-plated copper and not solid gold.[8] Having laden all of their ships with booty, including 'many thousands' of captives, the Vandals returned to Carthage.

Eudocia

Although certainty is impossible, as the few events recording Eudocia's exile in Africa are undated, it is probable that it was either late in 455 or early in 456 that Huneric was finally married to Eudocia as agreed in the Treaty of 442. Eudocia and Huneric's son Hilderic appears to have been born in the mid-late 450s, most likely in 456 or 457.[9] However, thanks to events surrounding the marriage neither the East nor the West accepted Eudocia's marriage as valid.

Hispania

In the meantime, learning of the confusion and distress in Italy caused by the deaths of Aetius and Valentinian III, and the assumption of power by Maximus, the Sueves resumed their attacks on Carthaginiensis.[10] As the majority of the 'barbarian' tribes settled in the West during the fifth century, the Sueves were to take every opportunity to enrich themselves and expand their sphere of influence when the Empire was unable to respond. Surprisingly, the fact that they had again resorted to attacking Roman territory was to be their undoing.

Illyricum

There is little direct information concerning Marcellinus' activities in Illyricum/ Dalmatia during this period. However, there is one sentence in Procopius that explains Marcellinus' reaction to the death of Aetius:

Now there was in Dalmatia a certain Marcellianus [Marcellinus], one of the acquaintances of Aetius and a man of repute, who, after Aetius had died in the manner told above, no longer deigned to yield obedience to the Emperor, but beginning a revolution and detaching all the others from allegiance, held the power of Dalmatia himself, since no one dared encounter him.

Procopius 3.6.7.

Using the period of devastation and calamity in Italy and Hispania as propaganda, Marcellinus expanded his influence throughout Illyricum: it is more than likely that the inhabitants of the Diocese would be happy to place themselves under the protection of a capable military commander with a viable army. The West seemed to be focused entirely upon events in Italy and Gaul, and the East similarly on Persia and the lower reaches of the Danube.

The Goths

Given the speed of communication in this period, it is almost certain that news of Maximus' death arrived in Toulouse before the Vandals had finished the Sack of Rome. At this point a major political event took place. Prior to 450 the Goths had been restrained within their original settlements in Aquitania. Although many Romano-Gauls will have had dealings with the Goths due to either their location near to the Gothic frontier, or because they felt that personal alliances with the new Gothic power would be useful as Roman power appeared to withdraw, such individuals will have been few and restricted to the south-west provinces of Gaul.[11] In part the growth of Gothic power will also have been restricted by the earlier establishment of the 'Council of the Seven Gauls' in which many Romano-Gauls could gain political influence. Evidence for the success of the Council is the fact that from 418–450 there were no attempted usurpations in Gaul using Gothic support.[12] On the other hand, it is almost certain that throughout this period 'local power blocks' quickly emerged, possibly linked with pre-Roman tribal identities.[13] The fragmentation of Gaul was to be slow but irreversible.

To some degree the status of the Goths had changed in the years following the Battle of the Catalaunian Plains. The alliance with Aetius had demonstrated that for the first time the Goths were at the focus of Imperial affairs, at least with reference to Gaul.[14] Yet their attempts to extend their own territories in Gaul had been thwarted by Aetius and their influence had remained peripheral.[15] Possibly the first attempt to co-opt the Goths directly was the attempt by Maximus to secure their support using Avitus as his envoy, as described above.[16] However, in the years from 451 to 455 circumstances had changed dramatically and it may be that the Goths themselves perceived a transformation in their importance.

Eparchius Avitus

Avitus had always been a major player in imperial politics. A native of Clermont, Avitus was descended from a very distinguished Senatorial family.[17] Having studied law, his introduction to the Gothic court came during the rule of Aetius.[18] He became a favourite of Theoderic I (418–451) and had an influence on the education of the future Theoderic II (reigned 453–466).[19] He had campaigned alongside Aetius against the Nori and Iuthungi in 430–1, and was probably made *magister militum per Gallias* in 437, in which position he defeated a group of Huns and helped to relieve the siege of Narbo by the then hostile Theoderic I.[20] His political career had reached its peak in 439 when he was appointed Praetorian Prefect of Gaul by Aetius, in which post he negotiated a much needed treaty with the Goths.[21]

Yet his most telling contribution to the Empire had been in 451, when he had used his influence to gain Theoderic II's support for Aetius when Attila and his Huns had invaded Gaul.[22] After the defeat of the Huns at the Battle of the Catalaunian Plains, Avitus had retired to his estates.[23] Given his strong connection to the Goths, it is obvious why he had been chosen by Maximus to journey as an envoy to Toulouse in order to gain Theoderic's support for Maximus' regime. Further, Maximus would have had little doubt concerning Avitus' loyalty: Avitus was also his brother-in-law. The esteem in which the Goths held Avitus is substantiated in the reports given by Sidonius Apollinaris that Avitus was met at the gate of Toulouse by King Theoderic II himself, as well as his brother.[24]

Sidonius goes on to relate a speech allegedly given by Theoderic after the news of Maximus' death had arrived, urging Avitus to become the new emperor of Rome.

> We do not force this on you, but we say to you: With you as leader, I am a friend of Rome; with you as Emperor, I am her soldier. You are not stealing the sovereignty from anyone; no emperor holds the Latian hills, a palace without a master is yours … I would that your imperial diadem might bring me the means to do your service. My part is but to urge you, but if Gaul should compel you, as she has the right to do, the world would cherish your rule.
>
> *Sidonius Apollinaris*, Carmina *7.510f.*

Avitus accepted Theoderic's 'nomination'.[25] Leaving Toulouse, Avitus travelled to Viernum (Ugernum), near Arles, where on either 9 or 10 July 455 he was officially proclaimed by the Gallic leaders, probably the 'Council of the Seven Gauls', as the new Western Emperor.[26] Sidonius claims that, like the Emperor Julian, Avitus was 'crowned' with a 'Celtic torc' rather than an imperial-style diadem.[27]

Although the dating of Avitus' appointments is insecure, we do know of several posts that Avitus filled, almost certainly before travelling to Italy later in the year. Wanting to cement his alliance with Theoderic, Avitus appointed a Goth named Remistus as the new *magister militum* and *patricius*.[28] Apart from this one position it would appear that the rest of Avitus' appointments were Gallic. For example, a man named Messianus, who, thanks to his connections is assumed to be from Gaul, was probably appointed as *magister militum per Gallias* and sent to continue negotiations with Theoderic.[29] It also appears that Consentius of Narbonne was appointed as *cura palatii* and Avitus' son-in-law Sidonius Apollinaris was made *tribunus et notarius*.[30]

There is not one recorded Italian serving in Avitus' administration.[31] The reasons for this are easy to understand. In the previous decades the fate of Gaul, especially of Gaul north of the River Loire, had been of ever decreasing interest to the imperial court in Italy. The net result was the increasing insularity of Gallic senators during the 450s, a time when the Empire needed to be united in order to reverse the decline in its power.[32] As a Gaul, Avitus appears to have been determined to reverse this trend and doubtless hoped that by including so many Gauls in his administration he would prove to the Gallic senators that they were still of central importance to the Empire: as part of his propaganda campaign Sidonius began to encourage his compatriots to serve Avitus in Italy.[33] These decisions were to be a mistake.

As the new 'Gallic' emperor, and determined to protect his power base, Avitus remained in Gaul for several weeks, possibly in the belief that his presence would deter attacks from across the Rhine or from groups such as the Franks who were already settled within the old imperial boundaries. Unfortunately for the Burgundians, it did not stop a Gepid warband from attacking and defeating them.[34] In the meantime, Avitus sent messengers to Italy informing the Senate of his acclamation. On 5 August he received news of his acceptance by the Senate in Rome.[35]

He also sent envoys to the Vandals, instructing them to stop their attacks and to return their hostages, and to Marcian, the Eastern Emperor, asking to be accepted as Emperor of the West and requesting support against the Vandals.[36] Over the winter of 455–456 Marcian did indeed send an envoy to Gaiseric demanding that the Vandals cease from attacking the West and release their royal captives.[37] It would appear that Marcian and Avitus had begun their joint rule with an act demonstrating that they 'harmoniously exercised imperial authority'.[38] Despite the political pressure, Gaiseric refused to bow to either embassy.[39]

In the meantime, Avitus had other things on his mind. He sent the *comes* Fronto to the Sueves demanding that they halt their attacks.[40] At the same time the Gothic King Theoderic, determined to help the recently elevated emperor, also sent envoys to the Sueves demanding that they respect the treaty they had signed with the Empire – an act which highlights the increasing level of Gothic autonomy.[41]

It was not until 21 September 455 that Avitus felt secure enough in Gaul and crossed into Italy, accompanied by an army composed of both Gallo-Roman and Gothic forces, plus his son-in-law Sidonius Apollinaris – the source for much of the information concerning Avitus' reign.[42] Interestingly, the choice of words used by the *Auctuarium Prosperi,* an Italian source, say much concerning the Senate's perception of Avitus' rule in Italy: 'And he entered Italy with his comrades in this appropriated honour on 21 September.'[43] Although the Senate had accepted Avitus, it is most likely that this was out of fear of his Gothic allies: Avitus would struggle to gain a favourable reception in Rome.

Rather than going directly to Rome it would appear that Avitus took his army across the north of Italy and crossed into the diocese of Illyricum: 'And his march alone recovered the Pannonias, lost for so many generations.'[44] There can be little doubt that Sidonius exaggerated his father-in-law's success in this campaign, and his description fails to reveal Avitus' intentions. The most obvious reason for such an operation would be to reassert the West's authority in the North of the diocese, and especially those areas which controlled the routes across the Julian Alps.[45] It may also have been an attempt to reduce the territories held by Marcellinus, who was still refusing to accept the suzerainty of the Western Emperor.

However the main reason for the attack into Illyricum was almost certainly an attempt by Avitus to assert the martial nature of his rule as early as possible: emperors had succeeded or failed as a result of their military success – or lack thereof. The last interpretation is supported somewhat by the knowledge that Avitus had already fought in this area alongside Aetius in campaigns against the Nori and Iuthungi in 430–431: Avitus knew the terrain and how to conduct a campaign immediately north-east of the Alps.[46] Returning through the north of Italy, Avitus left Remistus in Ravenna with a force of Goths before finally reaching Rome.

Once in Rome, if not before, and in order to forestall the appointment of a rival to the throne, Avitus announced that he would be retaining Majorian as *comes domesticorum*. It is certain that the political powers in Italy would have preferred Majorian, one of their own, to be emperor rather than Avitus, a Gaul, but Avitus' previous relationship with Majorian appears to have been cordial and doubtless Avitus hoped that the retention of Majorian in his position would forestall any attempt by the latter to rebel against his rule.

On 1 January 456 Avitus became consul: tradition dictated that an emperor become consul at the first opportunity. As part of the celebrations Sidonius delivered a panegyric to his father-in-law which emphasized both Avitus' previous exploits and the fact that Gallic nobles remained loyal to Rome, but not necessarily to individual emperors.[47] Unfortunately, at this point, if not before, Avitus became aware that the East was not going to accept his rule: although the West had proposed Avitus as their usual sole consul – traditionally, two consuls were nominated per year, each half of the Empire nominating one consul – the Eastern Emperor Marcian appointed two consuls from the Eastern Empire.[48] It would appear that Avitus was *persona non grata* in the East.

At this point it also became clear that Marcian, possibly encouraged by his *magister militum* Aspar, was not inclined to send military aid to the West to help against the Vandals.

Apart from not wanting to help a usurper, Aspar's earlier experience in fighting Gaiseric in Africa may have made him believe that an expedition against Gaiseric could end in disaster. As the obvious commander for such an expedition, Aspar will have been worried about his position, as leading an expedition that failed would doubtless damage his reputation. Better if the Vandals were left alone.[49]

The Vandals

In Africa, Gaiseric had realized the possibilities of the confusion inside the Empire and had resorted to the use of diplomacy to gain his ends. Although the Western Empire was now practically defenceless, Gaiseric was not yet free to act. If he sent all of his troops to ravage far-flung reaches of the West, the Moors would doubtless take advantage of his absence to wreak devastation on the Vandals themselves.

Although the exact timing is uncertain, as Procopius states that it was simply 'after the death of Valentinian', it is most likely that over the winter of 455 to 456 Gaiseric arranged a treaty with the Moors.[50] Doubtless as part of the agreement the Vandals and Moors would share the vast amount of predicted booty between them. The alliance was beneficial to both sides. Not only would it allow Gaiseric to dispatch more men on the sorties to Sicily, Italy, and other islands in the Mediterranean, but he could now use a mixed force of Vandal and Moorish troops to conquer those areas of Africa that were still under Roman control. For the Moors, the amount of booty they could seize in joint attacks on the Empire with the Vandals would be far greater than anything they could hope to accomplish on their own in Africa.

In the circumstances, Gaiseric certainly hoped to conquer new territory in Africa. Not only would expansion increase the Vandals' tax base, it would keep the Vandal troops and the Moors occupied, and maintain and even enhance Gaiseric's claim to be a successful warlord, giving him extra lands with which to reward his followers. Furthermore – and most importantly – it would eliminate any bases in Africa from which the Empire could launch a counter-attack on his kingdom.

The arrival of the embassies from both East and West late in 455 did not deter Gaiseric from his policy of assault, expansion and consolidation. A further embassy sent in 456 by Marcian from the East, including an Arian bishop named Bleda, also failed to discourage Gaiseric from his proposed conquests.[51] Finally, frustrated by Gaiseric's refusal to see reason, Marcian began preparations for war.[52]

In the meantime, a large Vandal army was sent west along the coast to conquer Roman North Africa.[53] Furthermore, once the sailing season arrived in March, a large raiding force of sixty ships was sent to harass the coasts of Italy and Sicily.[54]

Ricimer

Aware that due to the lack of opposition the Vandals would quickly renew their attacks, Avitus promoted a man who would quickly rise to fame in the Empire to the post of *comes* and sent him to Sicily to defend against the expected assault: the man's name was Ricimer.[55]

Little is known of Ricimer's parents. His father was apparently a member of the Suevian royal family, possibly a descendant of Hermeric, King of the Sueves. His mother was the daughter of Wallia, King of the Goths from 415–418/19. It is possible that his parents had married as part of a dynastic alliance between the Goths and the Sueves at some time in the years 417–418, although this is conjecture.[56] It is further inferred that, after the death of Wallia and the ascendancy of a new dynasty, Ricimer's father would have been seen as a political rival and so have thought it best to leave the new Gothic territory in Gaul in search of employment within the Empire.[57] Due to the confusion concerning Ricimer's origins it is impossible to state with certainty his date of birth and therefore his age. It is likely that he was in his mid thirties when he was appointed to the command in Sicily. One fact however seems certain: like his ancestors, Ricimer was an Arian: a lost inscription from the (presumed Arian) Church of St. Agatha in Rome demonstrates Ricimer's Arian belief.[58]

According to a panegyric delivered by Sidonius Apollinaris, Ricimer had earlier served under Aetius alongside Majorian, who had been retained by Avitus as *comes domesticorum*.[59] It would appear that their earlier service had resulted in some form of friendship between the two men. Although originally from a barbarian aristocratic background, Ricimer was now used to moving in established political circles in Rome.

The Battle of Agrigentum[60]

It would appear that the informant that carried news of the Vandal attack on Sicily also told Avitus of where to expect the ships to land: either that or Ricimer was extremely lucky in his choice of where to station his troops. Basing himself at Agrigentum, Ricimer awaited the expected invasion. His information/assumption was correct. As the Vandals left their boats and began their attempt to ravage the territory around the city Ricimer attacked them and 'with a ruse' – in all likelihood an ambush – defeated them.[61] The survivors retreated to their ships and set sail. When the news reached Rome Avitus would have been encouraged by this change in fortune: he immediately sent word to Theoderic in Gaul of the 'great victory'.[62]

Although precision is impossible, it is likely that this same embassy discussed the problem of the Sueves in Hispania. By this time it was clear that Rechiarus, King of the Sueves and brother-in-law of Theoderic, was not going to be persuaded by peaceful means to halt his attacks on Roman territory.[63] With the Vandals on the 'retreat' a victory over the Sueves would provide a major propaganda coup for Avitus and help to secure his position on the throne. Theoderic agreed to lead a campaign into Hispania to halt the Suevic attacks, although his motive was doubtless both to help Avitus and to increase his personal standing amongst his own people and in Rome.[64]

Unrest in Rome

The ensuing course of events is hard to disentangle, largely because the sources – and hence modern historians – are in disagreement.[65] As a result, what follows is an attempt to form a coherent narrative from a wide variety of disparate sources, both ancient and modern. It should be noted that these are not the only conclusions that can be drawn but are amongst the most logical.

It would appear that following his success in Sicily Ricimer was recalled to Rome, where at some point he fulfilled his vow and paid to have the Church of St Agatha embellished with new mosaics and the inscription mentioned above.[66] His victory in Sicily made the Vandals wary of attacking the island and as a result they appear to have concentrated their efforts on the mainland of Italy and the islands to the north of Sicily: Ricimer was better employed on the mainland.

Despite the victories, Avitus' position in Rome was rapidly deteriorating. There were two main causes of unhappiness. The first of these, and the one most important to the Senate, was that apart from Majorian and Ricimer there were few, if any, non-

Gallic senators in positions of power in Avitus' court. Naturally, the Italian senators who had previously enjoyed a virtual monopoly of the senior positions at court were unhappy with their loss of status and were inclined to rebel against Avitus' rule.[67] It is interesting to note that the attitude of the Italian senators – namely that co-operating with barbarians was not the 'Roman' way – contrasts sharply with the attitude of those in the provinces subjected to barbarian attack. For example, Hydatius, Paulinus of Pella and Marius of Avenches all had a positive view of the co-operation between Avitus and Theoderic.[68] This is further proof, if it were needed, that the senate of Rome had become ever more parochial in its outlook and had lost touch with the feelings of citizens in other parts of the Empire.

Of more importance to Avitus, however, was the fact that the common citizens of Rome were demonstrating against him. There were two main reasons for their unhappiness. The first of these was that the war with the Vandals had obviously cut off the supplies of grain from Africa which were used to feed Rome. Although Avitus almost certainly used local supplies during the emergency, not only were these insufficient but the transport network was in disarray thanks to the Vandals' attacks: neither the land nor sea route was free from threat.[69]

The second was the presence of Avitus' Gallic army. The large number of Gallic troops in the city only added to the problems of famine and Avitus bowed to the local demand to dismiss them and so relieve Rome of the burden of feeding them.[70] Similarly, his employment of Gothic auxiliaries to form his bodyguard and a large part of his personal army also aroused resentment. Determining that he needed to dismiss these men as well, Avitus now found that Maximus, his predecessor, had drained the Treasury in his pursuit of the throne: the donatives with which Maximus had secured the throne had depleted Imperial reserves to the point of no return. As a result, Avitus was forced to remove the bronze fitments from the statues and friezes throughout the city in order to sell them to local merchants as scrap metal, to raise funds with which to pay and dismiss his Gothic bodyguard. The defacement of these images of past glory further aroused the ire of the local population.[71] In these circumstances Avitus needed the support of a strong military commander with ties to the city of Rome. Thanks to his victory in Sicily, Ricimer was now in a strong position and Avitus decided to use him in an attempt to secure his throne. On an unknown date after the defeat of the Vandals Avitus gave Ricimer the post of *magister equitum* – Remistus, the *magister peditum*, was still in Ravenna.[72] He could have given the post to Majorian, but Majorian had already been dispatched elsewhere (see below). Despite these precautions, and as starvation loomed, there was rioting in the streets.[73]

Some ancient sources, for example Gregory of Tours, appear to claim that Avitus was a 'debauched' or 'extravagant' emperor. As the treasury was empty it is likely that Avitus was only 'extravagant' with regard to the extreme poverty of the state and this should not be taken as an indication of his 'immorality'.[74] On the other hand, later events concerning Agrippinus, the *magister militum* in Gaul, suggest that the nature of Avitus' elevation to the throne – and especially the involvement of the Goths – was causing resentment and anxiety in the capital, with some doubting the terms that had been agreed by Avitus with the Goths to secure their support (see Chapter Five).

In the meantime, and apparently unopposed, the Vandals ravaged parts of Southern Italy – possibly including the sack of the city of Capua.[75] It is sometimes claimed that either in 455 or 456 the Vandals sacked the city of Nola, as recorded by Gregory of Rome in his 'Dialogues', but it should be noted that the Paulinus referred to by Gregory died in 431 and so this attack relates to that of the Goths under Alaric in 410.[76]

It is probably at this point that Majorian was given command of troops and sent to Corsica in the hope of emulating Ricimer's success in Sicily. He was successful: 'In Corsica there was a slaughter of a multitude of Vandals.'[77] Although neither Majorian nor Ricimer is named in the sources, it is most likely that it was Majorian who was commanding this army.[78] Further, although usually attested as a naval battle, this is open to doubt: the passage in question can be translated in a variety of ways and, given the context, it is more likely that the Vandals landed and were defeated than they were beaten in a pitched battle at sea – especially as the status of the Roman navy in the Tyrrhenian Sea in this period is unknown.[79]

Pleased with the news but unhappy with the situation in Rome, Avitus decided to retire from the city, possibly intending to make an imperial journey to Arles in the south of Gaul: after all, many of his predecessors had not remained in the capital and Avitus may have feared the escalating violence in the city.[80]

With the Roman Senate unhappy with the emperor, with the Goths embroiled in a war in Hispania, and with the Vandal threat nullified by the approach of winter, Ricimer took his chance. Possibly acting with the agreement of the Senate (the sources do not make this clear) Ricimer led the available troops towards Ravenna. Surprising Remistus, the *magister peditum* was killed in the palace of Classis near Ravenna.[81] Returning to Rome Ricimer announced that Remistus was dead and his troops either killed, disbanded, or now serving the state. With the removal of the only potential threat in Italy, it may be that the Senate responded by declaring Avitus deposed.[82] Avitus, unaware of the scale of the revolt, was still en route to Gaul. Claims that he had already fled to Arles, raised an army, and then crossed back into Italy in the short time available are chronologically difficult to accept.[83]

Ricimer's Revolt

The assertion in modern sources that Ricimer was acting solely in an attempt to increase his own prestige and assume the same exalted position previously held by Aetius are based on preconceptions and do not appear to fit the facts. As will be shown, Ricimer's choices echoed the desires of the Senate in Rome and the citizens of Italy. It is clear that at this time Ricimer was acting within the context of Senatorial politics, which as always were focused upon the safety of Italy.[84] Although the accepted image of the 'Kingmaker' remains a possibility, at least in this first revolt against an emperor Ricimer was following the lead of the Senate, rather than simply imposing his own will.

The appointment of a Gallic emperor would always ensure conflict with the Senate, and as a by-product with the ambitious Ricimer. When looked at within this framework it becomes apparent that Avitus' main failing as an emperor was not simply his choice of Gallic appointees, but his failure to win the unquestioning support of Ricimer, Majorian, and the Italian army. It is also unfortunate for Avitus that 'strategic demands meant that an army was now needed in Italy [as a defence from the Vandals] and could be manipulated by Italian political factions'.[85] Avitus failed to ensure the loyalty of the Italian army upon which he relied for defence and upon which Aetius had previously relied for his political survival. It was a grave mistake.

Hispania

In 453 Frederic, the brother of the Gothic King Theoderic II, had invaded Hispania and attacked the *bacaudae* of Tarraconensis under instructions from Aetius – allegedly 'destroying the areas' of independent Roman leaders in the process.[86] He might also have been supported by seven shiploads of Heruls who at this time landed on the Gallaecian coast, only being driven off by the Sueves after they had caused considerable damage.[87] The campaign set a precedent of Gothic warfare in Hispania under the authority of the Imperial government.

As noted above, in late 455 the Suevic King Rechiarius had refused to accede to the demands of both Avitus and Theoderic that he stop attacking Roman territory. Once the Gothic envoys had been sent away empty-handed, a large force of Sueves invaded Tarraconensis, taking much booty and many captives back to Gallaecia.[88] Continuing the policy of joint action, and with the full agreement and support of Avitus, in the summer of 456 Theoderic gathered his forces and led them into Hispania.[89] The army included contingents from the Burgundians, although whether the two Burgundian kings, Gundioc and Chilperic (I), took part themselves is assumed but not clearly stated by Jordanes.[90] What is also not clear is whether Avitus sent any Roman troops from Gaul to take part, or whether any Roman forces still in Hispania immediately joined Theoderic.

In response to the invasion, Rechiarius gathered his own troops and on 5 October faced Theoderic on the River Urbicus, twelve miles from the city of Asturica. The battle proved to be short-lived:

> Soon after the onset of the engagement, they [the Sueves] were defeated. The Suevic rank and file were slaughtered, some were captured, but most were put to flight. Rechiarius himself, wounded and in flight, barely managed to make good his escape to the farthest inhabited areas of Gallaecia.
>
> *Hydatius s.a.* 456–7.

Theoderic followed up his success by invading Gallaecia itself. On 28 October he sacked the town of Bracara. Hydatius notes that in the sack of the town it was mainly the Roman population that suffered, a great many being taken captive. Rechiarius was captured and the remaining Sueves surrendered.[91] It was at this point that Hesychius, the envoy from Avitus, arrived and informed Theoderic both of the victory over the Vandals in Corsica and that Avitus was retiring towards Arles.[92] In December Theoderic had Rechiarius executed, and appointed a man named Aioulfus as the new King of the Sueves before withdrawing from Gallaecia to Lusitania.[93] The move backfired in more ways than one: first, shortly after his appointment Aioulfus asserted his independence and refused to obey Theoderic's orders; and second, not all of the Sueves were happy with the imposition of Aioulfus – the Sueves 'in the farthest reaches of Gallaecia' crowned a man named Maldras as their new king.[94] Theoderic's grip on north-western Hispania had loosened as soon as he had left the region.

The Defeat of Avitus: the 'Battle of Piacenza'

Back in Italy, Ricimer now knew that in order to avoid a full-scale civil war between Italy and Gaul Avitus needed to be stopped before he reached his power base and, more importantly, before he could rally the support of his major allies, the Goths of Theoderic, at the time preoccupied with affairs in Hispania.[95] Furthermore, either now or earlier, Majorian had returned to give a report of his victory over the Vandals. Joining the rebellion, Ricimer and Majorian set out in pursuit, but it would appear that Avitus only heard of the 'revolt' and of his 'deposition' as the enemy approached on 17 October. In desperation, Avitus took refuge in the city of Placentia (Piacenza). At last learning of Remistus' death, Avitus appointed Messianus as the new *magister militum* and *patricius*. It is most likely at this time that a man named Agrippinus was selected as the new *magister militum per Gallias* and immediately sent to Gaul.[96]

With the city surrounded, on the following day Avitus led his small force out of the city in a desperate attempt to break through the encircling forces and escape. It should be noted that the usual account – namely that Avitus had gone to Arles, acquired reinforcements and then led these in an attack from Placentia against vastly superior forces – should be discounted as propaganda aimed at establishing his bravery: in reality, no experienced military commander would attack a superior force in such a manner when he had the option of simply retiring to Gaul and gathering reinforcements.[97] Messianus was killed in the attempt and most of Avitus' forces were destroyed. Avitus and a small group of survivors took sanctuary in a nearby shrine, where they were besieged.[98] Eventually, it was agreed that his life would be spared if he agreed to be consecrated as a bishop and so be removed from political affairs. Consequently, Eusebius, the Bishop of Milan, was quickly summoned and Avitus was consecrated as Bishop of Piacenza.[99] Although the sparing of Avitus' life was to be an exception in Ricimer's methods, it is likely that Majorian, who was renowned for his concepts of fair play and mercy, had a hand in Avitus' survival.[100]

Death of Avitus[101]

The ordination of Avitus probably took place in late October (allowing time for Bishop Eusebius to be summoned), by which time the news of his deposition will have been spreading throughout Gaul. The fact that their nominee had been overthrown, plus the fact that Ricimer had assumed 'temporary' control of Italy, will have alarmed the Gallic nobility.[102]

In this context the details surrounding Avitus' death are intriguing. Gregory of Tours claims that, discovering that the Senate in Rome remained hostile and wished him dead, Avitus:

> Set out for the church of St Julian, the martyr of Clermont, taking with him many gifts. On the journey he died and his body was carried to the village of Brioude, where it was buried at the foot of the above named martyr.
>
> Gregory of Tours, 2.11.

It has been suggested that Gregory's claim concerning the nature of the 'gifts' is a later interpretation. It is possible that the money and goods he was carrying were instead intended to help fund a revolt in Gaul.[103] In this scenario, the plot was uncovered as Avitus fled to Gaul to start the revolt, but he was captured and killed on the orders of either Ricimer and/or Majorian. This interpretation has the benefit of explaining why the sources differ. Those sources from Gaul and Hispania, which are 'friendly' to Avitus, have him treacherously killed by Ricimer and/or Majorian, whereas hostile sources from Italy have him plotting a rebellion. The most likely explanation for his death is that neither Ricimer nor Majorian believed that Avitus was travelling to Gaul for religious reasons, instead judging that once in Gaul he would again claim the throne, leading to an all out civil war between Gaul and Italy. Obviously, rather than take the risk they decided to eliminate Avitus once and for all. However, as is usual, this interpretation should be seen as probable but not definite.[104]

Despite the Senate's assumed hostility, Avitus' three (known) children – Papianilla, Ecdicius and Agricola – survived his downfall: Sidonius even gave Ecdicius, his brother-in-law, the advice that he should retreat to his native town and avoid 'princes' who may see him as a threat.[105] Although Ecdicius appears to have taken this advice, the fact that all three children survived unharmed suggests that once Avitus was dead the senators and nobility of Gaul were no longer seen as a threat by the Senate in Rome.

The date of Avitus' death is unknown. The only clue is in the *Continuatio Prosper ad a 462*, which states that after his death there was an interregnum of fifteen months.[106] Although the precision of the entry, as well as the assumption inherent concerning the date of Avitus' death, is open to different interpretations, it would seem that Avitus died somewhere between late October 456 and early February 457.[107]

Interestingly, the *Gallic Chronicle of 511* claims that Avitus was killed by Majorian.[108] As Majorian is otherwise known for his clemency, the fact that on this occasion he is portrayed as being ruthless adds to the possibility that Avitus was indeed planning a revolt, and that, learning of this, Majorian had little option but to execute Avitus. Following his execution the *magister militum* Ricimer assumed full command of the West. He would spend the rest of his life ensuring that he never lost his position.

Gaul and Hispania

Understandably, the overthrow of their own Emperor infuriated the nobility of Gaul. This can be demonstrated by events at two separate locations in Gaul.

Lyon

In Lyon the senators were clearly angry at the death of Avitus – a factor which to some degree supports the claim that the Burgundians were settled in the region with the agreement of both Avitus and the nobles of the city: the nobles would otherwise have welcomed a new emperor to whom they could appeal for the Burgundians to be removed. Instead, the citizens of Lyon flatly refused to acknowledge the validity of any new emperor appointed in Italy to take Avitus' place, as demonstrated by an inscription set up in June 458.[109] Furthermore, and with complete disregard for the Western court, the citizens sent a delegation in the form of an archdeacon of the city to the Eastern Emperor Leo asking that their taxes be remitted.[110]

Narbonne: The *coniuratio Marcelliniana*

Alongside the evidence from Lyon, Sidonius relates a few snippets concerning the *coniuratio Marcelliniana*, an attempt to revolt instigated in Southern Gaul, centred on Narbonne.[111] Although details are limited and the identity of all concerned is open to doubt, it would appear that upon hearing of Avitus' deposition the citizens of Narbonne, possibly acting with the agreement of other cities, raised the standard of revolt.[112] The conspirators may have been attempting to force the restoration of Avitus, but such notions were quickly destroyed by his death. The conspirators may have then had the idea of appointing a second Gallic emperor, a man named Marcellus, 'of whom there are several attested in Gaul at this time', hence the name given by Sidonius to the revolt, or it may be that this was simply the name of the instigator of the uprising who had no intention of assuming the throne.[113] Certainty is impossible. The only other named individual was a man named Paeonius, who quickly assumed the office of Praetorian Prefect of Gaul.

Hispania

Avitus was probably still also recognized in Hispania as the legal emperor, since Theoderic, who was campaigning in Hispania, was his ally.[114] From Theoderic's later actions it is clear that he also was infuriated by the death of Avitus and this attitude will almost certainly have pervaded those areas of Hispania still loyal to the Empire, and especially those dominated by Theoderic.

Ricimer and Majorian

The reasons for Avitus' fall are clear, but the specific motives behind Ricimer and Majorian's involvement in the coup are unknown. This is underlined by the fact that following Avitus' downfall there was an interregnum lasting several months, during which neither Majorian nor Ricimer attempted to fill the vacant throne. The implication here is that neither man was reacting specifically in his own interests, but was instead acting in accord with general feeling both of the citizens and of the Senate of Rome. On the other hand, it was obvious that at some point a new emperor would be needed and that the primary candidate was Majorian.

Chapter Five

Majorian

1 April 457–August 461

Interregnum

After a brief reign Avitus was dead. Given the rioting that had earlier taken place, it is certain that the Senate and people of Rome were thankful that his reign was over. Sadly, there are no indications in the sources of precisely what happened next. It is feasible that Majorian was now accepted by all as the only possible successor to Avitus. On the other hand, there remained powerful men in the Senate who will have seen Avitus' removal as a chance to put forward their own claim.[1] That there was a division in opinion is likely, taking into consideration the fact that there was now a 'gaping interregnum' without an emperor: the delay may have been caused at least in part by dissension in the Senate.[2] Theoretically, the Empire was once more united under the Eastern emperor.[3] Yet there was little chance that anyone other than Majorian would be crowned as the new emperor in the West: Ricimer and Majorian commanded the loyalty of the army, and Ricimer appears to have backed Majorian from a very early date.[4]

Theoderic, Gaul and Hispania

Although the Roman populace and Senate were happy with the removal of Avitus, the feeling was not shared throughout the whole of the West. This was especially the case regarding the Goths and the Burgundians. Clarity is impossible and as usual there are a variety of interpretations, but it would appear that as part of the agreement between Avitus and the Goths regarding the invasion of Hispania, Theoderic had asked for help from the Burgundians and had arranged with Avitus that the Burgundians, recently defeated by the Gepids, would be given land around Lyon as a reward for their service.[5]

Despite the death of his ally Avitus, Theoderic was now in a strong position. His support for Avitus and the Gallic unhappiness with Avitus' death meant that it was unlikely that Theoderic would be attacked in 457. In the meantime, his authority in Hispania had been challenged by Aioulfus and Theoderic decided that he needed to secure his rear before challenging the Empire in Gaul.

However the Goths were not the only ones in Gaul to benefit from the confusion in Italy. The 'Ripuarian' Franks seized the opportunity to extend their dominion by invading imperial territory. At an unknown date in 457 they captured the cities of

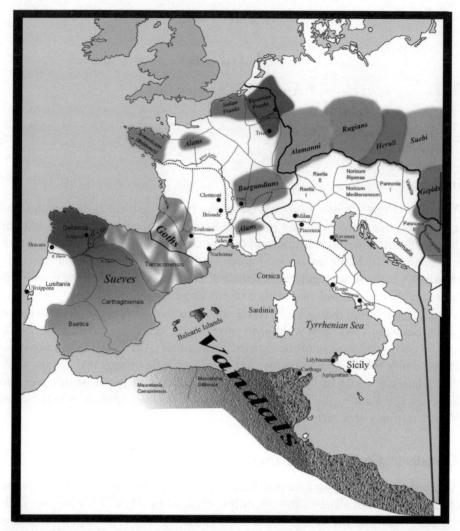

Map 8: The West during the early reign of Majorian. The Vandal presence around Lilybaeum in Sicily is assumed from later events.

both Cologne and Trier.[6] To the inhabitants of Gaul it must have seemed as if the Empire had simply forgotten their existence.

Majorian and the East

In the meantime, messages were sent to Marcian in the East asking for guidance, seeking news of Marcian's proposed campaign against the Vandals, and possibly putting forward Majorian's name as the West's preferred option as emperor.[7] Sadly for the West, the removal of Avitus coincided with a period of confusion in the East. It is possible that upon hearing the news Marcian 'toyed with the idea' of making an Eastern *magister militum* and *patricius* named Anthemius the Western Emperor.[8] However, on 26 January 457 the Emperor Marcian died. After a brief hiatus, on 7 February 457 the Eastern *magister militum* Aspar installed a man named Leo as the new emperor in the East. One of Leo's first actions was to send messengers to Rome, and on 27 February 457 Ricimer was appointed the new Western *patricius* and Majorian was made *magister equitum* (Ricimer retained the post of *magister peditum*).[9]

The reasons for the appointments are clear: Leo had only just been made the new emperor in the East and wanted time with which to deliberate over the appointment of a junior colleague in the West. Furthermore, the nature of his appointment meant that Western affairs were secondary to his need to firmly establish himself in the East: Marcian's proposed campaign against the Vandals was cancelled. In this context, it is clear that the modern suggestion that the interregnum was caused by Ricimer's attempt to rule the West as Marcian's regent is unfounded: Leo was simply allowing himself time to make an informed decision without having his judgement impaired by the demands of establishing his rule in the East.[10] In this Leo may have been following the example set by his predecessors Theodosius I and Theodosius II, although he would have known the danger of delaying: Theodosius I waited for too long a time over the elevation of a new emperor in 391–2, causing the civil war with the usurper Eugenius, and in 423 Theodosius II waited too long and the usurper John was elected by the West, again leading to civil war.

Italy Invaded

With affairs in Gaul becoming increasingly hostile, events in Italy also conspired against a peaceful transferral of power. What happened is, as usual, poorly recorded and open to interpretation, so the narrative given here is not definitive. However, when taking into account prior and later events it is believed to be the one that fits the facts and chronology the closest.

As of 27 March 457 Ricimer and Majorian were acknowledged as joint *magistri militiae*.[11] Certainty is impossible, but it would appear that Ricimer took command of the Italian forces and moved south to face the expected return of the Vandal 'pirates', who could be expected to raid Italy from March onwards if the weather was favourable. This made sense: Ricimer had recently defeated the Vandals in Sicily so had a record of victory over the invaders.

In the meantime, Majorian was to stay in the north – given later events he was based in Ravenna – and await further news from Gaul and the East. Although Majorian also had a successful military record against the Vandals and could have commanded the troops in the south, it may have been thought that Eastern envoys would react more positively when faced with a Roman rather than a 'barbarian' commander.

Unexpectedly, in very late March 457, a force of 900 Alamanni crossed the Alps from Raetia and invaded Italy.[12] Majorian responded by giving an otherwise unknown individual named Burco command of a small group of mixed units –

presumably the bulk of the army were in the south with Ricimer – and orders to face the Alamanni.[13] Burco gained a 'resounding victory' and the Alamanni were either crushed or forced to flee.[14] It is interesting to note the speed of this victory: over the winter of 357–8 the Emperor Julian had spent 54 days besieging 600 Franks in 'strongholds' in Gaul: there was no such delay here.[15]

Majorian the Emperor

It would seem that at this point the army demanded that Majorian become emperor: on 1 April 457 Majorian was acclaimed by the army, six miles outside Ravenna, at a place called *ad Columellas* (at the Little Columns), although he may have only accepted on the proviso that the East agreed to his elevation.[16] In this way he could ensure maximum support for his plans from the resource rich East. Accordingly, messengers were sent to Leo and negotiations begun to ensure amicable relations between the two courts, from later events including the proposal that Majorian be the Western nominee as consul for the following year. There is no evidence that at this date Majorian was appointed Caesar or 'junior emperor' by Leo.[17]

Theoderic

In June 457, shortly after the army had acclaimed Majorian as emperor but with Majorian still awaiting confirmation from the East, Theoderic once again invaded Hispania. In a very quick campaign he managed to defeat and kill Aioulfus in battle. Although by now it was clear that it would take several campaigns to quell the Sueves, at least he had limited their ability to dominate Hispania. Furthermore, his actions had ensured that some of the citizens of Hispania would look to him as their saviour and benefactor, rather than an ineffectual emperor in Italy. But not all: as part of his plan to prevent a resurgence of the Sueves, large areas of Roman Hispania were ravaged by the Goths.[18] Yet in one way the Sueves played into his hands: rather than uniting behind a single leader, some of the Sueves refused to accept Maldras, the man earlier raised in opposition to Aioulfus, as their king, electing instead an individual named Framtane to be their ruler.[19] At this point the Sueves themselves arranged a peace treaty with the peoples of Gallaecia:[20] the threat of further Gothic attacks had at least made them realize that they needed a secure and loyal base from which to resist Theoderic. With their rear secured the Sueves under Maldras attacked Lusitania and pillaged the city of Ulixippona (Lisbon).[21]

Returning to Gaul, Theoderic implemented the agreement he had reached with Avitus: 'The Burgundians took part of Gaul and divided the lands with the Gallic senators.'[22] The concept that the move was agreed with Avitus and backed by the citizens of Gaul in general and of Lyon in particular is supported by the fact that Sidonius, Avitus' *tribunus et notarius*, also took part in the settlement, a decision which would weigh against him in the coming years.[23] However, Theoderic had left some of his own troops and the Burgundian allies in Hispania. Whether against orders from Theoderic is unknown, but shortly after his departure these troops captured the Roman city of Asturica, looting the city and slaughtering the inhabitants.[24]

Ricimer and Campania

Earlier, Ricimer had moved south to counter any threat to the mainland from marauding Vandal pirates. One of the problems for the infant regime was that although the north of Italy had been the focus for attacks from across the Alps, and accordingly many northern cities had had walls built to defend them, the same does not appear to be true for the south. Safe from barbarian attacks, many southern cities did not have defences and so were vulnerable to attack by fast-moving marauders who had no access to siege engines.[25]

Gaiseric and his men already knew this and another raiding force was dispatched from Carthage, this time under the leadership of Gaiseric's son-in-law. The ensuing events are described in some detail by Sidonius:

> Lately … A savage foe was roaming at his ease over the unguarded sea. Under southerly breezes he invaded the Campanian soil and with his Moorish soldiery attacked the husbandmen when they dreamed not of danger; the fleshy Vandal sat on the thwarts waiting for the spoil, which he had bidden his captives to capture and bring thither. But, of a sudden thy bands had thrown themselves between the two enemy hosts into the plains which sunder the sea from the hills and fashion a harbour where the river makes a backward curve. First the multitude of plunderers flees in terror towards the mountains, and so, cut off from the ships they had left, they become the prey of their prey; then the pirates are aroused and mass their whole forces for the battle. Some land their well-trained steeds in hollow skiffs, some don the meshed mail of like hue to themselves, so get ready their shapely bows and the arrows made to carry poison on the iron point and to wound doubly with a single shot. Now the broidered Dragon speeds hither and thither in both armies, his throat swelling as the zephyrs dash against it … From everywhere a shower of steel comes down, but from our side it comes down on the throats of the foe … Soon as the Vandal began to turn and flee, carnage took the place of battle … In their panic flight the horsemen plunged pallid into the water and passed beyond the ships, then swam back in disgrace to their boats from the open sea.
>
> *Sidonius Apollinaris*, Carmina *5.385f.*

It would appear that the Moors were sent out to scout and ravage the countryside whilst the main Vandal contingent waited at their ships for news: the events of the previous year, when raids on both Sicily and Corsica had been heavily defeated, appears to have instilled a level of caution in Gaiseric's son-in-law. Sadly for the Vandals, it was not enough: Ricimer managed to insert his army between the Moors and the Vandals, forcing the Moors to flee to the mountains, where they were killed by the local inhabitants. Forming up, the Romans faced the Vandals in pitched battle.

After a brief period of contact the Vandals turned to flight, boarding their vessels and fleeing the scene of their defeat. Gaiseric's son-in-law was one of those killed in the attack. Ricimer's ability to 'ambush' the enemy had again ensured a victory.

The date of the attack is unknown, but the inference from Sidonius is that it was at some point early in the summer, as it is described as happening shortly after Majorian was acclaimed as emperor. The two rapid victories over the Alamanni and the Vandals enhanced the reputations of Burco and Ricimer, and by association Majorian: it would have appeared to the citizens of Italy that the tide of battle against the barbarians had turned.

There is little evidence for other events at court or in Italy in 457 so it may be assumed that other tribes who had been deliberating on whether to attack Italy were dissuaded by Burco's victory. Likewise, it is possible that a third defeat in two years, and this time including the death of his son-in-law, persuaded Gaiseric that further attacks on Italy would be unprofitable. It is probably from 457–458 that Gaiseric began the subjugation and annexation of the Mauretanian provinces, as well as Sardinia, Corsica, and the Balearic Islands.[26] Sadly, very little information survives regarding Vandal activity throughout these years so no precise dates can be given to any of these events.

What can be certain is that at some point late in the year envoys arrived from Leo accepting Majorian as the new Western emperor.[27] Furthermore, Leo acceded to Majorian's request to be named as the West's consul for 458. On 28 December Majorian was officially acclaimed emperor in Ravenna.[28] Four days later, on 1 January 458, Majorian followed tradition by celebrating his appointment as consul for the following year.[29]

Majorian and Ricimer

It is often assumed that the crowning of Majorian was Ricimer's first success at placing a 'puppet' emperor on the Western throne.[30] There are some arguments in favour of this proposition. Ricimer's later record of making and deposing emperors is naturally assumed to have begun at the first opportunity. However, there are several factors that are sometimes overlooked which suggest that this was not the case.

One piece of evidence that has often been used to determine the relationship between the two men is to be found in the *Novellae Maioriani* (New Laws of Majorian). In the first of these it is unmistakable that Majorian is accepting Ricimer as a 'partner', with the two men ruling jointly as emperor and *magister militum*. Unfortunately, this can be used to 'prove' both points of view. Some have used it as evidence that the two men were working in tandem and that Ricimer clearly accepted Majorian as his superior, and that he was content to hold the posts of *patricius* and *magister militum*, exactly as his predecessors Stilicho and Aetius.[31] Obviously, the law can also be used to suggest that even at this early stage Ricimer was the dominant 'partner', forcing Majorian to accept him as a virtual equal. As a result, the law is inconclusive.

What is possibly more telling is the previous connexion of the two men. Ricimer will have known of Majorian's military ability, of the senate's desire to have Majorian as emperor, and also of Majorian's personality, which does not appear to have been one willing to become a 'puppet' emperor dominated by Ricimer. Furthermore, Majorian was already the commander of the guard (*comes domesticorum*) when he was made emperor and so may have had the loyalty of a large part of the army: there was no chance of him accepting the role of 'junior partner' or 'puppet'.[32]

As a final note, it is common for a 'puppet' ruler to be kept isolated from events and surrounded by supporters of the 'puppeteer'. For example, Valentinian III had been left in Ravenna for the majority of his rule, with Aetius travelling throughout Gaul and Italy and supervising the defence of the Empire in his name. On the contrary, Majorian's actions from an early stage in his rule demonstrate a freedom of action incommensurate with that of a puppet ruler.

In light of this appraisal, it is certain that at the beginning of Majorian's reign the two men were working as partners, with Majorian as the dominant force behind imperial policy – a fact especially underlined by events during the first year of his rule. Yet it should be noted that in some ways Ricimer appears to have fulfilled much the same role as his predecessors, Stilicho and Aetius, having responsibilities 'that went well beyond the purely military'.[33] It was obvious to both men that the Empire was in dire straits and needed at least two competent military commanders and administrators in order to survive.

New Beginnings

It wasn't only the military situation which caused concern to Majorian. Financially and politically the situation in Rome was problematic. Majorian's *Novellae* gives some insight into how he attempted to rectify the situation. For example, with regards to the financial difficulties, *Novella 2* is concerned with the raising of tax.[34] Although it is granting the usual remission of tax arrears, what can be overlooked is the purpose behind the law itself: by cancelling the tax debts that had not been paid, Majorian will have hoped that those individuals who had not paid their taxes in the past would now feel relief and gratitude to the emperor and so be more willing to pay the current tax demands and help replenish the Treasury. Furthermore *Novellae 5* and *7*, concerned with the prevention of corruption and the continuing problems with *decurions* (city councillors) avoiding their duties, also in part attempted to solve the financial problems he faced.[35]

Politically, *Novellae 3, 6, 9, 10* and *11* (on the reopening of the post of *defensor civitatis*, female celibacy, inheritance, adultery, and enforced clerical ordination respectively), attempted to address some of the concerns amongst the aristocracy at this time, especially the decline in the aristocratic population due to the loss of high-status men and women to celibate lives within the Church.[36] On the other hand, and especially with regards to senators of powerful and long-lived families, *Novella 4* was concerned with the protection of public buildings: this would be of a special importance to senators concerned about the collapse of many monumental structures erected by their ancestors.[37] In an era of political and administrative upheaval, the Senate was intent on protecting both its past and its future and Majorian was attempting to ensure the Senate's support for his position.[38] For the time, he succeeded.

Ricimer

Throughout this period it would seem that Ricimer remained in the south of Italy, prepared to defend the coasts against any further attacks by the Vandals. With Gallic territory being seized by barbarians, whether with the agreement of the former administration or not, it was obvious that Gaul would need Majorian's personal intervention. Before he could go to Gaul in person Majorian needed to expand the *praesental* army of Italy to the point where it could be used for a major campaign of reconquest. The year of 458 would be a busy time for the new emperor.

Chapter Six

Majorian: Apotheosis – 458

Aegidius

As shown above, and despite some modern assertions that Majorian was simply a puppet of Ricimer from an early stage in his reign, it is clear that Majorian was his own man, appointing individuals of his own choosing to positions of power – as will quickly become clear.

One of Majorian's first decisions was certainly the recall of Agrippinus, *magister militum per Gallias*, who had been appointed by Avitus.[1] A man named Aegidius, a native of Gaul who had served alongside Majorian under Aetius and who was a strong supporter of Majorian, was appointed in his place.[2] From later events it is clear that Aegidius had a strong political base in the north of Gaul (see below) and this was to be of major importance later in his career.

The forces commanded by Aegidius (and his successor) are nowhere described so it is necessary to resort to hypothesis.[3] As a Roman general Aegidius would have had his own *bucellarii*, mercenaries serving under an individual within the Empire. In addition, he will also have taken command of the units of the Gallic field army. These men will have formed the core of his army and will have been supplemented from a variety of sources in northern Gaul, including *limitanei* and *coloni*. Furthermore, once it became known that Aegidius was intent on defending Gaul it is likely that he will have received fresh Gallic recruits who would otherwise not have joined, as they would have feared being transferred away from their native lands.

Travelling to his new command Aegidius was to suffer a major setback: at some time in 457, and doubtless taking advantage of perceived Roman weakness, the 'Ripuarian' Franks had expanded their sphere of control in Gaul, taking control of Cologne and Trier.[4] At the time, there was little he could do due to the 'rebellions' in Gaul and the threat posed by Theoderic, the sponsor of Avitus.

However, at around the same time Aegidius may have received some good news. Details are sparse but it is possible to associate the crowning of Majorian as emperor with events further to the north. The 'King' of the 'Salian' Franks was a man named Childeric. According to Gregory of Tours, in 457–8 he was driven out of his kingdom by the Franks and Aegidius was invited to take his place.[5] Childeric fled to the Thuringians, from where he schemed to regain his position amongst the Franks.[6] The implication here is that Childeric had been a supporter of Avitus and that his expulsion was an attempt by the Salian Franks to ensure that they were at peace with the Empire.[7] Given that their neighbours the Ripuarian Franks were advancing aggressively at this time, this would allow the

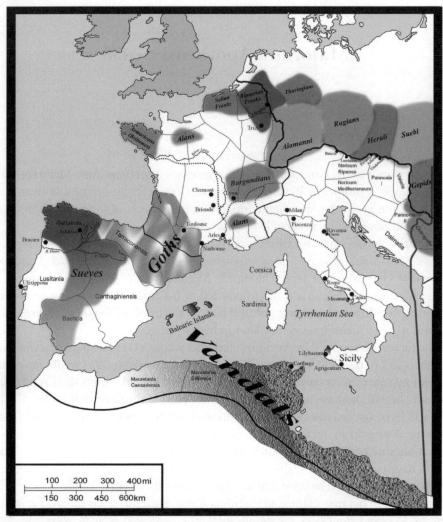

Map 9: Assumed Barbarian expansion during the early reign of Majorian.

Salians to concentrate upon one enemy at a time and also to call for Roman aid should the need arise. For the Romans, the alliance with the Salian Franks would act as a counter to the expansion of the Ripuarian Franks.[8] However, it is unlikely that Aegidius actually became their king. It is more likely that they accepted his protection on behalf of Rome and conducted all of their business via Aegidius, a man who they knew and trusted.[9]

In the meantime, Aegidius accused Agrippinus of planning to hand over territory in Gaul to the barbarians – possibly with regard to the settlement of the Burgundians, who had been granted land around Lyon for their own.[10] Doubtless Agrippinus' political enemies accused him of also planning to give further territory to other barbarian groups. He was found guilty of the charges and condemned to death, but according to one account fortunately managed to escape.[11] Although there may be some truth in the story of his escape, it is likely that he also had support in Rome which managed to convince Majorian to spare his life.[12] He would later return to the service of the Empire.[13]

Majorian the Politician

In order to recover lost territories, and especially to reassert control in Gaul when faced with the opposition of Theoderic, Majorian needed competent commanders and new troops. Where he obtained the money at such short notice is unknown, although it is possible that revenues were quickly raised by the law mentioned earlier in which delinquent taxes were remitted on the condition that current tax demands were met.[14] Furthermore, the law targeted the rich and powerful who had previously both refused to pay taxes and kept to their estates to avoid legal action.[15] However, the fact that this provision also applied to the Imperial estates is evidence that the phrase 'throughout the provinces' contained in the law is not proof that Majorian was annoyed by the fact that Gallic senators had ignored tax demands, but that the law instead applied to all 'loyal' provinces of the West.[16] Furthermore, at this early date Majorian will not have wanted to target only the nobles of Gaul, as he would not want to risk the rebellion in Lyon and Narbonne spreading by levying large taxes only in one area.

Whatever the source of income, Majorian used the money to hire mercenaries from the barbarian tribes 'living in the Danube basin'. This has been questioned, largely on the premise that this area was under the 'jurisdiction' of Leo.[17] This appears to be an odd conclusion. The tribes on the northern frontier across the Rhine were either hostile, such as the Ripuarian Franks, or defending their homes against such aggressive tribes, for example the Salian Franks.[18] As a result, the only tribes from which to recruit troops would be those on the Danube frontier. Leo would be happy for these men to serve in the West: after all, such service would remove them from the East's frontiers, so reducing the opposition to Leo if war broke out. Furthermore, in early 458 it is unlikely that Leo had the political power to stop mercenaries from the area serving wherever they wanted.

The list from Sidonius is more extensive than is often acknowledged. The new army allegedly consisted of the following tribesmen:

Bastarnian, Suebian, Pannonian, Neuran, Hun, Getan, Dacian, Alan, Bellonotan, Rugian, Burgundian, Visigoth, Alites, Bisaltan, Ostrogoth, Procrustian, Sarmatian, Maschan have ranged themselves behind thine eagles; in thy service are the whole Caucasus and the drinker of the Don's Scythian waters.

Carmina, 5.474–479.

Some of those listed are anachronistic and merely literary devices to emphasize the breadth of support for the new emperor, while others, such as the Pannonians,

Alans, and Burgundians, may have been recruited from settlers inside the Empire obliged to supply troops according to the terms of their *foedus* (treaty) with Rome.[19] Interestingly, as noted above, there is no mention of a Frankish contingent. Whatever their origin, it was clear that Majorian was intent upon regaining control of the West.

With a large army being gathered, and recognizing the importance of sea power if the Vandals were ever to be defeated, Majorian used at least some of the new taxes to finance the construction of a large navy, intent on retaking Africa:

> Meanwhile you built on the two shores fleets for the upper and lower sea. Down into the water falls every forest of the Apennines; for many a long day there is hewing on both slopes of those mountains so rich in ships' timber ...
> *Sidonius Apollinaris*, Carmina, 5.441–442.

The two fleets perhaps were those stationed traditionally at Misenum and Ravenna on the Tuscan and Adriatic Seas respectively.[20] The fleet at Misenum was doubtless to help defeat the Vandals. That at Ravenna would have two main duties. Their major task was to help in the reconquest of Africa. At the same time they were to facilitate Majorian's contacts with Marcellinus in Illyricum.

Marcellinus

It would appear that in 358 Majorian sent envoys to Marcellinus, who was still in control of Dalmatia. Marcellinus' refusal to accept orders from the court in Italy after the death of Aetius had lost the Empire a useful recruiting ground. Further, Marcellinus was now in a strong position and Majorian doubtless wanted to gain his support for the new regime. Later events clearly show that Marcellinus was willing to come to terms with Majorian, who had also earlier been a loyal supporter of Aetius. The eastern flank of the Western Empire now appeared to be secure. Although it has been suggested that Marcellinus only agreed to support Majorian because he had accepted the rule of Leo, the new Eastern emperor, and Leo now ordered Majorian to aid the West; this is not clearly corroborated by the evidence and appears to be an unnecessary and convoluted theory.[21] It is easier to accept that the elevation of one of Aetius' supporters to the throne eased Marcellinus' decision to accept the legal authority of the new emperor, secure in the belief that Majorian would not do anything to threaten Marcellinus' control of Dalmatia.

However, Marcellinus was unable to send immediate help to Majorian. The accession of two strong emperors gave Leo the confidence to attempt to reassert Roman authority over the whole of the Balkans. Accordingly, Leo stopped the payments the East had been giving to the barbarian settlers in Pannonia and the surrounding areas.[22] Obviously, these peoples were unhappy with the turn of events and were determined to seek revenge.

Hispania

Although the chaos surrounding the fall of Avitus was slowly easing, Theoderic, the Gothic king, now faced a dilemma: should he concentrate his forces against the Sueves in Hispania or attempt to take advantage of imperial weakness in Gaul? His decision was made by a series of embassies travelling early in the year. The first of these was sent by Gaiseric, who appears to have been hoping to form an anti-Roman alliance with his erstwhile enemies the Goths. Shortly after Theoderic sent these ambassadors, along with envoys of his own, to the Sueves, possibly hoping to form a triple alliance that would carve up the remnants of the Western Empire whilst confusion reigned in Rome. The embassy failed: the Sueves remained intent simply on pillaging Hispania and paid no heed to the request from the Goths and Vandals.[23] The response so angered Theoderic that, despite the need to keep troops in Gaul to repel any imperial attacks, he sent a commander named Cyrila with reinforcements to Hispania to maintain the pressure on the Sueves. By July this army had reached Baetica, but unfortunately no further information concerning Cyrila's actions are available.[24]

The appearance of a Gothic army was none too soon for the peoples in the area. Shortly after Easter 458 the Suevic 'King' Framtane had died from unknown causes.[25] Although still not fully united, as a part of the Sueves were now following a man named Rechimundus, whose origin and status is unclear, Maldras ignored the warnings of previous years and betrayed the people of Gallaecia, pillaging the areas of the province bordering the River Durius (Duero).[26] Interestingly, both the Goths and the Vandals now sent envoys to the Sueves: sadly, no hint of their business survives and so it is impossible to guess what the Vandals desired.[27] Doubtless the envoys from the Goths demanded a halt to the recent attacks and the return of the spoils and any captives to their place of origin.

Appointment of Nepotianus

Almost certainly at the same time as he began recruiting new troops Majorian promoted a man named Nepotianus to the post of *magister equitum*, the post he had himself vacated upon becoming emperor. Although not usually noted, the appointment may have had a two fold motive. The first was that, hopefully, Nepotianus would prove to be an accomplished military commander. The second was an astute political move on the part of Majorian. Nepotianus was married to the unnamed sister of Marcellinus in Dalmatia and they had a son, named Julius Nepos, who would be a main player in the story of the last years of the West.[28] Majorian may have hoped that the fact that his brother-in-law had been made *magister militum* would weigh in favour of Marcellinus joining the new regime.

Ricimer, of course, remained the *magister peditum*. Later events demonstrate that the plan was for Ricimer to remain in Italy whilst Nepotianus and Aegidius conducted campaigns in Gaul, in Nepotianus' case alongside the emperor. It has been suggested that this was a slight to Ricimer, as the new appointments meant that Ricimer was left 'idle' in Italy, in a position of 'great power'.[29] This is not the case. Past events had proved that unless Italy was safe, the Senate would support a commander willing to promise the safety of the city of Rome. Consequently, the appointments can instead be perceived as Majorian demonstrating his strength of personality – being willing to leave Italy to deal with the problems in Gaul – combined with the knowledge that Italy was safe in the hands of one of the emperor's most able and trusted commanders. Rather than being a slight, the fact that Ricimer was left in Italy was an honour, highlighting the man's importance to the Empire as a whole and to Majorian in particular.

Gaul

These arrangements will have taken time and, with the Empire seemingly still in turmoil, at some point in the early/mid campaign season of 458 Theoderic gave in to temptation and led a small force to attack Narbonne.[30] Theoderic may have been forced to take only the few available troops on the attack; he may have been hoping that the city, still in 'revolt' from the Empire and doubtless lacking a core of troops with which to defend itself, would capitulate if threatened, or even that it might be taken by surprise if he acted quickly. He was to be disappointed. The citizens held out until news from Italy forced Theoderic to retire before he was himself attacked.

Aegidius had taken up his command in Gaul. As usual, the sources give no specific chronology and so the nature of events has to be deduced from a consideration of other aspects of the story. As a consequence, some have suggested that the primary target of Majorian was the Goths under Theoderic and that it was only after defeating the Goths, and with their help, that Majorian or his *magistri* moved north to defeat the Burgundians. This is a misreading of the primary source, in this case Priscus, combined with the *assumption* that the Goths were the priority.[31] This is not the case: all emperors' main concern was that internal unrest was defeated prior to 'external' threats. Although Theoderic could do a lot of damage to the south of Gaul, he would never be able to occupy the throne and it was therefore only a matter of time before the superior Roman army would defeat him and drive him back to his own lands. On the other hand, Gaul had only recently promoted its own emperor and Majorian would have been worried in case a usurper arose who could command the loyalty of the Gallic army and so threaten his own position. Lyon, Arles and Narbonne had priority over Theoderic.

At some date after June, when an inscription was set up in the city which did not acknowledge Majorian's consulship, and so probably between July and September, Aegidius and his forces arrived at the city of Lyon.[32] Shortly after his arrival Aegidius overcame the resistance of the citizens of the city as well as the settled Burgundians, although whether this was simply by a show of force or whether a battle needed to be fought is unknown.[33] Upon hearing of the success Majorian sent his *magister epistularum* (Chief of Correspondence) Petrus to impose terms on the Burgundians.[34] Although the details are not outlined, it is likely that the Burgundians were forced to re-acknowledge their federate status under Majorian

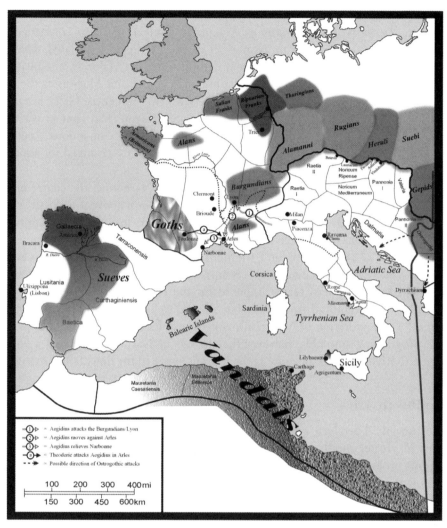

Map 10: Majorian's Recovery of the West. It is probable that the Goths relinquished their 'conquests' in Hispania but retained some of their Gallic extensions.

and that the Gallic senators had a tax penalty imposed: furthermore, either the Burgundians, or the senators, or both, were forced to give hostages to Majorian to ensure their fidelity to the treaty.[35] On the other hand, there is no mention in the sources that the Burgundians were removed from the city, so it is likely that they were allowed to remain in the area as long as they acknowledged the superiority of Majorian. Majorian had neither the time nor the resources to fight unnecessary campaigns.

Once affairs in Lyon had been settled, Aegidius took his forces to Arles. Earlier in the year Majorian had sent orders that Paeonius, who had 'usurped' the position of Praetorian Prefect of Gaul, should stand down and be replaced by Magnus of

Narbonne, who may have earlier been appointed as *magister officiorum* by Avitus. However, Paeonius' (brief) status as Praetorian Prefect was also confirmed by Majorian, allowing Paeonius to assume all of the privileges associated with ex-holders of the post.[36] Both choices clearly demonstrate that Majorian was an astute politician: by confirming Paeonius as the previous holder and Magnus as the new Prefect, Majorian was able to make an alliance with two influential Gallic senators, ensuring their support for his reign. Furthermore, Magnus had contact with the Goths and would be able to influence Theoderic in his choice of actions. Aegidius now confirmed all of the arrangements and almost certainly arranged for supplies to be gathered for his newly arrived army.

In the meantime, Aegidius turned his attention to Narbonne, the centre of the *coniuratio Marcelliniana*.[37] Events are unclear but as shown above it is possible that Theoderic had attacked the city earlier in the year but, hearing of the approach of Aegidius, he raised the siege and returned to his own territory. Determined to remain a part of the Empire, and frightened by Theoderic's readiness to attack them, it is likely that the citizens merely surrendered the city to Aegidius, a theory reinforced by the lenient terms imposed on the conspirators by Majorian: the ringleaders were removed from office but allowed to keep their old titles and their estates.[38] The restoration of Majorian's rule over at least Southern Gaul appeared to be progressing smoothly, however the citizens of Narbonne retained a hostile attitude to Ricimer, who they saw as the leading figure in the downfall of Avitus.[39]

Aegidius in Arles

Unfortunately, Theoderic's retreat from Narbonne was short-lived. Gathering fresh troops in greater numbers, late in the year Theoderic returned to the offensive. Aegidius probably returned to Arles after the restoration of Narbonne, since Arles was now the 'capital' of Gaul and all of the infrastructure for ruling the area was located in the city. Advancing into Imperial territory Theoderic trapped Aegidius in Arles and laid siege to the city.[40]

In Italy, with the situation in Gaul apparently calming and unaware of Theoderic's attack, Majorian decided that the Gauls were going to pay a large proportion of the taxes needed to finance the recovery of the Empire: 'No [tax] collector is to refuse a *solidus* of full weight, except for the Gallic *solidus*, whose gold is appraised at a lesser value.'[41] In effect, Majorian had increased the taxes for Gaul above those of the other provinces. With his punishment of Gaul for their disloyalty decided upon, shortly afterwards, and before the end of the year, Majorian headed towards Lyon.[42]

Leading his army across the Alps in person, Majorian suffered a setback both to his army's morale and to his personal authority.[43] A leader named Tuldila was in command of a section of troops in the army. Sidonius states that these men had 'withdrawn their untamed host from the Danube because they had lost their lords in warfare', implying that they were Huns who had moved away from their homeland due to the collapse of the Hunnic Empire after the Battle of the Nedao in 454. As they crossed the Alps, Tuldila led his men in 'unauthorized pillaging' of local Romans. Unwilling to risk his authority by punishing the Huns, Majorian pardoned them for their offence, but others in the army were unwilling to let this stand and massacred the Huns as they slept. According to Sidonius, the troops who had killed the Huns were allowed to keep the Huns' possessions as a 'reward'.[44]

The episode demonstrates both that Majorian was unable to control the newly enrolled troops, and that the force of his personality and strength of his rule was not strong enough to pass a judgement that the army was willing to accept. Although it is possible that the troops who massacred the Huns were members of the regular *praesental* army taking revenge for the devastation of Italian homes, the affair demonstrates that discipline in the army was poor.[45]

Once the situation had calmed, Majorian continued towards Gaul. It is likely that it was only as he crossed the Alps that he learned of Theoderic's attack and that Aegidius was besieged in Arles. Continuing his own journey it would appear that he ordered Nepotianus with a large detachment of troops to head south to relieve the siege.[46]

In the meantime, Aegidius had been defending the city against Theoderic. According to Gregory of Tours: 'Aegidius was being besieged by the enemy; reinforcements were not available. While he was being threatened and attacked, he prayed to the blessed man [Saint Martin].'[47] Given that Aegidius was allegedly praying for help, it is possible that the city was in dire straits, surrounded by an overwhelming number of Goths. On the other hand, it is just as likely that Gregory has simply played on the story to heighten tension and enhance the reputation of Saint Martin. It is possible that Theoderic was never going to be able to take the city.

Whatever the case, it is likely that Nepotianus' arrival was unexpected: Theoderic may have been unaware of the large numbers of mercenaries enrolled by Majorian and so not have expected to face a large Roman army. Although details have been lost, it appears that Nepotianus and Aegidius fought a battle against Theoderic, defeating the Goths in a face-to-face encounter.[48] Shortly after the battle Hydatius reported that:

> Envoys sent by the *magister militiae* Nepotianus and the *comes* Sunericus came to the Gallaecians and announced that *Augustus* Majorian and King Theodoric had established the strongest vows of peace between themselves, as a result of a Gothic defeat in a certain battle.
>
> *Hydatuis*, Chronicon, no. 197, *s.a.* 459.

Nepotianus had already proved his worth as a *magister militum* by both defeating Theoderic in battle and by arranging for a peace treaty to be signed between the two powers: and despite Gothic attacks, Majorian felt it necessary to integrate Theoderic into his new regime.[49] In Italy Ricimer may have felt a slight twinge of envy and alarm at the success of his junior *magister*.

459

Over the winter of 458–9 Majorian remained in Gaul. Not least of his problems was winning over the inhabitants of Gaul. Still angry at the death of Avitus, Majorian was to use all of his political ability to convert the Gallic senators into supporters of his regime. One of his first acts was to pardon Sidonius Apollinaris for Sidonius' involvement in the brief reign of Avitus, a pardon possibly eased by the fact that Sidonius had been simply following his own father-in-law and further helped by Majorian needing as much support in Gaul as he could get.

Thanks to the intervention of Petrus, Majorian's *magister epistolarum*, Sidonius was given permission to deliver a panegyric in honour of Majorian at Lyons, probably in early 459 – although the exact date is unknown.[50] In the panegyric Sidonius comments on the building of fleets and notes that: 'Gaul, though wearied by unceasing tribute, is now eager to gain approval by a new levy to this end, and feels not a burden wherein she holds a benefit.'[51] Although sometimes over interpreted, it would appear that the Emperor had retained the high taxes on Gaul in order to continue to build the necessary fleets: rather than being over critical of the emperor, Sidonius simply appears to be tactfully reminding Majorian that taxes were still very high, possibly in the hope that Majorian would relent.

Yet despite all of the 'praise' that is usual in such panegyrics it is clear that Sidonius was able to include much material that he hoped would influence the new emperor's future conduct. For example, Sidonius conveys his fear that Majorian was fighting solely to retain his throne rather than for the integrity of the Empire. 'All men fight for the emperor: I fear, alas! he now fights for himself.'[52] Further, Sidonius laments the fact that since the death of Gratian (383): 'My land of Gaul hath even till now been ignored by the lords of the world, and hath languished in slavery unheeded … for with the emperor … closely confined [Honorius and Valentinian III, in Ravenna] it has been the constant lot of the distant parts of a wretched world to be laid waste'.[53] For obvious reasons, in this diatribe he avoids any mention of Avitus, his father-in-law.[54]

After his delivery of the panegyric Sidonius was both pardoned and possibly raised to the rank of *comes spectabilis*.[55] This will have given hope to the members of Avitus' entourage that they too would be pardoned and at least allowed to retain their lands and titles. Much more effective as propaganda was Majorian's granting of the tax remission that the citizens of Lyon had earlier requested from Leo I in the East during the interregnum.[56] Yet despite these actions, and possibly because of Theoderic's incorporation into the political life of Rome, an 'ever larger proportion of the political classes of Southern Gaul was drawn into the Gothic orbit'.[57] The peoples of Gaul were to become ever more distrustful of the political ambitions of the Empire as time passed: Majorian was to be the last ruler accepted by the 'whole' of Gaul.[58]

Majorian's movements throughout 459 are unknown, mainly because none of the laws he passed at this time, which would have included the date and location of their writing, survive. Since the Council of the Seven Gauls was usually held at Arles it is probably safe to assume that a large proportion of his time was spent in the city, negotiating with the Gallic senators for their pardons, issuing laws aimed at the Roman provinces still held in Gaul, as well as continuing the preparations for an attack on Africa. As part of his programme of reconciliation, Majorian won Gallic support, partly by promoting Gauls to positions of power within Gaul.[59]

If not shortly before his departure from Italy, it was whilst he was in Gaul that Majorian will have learned of Leo's acceptance of the nomination of Ricimer as consul for the year. After only a short period in power Majorian appeared to be doing well. The East remained allied to his rule; the Goths under Theoderic had been defeated and reincorporated into the regime; the Gallic aristocrats had been converted to his cause, without alienating Avitus' supporters; and there seems to have been no sign of disquiet from Rome. There remained only two areas of concern: Hispania, where there was a running battle between the Goths and their Roman allies on the one hand and the Sueves on the other; and the continued Vandal presence in Africa.

Hispania

Now that he was again at peace with the Empire, and possibly having come to an agreement with Majorian similar to that he had earlier made with Avitus, Theoderic recalled Cyrila from Hispania and in his place sent the *dux* Suniericus with a detachment of troops.[60] Given that Gaul was now at peace it is likely that Suniericus was in command of a substantial number of men. Furthermore, and as earlier in 456, areas of Gallaecia were attacked by a number of Heruls on their way to Baetica, both attacks probably following orders from Theoderic.[61]

In the meantime, Maldras had further enhanced his power in Gallaecia. Before the Gothic reinforcements could arrive troops under Maldras had pillaged areas of Lusitania, those under 'King' Rechimundus parts of Gallaecia.[62] Due to the paucity of the sources, it is unknown whether the two men were acting in conjunction, possibly with Rechimundus following Maldras' directions, or independently. Shortly after, Maldras had his (unnamed) brother killed and intensified his attacks on Gallaecia, killing a number of Roman nobles and increasing the hostility of local Romans to his dominion.[63] The continued attempts to subdue Gallaecia demonstrate both that the Sueves were still unwelcome in the area, despite having been there since the early fifth century, and that resistance remained strong. According to Hydatius, it was now that the envoys arrived declaring that a peace treaty had been signed between the Goths and the Romans.[64] Since no further attacks are attested to this year, it would appear that the Sueves decided to withdraw to their own territory, doubtless fearful of events and expecting to be attacked by a combined Gothic and Roman force. Fortunately for them, they were to be given a respite: no allied attack was forthcoming for the rest of the year.

Illyricum

It is possible that Majorian had been hoping to transfer the army from Hispania to Africa in 459, but events thwarted any such plan. Negotiations between Majorian and Marcellinus in Illyricum may have resulted in an accord at this early date. However any attempts by Marcellinus to help Majorian were thwarted by external events. In 458 Leo had stopped the payments to the barbarian settlers in Pannonia and the surrounding areas, most notably the Amal Goths (Ostrogoths) under their ruler Valamir.[65] Valamir had earlier won fame by serving under Attila when the Hunnic Empire was at its zenith, taking part in the Battle of the Catalaunian Fields.[66] In response to the lack of payment, in 459 the Amali invaded the territory of Marcellinus, reaching the Adriatic and the city of Dyrrachium.[67] Under barbarian attack, there would be no possibility of Marcellinus helping Majorian in 459. It would be in the next year that the defining event of Majorian's reign would take place.

Chapter Seven

Majorian: The Fall

Hispania

Majorian's main objective for 460 was the obliteration of the Vandal kingdom in Africa and the restoration of Roman rule. Before he could begin, he needed the Sueves to accede to his peace proposals, and if not to be defeated, or at least to be restricted to the north-west of the Iberian Peninsula, as otherwise they could pose a threat to his lines of communication once he had crossed to Africa. An agreement was reached with Theoderic where a number of Gothic troops would serve the Empire in Hispania, although it should be noted that there is no evidence that they would be crossing to Africa and later events imply that the main use for the Gothic forces was to limit Suevic attacks. Probably even before the emperor had left for Hispania the *magister militum* Nepotianus was ordered into the peninsula, commanding troops alongside the Gothic *dux* Suniericus as the ships slowly gathered in Cartagena.[1]

As was by now usual, the envoys were not received favourably by the Sueves. In fact, it was to be at this point that in some respects the Sueves would turn into their own worst enemies. Rather than focusing upon events in Gaul and Italy, in 459 Maldras, the leader of one part of the Sueves, had killed his brother.[2] The murder was doubtless part of an ongoing series of political upheavals amongst the Sueves. In the New Year: 'At the end of February Maldras was assassinated and died the death he merited.'[3] The internal turmoil did little to dampen the Sueves' ardour for plunder and during the Easter period they attacked the city of Lucus, killing many people.[4] On the other hand, there was little chance of them uniting against the combined threat of the Goths and Rome.

Marcellinus

Yet although he was determined to invade Africa, Majorian was enough of a strategist to realize that Gaiseric had an easy way to prevent his invasion: to himself launch assaults against Sicily and Italy, resulting in the Senate in Rome demanding Majorian's return. Thankfully, Ricimer, who had already demonstrated his ability, had remained in Italy to defend against attack. This left only Sicily vulnerable.

It was now that Majorian's political ability shone through. Since Majorian had no link to the assassination of Aetius, and was almost certainly known by Marcellinus prior to Majorian's 'retirement' in 454, but mainly due to the common threat of the Vandals, in 460 Marcellinus agreed to help Majorian by moving with an army to

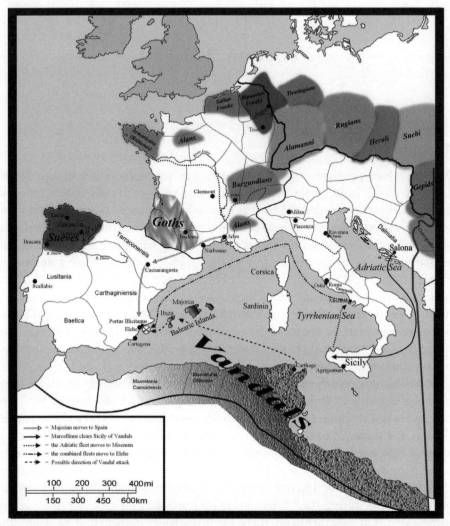

Map 11: The Vandalic War, including the campaign of Marcellinus.

Sicily, doubtless using transports from the new Adriatic fleet for the purpose.[5] In return he may have been made *magister militum Dalmatiae* by Majorian, although the post may have been given by Leo in 462 (see Chapter Eight).[6] Although sometimes assumed by scholars, there is no evidence that Marcellinus was either appointed by Leo at this date or that Leo put any pressure on Marcellinus to force him to serve in Sicily.[7] It is much easier to assume that all of the political manoeuvres of this period took place solely within the context of the Western Empire: there is absolutely no substantiation of Eastern involvement. Marcellinus soon proved his ability in the field: 'Marcellinus slaughtered the Vandals in Sicily and put them to flight from the island.'[8]

Hispania

At roughly the same time as Maldras' death, and at some point after 28 March, Majorian left Arles heading for Hispania.[9] In May he crossed the Pyrenees with his army and began the march to Carthaginiensis.[10] Further east, once spring had arrived, Marcellinus had attacked in Sicily. He may have arrived in Sicily earlier, but the weather conditions for this time of year were untrustworthy and he may have waited a little longer before beginning the sea journey down the Adriatic.

As usual the precise chronology is unknown, but it would seem likely that it was now that Nepotianus and Suniericus sent part of the allied force to Gallaecia to attack the Sueves.[11] The army moved as far as Lucus, where they pillaged areas under the control of the new Suevic 'King' Frumarius.[12] In the meantime, Suniericus took the remainder of his army in a more westerly direction to attack the Sueves and their allies around the city of Scallabis.[13] What Nepotianus did at this time is unclear: it may be that he secured the crossings of the Pyrenees to ensure good communications between Theoderic, Suniericus, and, not least, Majorian; or it may be that he remained at the 'base' for the operations, most likely to be Caesaraugusta. There also remains the possibility that he moved to take command of the navy as it assembled in the south, but this is nowhere mentioned and if he had been in control he would doubtless have been used in the sources as a scapegoat for what followed.[14]

With Marcellinus in Sicily, Ricimer in Italy, the Goths and Burgundians under control, and with the Sueves preoccupied in Hispania, Majorian prepared for the defining campaign of his career.

The Vandal Campaign

If Majorian was ever to recover the West it was clear that he had to eliminate the Vandals in Africa. This would solve many problems that the Empire was facing. In 455 the Vandals had sacked Rome itself and from that date onwards they had been attacking Italy and Sicily, and spreading their rule across North Africa and throughout the islands of the western Mediterranean, seemingly without end to their raids. Even when defeated, in the following year the attacks resumed. This was unacceptable to the Senate in Rome. Furthermore, the continued captivity of the imperial women was a constant embarrassment for the Empire. The detrimental effect on the morale of the inhabitants of the Western Empire will have been dramatic, not least the attitude outside Italy: if the Empire was unable to defend its home territory there was little chance that it could protect those inhabitants further afield.

The other reasons were financial and strategic. Obviously, Africa had been the breadbasket of Italy and without its grain Italy was finding it hard to feed itself. Furthermore, its taxes had gone a long way to keeping the Empire financially healthy. The loss had already resulted in the Empire becoming bankrupt. Food and taxes from the region had to be restored if the Empire was to rise again. Furthermore, the Vandal attacks will have disrupted trade, especially to Italy, the one area where such trade could be taxed and the money used by the central government. Strategically, it was necessary to first contain Gaiseric, allowing the resumption of trade, before retaking Africa itself. Not only would this restore the finances of the West, but with the seaborne threat to Italy removed the *praesental* army in Italy could more easily be deployed elsewhere without upsetting the rich nobles and senators in Rome. In addition, the released troops would allow the emperor to take a firmer control of those barbarian tribes settled inside the Empire. Furthermore, the propaganda effect of the resurgence of the Empire would help to deter external attack. Retaking Africa was vital.

The Navies[15]

Despite the many attempts to reconstruct the course of Majorian's project to reconquer Africa, few historians have analysed the events from a naval perspective, solely analysing the reasons for Majorian's decision to travel via Hispania from a logistical viewpoint.[16] In order to fully understand Majorian's dilemma it is necessary to look at the composition of the respective navies on the eve of the invasion.

Carthage
The nature of any ships captured by the Vandals in their annexation of Carthage in 439 is unclear. Although no naval force is attested as being stationed in the city, Carthage's main trade was the export of grain to Rome. Given the need to maintain ships and build new ones to replace any lost due to the weather or simple accidents, the port of Carthage will have stored large amounts of timber in the shipyards ready for use when the need arrived. Although the same is true, but possibly to a lesser extent, in Ostia, the Port of Rome, and possibly in Misenum, it is more likely that the majority of such repairs, along with the expense, were done in Carthage when at all possible: the province could easily afford the cost. As a result, Gaiseric will have had access to ship building materials and the expertise to use them for nearly two decades before war again broke out with Rome. Furthermore, the wood used will have been properly seasoned prior to use. It is likely that the majority of vessels built under Gaiseric's orders were transports to allow his men to conduct raids.

However, from 439–442 the Vandals were constantly concerned with the threat of the Empire uniting to crush their newly won kingdom. Although the Treaty of 442 will to some degree have lessened their worry, Gaiseric was a wily commander and will have been continuously preparing for a forthcoming war with the Empire. In addition, once Gaiseric had sacked Rome he will have been extremely wary of a Roman backlash, especially if the new Western rulers could organize a joint campaign with the East.

His decision to maintain vessels for the use of the Vandal army, rather than trade, may be implied by the speed at which he crossed to Italy and sacked Rome upon hearing of the death of Valentinian III, as well as by Victor of Vita, who mentioned the cutting of trees in Corsica 'for the King's ships'.[17] Although this is ascribed to the later reign of Huneric (477–84), the 'peaceful' reign of Huneric stands in contrast to the military expansion under Gaiseric, suggesting that Huneric followed his father's example. The evidence all implies that Gaiseric was building warships to defend his transport fleet as well as new transports.

In this context it is almost certain that Gaiseric will have ordered a 'large' number of *dromons* to be built, aimed at deterring an attack from the Empire, or at defeating an imperial fleet either en route to Africa, or at attacking the Romans as they disembarked troops in Africa itself, when they would be most vulnerable. These *dromons* were small agile ships with a single bank of oars, at this date the most common warship in the Mediterranean. Sadly, there is no evidence whatsoever of the composition or numbers of the Vandal fleet. The only clue that survives is Gaiseric's response to Majorian's building of a large fleet – as will be seen.

Rome

The Vandals had previously been defeated on Mediterranean islands by Majorian and Ricimer. In order for the Romans to transport troops to Sicily and Corsica it was necessary to have a fleet in the Tyrrhenian Sea capable of transporting substantial numbers of men. In the narrow seas between Italy and the adjoining islands the fleet was almost certainly composed of transports and conscripted merchant vessels, with few, if any, warships: they had simply not been needed and the Empire did not have the monetary surplus to allow the building and maintaining of a war fleet prior to the attack on Rome in 455: such a measure would have been seen simply as an unnecessary luxury.

In this context the information given by Sidonius, that Majorian had built two fleets (quoted above[18]), needs to be assessed. Although the existence of at least one small fleet in the Mediterranean prior to Majorian's reign is obvious, the lack of warships was a major failing. It is certain that at least some of the new ships being built were *dromons*, built to face Gaiseric's warships in battle. Unfortunately, such ships needed skilled crews and Majorian did not have access to a ready supply of such men: most of the peoples with a long tradition serving in ships were either under barbarian control (e.g. Carthage) or were in the East (e.g. Rhodes or the Phoenician ports). As a result, and with raw crews, it is likely that Majorian was unwilling to risk losing both the new *dromons* and the accompanying fleet of transports in a single sea encounter off the coast of Africa.

Furthermore, a major landing on the coast near to Carthage would be an extremely hazardous undertaking. A large army would take a long time to disembark and be exceptionally vulnerable to an attack by a mobile army that could move fast and catch them when they were disorganized. At the same time, the fleet itself would be exposed to a naval assault from the Vandal fleet. Even with a large number of *dromons*, to attempt such a landing with untrained crews was an exceptional risk and one that Majorian did not wish to try.

In fact, given the size of the 'invading' army, the majority of the ships being built were undoubtedly transport vessels aimed at moving as many men as possible as quickly as possible from one continent to the other. Such vessels would be easy targets for the Vandals' warships, and it is in this context that Majorian decided to use his fleet to transport his troops across the Straits of Gibraltar, a long way from Carthage and where he hoped to avoid armed resistance. In this context the modern hypothesis that the decision not to attack direct from Sicily to Africa was either a mistake or seems 'odd' appears to be mistaken.[19]

The African Campaign

At some point Gaiseric became aware of the Roman intentions to land in Africa. Accordingly, he sent 'insincere' envoys to Majorian in an attempt to negotiate peace, probably including the request that Eudocia's marriage to Huneric be recognized as legitimate.[20] His envoys were rebuffed and his reaction demonstrates that he was also aware of Majorian's decision to cross the Mediterranean from southern Hispania: he laid waste to those areas of Mauritania that Majorian would traverse and allegedly poisoned the wells that the Roman army would have to use.[21] These are not the actions of a ruler convinced that he would win: instead, they demonstrate that Majorian's forces were large enough to cause at least serious damage to the Vandal presence in Africa, if not to wipe it out completely. Gaiseric's panic also implies that the newly made Roman fleet was far larger than his own, even though the majority were only transport vessels.

Having rejected Gaiseric's negotiations, Majorian carried on with his invasion plans. He had given the fleet orders to meet at Portus Illicitanus, near Elche, on the Bay of Alicante forty miles from Cartagena. Marching separately with his army, Majorian moved slowly south and reached the city of Caesaraugusta.[22] As noted above, the city may have been acting as the base of operations for the campaign against the Sueves and most likely Nepotianus was here, ready to give reports on the course of the war. Not long after his arrival Majorian left the city and travelled onwards. It was during this journey, and probably after reaching Carthaginiensis, that he received devastating news.[23]

The Battle of Elche
According to their instructions, the fleet had moved to Elche and now awaited the arrival of Majorian with the army. Gaiseric, a cunning strategist who was unwilling to await the fall of the Roman axe, had decided upon a pre-emptive strike. Gathering his limited naval forces together Gaiseric had sent them west against the Romans, possibly using ports on the North African shoreline as bases. However, given Gaiseric's military abilities, plus the possibility that by this time he had already conquered the Balearic Islands, it is perhaps more likely that the fleet was sent to Majorca or Ibiza, from which position they could monitor activity along the whole of the eastern coast of Hispania. Although certainty is impossible, it is likely that Gaiseric remained in Carthage: Hydatius only states that the fleet was composed of Vandals, not led by Gaiseric in person.[24]

Informed of the location and composition of the Roman fleet, according to Hydatius by 'traitors', the Vandal commander decided to attack.[25] The fact that the attack was a complete surprise suggests that the Vandals did not have to sail along the coast of Hispania, however an attack from the direction of Ibiza would have been unexpected and unseen (see Map 11). The Roman fleet was either captured or destroyed: sadly, no details concerning the course or specific outcome of the battle have survived.[26] The news was a devastating blow to Majorian: his much vaunted fleet was either sunk or in the hands of the enemy and with its loss his dream of conquering Africa was at an end. Any attempt to raise taxes in order to build a second armada would almost certainly lead to discontent, if not outright rebellion. Majorian now had to decide what course of action to take.

Analysis

Hydatius' claim that the fleet was 'betrayed by traitors' has usually been accepted by modern historians.[27] Although this remains a possibility, it would appear to be unlikely. There were doubtless merchants and other seagoing craft, such as fishermen, who could be either paid or forced to give the Vandals news of the movement of the Roman fleet. Such individuals, whether voluntarily or under pressure, would be able to inform the Vandals of both the composition and the manpower of the Roman fleet. It is likely such people were the ones called 'traitors' by Hydatius.

There remains the question of why such a large fleet was so easily defeated by the Vandals. The first factor will be the experience of the Vandal sailors when compared to the inexperience of many of the Romans. Any manoeuvres attempted by the Roman fleet would be easily countered by a Vandal fleet with years of experience behind them. In addition, there is the question of the manpower of the Roman fleet. Given the Empire's near bankruptcy and the fact that Majorian had recruited a large number of land forces, it is more than likely that the ships were only manned by skeleton crews – enough men to move the ships to the south of Hispania and transport the army to Africa, but not enough to fight a battle. Finally, it should be noted that the Vandal attack took place in the 'harbour', leaving little room for even a well-trained navy to outmanoeuvre their less-numerous opponents. Taken by surprise and with their untrained crews on shore, there was little doubt about the outcome of the attack: the fully equipped and manned experienced Vandal fleet had little difficulty in defeating the Roman armada, even though heavily outnumbered in ships.

Several sources claim that the Roman fleet was captured, but the chances are that the majority, if not all, of the transport ships were destroyed, whereas wherever possible the Roman *dromons* will have been captured and taken for use by the Vandals.[28] The Vandals had enough ships to transport their raiding parties, but additional combat vessels to face further threats would be welcomed. In this light the despair of Majorian and the instant collapse of any attempt to recapture Vandal Africa are understandable: even a rebuilt Roman fleet would now struggle to compete with the newly enlarged Vandal navy.

Aftermath

When news of the defeat became widespread the anger and despair felt in Rome will have been the complete opposite to the relief and elation felt in Carthage. All of the surviving sources demonstrate that Majorian now suffered a complete loss of confidence. He was far from Italy, and the defeat had damaged his reputation. Under these circumstances he could not be sure of his reception in Italy nor the reaction of his erstwhile ally Theoderic.[29] Throughout the remainder of the year it would appear that envoys were passing between Majorian in Hispania and Gaiseric in Africa: from his position of newfound strength, 'King Gaiseric sought peace from the emperor Majorian through envoys'.[30] Eventually an agreement was reached and a peace treaty was signed 'on shameful terms'.[31]

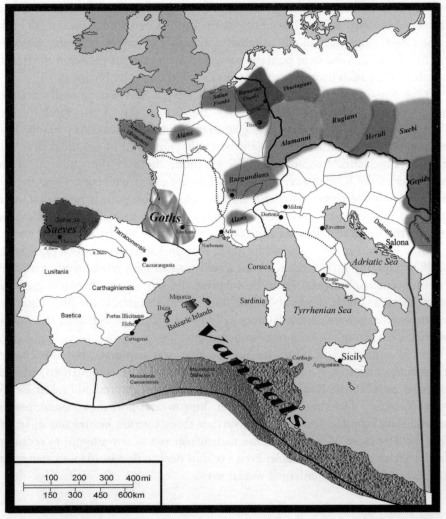

Map 12: Vandal Expansion in Africa and the Fall of Majorian. The extent of the western conquests in Africa are unclear.

What these terms were is nowhere described by the sources. The most likely conditions included the West's acceptance of the Vandal possession of the whole of the North African coastline west of Carthage, including those provinces retained by Rome in the Treaty of 442, as well as any islands in the Mediterranean that Gaiseric had occupied. In return, Gaiseric will have consented to the restoration of the grain supply from Africa to Rome.

It is possible that also included in the treaty, and perhaps an attempt by Majorian to save face and allow him to present the campaign as at least a marginal success, was Gaiseric's agreement to return Eudoxia and Placidia, the wife and daughter of Valentinian III, taken as captives by the Vandals in 455.[32] Although Placidia may already have been engaged, if not married, to a man named Olybrius, in 454 the Empress Eudoxia had attempted to arrange a marriage between Placidia and Majorian.[33] It is possible that Majorian saw Placidia's release as a chance to marry her, which would give him a legitimate claim to continuity from the dynasty of Theodosius. It should be noted, however, that including the return of the Imperial women to Rome as part of the agreement is speculation, although possibly reinforced by the circumstances surrounding the actual return of the captives in 462 (see Chapter Eight). Also included may have been the acceptance that Eudocia's marriage to Gaiseric's son Huneric, as per the Treaty of 442, was legitimate: Majorian may even have been forced to pay a 'dowry' to Eudocia. Once the negotiations with Gaiseric were complete, if not before, Majorian returned to Arles.[34]

Hispania

Given the distances between Hispania and Carthage, and the complex negotiations involved in the discussions, it is probable that the peace treaty was only concluded either late in 460 or early in 461. In the meantime, the Gothic forces in the Iberian Peninsula continued their campaigns against the Sueves. Prior to the disaster at Elche, Suniericus and Nepotianus had dispatched an army towards Gallaecia. The Gothic army had pillaged the Suevic settlements around Lucus, but almost as if to confirm that Majorian's luck was at an end the army was betrayed by three 'informers', Dictynius, Spinio and Ascanius. Demoralized and terrified, the army retreated to its 'base', probably Caesaraugusta.[35] In addition, and probably under the command of a man named Frumarius, the three 'traitors' then helped the Sueves, in an attack on the town of Aquae Flaviae (Chaves) dated to 26 July 460, where they captured Hydatius himself – hence the specific dating.[36]

At the same time, the other Suevic leader, Rechimundus, pillaged areas contiguous with his own territory, including the coastal region near to Lucus – territory nominally under the control of Frumarius.[37] This resulted in the Sueves turning on each other, leading to a temporary peace with the native Gallaecians.[38] The one piece of good news for Majorian was that further south Sunieric had finally gained control of the city of Scallabis, effectively pinning the Sueves back towards their own territory.[39]

461

The loss of the Battle of Elche was the final straw for Ricimer and members of the Roman Senate. Majorian had stripped Italy, and especially the Senate, of much of its wealth to pay for the mercenaries and fleet for the campaign; had left the Goths in situ as a major power in Gaul (although the Gallic senators seemed happy with the arrangement); the Sueves remained at war with the Empire; and now the effort and cost of the African campaign had been for nothing. It may have seemed to the senators in Italy that Majorian had failed in everything that he had promised since taking power. Furthermore, his legislation had demonstrated that he was intent on addressing the many issues faced by the whole Empire, even if such laws went against the interests of the minority Senate in Rome.[40] Opposition to his rule continued to grow.[41]

In the meantime, Majorian dismissed the mercenaries, and, retaining only his personal *bucellarii*, headed for Rome, where he appears to have been planning to continue with his political reforms.[42] He may have been surprised when, on 3 August, near to Dertona (Tortona) in Northern Italy, he was met by Ricimer and a strong military force.[43] When the two men met, 'Ricimer's men seized [Majorian], stripped him of his purple and his diadem, beat him, and cut off his head.'[44] According to the *Fasti Vindobonenses Priori*, Majorian was beheaded on the fifth day after the meeting, close to the River Ira.[45] Surprisingly, Procopius claims that Majorian died of dysentery: it is possible that this was the version of events Ricimer sent by envoys to the East to announce Majorian's death to Leo.[46] Even more surprisingly, Victor of Tonnena not only claims that Majorian was killed in Rome, but dates his death to 463.[47] In contrast Jordanes claims that he was killed whilst preparing for a campaign against the Alans, who were allegedly 'disturbing' Gaul, but there is no other record of such a conflict and Jordanes simply appears to be mistaken.[48]

The Church of San Matteo in Tortona contains a building traditionally identified as the 'Mausoleum of Majorian', although the fact that the building has no original inscriptions to this effect makes the claim debatable. Ennodius, Bishop of Pavia fifty years after the death of Majorian, in his *Epigrams*, simply states that the tomb was 'flat and obscure', as was the case for all 'good' emperors.[49]

Analysis

The brief reign of Majorian, the 'Last Hope of the West', was over. He had died at around the age of 40. Majorian had been a realist: he knew that for the West to survive he needed to re-establish firm control over Gaul, Hispania and – most importantly – Africa. Without the lost revenues the West could not survive militarily, as by Majorian's reign the cost of hiring mercenaries, never mind recruiting Roman troops, was prohibitive to the depleted treasury.

His death is always laid at the feet of Ricimer: for example, 'While the Emperor was busy away from Italy, the barbarian *patricius et magister militum* had gathered around himself the aristocratic opposition to his former comrade with whom, just a few years earlier, he had cultivated dreams of power.'[50] This is mirrored by: 'Ricimer must have decided long before [the loss of the fleet] that he would have to rid himself of this emperor, and was simply awaiting his chance.'[51] The vast majority of historians have followed this viewpoint, claiming that: 'Ricimer, who had made an emperor, felt fully entitled to unmake him at will' and 'now that he [Majorian] had proved himself unable to "preserve the state of the Roman world", Ricimer, who was thoroughly dissatisfied with him, could venture to take action against him'.[52] In this context Ricimer is seen as the successor of Aetius, doing anything in his power to ensure that he retained the control over the West achieved by his predecessor.

This is not the whole story. The 'evil' Ricimer is contrasted with the 'good' Majorian, who has received praise from modern writers for the laws he passed while emperor. For example:

> During A.D. 458 Majorian had attempted much remedial legislation. He alleviated the public burdens by a remission of arrears (*Nov.* 2) and resuscitated the office of *defensor civitatis* (*Nov.* 3). He enacted a much-needed law for preserving the public buildings of Rome, to check the 'disfigurement of the face of the venerable city' (*Nov.* 4). He also endeavoured to deal with the social evil of celibacy (*Nov.* 6).
>
> *Bury*, 1923, *I 332, n. 80.*

Unfortunately, such views do not stand up to scrutiny. *Novella 2* was not so much an attempt to curry favour and 'alleviate the public burden' so much as a piece of legislation that would be expected of an emperor in a weak position. In reality it was an attempt to encourage the payment of current tax demands, which were desperately needed if Majorian's plans to reunite the West were to succeed. Furthermore, *Novella 6* did not 'deal with the social evil of celibacy' in the way envisaged: the main point of the law was to attack 'abusive marriage strategies ... [such as] ... the practice of families forcing daughters to take the veil ... [and Majorian] ... felt that the fecundity of young women was needed to help the Roman state (which was rapidly disintegrating in the West)'.[53] Such practices were undoubtedly endemic amongst the rich and powerful and it is likely that Majorian garnered a fair amount of hostility with these laws.

However, as far as the Senate in Rome may have been concerned, Majorian's greatest failings were military. Although the peoples of Gaul had 'rebelled', both with the elevation of Avitus and during the months after Avitus' death, Majorian had not punished them for their crimes. In addition, after the defeat of the Goths following their siege of Arles, Majorian had not then gone on to penalize them for their attacks on the Empire. Instead, they had been allowed to maintain their dominant position in Gaul, a decision which was anathema to the anachronistic viewpoint of a Senate that still very much believed that barbarians were there to be defeated and the might of Rome had to be upheld by strength of arms. Finally, Majorian had levied high taxes to build a fleet and raise an army, and had promised to reunite the Empire. These promises had been dashed in a single battle. At this point the Senate might have expected Majorian to somehow uphold Roman military tradition by not giving up and instead continuing with his plans to cross the Straits of Gibraltar.[54] Instead of continuing the war, the defeated Emperor, with his army still fully intact, had instead negotiated with the enemy and given away territory.

The reasons for Majorian's loss of heart are nowhere explained. Given his 'youth' (he was about 40-years-old at the time of the battle), and his previous disappointments – especially the failure of his proposed marriage to Placidia – it is possible that the defeat at Elche drained his willingness to fight. However, what is more likely is that in gathering the invasion fleet he had used all of the available ships and so had none left to even manage a staged crossing of the Straits of Gibraltar. In these circumstances, a peace treaty would be a good thing for the Empire, as it would allow the Empire time to recover and rebuild its forces. Yet there is one further factor: at the time of the Treaty Gaiseric was about 70-years-old. It is possible that Majorian believed that if he waited only a short time, the elderly and brilliant Gaiseric would die and be replaced by his son Huneric, whose reputation may have suggested that he would be a far weaker adversary than his wily father.

Taking all of the above into consideration, it is certain that a large part of the Senate and People of Rome, not just Ricimer, will have been very unhappy with Majorian's rule. This is reinforced by the observation of Hydatius that:

> While returning to Rome from Gaul … Majorian was treacherously ensnared and murdered by Ricimer, who was driven by spite and supported by the counsel of jealous men.
>
> *Hydatius*, 205 [210], *s.a.* 461.

Sadly, Hydatius does not name any of the 'jealous men'.

The concept that Ricimer was acting out of spite is usually accepted at face value, fitting in as it does with the concept of Ricimer the 'Kingmaker' becoming worried by the apparent ability of his 'underling' – despite Majorian's failed campaign. In some ways Majorian's strength of character must remain a possibility in Ricimer's decision to eliminate Majorian: Ricimer may have been concerned that Majorian would eventually replace him with another commander as *magister militum et patricius*.

Yet the fact that Ricimer did not act alone has often been overlooked. Instead of seeing Majorian's death as Ricimer losing patience with his 'protégé', it is better to analyse the event in a wider context. It is clear that there is a strong likelihood that Ricimer was acting as the focus of a large anti–Majorian faction within the Senate, appalled by Majorian's legislation and upset by Majorian's inability to fulfill the functions of an Emperor by defending Italy and defeating all enemies.[55] But most of all it was his 'cowardly' decision to surrender after only one defeat – a situation anathema to the inheritors of the traditions of the Second Punic War, when the determination to carry on was the factor which ensured eventual success. This was almost certainly the defining rationale that ensured that the Senate lost patience with their young, inexperienced and obviously 'incompetent' emperor. The defeat at Elche and Majorian's instant negotiations with Gaiseric were the major cause of his death, not Ricimer's desire to try with a new subordinate emperor.

Chapter Eight

Libius Severus

19 November 461–15 August/post 25 September 465

The Fallout: Marcellinus, Aegidius and Nepotianus

Majorian was dead. One reason to suspect that the assassination of Majorian was part of a wider political backlash to the failed African campaign is that Ricimer was certainly aware of the possible ramifications: the majority, if not all, of the military commanders currently in office had been appointed by, and were hence loyal to, Majorian. Although the Senate may have blithely expected these men to follow the orders of the 'Senate and People of Rome', Ricimer must have had qualms, and especially will have known that at least one general would immediately renounce his loyalty; Marcellinus in Dalmatia. In this context it is extremely unlikely that Ricimer acted alone, and more likely that he acted under instruction from the Senate.

Foreseeing the inevitable, at the same time as Majorian was being executed Ricimer had sent men with money to Sicily in order to tempt Marcellinus' Hunnic troops, who formed the backbone of the army in Sicily, to accept service in Italy. The attempt succeeded and early in 461 the Huns took ship for the mainland.[1] As a consequence, Marcellinus had no option but to quit the island and return to his stronghold in Dalmatia. Ricimer and the Senate had lost the Empire's jurisdiction over the western Balkans. Although Marcellinus and his heirs would accept service under later Western emperors, only for one short period would Dalmatia/Illyricum be directly attached to the West. For the most part it would be an 'independent' region more often looking to the East for guidance and support.

Ricimer will have known all along that Marcellinus would secede from the West upon the death of Majorian. More worrying was the fact that upon hearing of Majorian's fate Aegidius, the *magister militum per Gallias*, also renounced his loyalty, refusing to accept Ricimer's right to 'rule' as valid.[2] Instead, he retired to northern Gaul, relying on the Gallic field army and the Salian Franks to support him in his stance. He may also have been able to recruit some of the troops recently dismissed by Majorian after the failure of the campaign against the Vandals.[3]

Furthermore, recognizing that at some point he would be attacked by either the Goths, Ricimer, or an alliance of the two, Aegidius cast around for further allies. It is probable that this included a contingent of Saxon 'pirates', better described as Saxon mercenaries, willing to serve Aegidius under their commander Adovacrius.[4] Although sometimes called Odoacer, this man is not the same as the later individual of that name.[5] The changing of the name Adovacrius, as given by Gregory of Tours,

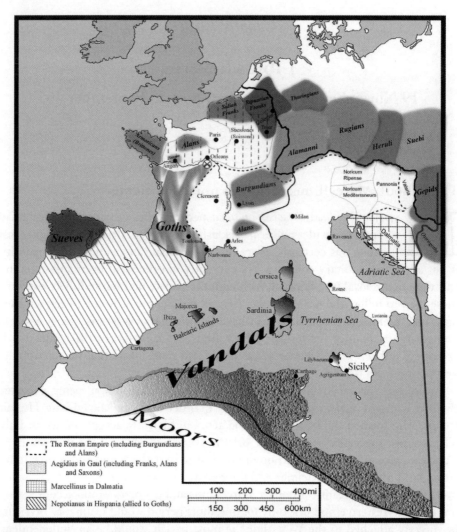

Map 13: The division of the West. Note the Vandal expansion and that all borders are approximate.

into Odovacar reflects an earlier tradition that Adovacrius is the same individual later known by the name Odoacer.[6] The men were two separate individuals.[7]

It has been suggested that these Saxons were allied to the Goths, based upon the concept that they must have arrived by sea and the Goths had an active navy defending the coast.[8] This overlooks the fact that a large group of warriors could easily land undetected before entering Aegidius' service and therefore not need to return to their ships. These men were stationed in the region of Angers, doubtless to protect the city from attack.

It is possibly at this time, with Aegidius being forced to focus on the border between his own territory and that of the Goths, that the Franks relented from their previous position and invited their 'King' Childeric back from his exile.[9] Childeric's presence as a war leader may have been needed in the north to counter threats that Aegidius would be unable to face alone.

Although Ricimer may have feared that Aegidius would gather his army and lead an assault on Italy, Aegidius was intent on first establishing his position and assessing his options before acting: prior to any attempt to invade Italy Aegidius would need to ensure the loyalty of his troops. In fact, Aegidius may have been hoping that the deaths of first Avitus and then Majorian would poison relations between Theoderic and Italy, meaning that a joint operation of Gauls and Goths could be launched against Ricimer. However his plans are a mystery as no source gives any indication of what he hoped to achieve.

On the other hand, there is one major difference between the secession of Aegidius and that of earlier commanders: at no point did Aegidius nominate either himself or a pliable candidate as emperor in opposition to Ricimer. Although often overlooked, his decision marks 'a radical change in political realities': while part of the reason may have been that he did not have enough troops to force the issue, nonetheless the 'title of emperor was by now hardly worth usurping outside Italy' and consequently no longer worth aiming for.[10] Nevertheless, with Aegidius' action Ricimer and the Senate had lost control of northern Gaul. It would never be recovered.

Also usually overlooked by modern historians, and possibly by Ricimer, there was a third *magister militum* at this time: Nepotianus in Hispania. He had been campaigning alongside the Goths against the Sueves and from later evidence it would appear that he followed the example set by his brother-in-law Marcellinus and disavowed allegiance to Ricimer and the imperial court, instead for a short period continuing to serve in a semi-independent position in Hispania.[11] The population of Iberia, who had benefitted from Majorian's campaigns in the peninsula, also appeared to have been dismayed by Majorian's death, opting to follow Nepotianus in his 'rebellion' against the court. As a result, from this point onwards the peoples of Iberia would look more often to Theoderic in Gaul or themselves rather than to the emperor in Italy for support and defence. Like northern Gaul, the Empire would never regain control of Iberia.[12]

The Army

The death of Majorian marks the end of an epoch in Roman history. As with the third century crisis, or the civil wars following the abdication of Diocletian in 305, the army in the separate regions of the Western Empire abandoned their loyalty to the emperor in Italy and gave it instead to their own commanders: Aegidius in Gaul, Marcellinus in Dalmatia, and Ricimer in Italy. Unlike previous eras, these armies were to retain their independence, meaning that from this point until the end of the Empire they were all 'separate agents which had to be reconciled individually to imperial regimes'.[13] As will be seen, some emperors almost managed the balancing act of integrating the three armies into their Empire. However, this was to be a rare and short-lived phenomenon.

Certainty is impossible but it is probably at this point that the Roman army in Italy began to lose the remainder of its native troops. The loss of the revenues from Africa had caused Valentinian III to declare the Empire bankrupt in 442 and although he then issued a levy in 443, after that date it is likely that the number of new regular recruits dropped dramatically.[14] Instead, the existing troops would be allowed to complete their service, upon their retirement their place increasingly being taken by mercenaries. However in some regions, such as Noricum, where Roman troops were still serving after 450, and Gaul, where some troops were attested as surviving into the Frankish era, service in the Roman army still retained some allure and troops could continue to serve long after the Fall of the West.[15]

The execution of Majorian and the loss of northern Gaul, Hispania and Illyricum in 461 further weakened the treasury. As was noted earlier, Avitus was forced to strip marble monuments of their metal adornments in order to pay his Gothic bodyguard, clearly demonstrating that the Empire was penniless. Majorian had imposed heavy taxes on all of the remaining Empire, including the rich, in order to attempt the reconquest of Africa. The decision had allowed him to build a fleet and army, but the attempt simply added to the demoralization of the Empire's inhabitants when the massive financial effort failed at the first hurdle. Further, the defeat had alienated the Senate. The long-term consequence was that the Senate would fear and distrust any emperor who proclaimed his desire to fight offensive wars in Africa.

As a consequence, it is probably safe to assume that from this point on the 'Roman army' had increasingly few 'Romans' in its employment, as these were expensive to recruit, train and equip. It is more likely that as regular troops were released or died the majority of the armed forces quickly became mercenaries, trained and equipped by themselves and hired by the powerful to act as both army and bodyguard. This would explain why Marcellinus, with few sources of income in Dalmatia, could not match the offer from Ricimer when the latter bribed his Huns in Sicily and why the Huns so quickly changed sides.

The inability to equip troops was not helped by the loss of the *fabricae* (armour and weapons factories/arsenals) in northern Gaul (see Map 6). Those at Amiens (broadswords and shields), at Soissons (manufacture unknown), and at Rheims (swords) were now under the control of Aegidius, who would put the weapons to good use in the next few years. Sadly for Aegidius, that at Trier (shields and *ballistae*) had earlier been lost to the Ripuarian Franks. Further south, those at Argenton (all weapons), at Macon (arrows), and at Autun (corselets, *ballistae*, mail and shields) were now very close to the Goths. However, it is likely that prior to the Gothic advance these had already been closed, both to save on money and to prevent them and their arsenals from falling into the hands of a potential enemy.

With all of these losses it was becoming clear to all that the 'Empire' was no longer the financial and political power it had been. It was now degenerating to a localized power based on Italy, Sicily, and a small part of Southern Gaul. This hypothesis is reinforced by the fact that from this point onwards the West lacked the means to take the offensive unless supported by the much wealthier East. Rather than being the mighty power of old, the new imperial order was becoming reduced to a handful of rich individuals who could pay for a retine of mercenaries. In this context later events become easier to understand.

Interregnum

Prior to the crowning of Majorian there had been a short interregnum. In a similar manner, following Majorian's death there was another. The reasons for this are unclear and several possibilities present themselves. One is that Ricimer had sent messengers to Leo I and was waiting for a reply and possibly a nomination from the East. Sadly, Leo was preoccupied by a war with Valamer, 'King' of the Ostrogoths, who had taken part alongside Attila when the Huns had invaded Gaul in 451.[16] Following Attila's death in 453, the Ostrogoths had rebelled against the Huns and been settled in Pannonia by Marcian.[17] However, in 459 the Ostrogoths had not received their annual 'subsidy' and, worried that his rival Theoderic Strabo was receiving more honour from the East Romans, Valamer led his men in attacks upon Illyricum. Affairs would not be settled with the Ostrogoths until late 461 or 462, when Leo agreed to resume the payments, in return receiving as a hostage Valamer's nephew, a boy named Theoderic.[18] In this context it is not surprising that Leo refused to become embroiled in the nomination of a new emperor for the West.

It has sometimes been suggested that Ricimer also asked Leo for permission to rule the West in Leo's name, obviating the need for a separate Western Emperor. This must remain a possibility but the complete lack of supporting evidence means that it is impossible to prove one way or the other. It is more likely that Leo did not have a suitable nominee that could be spared. Furthermore, Leo was being guided in political matters by his *magister militum* Aspar, who did not want to become embroiled in Western affairs.[19] The conclusion is reinforced by the fact that when Ricimer did nominate a Western Emperor, despite refusing to recognize the new ruler the East did not take any military action to implant their own nominee, as had happened earlier.[20]

Gaiseric

In Africa, Gaiseric's reaction to Majorian's death was instant and predictable: disavowing the treaty he had made with Majorian, he speedily marshalled his men and sent a mixed force of Vandals and Moors to ravage Italy and Sicily. The attacks will have been almost completely undefended: Ricimer had led a sizeable force into Northern Italy to ensure success against Majorian. Although it is likely that these men had returned with Majorian to Rome to forestall any dissent following Majorian's death, there were now few troops and no commanders in the south of the peninsula to defend against the Vandals. Furthermore, Sicily, previously protected by Marcellinus, was left defenceless when Marcellinus retreated to Dalmatia.

In response, Ricimer sent an embassy to Gaiseric saying that he 'ought not utterly to neglect the treaty'.[21] In addition, and despite his unwillingness to intervene directly in the West, one thing that Leo did agree to was a continuation of the political pressure on Gaiseric both to stop his attacks and to return the imperial women. Between the death of Valentinian in 455 and that of Majorian in 461 many embassies had been sent to Gaiseric hoping to stop attacks on the West and to secure the release of Eudoxia and Placidia.[22] Sadly, none of the dates for these embassies are known, so it is impossible to outline the nature of the Eastern Empire's relations with Gaiseric in detail. Unfortunately for the West, Gaiseric had learned of the division between the two halves of the Empire, and, realizing that on his own Ricimer had no army with which to oppose him, Gaiseric ignored the requests and prepared for war in the New Year.

Libius Severus

Finally, after nearly three months, on 19 November 461 a new emperor was proclaimed at Ravenna.[23] Shortly afterwards he was recognized as emperor by the Senate in Rome.[24] The reign of Libius Severus is one of the most poorly documented in the fifth century, especially when the fact that he reigned for four years is taken into account.[25] Doubtless the main reason for this is that he was not recognized in the East and as a consequence the majority of the Eastern sources fail to give details concerning his reign, only relating major events in a vague manner.[26] The sole fact concerning Severus that is known with certainty is that he was a native of Lucania in Italy.[27] However, he did manage to gain a reputation for 'living piously', although the precise nature of the epithet is unclear.[28]

Two other sources suggest that Severus was given the nickname 'Serpentius' (serpent, snake, reptile).[29] Unfortunately, at this point the text of Theophanes is corrupt and the meaning of the word is uncertain.[30] However a man named 'Serpentius' is acknowledged in the *Chronicon Paschale* as being consul alongside Leo I in 462.[31] This can only mean Severus, as the Eastern lists have Leo as sole consul. As a consequence it is likely that the nickname is correct, but, as with the claim that he lived 'piously', the exact meaning is unclear. It may mean either that Severus resembled a snake physically in some way, or that he had the morals of a serpent, or that his family had connections with snakes, or any of a variety of similar meanings.[32] Without context it is hard to ascribe any specific attribution to the name and it is therefore probably best ignored.

The fact that so little is known about Severus' background has led some historians to propose that his lack of experience in public office suggests that he was both a pliable and unresisting tool in the hands of Ricimer, as well as being unacceptable to the Senate.[33] Given the paucity of the sources for this period such arguments from negative evidence are weak and need further support from any other available information.

One such piece is a bronze plate found in Italy with an inscription, the obverse reading '*salvis dd. nn.* [Severus and Leo] *et patricio Ricimere*', and the reverse, '*Plotinus Eustathius v. c. urb. pr. fecit*'.[34] At first glance this is a staggering inscription, placing Ricimer on a par with the two emperors. However, it should not be taken at face value: it is a bronze plate, not a monument, and it is likely that it was a personal possession of the named Eustathius, who in turn was Prefect of Rome and almost certainly a dedicated supporter of Ricimer.[35]

A piece of numismatic evidence has also been offered as proof that Ricimer controlled Severus. Coins of Severus bearing the apparent monogram 'RCM' (interpreted as meaning 'Ricimer') on the reverse have usually been taken as implying that Ricimer was at least the equal of Severus. However recent research and reinterpretation has resulted in the conclusion that the monogram is actually a variant of 'Severus', comprised of Latin, Greek, and joined letters.[36] Although a complex and detailed analysis, this work has clearly demonstrated that the assumption that Ricimer had his name on imperial coins alongside the emperor, which would be a major concession of power, is at least open to question, if not a mistake.

One possibility usually ignored is that Severus' lack of 'credentials' was the reason for his appointment. If, as stipulated, there was a body of support for Ricimer's execution of Majorian, then by default there is likely to have been a section of the Senate that was unhappy with Majorian's death. It is often forgotten that 'certainly there are groups, or factions, but they are fluid and changing, in typical Roman fashion after the political habits of centuries, and depend more on personal interest than on ideology'.[37] Given the previous history of the Senate it is clear that there were at least two political 'cliques' in Rome: it is possible to suggest that one hungered for lost imperial glory and wanted to reconquer lost territories whilst the other believed that only Italy, the Imperial homeland, was important and should be defended at all costs.

In this context one of the reasons for the interregnum and for Severus' appointment may have been that the Senate had been deadlocked and that Severus was a compromise candidate, chosen precisely because his career had not placed him specifically in either camp. Accordingly, he was selected due to his acceptability by both parties. Although impossible to prove, the theory gives a viable hypothesis with which to work.

As a result of these deliberations it is apparent that the nature of Severus' rule is not as clear-cut as some historians believe. Instead, a more detailed analysis of what is known of his reign needs to be undertaken before any conclusions are reached. However, there is a problem with this approach: the lack of sources.

The difficulty appears to be a simple lack of 'interesting' events, especially in Italy, for the chroniclers to record. In Gaul the Goths were temporarily inhibiting Aegidius from acting; Hispania was now separate from the Empire and as a result Spanish writers have little to say about Italy, focusing instead on their own troubles; and finally, as will be seen, Marcellinus was to remain quiet in Illyricum. As a result, the only enemy directly affecting Severus were the Vandals. Even here, the monotonous round of raids and attempts to intercept them means that all that is noted in the sources is that the Vandals attacked every year in spring. With nothing happening in Italy to interest ancient writers, and with his rule not being recognized in the East, it is no wonder that so little is known of Severus' reign except for a few major events.

As was to be expected given the circumstances, Severus' rule began inauspiciously. Predictably, nominated by Ricimer as the new emperor, Severus had not been recognized by either Aegidius, Marcellinus, or Nepotianus.[38] The new regime had no option but to take steps to neutralize opposition to its rule: the peninsula was under severe threat. Despite the loss of some troops to Ricimer, an attack by Marcellinus from Illyricum remained a distinct possibility. Even more worrying, there were three major opponents to the regime in Gaul and Hispania: Aegidius, Theoderic and Nepotianus. A worst-case scenario would be an alliance of the three men and a joint attack over the Alps. The army of Italy almost certainly did not have the manpower to face such a crisis.

In response to these threats, Severus sent envoys to Leo asking for support to prevent an attack by Marcellinus. Surprisingly, given that Severus' regime was not recognized, help was given and a man named Phylarchus was sent to Marcellinus, who in turn was persuaded not to attack Italy: in fact, he was to remain inactive in Western affairs for several years.[39] It may be that as part of the agreement Leo agreed to recognize Marcellinus' power in the region by giving him the title *magister militum Dalmatiae* (Master of Soldiers in Dalmatia), a title later borne by his nephew and successor Julius Nepos, but sadly the fragmentary nature of the sources makes this uncertain.[40]

Doubtless part of the reason for accepting the plea from the western court concerning Marcellinus was the fear of a major invasion from across the northern frontier: the last thing Leo needed with the continued war against Valamer was a weak West stimulating attacks all along the Rhine and Danube which would threaten both the West and Illyricum. The event marks a major watershed for Dalmatia: from this point onwards Marcellinus and his successor would look to Constantinople and not Rome for leadership.

462

On 1 January 462, and in accordance with tradition, Libius Severus was proclaimed consul in the West, although as previously noted his nomination was not accepted in the East.[41] Instead, in the East Leo was chosen as the sole consul.

Despite the political setback, and with hope that Marcellinus was now at least neutralized, Severus and Ricimer* turned their attention to Gaul. Assessing their options, it was clear that Aegidius would only be able to act against Italy if he was allied to Theoderic, as otherwise the Goths could either threaten Aegidius' communications across the Alps or even devastate Aegidius' power base when Aegidius was away. Similarly, Nepotianus would be unable to reach Italy from Hispania without access through Gaul, leaving his lines of communication open to attack. It was obvious that the key to securing Italy from attack across the Alps was an alliance with Theoderic. With this in mind, Severus turned to the previous holder of Aegidius' post of *magister militum per Gallias*, Agrippinus.

---

* Unless otherwise specified, and to avoid repetition, when Severus is specified as the political mover Ricimer may also be implicit – and vice versa – but no proof is available.

Since his removal from office Agrippinus had been tried and convicted of 'treasonously' attempting to hand over cities in Gaul to barbarians.[42] Escaping the death penalty, his actions between his conviction and Severus' summons to serve are unknown. What is known is that he was 'a native of Gaul ... [with] ... ties ... concentrated in the eastern part of Lugdunensis' (see Map 1).[43] It may have been these ties that convinced Severus that Agrippinus would be useful in dealing with affairs in Gaul, and especially with Theoderic.

Unless otherwise specified, and to avoid repetition, when Severus is specified as the political mover it should be taken that Ricimer may also have been implicit in the action, and vice versa, but that no proof is available.

Whatever the case, in either late 461 or early 462 Agrippinus was made *magister militum per Gallias* once more and entered into negotiations with Theoderic, a man who had already supported Avitus as emperor before transferring his allegiance to Majorian. With two of the emperors he had supported removed, the price for his continued friendship and support of a third emperor would be high, but Severus had little choice but to accede to Theoderic's demands. At an unknown date in 462 the city of Narbonne was 'betrayed ... to Theoderic in order to win the assistance of the Goths'.[44] On the other hand, the Goths now controlled Southern Gaul all the way to the Mediterranean, meaning that Italy was now safe from invasion by Nepotianus in Hispania.

In addition, it would appear that Theoderic was given the right to appoint a *magister militum* for Hispania. Not only would this allow him to assume control of all of Roman Hispania via his appointee, but in the eyes of the population of the peninsula he now became as important, if not more so, as the emperor in Rome: from this time Hydatius records more envoys going to the Goths than to Italy. Theoderic wasted no time in replacing Nepotianus with a more pliable and/or acceptable *magister militum*: a man named Arborius became the new Roman commander in Hispania.[45] Despite his opposition to Ricimer, Nepotianus was able to live on peacefully until 465 – almost certainly in Hispania, as his death is recorded by Hydatius, a Spanish chronicler.[46]

Despite his success in arranging the alliance with the Goths, Agrippinus was not to remain as *magister militum per Gallias* for long. In early-mid 462, and with his job done, Agrippinus was replaced. No account gives details concerning his removal, but it may have been political pressure from the Senate: the cession of Narbonne was doubtless seen by many as a betrayal of Roman principles and it is likely that Agrippinus acted as the scapegoat, being removed from his post as 'punishment' for the 'betrayal'.

Severus quickly found a replacement for Agrippinus. Before October 463 Gundioc, the King of the Burgundians, was appointed as the new *magister militum per Gallias*.[47] His alliance to the regime was cemented by his marriage to one of Ricimer's sisters, with whom he had several sons.[48] This was a major break in Roman tradition: although there had been many barbarian *magistri* before this date, it was the first time that any of them had been simultaneously a king of their own people. It is obvious that if the Burgundians had earlier been defeated and forced to retire by Majorian, they were now allowed to resettle around Lyon, as had been promised earlier as reward for their assistance in Hispania.[49]

Repercussions/Analysis

The implications and repercussions of the treaty with Theoderic are often overlooked. For Theoderic, the treaty was a major breakthrough. Alongside his accepted control of Hispania, in many respects he was now the equal, if not of the emperor himself, then at least of the *magister militum*, Ricimer.

Furthermore, the fact that he was allowed to nominate his own *magister militum* in Hispania is often ignored by historians but may be a hint that Severus was not Ricimer's docile puppet, as is often claimed. In theory only the emperor or his dominant *magister militum* could appoint senior commanders. That Theoderic was now given equivalent power implies that he was theoretically the equal of Ricimer, a position untenable to a man who was dominating the imperial court.[50] Although based on weak evidence, it is possible that even at this early stage Severus had asserted some form of independence from Ricimer.

Whatever the case, the acquisition of Narbonne gave Theoderic one major bonus: access to the Mediterranean. Not only did this increase his power by cutting Rome off from land contact with Hispania, it also gave him a port on the Mediterranean coast from which he could access Mediterranean trade, with its concomitant supply of luxury goods and import taxes. From this time onwards the financial security and increased status of the Gothic kingdom resulted in the Goths paying less attention to the demands of Rome than ever before.

For Italy too the treaty was a milestone. For the first time in centuries the Empire was no longer connected by land to Hispania. Furthermore, alongside the loss of northern Gaul, Hispania and Dalmatia, the loss of the major port of Narbonne further reduced the income from taxes for the emperor.

Aegidius

The treaty came none too soon for the Empire. Implied by Priscus is the fact that Aegidius had marshalled his forces, arranged treaties with the Franks to the north, and was contemplating invading Italy.[51] It is possible, from later events, that some of the Ripuarian Franks also entered into a treaty with Aegidius, giving him control over Cologne and possibly Trier.[52] Once details of the treaty between Theoderic and Severus became known it was clear that Theoderic was no longer available as an ally and that instead war with the Goths was inevitable.[53] Given later events, it is also likely that Aegidius arranged for treaties with the Alans settled in the north of Gaul: the Goths had a habit of attempting to expand their territory and the Alans had been attacked before.[54] With the Empire in retreat and the Goths gaining in influence and power, it is only logical both that the Alans would be fearful of Gothic aggression and that they would take steps to gain support against Theoderic. Aegidius would be a natural ally.[55] Luckily for Aegidius the Goths would not be ready to campaign against him until the following year.

Gaiseric

The Empire's weakness was now clear to all and Gaiseric was determined to take advantage. The death of Majorian, the man with whom he had signed a treaty, was to be used as a pretext for renewing the war against Rome. Having already rebuffed Ricimer's envoys, Gaiseric may have been a little surprised when, early in the New Year, Phylarchus, the envoy who had arranged peace with Marcellinus, arrived from Leo in the East.[56]

Although the absolute accuracy of the text is uncertain, it is possible that Priscus gives some idea of the nature of the talks. Obviously the envoys from Ricimer (either new envoys or those dispatched in the previous year) had focused upon Gaiseric refraining from attacks upon the West. Those from the East echoed these sentiments, but also stressed the need for Gaiseric to release the Imperial women he had kept in Africa since the Sack of Rome in 455.[57] Gaiseric appears to have presented his terms for the cessation of attacks and the return of the women: from the East he demanded the patrimony – a part of the property of the deceased Emperor Valentinian III – be given to him for Eudocia, possibly as part of a dowry, plus an acknowledgement of the validity of Eudocia's marriage to Huneric. Likewise, from the West he demanded property for Eudocia, plus the property previously owned by Aetius to be given to Aetius' son Gaudentius, who was also in Africa.[58]

Leo, under pressure not to become involved in Western affairs, acceded to the demands and the ownership of part of the lands previously owned by Valentinian were allotted to Gaiseric on behalf of Eudocia.[59] It is also possible that a small payment was made to ensure the release of Eudoxia, although this is not supported by all of the sources.[60]

The West, crippled by the loss of taxes and the need to maintain a large army to face the threat of Aegidius and the Vandal raids, refused the terms. In many respects this was a mistake: Gaiseric had already almost certainly gained Majorian's acceptance of the marriage and had now secured Leo's recognition of Gaiseric's son Huneric as an accepted member of the Theodosian House, although with the caveat that he was not eligible to be emperor. Gaiseric, probably the most politically astute of the 'barbarian' kings, would be able to use the newly accepted family relationships to his advantage.

At this point Gaiseric may have had a choice: as the West was refusing his demands he could either keep the imperial women in Carthage, or he could uphold his agreement with the East and release them. Keeping them could cause Leo to finally submit to Italian demands for aid from the beleaguered West. However, other events now made Gaiseric reconsider at least some of his options. By early 462 it was clear that Leo I was regaining control of the Balkans and that the war against the Ostrogoths would soon be coming to an end, even if they had lasted into the New Year. Further, peace with the Persians continued so it was clear that, with Eastern military commitments declining, Leo could easily commit unused forces to the aid of the West. Although Gaiseric's army and navy were both powerful, they would be dwarfed by the combined might of the whole Roman Empire.

Determined to prevent the two halves of Empire uniting against him, Gaiseric decided to release Eudoxia and Pulcheria into the custody of Leo in the East. Their long captivity in Carthage was over. In many respects they had served their purpose: Eudocia's marriage to Huneric had now been recognized by legitimate Emperors in both East and West and there was no value in keeping the other women hostage. Pulcheria travelled with her mother to Constantinople, where according to Hydatius, she was finally married to the Western Senator Olybrius, who appears to have remained in the East rather than returning West after 455.[61] Although, as noted above, there is the possibility that she was already married to Olybrius, there is no definitive account of events on which to place any certainty.

In the East, the Treaty was probably accepted with relief. At a small price Leo had ensured that the Empire would not come under Vandal attack. In the West, the opposite was true. Severus knew that come the New Year the attacks on Sicily and Italy would resume and that no help would come from the East.

463

As expected, with the opening of spring the Vandals renewed their attacks. The raids seem to have increased in intensity from the previous year. Although certainty is impossible, several factors could have united to ensure that the Vandals' offensives were at their severest for a long time. The first of these is that, following the signing of a treaty with Leo, Gaiseric no longer feared an attack from the East and so was willing to allow more men than previously to go on raids rather than stay in Carthage to defend the homeland.

Another, and evidence of Gaiseric's high political ability, was his avowed claim to be fighting on behalf, not of himself, but of three other people. First, in the name of Olybrius (married to his son's wife's sister), who as the last member of the Theodosian dynasty by marriage should now be Western Emperor. Second, for Eudocia, who had not been given her due share of her father Valentinian III's inheritance. Third, for Gaudentius, who likewise had been bereft of his father Aetius' inheritance after Aetius had been assassinated – Gaudentius had been held in Carthage since the Sack in 455.[62]

Obviously, the West ignored these claims, but it is possibly at this date, after the fighting in the previous year had revealed the full extent of Roman weakness, that Gaiseric determined on further expanding his dominions. The loss of the Roman fleet at the Battle of Elche was now to have severe repercussions. Although this is nowhere explicitly stated, the Mediterranean islands which had been retaken by Rome but which may not have been seen as vital by the Romans – who were almost certainly intent on defending the arable areas in Italy and Sicily to feed the capital and surrounding regions – were undoubtedly left unguarded. Further, Priscus notes that only 'defended' areas were avoided by the Vandals.[63] As they were undefended, it is most likely at this point that Gaiseric sent troops to annexe Corsica and Sardinia. He may also have attacked Sicily with the intention of regaining a foothold in the west of the island, both to act as a diversion and to determine the strength of Roman resistance.

Severus

In spite of the continued assaults, business in Italy continued in as normal a fashion as possible. In the court, Severus passed one of only two pieces of legislation that have survived. On 20 February 463 *Novella Severa I* was distributed from Rome, which abrogated (cancelled) the sixth novel of Majorian concerning the succession of widows and the entering of holy orders by single and married women, with only some specific clauses being retained. Although this has been assessed as being an attack on the 'anti-clerical legislation' of Majorian, the exact cause of the novel is unclear: after all, if the law was seen as being poor and in need of removal, the question remains as to why it took nearly one-and-a-half years to remove.[64] It may be better to interpret the new law as part of a series aimed at protecting the interests of the Senate rather than being an attempt to nullify the laws of Majorian – a hypothesis reinforced by the fact that many of the laws passed by Majorian remained in force and so were recorded later. It is also possible evidence that the Senate were once more in a powerful position, able to extract concessions from Severus and Ricimer.

Although Italy was only threatened by the Vandals in this year, due to them concentrating on the defenceless islands, in Gaul affairs were reaching a climax. The battles and manoeuvres of the previous year between Aegidius and the Goths continued into the New Year, with hard fighting going on in a 'dispute over border lands'.[65] Finally, the opponents faced each other in a major battle. At an unknown date in 463 the Goths, under Frederic the brother of Theoderic, faced Aegidius near Orleans. By this time Frederic appears to have been 'associated' with Theoderic in the rule of the Goths, possibly being nominated as Theoderic's successor.[66] The fact that Frederic was commanding at the battle suggests that this was a major campaign aimed at eliminating Aegidius from northern Gaul.

The location of the battle near Orleans suggests that Aegidius was in alliance with the Alans settled in the area, and that Frederic's main objective at this point may have been the establishment of Gothic control over the city, although this is not mentioned in the sources. Allied to Aegidius and also present on the battlefield was a contingent of Franks under Childeric.[67] The details of the encounter are unknown, but the outcome was an outright victory for Aegidius, with Frederic being killed.[68] No surviving sources give any indication of how Aegidius followed up his victory over Frederic. Although the two sides appear to have continued fighting in the months after the battle, the victory ensured that the region around Orleans and Soissons remained under 'Roman' rather than Gothic control. The most likely outcome is that Aegidius extended his control into territories previously held by the Goths, so weakening their prestige, but sadly no detailed information has survived.

On the other hand, it is important to note that not all of the Franks sided with Childeric and Aegidius: the *Liber Historium Francorum* claims that one section of

Franks drove Aegidius' allies from Cologne.[69] It is important to remember that Roman authors could use tribal names indiscriminately and that even when single 'tribes' are mentioned, unity should not be assumed: large numbers of tribes were given titles that reflect a unity that was not real and there remains the likelihood of 'inter-tribal' strife. Who exactly these Franks were remains unclear.

In the meantime, in Hispania affairs continued as normal. Recognizing that the Goths were intent on continuing their war with Aegidius, the Sueves took their opportunity. Despite exchanging envoys with Theoderic, 'the Sueves, treacherous and characteristically false to their promises, pillaged different parts of unhappy Gallaecia in their usual manner'.[70] Although Theodosius sent more envoys, the Sueves ignored these too and 'lawless disorder dominated relations between the Gallaecians and the Sueves'.[71] Despite the fact that the attacks were focused upon Gallaecia, the whole of the peninsula was doubtless worried about the spread of the troubles to other areas.

464

The Vandal attacks were now becoming a serious threat to the existence of the Empire. Desperate, Severus sent envoys to the East begging for the use of a fleet with which to defeat the Vandals. Leo refused the request, citing the existing treaty he had with Gaiseric as the cause, but he did agree to send an envoy to Africa. A man named Tatianus was sent to intercede with Gaiseric on behalf of the West, but to no avail.[72]

In Northern Italy a new danger threatened. An invasion led by Beorgor, 'King of the Alans', crossed the Alps and advanced as far as Bergamum (Bergamo).[73] The nature of this group has been scrutinized and several origins have been postulated.[74] Since they are not mentioned by the Gallic sources, it is unlikely that they were allies of Aegidius sent to attack Italy. In addition, they are noted as 'invading' Italy by the sources so their being a group previously employed by the Empire and settled in Northern Italy also appears to be unlikely. The most obvious source for these 'Alans' would be from beyond the northern frontiers, a theory supported by the fact that at this time similar tribes were disturbing the Danubian frontier.[75] With the Empire in turmoil they had attacked Italy in the expectation of easy pickings. They were to be disappointed: an army led by Ricimer in person defeated them in battle at Bergamum.[76] Sadly, no details exist of the conflict apart from what has already been noted. However the fact that so many disparate sources mention the affair suggests that the threat, and hence the ensuing victory, had been significant.

Gaul

Although otherwise unattested and difficult to date, it is possible that during the previous years of warfare in the north of Gaul, Childeric and/or Aegidius had repeatedly attempted to capture the strategically useful city of Paris. Finally, and possibly following the successful battle against Frederic in 463 after which a large number of troops had been released to campaign against enemies other than the Goths, Childeric I besieged the city in 464 and despite a stout defence it was captured. Allegedly, thanks to the intervention of Saint Genevieve (Genofeva) Childeric spared the lives of many prisoners and the 'sack' of Paris was less severe than it might have been.[77] At around the same time, Aegidius appears to have retaken control of Trier and Cologne, as he is later described defending the city.[78] Apparently, Aegidius and his allies were slowly beginning to establish their rule in the north of Gaul.

Hispania

Suevic unreliability, in the person of Frumarius, had been an ongoing problem in Hispania for many years. In 464 the Goths, and by association the Romans, received some good news: Frumarius died. At this point a major political victory was scored by Theodosius: the choice of the Sueves fell on a man named Remismund, who had long associations with the Gothic king and appears to have been working on behalf of Theoderic in the previous year.[79] Attacks on the Gallaecians ceased and an uneasy peace settled in Hispania. This was extended by the exchange of numerous embassies and gifts, including the wife of Remismund, who for a short period had remained with the Gothic king.[80]

465

On 25 September the last of the two known laws (*Novella Severa 2*) given by Severus was passed.[81] As with the previous law, the Senate may have insisted that this law was passed, concerned as it was with the clarification of a child's status if its parents were of mixed ranks: more especially, if one was the member of a guild and the other was either of *coloni* or slave status. The reason for the belief that this was desired by the Senate was that senators appear to have been losing manpower at an alarming rate, with *coloni* or slaves marrying higher-status individuals and so gaining their 'freedom'. A simple way to curb the losses was to ensure that all children of 'mixed' parentage remained as either slaves or *coloni* unless it could be proved that the marriage of the parents took place prior to the issuance of the law. The Senate were determined to 'shut the escape route' for those *coloni* and slaves who had managed to free themselves from their onerous status, demonstrating that even at this late stage the Senate was determined to uphold its privileges.[82]

Death of Aegidius and Succession of Syagrius

In the previous year Aegidius had been unable to convince the Goths to accept peace terms. In this context the information given by Hydatius, who records that Aegidius sent an embassy to the Vandals in May and received their reply in September, could be telling.[83] The nature and consequence of this embassy are unknown. It is possible that Aegidius was seeking a treaty with Gaiseric against their common enemy

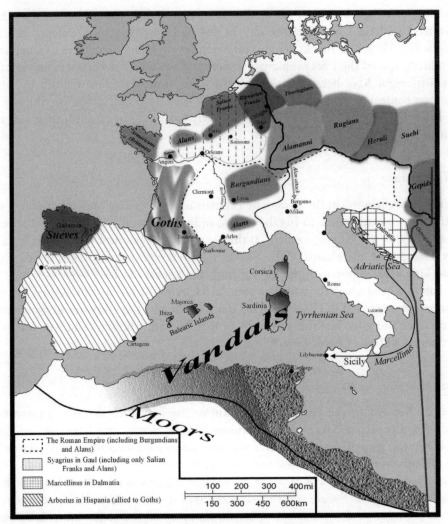

Map 14: The Empire at the deaths of Aegidius and Severus.

Ricimer, or that Aegidius was simply putting out feelers in an attempt to make an alliance with which to threaten Ricimer. Possibly more likely given the ongoing war with the Goths, Aegidius may have been hoping to persuade Gaiseric to declare war on Theoderic. Vandal attacks on Narbonne in alliance with Aegidius could easily persuade Theoderic to make peace.

Unfortunately, due to the lack of information, it is impossible to say what was happening and it is dangerous to read too much into the event. Whatever the talks, before an agreement could be reached events in northern Gaul intervened. The *Liber Historiae Francorum* (The Book of the History of the Franks) records:

In those days the Franks took the city of Agrippina on the Rhine, known as Colonia [Cologne], as if *coloni* inhabited it. There they massacred many of the people belonging to Aegidius' faction. Aegidius himself escaped by flight. They then moved on to the city of Trier on the River Moselle, devastating its lands, and took and burnt it.

Liber Historiae Francorum 8, trans. MacGeorge, 2002, 107.

Although it is sometimes assumed that the 'Franks' were being led by Childeric, the ally of Aegidius, this is not actually stated and is unlikely given previous and subsequent events. It is possible that Aegidius was taken by surprise by a separate Frankish contingent – possibly part of the 'Ripuarian Franks' (see above) – and with only a few troops was defeated and forced to retire. Further, given later events, it is feasible – although impossible to prove – that the Franks in question were acting as allies of Theoderic.[84]

At around this time Aegidius died. Given the context, the rumour recorded by Hydatius that Aegidius was either 'trapped' or 'poisoned' is interesting.[85] Although Aegidius appears to have been an excellent military commander, it is possible that after his defeat he was pursued by the Franks and finally trapped and killed.

There remains the question of whether he was poisoned. If true, several architects of the deed are possible, including Childeric, Severus, and, of course, Theoderic. There are no records of Roman involvement in affairs in Gaul, so, although an argument from negative evidence, it would appear that an order to poison Aegidius would not have originated with either Severus or Ricimer. Only the year before Childeric had fought alongside Aegidius against the Goths, so although possible it would appear that his involvement in the affair is also unlikely.

That leaves Theoderic as a candidate. His motives are easy to understand. Firstly, his brother Fredericus had been defeated and killed by Aegidius and revenge would be a strong motive. Secondly, and just as pertinent, Aegidius had proved beyond doubt that he was the equal of the Goths in battle. Theoderic may have despaired of ever defeating Aegidius and either killing or removing him in a 'fair fight'. The only resort was to use poison. Although conjecture, if Aegidius was indeed poisoned, Theoderic is the most likely culprit for the decision.

On the whole, however, it seems more likely that Aegidius was unexpectedly attacked by unfriendly Franks, driven into a corner – possibly in or near Trier – and killed. Unfortunately, the truth surrounding his death is unlikely to be solved unless fresh evidence comes to light.

Although only two ancient sources describe Aegidius, both are extremely complimentary. Hydatius states that he was: 'a man who both enjoyed an excellent reputation and was very pleasing to God because of his good works'.[86] Likewise, Paul of Perigueux declares that Aegidius was an 'outstanding man of courage and character', clearly affirming Aegidius' positive qualities and implying that his loyalty to Majorian was appreciated in Gaul and Hispania.[87] The fact that his troops supported him against both the 'official' emperor as well as Theoderic gives further support to the description of Aegidius as an exceptional leader of men.

With Aegidius' removal the Goths and Romans may have both hoped to move in to the vacuum left by his death. It was not to be. The Roman army in Gaul refused to accept defeat and, loyal to Aegidius' memory, chose his son Syagrius to be the new leader of the Gallic field army in the north.[88] Syagrius was to have a long and distinguished career.

It is usually asserted that in order to succeed his father Syagrius must have been born c. 430, meaning that in 465 he was in his mid thirties.[89] There is no evidence for this claim. On the contrary, the fact that Syagrius himself is nowhere documented as leading campaigns in person implies that in fact he was much younger and was chosen by the army to succeed his father out of dynastic loyalty, not out of respect for his military ability. This would account for his absence in the sources from his succession until after the death of Childeric. Instead, the army may have been led by loyal commanders with the title of *comes*.[90] Although hypothesis, this interpretation appears to fit with records of the years 465–472, and explains many otherwise confusing events. These will be described at the appropriate time.

Goths and Saxons

Learning of Aegidius' death, the Goths immediately attempted to take advantage of the situation: 'On the death of Aegidius the Goths invaded regions he had protected in the name of Rome', sending small contingents to test the strength of Syagrius and his alliance with Childeric.[91] The Goths may have expected to begin a major assault in 466: events at court in Toulouse were to confound their expectations.

In a similar manner to the Goths, the Saxon mercenaries under Adovacrius who had been serving Aegidius took the opportunity of his death to assert their independence, taking hostages from Angers and other cities in the vicinity.[92] The result was yet another competing warband in the north of Gaul that both Syagrius and the Goths had to contend with.

Hispania

Given the events of the previous year, many in Hispania may have had great hopes of a continuing peace with the Sueves. They were to be disappointed. Affairs soon returned to normal, with the Sueves attacking the city of Conimbrica.[93] Theoderic dispatched two envoys, both of which failed to secure peace, before Arborius, the *magister militum Hispaniae*, was also sent, but to no avail. When the latter envoys returned they were met with news from Italy.[94]

Leo and Marcellinus

With the Empire seemingly disintegrating, the West desperately needed help from the East and it is likely that an unrecorded series of envoys were in continuous motion between the two emperors. In 465 a major change took place in the East. Up until this time the leading military commander in the East had been Aspar. During his period controlling the army Aspar had maintained that the East should not become involved militarily in Western affairs.

Yet now Gaiseric's refusal to stop the attacks on the West appears to have become too much for Leo, but without the approval of Aspar sending aid was difficult. Although he could not send the main army, Leo could order help to go from other quarters. The evidence is fragmentary and open to different interpretations, yet it would appear that in 465, following orders from Leo, Marcellinus landed in Sicily.

The theory that Marcellinus acted either on his own initiative or at the request of Ricimer can be discounted. It is unlikely that he had the ships needed to transport troops and supplies to the island on his own, and, even more telling, when last in Sicily his troops had been bribed by Ricimer and unless under instruction from and assisted by Leo he will almost certainly have been unwilling to risk a repeat of the episode.[95] Surprised, the Vandals were easily defeated and evicted from the island.[96] In the meantime, Leo began political manoeuvres to reduce Aspar's power.[97]

Death of Severus

As summer turned to autumn, on 25 September *Novella Severa 2* was passed by Severus. The law is his last known act. On 14 November 465 he died in Rome.[98] None of the contemporary primary sources suggest foul play in his death: Sidonius Apollinaris even states outright that it was due to natural causes.[99] Unfortunately, Cassiodorus, a sixth century source, suggests that the 'deceitful' Ricimer had Severus poisoned in the palace in Rome.[100] This has resulted in Ricimer being seen as the sinister power behind the throne, fitting with and encouraging the theory that throughout his time as *magister militum* Ricimer was intent on having 'puppet' emperors obeying his every order.[101] However, it is best to take the statements of Sidonius and the silence of other contemporary writers such Hydatius at face value and acknowledge that Severus died of natural causes.

Analysis

Severus is almost always portrayed as Ricimer's docile stooge, acting as emperor but following orders from Ricimer to the letter. Only when he is assumed to have displayed any form of initiative is he considered to be no longer of use and so have been killed by Ricimer.[102] A closer examination demonstrates that there is no evidence for the assumption. That permission was given to Theoderic to appoint a new *magister militum per Hispaniae* suggests that Ricimer was not the power behind the throne, implying instead that there was severe political infighting taking place in Rome between Ricimer and his opponents and that the grant of such power to Theoderic may have been an attempt to curb the excessive power of Ricimer by establishing Theoderic as a viable alternative should Ricimer overstep the mark.

Nevertheless, the little evidence that survives implies that Ricimer did not kill Severus and throughout his reign may have supported the emperor in the majority of the political debates in Rome. With the emperor dead Ricimer would again have to face the problem of finding a replacement. As with both Majorian and Severus there would be an interregnum before the choice would be made.

Chapter Nine

Anthemius: Hope Renewed

12 April 467–11 July 472

Interregnum

As with the deaths of Avitus and Majorian, after the death of Severus there was an interregnum, although in this case it lasted far longer than those occurring previously. Part of the problem lay with the political implications of the possible candidates. As is usual, there is no evidence in the sources saying why Ricimer did not immediately choose a successor to Severus, which would be expected if Ricimer was simply a barbarian general determined to maintain control of the Empire. Instead it is necessary to resort to hypothesis. Following the earlier analysis of events surrounding the elevation of Severus, it is plausible to suggest that after Severus' death there was no outstanding candidate who could unite the divided Senate in Rome.

There was an obvious successor in the form of Olybrius – the husband of Placidia, daughter of Valentinian III – yet at this stage there may have been little chance of him being crowned. There are several reasons for this hypothesis. One is that it would appear that at the time of Severus' death he was still in the East, and so simply not available for a coronation in the West. A further, and possibly more important factor, is that his marriage to Placidia gave him a legitimate claim to be the heir of the House of Theodosius, so he could easily become more independent than either Ricimer or the Senate were willing to risk. This is especially the case when Ricimer's position is considered, since Olybrius' legitimacy could result in the army changing their allegiance away from Ricimer to Olybrius – a possibility that may have alarmed Ricimer. Finally, and most importantly, Gaiseric was still campaigning on behalf of Olybrius as the new Emperor.[1] Accepting Olybrius may have been perceived by some as unacceptable, as it could be interpreted as the Senate bowing to political pressure from a barbarian with whom they were at war. As if to ensure that Olybrius would not be chosen, Gaiseric continued his attacks on Italy throughout 465 and 466.

With no suitable candidate, Ricimer was forced to send envoys to the East asking Leo to appoint a new emperor for the West. It has been suggested that Ricimer would have preferred to 'govern the West as a *generalissimo* under Leo, but the time was not yet ripe'.[2] This remains a possibility but seems unlikely: at no time did Ricimer attempt to rule on his own.[3]

Unfortunately, as noted in the previous chapter, the request for an emperor coincided with a period of political turmoil in the East. Aspar had remained the

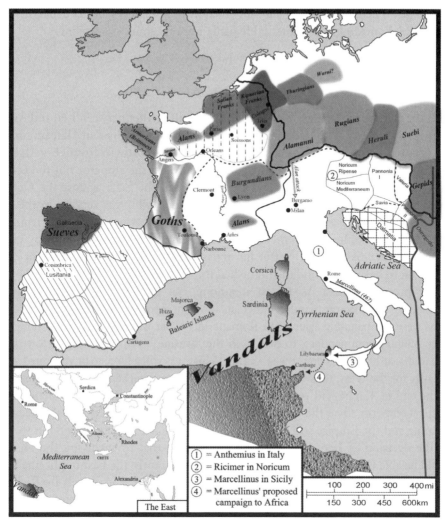

Map 15: The Early Reign of Anthemius, including Marcellius' possible proposed campaign.

dominant military commander for many years, but Leo was now determined to either raise up a rival to balance Aspar's influence, or to eliminate Aspar once and for all. Ricimer would have to wait for the emperor's decision.

Hispania

Encouraged by the news from Italy of Severus' death, the Sueves attacked Aunona. In this they may have been advised by a 'leading Arian apostate', a Greek named Ajax. According to Hydatius, Ajax had abandoned the Catholic faith, become an Arian, and at first worked amongst the Goths in Gaul, but afterwards he had moved to Hispania and was now preaching a radical form of Arianism amongst the Sueves.[4]

In response Theoderic sent yet another embassy to the Sueves, but as usual this was ignored by Remismund.[5] Affairs in Hispania were reaching crisis point.

466

Leo

With the coming of the New Year tensions rose still further between Leo and Aspar, his *magister militum*. As noted earlier, Aspar was either a Goth or an Alan and in 466 war erupted between the Goths and the Sciri on the northern frontier, with both sending envoys to Leo asking for help.[6] Aspar advised the emperor not to become involved, but he was overruled and Leo supported the Sciri against the Goths.[7] Presumably shortly afterwards Aspar's son Ardabur, who was serving in the east as *magister militum per Orientem*, was accused of treachery and removed from his post.[8] The proof of his involvement were letters carried to Constantinople by a man named Tarasicodissa:[9] shortly after his arrival he would change his name to Zeno and go on to have a long and distinguished imperial career.[10]

The pressure against Aspar was mounting, but he was still recognized as an outstanding military commander: either late in 466 or at some time in 467 the Goths and Huns were campaigning against the Romans and Aspar was sent to Thrace, alongside other military commanders, to deal with the invasion.[11] Aspar quickly defeated the barbarians: although his power was waning, Aspar was still a force to be reckoned with.

Sadly for the West, these events in Constantinople absorbed Leo's attentions and by the end of 466 he had yet to make a decision about whether to nominate a new Western emperor. Over the winter Ricimer decided that, despite political indecision in Rome and the Empire still being under attack, he still had no option but to wait for the decision of Leo. Doubtless he was hoping that by involving the East he would be able to bypass the Senate and, more importantly, the East might finally be encouraged to lend direct support to the beleaguered West. Fortunately for Ricimer, by sending Marcellinus to Sicily in 465 Leo had already made a fateful decision that would gain the West a breathing space and finally bring the East into direct opposition to Gaiseric.[12]

Gaiseric

As usual, the exact sequence of events is impossible to determine with confidence, but the meagre sources suggest that over the winter of 465–6 Gaiseric learned that Marcellinus' attack had been promoted by the East.[13] In response, in 466 Gaiseric diverted the spring raids away from Italy and the surrounding islands to the eastern Mediterranean.[14] Not expecting war, the East was unprepared and Procopius claims that Gaiseric 'plundered Illyricum and most of the Peloponnesus and the rest of Greece and all the islands which lie near it'.[15] Possibly knowing that Marcellinus was defending Sicily, Gaiseric had attacked Marcellinus' territories. This would help to explain the instant success enjoyed by Gaiseric's raids. The attacks would both negate Aspar's policy of non–intervention and also spur Leo into taking direct action against the Vandals.

Euric

In 465 the Sueves had yet again raided Roman territory in Hispania and ignored Gothic requests to stop. In the New Year Theoderic sent even more envoys, including a man named Salla, to Remismund in Hispania. As usual the envoys were rebuffed but when they returned to Toulouse they found that Theoderic was dead and a new king was in command. Euric, Theoderic's brother, had assassinated the king and taken his place.[16]

The reasons behind Euric's decision to kill Theoderic are unknown, but if, as mentioned earlier, Theoderic had associated Frederic with his rule then a theory presents itself. After Frederic's death it is possible that Euric was expecting to take Frederic's place as 'under-king'. When this did not happen, Euric lost patience with Theoderic.[17] Later, the change was to mark a watershed in Romano-Gothic politics, but at this early date the transition was simply marked by the traditional envoys to the 'emperor' and the Sueves.[18]

Unfortunately, Hydatius appears to be a little confused in his chronology at this point and it is likely that these envoys were received by Ricimer in Rome.[19] These almost certainly gave assurances that peace would prevail: although the sources are silent, for the remainder of 466 and 467 Euric remained quiescent in Aquitaine. The most likely cause would be his need to quell internal unrest due to the killing of his brother, a man who had reigned over the Goths for thirteen years: many of the Gothic nobles will have been unhappy about the abrupt change of ruler.

The envoys to the Suevic King Remismund were immediately returned. Instead, Remismund dispatched envoys of his own to Italy, the Vandals and the Gothic court.[20] Sadly, the nature of these envoys is unknown but it is likely that Remismund was endeavouring to create as much confusion as possible so that he could continue to raid throughout Hispania without interference. At roughly the same time the people of Aunona, continuously attacked by the Sueves, sent envoys to Gaul to appeal for help from the new king.[21] The court in Italy was no longer seen as being capable of interfering in events in Hispania.

Interestingly, Cassiodorus claims that Euric also attempted to establish good relations with northern tribes, especially the Thuringi and possibly also the Heruli and the Warni, sending them gifts and helping them against their hostile neighbours.[22] In this way Euric would create a coalition of forces that would help him to survive any civil wars, as well as against any hostile reaction from the Empire. It would also help to stop attacks from Syagrius' forces in northern Gaul.

467

Anthemius

Over the winter of 466–7 Leo and the Eastern court debated their options. Gaiseric's attacks had resulted in a state of war between the East and the Vandals, and Leo now had decisions to make. Finally, Leo nominated an emperor for the West: the *magister militum* and *patricius* Anthemius. In the previous decade, over the winter of 456–7, the Emperor Marcian may have planned to make Anthemius the Western Emperor but had died before this could take effect.[23] Eventually, Majorian had been made emperor. Anthemius would now get his chance.

Anthemius was born in Constantinople at some time around 420.[24] Descended from a line of powerful men, including consuls and possibly the usurper Procopius (d. 366), around the year 453 Anthemius was married to Aelia Marcia Euphemia, the only daughter of the Emperor Marcian, making him a distant successor to the House of Theodosius.[25] Together, they had four (known) sons, Anthemiolus, Marcianus, Procopius Anthemius, and Romulus, and one daughter, Alypia.[26]

In his youth he either went or was sent to Alexandria to study in the Neoplatonic school in the city. This gave rise to the later claims from hostile sources that Anthemius was not a Christian but a pagan, although this is now discounted.[27] It is probable that studying at the same time were men who would later become important, for example Pusaeus, who would become Praetorian Prefect of the East and was to be Eastern consul in 467, and Messius Phoebus Severus, who would be the Eastern consul in 470.[28] However, for later events the most important man at the school was Marcellinus, now, in 467, the *magister militum per Illyricum* and opponent of Ricimer.

Following his father in a military career and after his marriage to Euphemia, in 454 Anthemius was probably made *comes rei militaris per Thracias* (Count of the Military in Thrace) and sent to re-establish the Roman frontier on the Danube after the death of Attila the Hun. Following his successful tenure, Marcian gave him the rank of *magister utriusque militiae*, nominated him as consul for 455, and gave him the title *patricius*.[29] After Marcian's death he was a potential nominee for emperor, but thanks to the support of Aspar the throne went to Leo. Nevertheless, Anthemius' services were retained and at some point between 459 and 462 he defeated an Ostrogothic force led by King Valamer in battle before triumphing over a force of Huns that had captured Serdica, possibly in the winter of 466–467.[30] He was almost certainly a capable commander, his military ability outweighing the threat he posed as an alternative candidate for the throne.

In the spring of 467 Leo ordered Anthemius to travel to Italy, according to Procopius with the 'explicit task' of making war on the Vandals.[31] To ensure his acceptance by Ricimer and the Senate in Rome he was accompanied by an army led by Marcellinus. It is sometimes claimed that Marcellinus 'provided the fleet to transport Anthemius' army', but this is nowhere stated by the sources and more recent analysis has suggested that Marcellinus actually possessed few ships.[32]

Although the fact that Marcellinus led the troops is usually glossed over, the appointment needs to be examined in detail. It is clear that Leo was not going to allow Ricimer to remain in uncontested control of the West with a puppet emperor. In the East, there were a number of *magistri militiae* who counterbalanced one another in order to ensure that there was less chance of a rebellion against the ruling emperor. Although in theory this could have been true of the West, the fact that the *magister peditum* had been senior since the rule of Honorius (395–423) had resulted in one man dominating affairs in the West. For Anthemius to achieve an independent status there needed to be a counterbalance to Ricimer. The most obvious individual was Marcellinus: as an opponent of Ricimer he was unlikely to become a pawn in Ricimer's hands. As if to emphasize the new division of power, Marcellinus was also made *patricius*.[33]

At this point the military power of the East when compared to the impoverished West was clearly demonstrated to all: Anthemius arrived in Italy with a 'well-equipped army of vast proportions'.[34] Marching towards Rome, on 12 April 467, possibly at Brontotas, three miles from Rome, Anthemius was proclaimed emperor.[35] Although it is sometimes claimed that Anthemius was only appointed as Caesar by Leo, there is no evidence on this from the sources.[36] He then entered the city, although at the time a raging pestilence was devastating Rome.[37]

As part of the long negotiations which had taken place it had been agreed that Ricimer would marry Anthemius' daughter, Alypia.[38] The wedding was celebrated in 'extravagant style', with the approval of 'all factions of Rome', giving 'hope for the future security of the state'.[39] Anthemius may have seen the marriage as a major concession to the barbarian general and have hoped that the marriage would ensure the loyalty of the most powerful individual in his new domain.[40] He may also have hoped that the marriage would help to alleviate Ricimer's anger at Marcellinus being made joint *patricius*.[41] Similarly, Ricimer may have begun by valuing the marriage, hoping that his position as son-in-law would help him to achieve a position greater than that achieved by either Stilicho (brother-in-law by adoption of Honorius) or Aetius (prospective father-in-law of Valentinian III's daughter Placidia), both of whom had attempted to join their descendants directly to the imperial House without success.[42] Sadly for Ricimer, it soon became apparent that Alypia did not like her new husband.[43] This may be one of the reasons for there being no record of the couple having children.

One thing that was achieved by the marriage was the acceptance by Ricimer of the new regime, and an open sign of his loyalty to Anthemius. This is nowhere better demonstrated than by Ennodius' claim that Ricimer was 'second only to the Emperor Anthemius'.[44] Furthermore, despite Marcellinus' arrival at court, Ricimer still had a military role to play: earlier, in 466, war had broken out between the Goths and the Sciri and Leo had supported the Sciri against the Goths.[45] It is possibly in this context that as part of the conflict a section of the Ostrogoths invaded Noricum early in Anthemius' reign.[46] Rather than sending Marcellinus, Anthemius ordered Ricimer to repel the invaders. He defeated them whilst they were still in Noricum.[47]

In the summer of 367 Sidonius was sent as an ambassador from the Auvergne to the royal court, although his mission is unknown.[48] Once in Rome, he was convinced by one friend to write a panegyric to Anthemius, and another friend helped him to gain access to the emperor.[49] On 1 January 468 he delivered the panegyric, heavily imbued with the hopes of victory over the Vandals and the unity of East and West, and was rewarded with the Urban Prefecture for 468.[50] Circumstances would ensure that he would not serve the full year in the post.

Anthemius, the husband of an imperial princess and so a candidate for the Eastern throne, had not only survived under Leo's rule, but had been nominated as Western Emperor. Although Leo may have acted in part to remove a rival from the Eastern court, it is a testament to Anthemius' ability that he had managed to survive for so long in the Byzantine politics of the Eastern court. He now attempted to put his political abilities to work in the West.

Ricimer

It is possible that Ricimer's main allies were the barbarian peoples with whom he had blood ties and, not least, the army. In the later days of Imperial Rome these may have been of more value than the aristocratic support found in the Senate, although earlier analysis suggests that Ricimer did have sections of support in the Senate. In order to secure his own position Anthemius needed to reduce Ricimer's support, both in court, in Gaul, in Hispania, and with the army.[51]

Doubtless it was hoped that Anthemius' long military career and his distant connection to the Theodosian house would make him acceptable to the 'conservative faction' in Rome, but of overriding concern was the hope that it would help him secure the loyalty of the army.[52] With any luck, Italy would be swayed to support Anthemius rather than Ricimer. It is possible that the place of Anthemius' acclamation, at a point somewhere outside Rome, may have been at a military camp, in a similar fashion to the previous acclamations of Valens at Hebdomon (a known military base outside Constantinople) and Majorian at 'Columellas'.[53] If this is true, the attempt to sway the loyalty of the army began at a very early stage of his reign.

In this context the giving of the Urban Prefecture to Sidonius also becomes more understandable. Anthemius also gave leading positions to other Gauls, doubtless in the hope of fostering Gallic support for his new regime.[54] At the same time he attempted to establish good relations with the Goths, the Sueves, the Salian Franks, and the *Brittones* (Bretons). Although several of these missions – notably those to the Goths, the Sueves and the Franks – would be failures, the attempt demonstrates that Anthemius had a good grasp of Imperial politics: gaining the support of barbarian leaders would strengthen his position as emperor, and the ongoing discussions at least managed to sow doubt in the minds of his opponents.

It has been suggested that these attempts to negotiate with the barbarian kingdoms was 'an encroachment on Ricimer's territory', but this has rightly been refuted: there is no reason to suppose that Ricimer was left out of these negotiations. At this early stage the regime was still united and Ricimer's connections would have been of great value to Anthemius.[55]

Yet even very early in his reign the omens were against the new emperor: at an unknown date in 467 there was an earthquake in Ravenna.[56] At roughly the same time there were famines, a pestilence in Italy focused on Campania, strange celestial phenomena, and an outbreak of cattle disease – the last two specifically dated to 467.[57]

Gaiseric

As a response to Gaiseric's attempts to pressure the Empire into accepting Olybrius as Western emperor, and as a demonstration of the new unity between East and West, Leo sent envoys to Gaiseric telling him to stop his attacks on, and his interference in, the politics of the West. In response, Gaiseric flatly refused the demands, instead accusing the East of breaking the Treaty of 462 and effectively declaring outright war.[58]

News of the rebuff spread quickly. Although previous Vandal attacks on the East had focused upon Greece and its environs, this could easily change. Following the Sack of Rome in 455 Gaiseric had conquered the whole of the North Africa littoral from Carthage to the Straits of Gibraltar.[59] Now at war with the East, it was possible that he would attack along the coast towards Egypt. The citizens of Egypt clearly recognized the threat, as the *Life of Saint Daniel Stylites* mentions that panic spread in Alexandria with rumours that Gaiseric was going to attack.[60] From internal evidence within the source it is clear that the story was rife in 467.[61] The citizens of the East were correct in their assumption that Gaiseric would attack: later that same year, probably as soon as the sailing season began in early-mid spring, the Vandals attacked, in this year focusing upon the areas around Rhodes.[62]

Anthemius Reacts

In Italy, events are complicated by the meagre nature of the sources and the subsequent confusion in dating events, especially with regards to the information stated by Hydatius.[63] As noted in the previous chapter, Hydatius claims that in 465: 'Marcellinus slaughtered the Vandals in Sicily and put them to flight from the island.'[64] This is accepted as being prompted by Leo in opposition to Gaiseric's continued attacks.[65] However, later, in 467, Hydatius writes that: 'An expedition to Africa organized against the Vandals was recalled because of "a change of weather" and the unsuitability of sailing.'[66] Sadly, Hydatius gives no context for the claim that an attack in 467 was halted by bad weather and no other source mentions the event. As a result, it is necessary to reconcile Hydatius' claim with what may actually have occurred.

It is feasible that Hydatius, living in Hispania, had heard two stories in different years relating to the same event and has consequently misreported that Marcellinus was in Sicily on two separate occasions: once in 465, the other in 467. Hydatius had simply not realized that the two stories are of the same event.

However, it is possible that Hydatius is correct in describing two attacks, the first, in 465, being at Leo's request, the second, in 467, under orders from Anthemius. If this is the case, it is possible to theorize that in 465 Marcellinus was sent by Leo to relieve the pressure on Sicily. After Gaiseric had attacked his homeland, Marcellinus may have returned home in 466, before returning to Sicily in 467 once it became clear that Gaiseric's attacks were focused further to the East, rather than on Illyricum again.

The hypothesis makes sense. The West needed at least three commanders in 467: Anthemius to defend the mainland in person, Ricimer in Noricum repelling invaders and dissuading attacks on Northern Italy, and now Marcellinus in Sicily to complete the defence of what was left of the Western Empire.

In addition, it is possible – though impossible to prove – that on this occasion Marcellinus was given further orders. With Euric quiescent due to his need to cement his rule, Anthemius did not need a large army to garrison Italy. It is possible that extra troops were available and were placed under the command of Marcellinus.

Since Gaiseric was now at war with the East it may have been expected that the majority of his troops would be away from Africa raiding the eastern Mediterranean. Should this be the case, it is possible that a lightning attack on Africa from Sicily using the few forces available would destroy the Vandal kingdom.

Such a victory would have been a major political coup for Anthemius. In addition, since over the years the Vandals had amassed vast amounts of booty from their raids, the 'reconquest' could even have made the West financially viable for the vital first years of Anthemius' reign, possibly even financing the reconquest of further regions of the West. Sadly for Anthemius and Marcellinus, the chance was ruined by bad weather.[67]

Hispania

In Hispania the envoys sent by Remismund on Anthemius' acclamation returned bringing the dire news that the Empire had raised a very large army headed by three capable commanders. The Sueves panicked and their raiding parties were hastily withdrawn.[68] In a similar fashion, in Gaul the Goths quickly recalled their envoys to the Vandals.[69] Sadly, once it was realized that Anthemius was concentrating upon the Vandals, the Sueves resumed their raids, with Remismund himself leading an attack into Lusitania.[70] Late in the year the city of Conimbrica was attacked once again and this time heavily sacked by the rampaging Sueves.[71] Hispania was no longer connected to the Empire except in the minds of a few nobles reminiscing about the glory days of old. That would quickly change should Anthemius be able to conquer Africa from the Vandals.

Chapter Ten

The African Campaign

T he major event and defining moment of Anthemius' reign was the joint campaign of East and West against the Vandals in Africa in 468. Although this has often been described in terms of its outcome, its objectives and course have seldom been analysed from a military point of view.

The most detailed description we have of what happened comes from Procopius' *War Against the Vandals*.[1] As is usual, care needs to be taken when analysing such texts: for example, it derives from other sources and Procopius may have edited events described in the originals to fit into his own narrative, which aimed to promote the military achievements of his hero, Belisarius, who conquered the Vandals in a swift campaign in 533–4. Further, it is uncertain how the original sources gained their knowledge so their accuracy is also indeterminate. However, as it is the source with the greatest level of detail it must be used in order to attempt an analysis of the campaign. When utilized in conjunction with other sources an even more detailed picture of events can be reached.

Anthemius, and probably Marcellinus, had input when planning the campaign against the Vandals, but overall it was masterminded by Leo in Constantinople, who supplied most of the men, ships and resources for the operation.[2] Yet although Leo was the mastermind behind the campaign in Africa, it is likely that Anthemius had a greater degree of control of operations in Italy and the surrounding islands due to his proximity to the area and access to up to date intelligence.

A study of all of the sources demonstrates that Leo had a grand strategy, based upon a three-pronged approach. One force would attack the Vandals' possessions in the western Mediterranean. A second force was to muster in Egypt before travelling across the northern coast of Africa, seizing Tripolitana before moving on to Carthage itself. The third and main attack would be a direct assault on the Vandals' African territories, carried out by a large fleet and supporting army.

To this effect, command of the first task force was given to Marcellinus, now *magister militum* in Italy, and he was sent with a mixed army of Eastern and Western troops to seize Sardinia, one of the Vandals' major holdings west of Italy.[3] The decision to invade Sardinia made sound strategic sense, as it eliminated one of the Vandals' major threats to Italy. Further, the decision may have been swayed by the urgings of Pope Hilarius, himself a native of Sardinia.[4] Despite the fact that Marcellinus' army is sometimes seen as being composed only of Eastern troops, the fact that Hydatius describes it as an 'Allied' force implies that the army was a mix of Eastern and Western troops, doubtless being based around a core formed of Marcellinus' *comitatus*.[5] Doubtless the intention was to reconquer Sardinia,

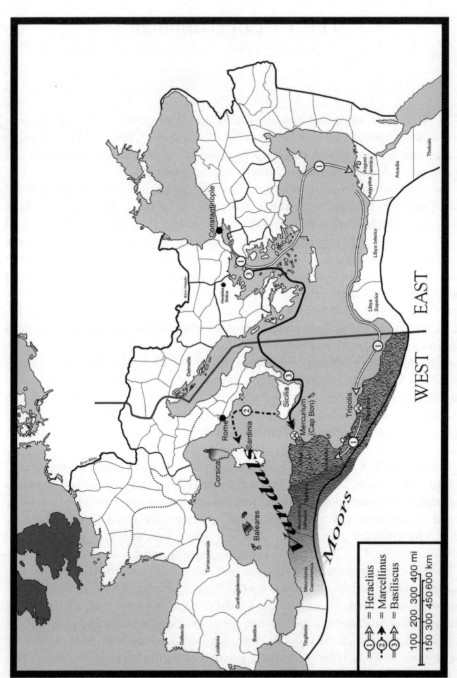

Map 16: The African Campaign of 468.

distracting the Vandal garrison and either destroying it or at least ensuring that it could not be removed to protect Africa until after it had been heavily defeated and demoralized.

The second attack was led by a man named Heraclius, alongside an Isaurian named Marsus.[6] Previously probably a *comes rei militaris*, Heraclius had gained experience fighting the Iberians (in the Caucasus) and the Persians on behalf of the Lazi, although the campaign had been cut short thanks to the poor logistical organization of the Lazi.[7] As with the campaign in Sardinia, the plan appears to have been to attack peripheral areas where the Vandals had key garrisons, pinning the garrisons before defeating them. In this way any men that escaped would be demoralized and return to Carthage telling of the superiority of the Roman troops. Further, it would limit the options available to Gaiseric, as he would not be able to mount a diversionary attack on Egypt from Tripolitana.

To command the main invasion fleet Leo chose a man named Basiliscus. Basiliscus has long been the subject of biased reporting, largely because he is seen as an incompetent commander who was only appointed to the command since he was brother-in-law of Leo – the brother of Leo's wife Verina.[8] For example, Priscus describes him as: 'a successful soldier but slow-witted and easily taken in by deceivers'.[9]

Yet he appears to have been *magister militum per Thracias* between 464 and 467–8, having 'many successes against the [Ostro-]Goths and Huns'.[10] This may be confirmed by the fact that in 465 he was awarded the consulship, possibly as a reward for his service in Thrace.[11] Furthermore, at an unknown date he was declared *patricius*, and although this may date to later (471/2) it is probable that he was given the title prior to the campaign against the Vandals.[12] For the upcoming campaign he was recalled from Thrace and almost certainly given the post of *magister militum praesentalis*.[13] There may have been more qualified generals available for the command, but there was little chance of any other commander being chosen due to his relationship with the emperor.

It is interesting to note that the military services of Ricimer were not utilized for the campaign. There are at least three obvious reasons for this. One is that his military abilities were an unknown quantity as far as Anthemius and Leo were concerned. They almost certainly decided that for the proposed campaign they should use commanders whose abilities and methods were known to them. A second is that despite his joining the 'royal family', his loyalty may still have been of concern, especially when it came to placing large numbers of troops at his disposal. The third, and possibly decisive factor, is that as the campaign was primarily funded by the East Leo may have decided that only Eastern generals – and by extension Leo himself – would get the credit for the upcoming victory.

For the campaign Leo emptied the Eastern treasury, possibly spending four years' worth of revenues, in order to gather a formidable army:[14]

And the Emperor Leo … was gathering an army against them [the Vandals]; and they say that this army amounted to about one hundred thousand men.

And he collected a fleet of ships from the whole of the eastern Mediterranean ... [and] ... they say, thirteen hundred *centenaria* were expended by him.'

Procopius 3.6.1–2, *trans. Gordon, 205.*

Whereupon the emperor, aroused to anger, collected from all the eastern sea 1,100 ships, filled them with soldiers and arms and sent them against Gaiseric. They say that he spent 1,300 *centenaria* of gold on this expedition.

Priscus fr. 42, *trans. Gordon, 120–1.*

According to the original text the number given by Priscus was 100,000 ships. This has been emended by Gordon, the translator, to 1,100, as the original number is obviously far too large and the latter corresponds to the 1,113 vessels claimed by Cedrenus.[15]

Joannes Lydas [Lydus – John the Lydian] ... says that 65,000 pounds of gold and 700,000 pounds of silver were collected. [and] ... those that administered these things reveal, 47,000 pounds of gold were raised through the prefects, 17,000 pounds of gold through the count of the treasury, and 700,0000 pounds of silver, apart from adequate amounts raised from the public funds and from the Emperor Anthemius.

Candidus fr. 2, *trans. Gordon, 121.*

In addition, Theodorus Lector gives a figure of 7,000 sailors/marines to man the fleet.[16] Although possibly a realistic number, there is then the problem that if the Latin word *nauta* is translated as the usual 'sailor', this gives an average of only six sailors per vessel: in that case, the fleet was probably not as large as the sources claim. Assuming that it would, for example, take only 20 sailors to man a vessel, this would give a fleet of 350 ships. This may be more likely than the 1,000 vessels assumed by Cedrenus, but if the latter is to be accepted then the 7,000 men attested by Theodorus needs correction. This has led to at least one modern historian translating *nauta* as 'marines', so bypassing the need to lower the number of ships.[17] Obviously, certainty is impossible but it is feasible that the lower number of ships is more reasonable. This would account for the speed and decisiveness of later events.

The logistical problems of supplying the extremely large force over long distances also needs to be assessed before the number of troops given by Procopius can be accepted at face value. Sadly, there is no other information concerning the origins or numbers of men used so the details are unknown. As a result, any attempt to estimate them is merely guesswork: all that can be said with certainty is that from the context this was the largest military force assembled to campaign in the West in the last days of the Western Empire.

In addition to these difficulties, Leo had planned a three-fold attack. Unfortunately it is not made clear whether the troops used by Marcellinus and Heraclius were included in the total given by Procopius. If so, as seems likely, then obviously the invasion fleet aimed at Africa will have been far smaller than that given for the whole campaign. Marcellinus would need a large fleet to carry his troops and ensure that they could land safely in Sardinia, and it is clear from later evidence that Heraclius was accompanied by a fleet as he traversed the North African coast.[18]

Despite modern estimates, no numbers are given for the men assigned to either Marcellinus or Heraclius and all of the numbers suggested are based upon figures proposed for other armies, which are themselves often conjecture, usually based upon the *Notitia Dignitatum*, a document seventy years out of date. As a result, and despite temptation, no numbers will be given for any of the armies used by Marcellinus, Heraclius and Basiliscus. Yet one thing is certain: the diversion of ships and men away from the main projected invasion of Africa means that Basiliscus probably would not have the overwhelming superiority in men and ships usually accorded in the sources and accepted by some more modern accounts.

Sardinia and Tripolitana

The campaign began well. Following his orders Marcellinus landed in Sardinia, where 'he drove out the Vandals and gained possession of it with no great difficulty'.[19] This is unsurprising. Since Leo had spent time gathering ships for the invasion of Africa it is almost certain that rumour of the planned invasion will have reached Gaiseric. In this context, it is likely that the majority of the Vandal garrison of Sardinia was recalled to help in the defence of the homeland. The chances are that Marcellinus was met with little resistance from only a few troops left behind to ensure that the island did not spontaneously rebel.

Leaving Constantinople, Heraclius travelled first to Egypt to collect 'an army drawn from Egypt, the Thebaid and the desert'.[20] As noted above, it is impossible to decide the number of troops Heraclius had under his command. The out of date *Notitia Dignitatum* lists over seventy units in the regions of Egypt and the Thebaid. Heraclius could have had command of a vast army. The only hint of any sort is the inclusion of 'the desert', which suggests that Heraclius may have had a contingent of 'Saracen' (Arab) allies. Travelling west, they caught the Vandals by surprise.[21] However, unlike Marcellinus, Heraclius had to defeat the enemy in a pitched battle:

> And Heraclius was sent from Byzantium to Tripolis in Libya, and after conquering the Vandals of that district in battle, he easily captured the cities, and leaving his ships there, led his army on foot toward Carthage. Such, then, was the sequence of events which formed the prelude of the war.
>
> *Procopius* 3.6.9.

It would appear that Heraclius had been transported by a fleet from Egypt to near Tripolis, where he had landed and fought the Vandals. After this, wary of the threat of the Vandal fleet nearer to Carthage, he had left the ships in Tripolis. As already noted, when combined with the campaign against Sardinia, the strategy of attacking on three fronts was to seriously weaken the fleet available for Basiliscus.

Africa

As noted above, Leo gave command of the main assault to his brother-in-law Basiliscus. Despite the evidence suggesting that Basiliscus may have been a competent commander, Procopius has a different view of the man, and includes information concerning Aspar's loyalty to Leo and attitude to the campaign:

> He [Leo] made Basiliscus commander-in-chief, the brother of his wife Berine [Verina], a man who was extraordinarily desirous of the royal power, which he hoped would come to him without a struggle if he won the friendship of Aspar. For Aspar himself, being an adherent of the Arian faith, and having no intention of changing it for another, was unable to enter upon the imperial office, but he was easily strong enough to establish another in it, and it already seemed likely that he would plot against the Emperor Leo, who had given him offence. So they say that since Aspar was then fearful lest, if the Vandals were defeated, Leo should establish his power most securely, he repeatedly urged upon Basiliscus that he should spare the Vandals and Gaiseric.
>
> *Procopius* 3.6.2–4.

There are two main difficulties with accepting this information at face value. One is that Procopius, or at least his sources, appear to be acquainted with 'secret' information: the idea that Basiliscus' ambitions were well-known is unacceptable. There is little doubt that had Leo believed that Basiliscus was aiming for the throne then Basiliscus would have been executed rather than being put in command of the African campaign. The report concerning Basiliscus' ambition as given by Procopius was an assumption based upon the *topos* (a traditional theme or motif; a literary convention) of ancient historians that events were usually decided by the integrity or lack thereof of an individual and upon the hindsight that Basiliscus would later become emperor.

On the other hand, it is likely that the report that Aspar was opposed to the campaign is accurate. Such overt opposition would be well known. It is even possible that Aspar's motive for his opposition – that he feared lest Leo grow too strong to be 'guided' – is near to the truth, although Aspar's long-established resistance to supporting the West may simply be that he believed that such assistance was futile and that the West could not long survive. In this context it should be noted that Aspar had spent time campaigning against Gaiseric in Africa in 431, alongside the *comes Africae* Bonifatius, and had found that Gaiseric was a worthy opponent.[22] Although Aspar had fought Gaiseric to a standstill, he had been unable to defeat the Vandals. As a consequence, it may be that Aspar was simply worried about the consequences for the East should the attack fail. The likelihood is that Aspar's motives were a combination of all of the above, resulting in a determination not to interfere in the West that was well known at court.

Not waiting for the whole fleet to be amassed, Basiliscus apparently used part of his newly acquired navy to attack Vandal shipping: 'When no small force from the

East had been collected, he engaged frequently in sea fights with Gaiseric and sent "a large number of ships to the bottom".[23] Sadly, no source describes the strength of this fleet, nor the battles fought.

Whilst Marcellinus in Sardinia and Heraclius in Tripolis had been leading successful campaigns, Basiliscus had been assembling and organizing his forces. Finally, he set sail for Africa, doubtless using the newly-subdued Sicily as a staging point for the landings – later, Belisarius was to use the same route in his assault on Africa. Unlike Majorian, Leo had eschewed the subtle approach of a landing via Hispania for a direct frontal assault on Carthage with his main force.

> But Basiliscus with his whole fleet put in at a town distant from Carthage no less than two hundred and eighty *stades* [a *stadion* was 185 metres in length: therefore the landing was around 52 kilometres or c. 32 miles from Carthage] ...[at a place that was] named Mercurium [Cap Bon].
>
> *Procopius* 3.6.10.

The fact that Basiliscus landed so near to Carthage was obviously seen by Procopius as a mistake, reinforcing his depiction of Basiliscus as a poor commander. However, it is possible that Procopius' bias is misleading. He is comparing Basiliscus, whose expedition ended in failure, with his hero Belisarius, the epitome of how Procopius thinks a general should act. Obviously, this is unfair. In an era where major naval expeditions were extremely rare – the only other example is Majorian's failed expedition – Basiliscus was breaking new ground. Doubtless his idea was to land near Carthage, immediately cow the Vandals into submission, capture the city and end Vandal rule in Africa. However, by opting to land very near to Carthage he left himself open to rapid counter-attacks, a problem exacerbated by later events – as will be seen.

Finally, Basiliscus landed in Africa with the troops.[24] Procopius sees this as the defining moment of the campaign:

> If he [Basiliscus] had not purposely played the coward and hesitated, but had undertaken to go straight for Carthage, he would have captured it at the first onset, and he would have reduced the Vandals to subjection without their even thinking of resistance; so overcome was Gaiseric with awe of Leo as an invincible emperor, when the report was brought to him that Sardinia and Tripolis had been captured, and he saw the fleet of Basiliscus to be such as the Romans were said never to have had before. But, as it was, the general's hesitation, whether caused by cowardice or treachery, prevented this success.
>
> *Procopius* 3.6.11–12.

As is usual with ancient historians, the fate of a whole campaign rests solely on the negative interpretation of a commander's actions. But in this case the narrative is more biased than normal. When leading the later expedition in 533, Belisarius learned from his predecessor's mistake and opted to land further from Carthage.[25]

He was also able to take Gelimer, the Vandal king at the time, by surprise. In addition, the speed of Belisarius' attack resulted in the collapse of the Vandal Kingdom.

In this context it is unsurprising that Procopius is scathing of Basiliscus' abilities. Yet in Basiliscus' defence, it should be noted that he had no previous examples to consult and was breaking new ground. In addition, coordinating the movement of a large fleet of ships over a large distance without the communication equipment now available was fraught with danger: the least that could be expected was that the ships would become dispersed as they travelled. Therefore, the shortest route available would result in less chance of the fleet becoming dispersed. Yet choosing a place close to Carthage, and therefore open to swift countermeasures, was clearly a mistake. Belisarius later recognized this and made sure that he did not follow in Basiliscus' footsteps.

In a similar vein, although it is possible to conclude that Basiliscus acted too cautiously in not advancing directly on Carthage, the majority of military experience tells against such a hasty interpretation. Basiliscus had used newly-pacified Sicily as a staging post on his way to Africa. Consequently, he will have known that news of the victories in Sardinia and Tripolis will have reached Gaiseric.

The most likely response to being attacked would surely have been for Gaiseric to recall as many of his troops as possible and gather them at the capital in preparation for a counter-strike.[26] If that was the case, Basiliscus would have erred on the side of recklessness to order his men to land and then move quickly against Carthage: an attack on Basiliscus' ill-prepared forces as they marched towards the city would have been devastating. Basiliscus did the correct thing in landing, making a beachhead secure and sending out scouts for information on Gaiseric's activity: later Byzantine military manuals also stress the benefits of avoiding pitched battles.

According to Procopius, Gaiseric took advantage of the lull in Roman activity:

> And Gaiseric, profiting by the negligence of Basiliscus, did as follows. Arming all his subjects in the best way he could, he filled his ships, but not all, for some he kept in readiness empty, and they were the ships which sailed most swiftly. And sending envoys to Basiliscus, he begged him to defer the war for the space of five days, in order that in the meantime he might take counsel and do those things which were especially desired by the emperor. They say, too, that he sent also a great amount of gold without the knowledge of the army of Basiliscus and thus purchased this armistice.
>
> Procopius 3.5.12f.

By the early sixth century the story that Basiliscus had been 'bribed' by Gaiseric was common, since this is also included in the history of Theodorus Lector.[27] Procopius' claim concerning the 'perfidious' nature of Gaiseric's negotiations, stating that he only asked for an armistice in order to amass his forces, also has a precedence in Roman historiography: for example, Ammianus states that the Gothic leader Fritigern had fraudulently opened negotiations with Valens prior to the Battle of Adrianople in 378.[28] Interestingly, in both cases the end result was a catastrophic defeat and it may simply be a common Roman excuse that they could only be defeated by the treacherous nature of their barbarian enemies.

Basiliscus' reaction to the Vandals' envoys is understandable. He was at the head of (probably) the largest army assembled by the Empire for many years, and, in conjunction with his overwhelming fleet, it was only natural for him to believe that Gaiseric would want to come to terms with the Empire before his 'kingdom' was annihilated.

What Basiliscus did not take into account was that Gaiseric was one of the greatest commanders the barbarian kingdoms would ever produce. A study of Gaiseric's history clearly shows that he was a superb military and political leader. He had taken control of Africa in two campaigns, one ending in 435, when he made a treaty with Rome, and the other in 442, when his conquest of Carthage was accepted by both East and West.[29] Furthermore, he had easily defeated Majorian's attempt at reconquest and had then been able to politically isolate the West from the East. Sadly, Basiliscus appears to have underestimated his opponent.

Unfortunately for Basiliscus, Gaiseric had quickly recognized that without the support of the fleet the Roman army would struggle to feed itself in a hostile environment. Gaiseric had enough troops to ensure that Africa remained hostile to the Romans. What Gaiseric needed was to destroy the 'mobile supply base' that was the Roman fleet. He used the negotiations as a way of both buying the time necessary to make his own preparations and for the weather to come to his assistance.

The Battle of Cap Bon

> And [Gaiseric arranged for the truce], thinking, as actually did happen, that a favouring wind would rise for him during this time ... The Vandals, as soon as the wind had arisen for them which they had been expecting ... raised their sails and, taking in tow the boats which, as has been stated above, they had made ready with no men in them, they sailed against the enemy. And when they came near, they set fire to the boats which they were towing, when their sails were bellied by the wind, and let them go against the Roman fleet. And since there were a great number of ships there, these boats easily spread fire wherever they struck, and were themselves readily destroyed together with those with which they came in contact. And as the fire advanced in this way the Roman fleet was filled with tumult, as was natural, and with a great din that rivalled the noise caused by the wind and the roaring of the flames, as the soldiers together with the sailors shouted orders to one another and pushed off with their poles the fire-boats and their own ships as well, which were being destroyed by one another in complete disorder.[30]
>
> *Procopius* 3.6.17–21

Although as already noted the whole disaster is usually laid at the feet of Basiliscus, it is clear that Gaiseric deserves a great deal of the credit for the victory. By agreeing to an armistice he had bought time for himself to organize his defences in case the opportunity to strike presented itself. When the time came he acted with speed and determination, and his ability is highlighted by the decisiveness of the attack. However the Vandals were not willing to simply let the fireships go in and await the outcome. Even as the fires were spreading amongst the Roman fleet:

> Already the Vandals too were at hand ramming and sinking the ships, and making booty of such of the soldiers as attempted to escape, and of their arms as well. But there were also some of the Romans who proved themselves brave men in this struggle, and most of all John, who was a general under Basiliscus and who had no share whatever in his treason. For a great throng having surrounded his ship, he stood on the deck, and turning from side to side kept killing very great numbers of the enemy from there, and when he perceived that the ship was being captured, he leaped with his whole equipment of arms from the deck into the sea. And though Genzon, the son of Gaiseric, entreated him earnestly not to do this, offering pledges and holding out promises of safety, he nevertheless threw himself into the sea, uttering this one word, that John would never come under the hands of dogs.
>
> *Procopius* 3.6.22–4

In 1588 the use of fireships by the English navy scattered the Spanish Armada, but it was the ensuing storm that finally destroyed the Spanish fleet. In 468 there was no storm: the Roman fleet was disordered and many ships were burnt by the fireships, but the decisive action was the follow-up by the Vandal fleet, ensuring that the Romans were so heavily defeated that their fleet ceased to exist as an effective fighting force. Furthermore, it is likely that the vast majority of surviving ships fled to Sicily, leaving the army to its fate.

Basiliscus was now cut off from supplies except for what he could forage in Africa, which was probably not enough to feed his large army on enemy soil. Not only could the Vandals harass any Roman troops gathering food, but it is probable that the Vandals had continued the Roman practice of storing food in cities in order to deny access to potential enemies in Africa. Further, without a fleet Basiliscus had no way of effectively laying siege to the city of Carthage: the Vandal fleet could not only keep the city supplied with food, but could transport reinforcements into the city. In addition, the Vandal fleet could take troops out of the city and land them to the rear of the Roman siege lines, possibly with devastating results. There was now little chance of the campaign successfully taking Carthage. Using the remaining ships Basiliscus embarked the army and sailed to Sicily, where he was joined by Marcellinus.[31]

Analysis and Aftermath

Basiliscus

Ancient historians almost universally believed that individuals were responsible for victories and defeats. An energetic and capable commander won: an ineffective and incapable commander lost. In addition, where the Romans had (apparently) overwhelming superiority then the ancient sources rarely accepted that the ability of enemy commanders could account for a defeat. The traditional method of assigning blame for such defeats, especially in the Later Empire, was 'treachery'. Where exactly the blame was to lie depended upon the popularity of the military commander. In 460 the failure of Majorian's campaign against the Vandals was given as 'treachery' on behalf of unknown individuals: Majorian was popular and the failure could not be ascribed to him.[32] Basiliscus was not popular. The fact that he had lost a campaign that seemingly could not be lost meant that although Gaiseric was castigated for his 'treachery', Basiliscus was the scapegoat for some contemporary historians. As a result, the majority of the sources castigate Basiliscus.

Over time Basiliscus' failure was transformed. Procopius' claimed that 'Basiliscus, either as doing a favour to Aspar in accordance with what he had promised, or selling the moment of opportunity for money, or perhaps thinking it the better course' waited blindly for Gaiseric to strike, and so a large part of the fleet was either destroyed or captured.[33] Later, the tale took a more sinister twist. For example, according to Malalas, Basiliscus 'accepted bribes from Gaiseric and betrayed the ships and all the men in them. Basiliscus was in the only ship to escape, all the rest being sunk.'[34] Possibly the only deviation from the theme is that of Theophanes, who claims that Leo was willing to accept the defeat as he was more concerned about the primacy of Aspar, needing Basiliscus, Heraclius and Marsus for his plot against Aspar.[35] In this narrative, although Basiliscus is still at fault, the defeat was in some ways a blessing for Leo, as he could from then on focus upon internal affairs and the removal of Aspar from his seat of power.

Whether caused by incompetence, treachery, or simply due to the underestimation of an opponent, Basiliscus knew that his failure had been catastrophic. On his return to Constantinople, and fearing for his life, he immediately sought sanctuary in the Church of St. Sophia. Fortunately for Basiliscus, his sister Verina interceded with her husband in order to save his life.[36] As noted, possibly of more importance, Leo still needed supporters in his escalating conflict with Aspar. In this context, Basiliscus' survival is less surprising. However, for a period after the defeat it would be inappropriate to restore Basiliscus to his previous status and he was exiled to Heraclea Sintica in Thrace.[37] Despite this, he would have been able to influence events at court due to his connections: although he is not recorded as being active until after the death of Leo, this is unlikely given the complex nature of political developments prior to Aspar's overthrow. It is also probable that he returned to court much earlier than is recorded in the sources.

Despite his personal reprieve, Basiliscus' reputation amongst later generations was to be secured by events in the mid 470s. In January 475 Basiliscus was officially proclaimed emperor, evicting Zeno, Leo's successor.[38] Unfortunately, his rule was so inept that after only twenty months, in August 476, Zeno was able to return to Constantinople. Basiliscus died shortly afterwards in captivity. The nature of his rule assured that later historians would ridicule his memory, leaving us with the image of a misguided, inept commander who was easily duped by Gaiseric, when in reality he was probably a competent, if cautious, commander who failed to take into account Gaiseric's outstanding military ability and his willingness to take a risk.

Heraclius

When he received news of Basiliscus' defeat Heraclius was still on the way towards Carthage. Realizing the futility of continuing the advance, Heraclius withdrew – probably to Tripolitana – before taking ship to Constantinople where later, in 471, he aided Leo in the final overthrow of Aspar.[39]

Marcellinus

After the reconquest of Sardinia it seems that Marcellinus returned to Sicily, possibly to prepare to join the campaign in Africa. He was never to leave the island. Shortly after Basiliscus' return, in August 468 he was 'destroyed treacherously by one of his fellow officers'.[40] Although Marcellinus' *comes* claims that Marcellinus was in Africa at this point, this would seem to be in error.[41]

The main consensus in the ancient sources is that Marcellinus was killed by one of his fellow officers: interestingly, none make a connection between his death and Ricimer. Despite this, the main suspect for the origins of the plot in most modern histories remains Ricimer.[42] In some ways this is understandable: Marcellinus was one of Anthemius' main supporters and, despite his marriage to Anthemius' daughter, Ricimer would live in constant fear of being supplanted by Marcellinus in the near future.

However, nineteenth and early-twentieth century historians did not make this connection: 'But why or by whom Marcellinus died remains a mystery.'[43] It would appear that the theory has evolved in the twentieth century to fit in with the hypothesis that Ricimer was the sinister moving force behind all decisions in the West.

The only fragment of evidence that can be used to support the theory can be found in Damascius: 'When Gaiseric ... heard that the Romans had killed Marcellinus, their ally against him, treacherously and contrary to the oaths they had sworn ... '.[44] Obviously, the need to support the modern hypothesis that Ricimer was responsible has resulted in the words 'their ally' and 'contrary to oaths' being transformed into a hypothetical meeting between Ricimer and Marcellinus when Anthemius became emperor, during which the two men were forced to swear allegiance to each other.[45] There can be little doubt that Marcellinus and Ricimer were forced to reconcile when Anthemius became emperor. It is also likely that they took oaths of loyalty, if not to each other, at least to the emperor. Although an attempt to make a poorly understood fragment of Priscus support this view, and so allow it to be used to prove Ricimer's guilt, the wording is ambiguous and can easily end in different interpretations.[46]

As a further attempt to support the idea that Ricimer was responsible for Marcellinus' death, it has been suggested that, in the same way that Majorian left Ricimer in Italy during his campaign against Gaiseric in 460, Ricimer was once again insulted by being left behind during the invasion of Africa in 468. The slight to his authority has been interpreted as a major factor in Ricimer's decision to eliminate Marcellinus.[47] This remains a possibility, but his marriage to Alypia and immediate employment as a military commander implies that no insult was intended: as with the campaign of 460, a strong military commander was needed on the mainland, in this instance in the north of Italy and in Noricum to defeat invaders and ensure the quiescence of the frontiers.

A more compelling reason for Ricimer's involvement in Marcellinus' death lies with the fact that Marcellinus was popular with his men, was obviously a capable military leader, and was obviously being promoted to a position where he could counterbalance Ricimer's influence.[48] This is almost certainly true. It is very likely that Ricimer wanted to remove Marcellinus due to these factors. Yet having a motive is not proof of guilt.

Unfortunately, no culprit for Marcellinus' death is named in the sources. For example, Procopius' statement that Marcellinus was 'murdered by officers in his army' can be taken two ways.[49] One is that military commanders loyal to Ricimer had taken their chance to kill Marcellinus in the confusion after the failure of the African invasion, either on their own initiative or following Ricimer's orders. The other is that during the course of the campaign in Sardinia Marcellinus had either alienated one of his lieutenants in some way, or that an individual with an unknown grudge struck Marcellinus down on his own.

In defence of Ricimer it has been noted that Sicily was a long way from Northern Italy and that 'long-distance assassinations are difficult to organize'.[50] This is true, but earlier it was suggested that Marcellinus was in command of an army composed of both Eastern and Western elements. In that case, Ricimer could easily have given one of his own supporters, who had been assigned to Marcellinus' command, orders to kill Marcellinus when the opportunity presented itself. There can hardly have been a better opportunity than when the two armies of Marcellinus and Basiliscus arrived in Sicily: after the defeat in Africa confusion will have reigned. In those circumstances an assassin who had long awaited his opportunity would find it easy to carry out his orders without being caught.

With such a diversity of opportunity and motive certainty is impossible and explains the wide variety of opinion in more modern histories. Without concrete information, all that can be stated is that because Ricimer is not implicated by any of the contemporary ancient sources it is unlikely that Ricimer was directly involved in the death of Marcellinus.[51] Unfortunately, unless some further ancient documents come to light the truth will never be known.

Chapter Eleven

Anthemius: Disintegration And Civil War

468

D espite the focus of both ancient and modern historians being on the African campaign, many other events unfolded whilst the West was concentrating its attention upon Africa.

The joint campaign of East and West was meant to demonstrate that the two were once again united and in accord. Unfortunately for Anthemius there was a problem: the increasing insularity of the court in Italy, coupled with the fact that the Western Empire was fragmenting and old loyalties were dying, meant that in some respects Greek-speaking Easterners were now seen as 'just another national group': in addition, it is likely that Anthemius spoke Latin with a strong Eastern accent.[1]

In this context an event that occurred in the West is easier to understand. In 468 the Praetorian Prefect of Gaul, a friend of Sidonius named Arvandus, was alleged to have sent a letter to Euric urging him not to make peace with the 'Graecus Imperator' (Greek Emperor) and that 'instead he should attack the Bretons north of the Loire, ... asserting that the Law of Nations called for a division of Gaul between the Visigoths and Burgundians'.[2] This was not the only example of such thoughts: Ennodius describes Anthemius as *Graeculus* (the Little Greek).[3]

Such feelings are easier to understand when Anthemius' attitude to religion is analysed. At some point after his acclamation Anthemius had come into conflict with Hilarius, Bishop of Rome. Apart from the Donatists in Africa, and to a lesser extent other groups such as the Pelagians and the Priscillianists, Western Christianity had largely remained unaffected by the schisms that had wracked the East. On his way West, Anthemius had been accompanied by an unnamed man who was a firm adherent of the so-called 'Macedonian heresy'. This man had attempted to introduce a measure of 'toleration' by allowing Christian sects to hold canticles in Rome. Obviously, this was anathema to Bishop Hilarius and he had protested. Anthemius had been forced to back down, in this way losing both face and the unconditional support of the Church.[4] Since the reigns of Valentinian and Valens, East and West had gone their separate ways in both the political and religious spheres. These differences would now come back to haunt Anthemius.

At this time Arvandus was in his second appointment to the office of Praetorian Prefect of Gaul and was heavily in debt. Thanks to his arrogance it is undoubted that he had made many enemies in Gaul and these men ensured that the letter described above was sent to Anthemius in Italy. Sidonius, as Prefect of Rome, would be expected to preside at Arvandus' trial: unwilling to act against his friend, Sidonius resigned his position.

Plate 01: Coin of Petronius Maximus, © CNG

Plate 02: Tremissis of Avitus, © CNG

Plate 03: Coin of Majorian, © CNG

Plate 04: Tremissis of Majorian, © Wildwind coins

Plate 05: Coin of Libius Severus, © CNG

Plate 06: Gothic coin of Libius Severus. This clearly shows that Severus' reign was accepted by the Goths, © CNG

Plate 07: Tremissis of Anthemius, © CNG

Plate 08: Coin of Olybrius, © CNG

Plate 09: Coin of Glycerius, © CNG

Plate 10: Coin of Julius Nepos minted during his reign in Italy, © www.romancoins

Plate 11: Coin of Julius Nepos minted by Odovacar in Ravenna after Nepos' exile to Dalmatia. Such evidence proves that Odovacer was a consummate politician, © www.romancoins

Plate 12: Coin of Romulus Augustus, © www.romancoins

Plate 13: Coin of Romulus Augustus, © CNG

Plate 14: Coin of Leo II (Public Domain)

Plate 15: Coin of Ricimer showing disputed inscription (Public Domain)

Plate 16: Solidus minted by Odovacer depicting Zeno. The coin dates to after the death of Nepos, © CNG

Plate 17: A rare coin possibly depicting Ricimer, not an emperor (Public Domain)

Plate 18: Coin of Zeno (Public Domain)

Plate 19: Coin of Euric. The coin clearly demonstrates the influence the Empire had on the 'successor' states, © CNG

Plate 20: Coin of Gaiseric. Such coins are the only depiction of Gaiseric on record, © CNG

Plate 21: The 'Ricimer Plaque', © Professor Manfred Clauss, Epigraphische Datenbank Clauss-Slaby (http://www.manfredclauss.de/)

Plate 22: Bust of the Eastern Emperor Leo I, now in the Louvre, (Public Domain)

Plate 23: The Mausoleum of Majorian, Rectory of the Church of San Matteo, Tortona

Plate 24: The Castel dell'Ovo, alleged retirement place of Romulus Augustus

Plate 25: A detail of the Missorium of Aspar, depicting Aspar and his elder son Ardabur

Plate 26: The Tomb of Clovis I in the Basilica of St Denis, Saint Denis, France (Public Domain)

Plate 27: Signet ring of Childeric I. Inscription reads CHILDIRICI REGIS ('belonging to Childeric the king'). Found in his tomb at Tournai, now in the Monnaie de Paris (Public Domain)

Plate 29: Statue of Euric at the Plaza de Oriente in Madrid, sculpted in white stone by Juan Porcel

Plate 28: Golden Bees with Garnet inserts, found in Childerics tomb at Tournai, now in the Monnaie de Paris (Public Domain)

ROMULUS AUGUSTULUS SURRENDERS TO ODOACER THE INSIGNIA OF EMPIRE.

Plate 30: Romulus Augustulus Surrenders to Odovacer, William Zimmerman c.1890

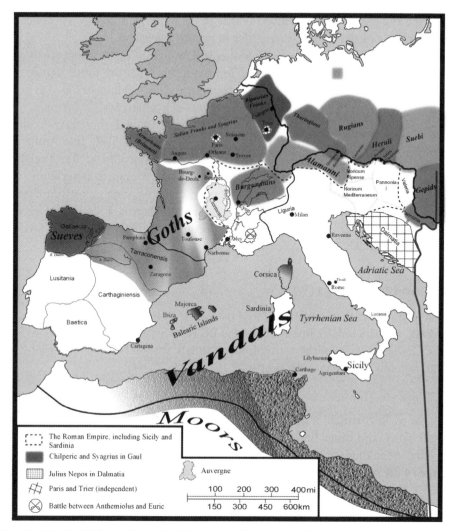

Map 17: The Civil War and Barbarian Expansion. Note that by this time the boundaries between the northern tribes are extremely conjectural. Also note the Ostrogoths have left Pannonia and been replaced by the Gepids.

Arvandus was now in grave peril. According to Sidonius, Arvandus refused to take the charge seriously, accepting that he had written the letter but convinced that only men who aimed at becoming emperor could be found guilty of treason.[5] Unsurprisingly, given the evidence, Arvandus was found guilty of treason and was sentenced to death.

Yet, contrary to Sidonius, Cassiodorus claims that Arvandus in fact did have designs on becoming emperor: 'At the order of Anthemius, Arvandus, who had attempted to become emperor, was sent into exile.'[6] Given Cassiodorus' access to imperial records it is likely that this was the main thrust of the court case, but as there was no proof of him intriguing to gain the throne, he was simply found guilty of writing the letter.[7] The likelihood is that in his writings Sidonius has concealed the true nature of the court case in order to protect his friend.

As noted by Cassiodorus above, Sidonius and Arvandus' other friends petitioned the emperor and were successful in saving Arvandus from the death penalty: his sentence was commuted to exile.[8] Yet the court case clearly demonstrates that not all Western 'nobles' were happy to accept the rule of the 'Easterner' Anthemius.

Included in the list of unhappy people is Ricimer. Although there is no evidence that Ricimer was involved in the death of Marcellinus, it is likely that Anthemius suspected him of being embroiled in the murder. After Marcellinus' death relations between the two most powerful men at court quickly began to deteriorate. It is recorded by Ennodius that the two men began exchanging insults, with Anthemius calling Ricimer *Pellitus Geta* (A skin-clad Goth) whereas Ricimer referred to Anthemius as *Galata concitatus* (Excitable [Temperamental?] Galatian).[9] Tensions in the capital quickly began to escalate.

Euric and the Sueves

It is almost certain that news of the trial reached the Gothic court, where Euric, the new king, appears to have finally cemented his rule. Styled *Rex Visigothorum* (King of the Goths) in many of the contemporary annals, it soon became clear that Euric was completely different to his brother.[10]

Rex

His title of *Rex*, which is also given to the rulers of the Sueves, the Franks, the Burgundians, and other barbarian tribes, as well as some 'Romans', has aroused much debate in modern literature.[11] The main cause of controversy has surrounded the use of the word *Rex* (King) by Romans who traditionally had an aversion to the title.

Although in earlier years this may have been true, by the time of the late Empire the meaning of the word seems to have changed. It is often forgotten that the usage and meaning of words from the days of the Republic and early Empire differ in time from the late Empire by a lapse the same as between Elizabethan England and the present day. Although no historian would assume that all words found in the works of Shakespeare continue to have the same meaning and implications as they did at the time of writing, classical historians rarely allow for such changes in the ancient world. This accounts for examples throughout late antiquity of the use of *rex* in otherwise unexpected or innocuous circumstances – for example, the reference found in Marcellinus' *comes* to Ricimer as *rex*, which is patently absurd under the original meaning of the word.[12]

As a result of these deliberations it is possible to assert that by the time of the later Roman Empire, and especially the fifth century, the meaning had changed. Apart from the upper classes – where training in rhetoric, grammar and the Classics appears to have continued – the word *Rex* no longer had severe negative connotations and came to have the meaning of 'ruler', or 'warlord not employed directly by Rome', or something similar. These deliberations will have a profound impact on interpreting events between 468 and the end of the West.

Euric in Hispania

At the start of his reign in the previous year Euric had sent envoys to the Emperor, the Sueves, the Vandals, and the Ostrogoths.[13] By 468 these men had either returned or been recalled due to the massing of the Roman troops which were eventually to be used in the campaign against the Vandals.

As usual the Gothic envoys to the Sueves came back empty-handed and the Sueves continued their depredations against the inhabitants of Gallaecia and further afield. At this point Euric made his first break with tradition. Acting whilst the focus of the West was on the campaign against Gaiseric, in 468 Euric launched a 'massive and devastating' attack on Lusitania.[14] There is no evidence suggesting that he acted with either the knowledge or the approval of Anthemius. Successfully overcoming all opposition, he then moved on and attacked Pamplona and Zaragoza, before subjecting all of Northern Hispania to his rule.[15] The Sueves withdrew in front of his assault and retreated into their north-western stronghold. Although Euric may have claimed that his actions were as an ally of the Roman emperor, it is clear that not all of the native peoples accepted this: in fact, the 'Roman nobles' of Hispania, especially in the south, resisted his attacks.[16] Although it has been suggested that these nobles were 'maintaining themselves as Roman', it is just as likely that, knowing that Euric was acting on his own initiative, they were simply determined to oppose him.[17] Despite their resistance, before the end of the year Euric had established a large 'protectorate' in the north of Hispania.

Knowing that the Romans were going to be focused upon the Vandalic War for at least one campaign season, Euric then took his troops further south, where he quickly 'overthrew Tarraconensis'.[18] Although probably still claiming to be acting in the interests of the Empire, before the end of the Vandalic War his aggressive actions were to provoke a response from Anthemius. Euric had now 'conquered' large parts of northern Spain. In direct contrast, the south was to remain independent until conquered by Euric's successors in the late sixth and early seventh century.[19]

Gaul

Affairs in Gaul are difficult to unravel, largely because the disjointed sources include no dates and it is therefore impossible to narrate a secure sequence of events. Nevertheless, it is possible to trace the continuing disintegration of Roman society and its replacement by a fragmented, parochial system based upon loyalty to a single city or leader, or the transferral of loyalty to one of the encroaching barbarian 'kings'.

Childeric

In the north of Gaul the main personality was the Frankish King Childeric. Formerly allied to Aegidius, after the latter's death in 465 Childeric assumed the dominant position north of the Loire. In this he may have been aided by Syagrius, son of Aegidius. Syagrius appears to have succeeded to his father's position as commander of the Gallic army based in the region of Soissons.[20] As the junior partner, it appears that Syagrius – or his advisors – was willing on the whole to accede to the direction of Childeric. Thanks to their alliance the territory north of the Loire was protected and during the late 460s and early 470s Childeric would use the combined army in an attempt to expand his influence.[21] Obviously, this would bring him into conflict with Euric.

Elsewhere in Gaul the situation is even more unclear. It is known from Sidonius' letters and other fragmentary and undated sources that cities including Trier (under the *comes* Arbogast, a descendant of the fourth century *magister militum*) and Paris managed to maintain some form of independence from the rival barbarian factions, but how they managed to do so is unknown, and nor is the date of their final surrender.[22]

Anthemius and the Goths

It would appear that, when he learned of Euric's attacks in Hispania, Anthemius realized that the Goths were now becoming too powerful and he became determined to arrange a coalition of forces against them – in a similar manner to that arranged by Aetius against the Huns in 451 – although whether he intended aggressive or defensive action is unclear.

Whereas the Burgundians under their King Gundioc remained staunch Roman allies, it was obvious that the Franks and Romans under Childeric and Syagrius would not join any coalition involving Ricimer. On the other hand, there was a new military and political force in northern Gaul that could be tapped: the *Brittones* under their King Riothamus.[23] The origin of the 'Brittones' has been disputed. Jordanes states that:

> The Emperor Anthemius … asked the Brittones for aid. Their King Riotimus came with twelve thousand men into the state of the Bituriges by the way of Ocean, and was received as he disembarked from his ships.
>
> *Jordanes*, Getica, *237.*

Jordanes' claim that they travelled 'by the way of Ocean' implies that they may have come from Britain specifically for the campaign. However it would appear unlikely that, under pressure from invading peoples, the Britons could afford to send a large army to the continent.

In this context, the fact that Riothamus is attested as having as many as 12,000 men under his command reinforces the idea that this was not a mercenary force joining Anthemius after fleeing Britain.[24] In addition, Sidonius wrote a letter to Riothamus complaining about his troops' behaviour towards the Romans under Riothamus' control, which suggests that Riothamus was king of a settled people who were impinging on the rights of the natives, which adds further weight to the concept that this was not a migratory band of mercenaries.[25]

It is more likely that *Brittones* was the name given to those people from Britain who had earlier emigrated to the area later called Brittany in order to escape the Saxon advance across southern England in the 450s and 460s.[26] Jordanes has simply linked *Brittones* with Britain and concluded that Riothamus must have originated on the island and must therefore have landed by boat. Writing after events, he has failed to realize that the name *Brittones* was at the time given to the new settlers. The *Brittones* were the descendants of the Armoriciani allied to Aetius against the Huns in 451 whose origin was now demonstrated by their name, and whose name would later be applied to Brittany.[27] This would account for Riothamus being able to field a very large army.

It was probably late summer 468 that Riothamus gathered his forces and moved to Bourges in central Gaul.[28] It is possible that he was simply to act as a garrison in the face of expected Gothic aggression, or that he was to await a contingent of Roman troops preparatory to an attack on the Gothic homeland, as suggested by Jordanes.[29] Whatever the case, the plan backfired.

It is almost certain that, with Euric campaigning in Hispania, the defence of Gaul was left to local leaders. It is possible that even at this earlier date Euric had delegated command in Gaul to a man named Victorius, although it should be noted that Victorius is only definitely attested as holding command from c. 470.[30] Whatever the case, prior to any contact with Roman forces the *Brittones* were attacked by a Gothic army and forced to retire. Either the same force or a detachment of the *Brittones* was forced to face the enemy at Bourg-de-Déols, where Riothamus was heavily defeated.[31] Unsupported by Rome, and with the enemy blocking his retreat to Armorica, with his remaining forces Riothamus was forced to seek sanctuary with the Burgundians, whose King Gundioc was still *magister militum*.[32] The fact that Riothamus joined Gundioc, a staunch ally of Ricimer, clearly demonstrates that the *Brittones* were acting as allies to Anthemius/Ricimer and not to Childeric/Syagrius.

At this point Gregory of Tours includes a piece of information that has confused historians ever since:

> The Bretons were expelled from Bourges and many were killed at Bourg-de-Déols. Count Paul, who had Roman and Frankish troops under his command, attacked the Goths and seized booty from them.'
>
> *Gregory Turensis* 2.18.

The question of who 'Count Paul' was has vexed historians for many years. As is usual, many possibilities exist and at some time the majority of these have been proposed by historians. For example, one modern historian has suggested that he may have been an officer who had served under Aegidius but who now served Childeric.[33] However, in this instance it is possibly better to slightly modify the views of earlier historians, who claim that he was the 'successor' to Aegidius.[34] In fact, with Aegidius' son as his successor, it is probably better to accept that Paul was acting as one of Syagrius' commanders. In this context Paul's alliance with Childeric is understandable. This would also explain why he was leading a mix of Roman and Frankish forces, as well as explain the fact that after his death there is no mention of the fate of his Roman troops: they simply returned to Syagrius at Soissons.

Whatever the case, Paul appears to have been a capable military commander, as he took advantage of the confusion surrounding the Battle of Bourg-de-Déols. The brief description by Gregory of Tours translated above suggests that after the battle Paul used his coalition forces to attack the Goths who had recently gained a victory over the *Brittones*. He defeated them and captured the booty they had taken from the *Brittones*, as well as their original belongings.

Despite this success, the fact that the 'Bretons were expelled from Bourges' implies that at this point a separate Gothic force finally captured the city.[35] Slowly the Goths were forcing their way north towards the Loire and the heartland of Childeric and Syagrius.

469

Illyricum and Pannonia

In Illyricum the death of Marcellinus was doubtless a blow to the people who had depended upon his military and political skills to survive. Although it was possible that either Leo or Anthemius could have appointed a successor, as elsewhere in the Empire dynastic sensibilities were to the fore and it would appear that Marcellinus' nephew Julius Nepos succeeded to the command.[36] He was the first to be securely attested as *magister militum Dalmatiae*, and although this dates to 473 he may have gained the title after Marcellinus' death, either in 468 or, given the amount of time to complete the necessary correspondence with Leo in Constantinople, possibly in 469.[37] Unfortunately, little is known of his governance of the region until much later, in 474.[38]

At the same time, a little heralded event occurred in Pannonia, where the Sciri and their allies attacked the Ostrogoths. At the Battle of the River Bolia (which is sadly unidentified) the Sciri were defeated. This would not be of major importance except for the fact that after the defeat a group of Sciri sought sanctuary and employment in Italy. One of their number was named Odovacer and he would rise to prominence in the following decade.[39]

Gaul

Following the conflict of the previous year Euric almost certainly returned from Hispania either late in 468 or early in 469 – with the earlier date being preferred. Although there had been at least two battles in Gaul in 468, it would appear that Euric trusted his subordinates to maintain the status quo in Gaul whilst he dealt with affairs in Hispania. Although there can be little doubt that by 469 he had returned to Gaul, he would still not have his full forces available as these would be needed in Hispania to secure that area. The absence of many of his troops would explain why Euric embarked on no significant campaign in Gaul in 469.

Euric's actions in Hispania had clearly demonstrated that he no longer needed the approval of the court in Italy to embark on campaigns which he felt would benefit the Gothic kingdom. Yet in one aspect Euric continued the policies of his predecessors: he continued to use 'Roman notables' from Gaul in his administration. The Gallic nobles were now being forced to choose: Sidonius himself notes that many Gallic aristocrats were torn between serving either the Roman Empire or the Goths. One example of a Gallo-Roman working for Euric is that of Leo, Euric's *consiliarius* (advisor), who is said to have drafted Euric's speeches and may have taken a major role in drafting the Law Code of Euric.[40]

Part of the problem faced by Gallo-Romans was the political status of the Goths. When Euric or his predecessors were allied to Rome, Sidonius and his compatriots were only too willing to work in tandem with the Goths.[41] On the other hand, when the Goths 'rebelled' against Roman rule, Sidonius and his ilk resisted Euric's attempts at expansion in Gaul. In the coming years it would be seen that one of the major impacts of Euric's aggressive policy was that it forced Gallic notables to choose between the expanding and successful Goths and the diminishing force of the Empire. To Sidonius' horror, many would choose the Goths.[42]

North of the Loire the alliance of Childeric and Syagrius continued to expand its authority, with Childeric campaigning throughout the region.[43] What happened next is described by Gregory of Tours. Unfortunately, the text is confusing and open to several different translations/interpretations. However, having decided that Count Paul was serving under Syagrius and was in alliance with Childeric it is probably best to use only one of the many translations offered:

Odovacar [Adovacrius] reached Angers, but King Childeric arrived there on the following day: Count Paul was killed and Childeric occupied the city. On that day the church-house was burned down in a great fire.
Gregory Turensis 2.18, trans. *Thorpe, 1982, 132.*

The most obvious explanation for this account is that Childeric had taken over command of the allied forces campaigning against Adovacrius from Paul when Adovacrius was forced to retire to Angers. On the following day Childeric and Paul arrived and stormed the city, but Paul was killed in the attack.

It would appear from Gregory that this is just one part of the ongoing campaigns being fought by Childeric and Syagrius. At the same time they secured another much-needed victory: Saxon 'pirates' had been attacking the surrounding territory from bases on islands in the Loire, but:

A great war was waged between the Saxons and the Romans. The Saxons fled and many of their men were cut down by the Romans who pursued them. Their islands were captured and laid waste by the Franks and many people were killed.
Gregory Turensis 2.19.

The alliance between the Franks under Childeric and the Romans of Syagrius was helping to stabilize affairs north of the Loire.

Noricum and the North

It is probably after the failure of the Vandalic Campaign that the Alamanni began to assert their independence. Prior to this the Alamanni appear to have been loyal defenders of their assigned region of the Empire's northern frontier, although the fact that they had settlements on the Roman bank of the Rhine was earlier 'admonished' by Sidonius.[44]

The Alamannic King Gibuldus began extending his authority into Noricum by 470 at the latest, attacking the towns of Quintanis and Batavis, before pushing 'into the heart of Noricum Mediterraneum'.[45] In the process he became involved with Saint Severinus, as described by Eugippius.[46] Surprisingly, however, Gibuldus' advance was halted and it was the Thoringi (Thuringians), coming into Noricum from the north-west, who eventually took Batavis: but only after most of the city's inhabitants had gone with Severinus to Lauriacum.[47] The disintegration of the West was slowly gathering momentum.

As well as advancing towards Noricum, it should also be noted that Alamannic tribes are by this time attested as being as far west as Troyes.[48] Although such an extended political dominance may be unlikely, it is possible that, due to the confusion caused by the failure of the Roman campaign against the Vandals and the resultant upsurge in barbarian attacks, a large force of Alamannic raiders did indeed penetrate as far as Troyes, where their presence is attested and interpreted as an attempt at settlement and/or expansion rather than simply a raid in strength. Whatever the case, the pressure on the Imperial frontiers was escalating and the borders themselves were slowly eroding in the face of the barbarians.

470

Coupled with the barbarian attacks on the northern frontiers in 469, it is possible that, having spent the previous year securing his control of the Western Mediterranean islands and campaigning to reconquer Tripolis (see Map 16), in 470 Gaiseric finally ordered the raids on Italy to resume – although it should be noted that the evidence for this is rather weak.[49] According to John of Antioch, Ricimer assumed responsibility for the defence of Italy against the Vandals – an obvious appointment as following Marcellinus' death he was the sole *magister militum* in the West.[50]

In this critical time the remnants of the Empire needed to be united in order to repel the invaders and begin to re-establish some form of control over the West. Circumstances decreed otherwise:[51]

> Anthemius, the emperor of the West, fell into a serious sickness by sorcery and punished many men involved in this crime, especially Romanus, who held the post of Master of the Offices [*magister officiorum*] and was enrolled among the patricians, being a very close friend of Ricimer.
>
> *John of Antioch* fr. 207.

The exact situation surrounding the affair is unclear. It is possible that Anthemius had simply become ill and, associating his illness with sorcery, had launched an investigation which implicated Romanus. Happy to use the incident to rid himself of one of Ricimer's more powerful supporters, Anthemius acted. On the other hand, and as claimed by Cassiodorus, it may be that there was actually a plot to put Romanus on the throne.[52] If Romanus was aiming for the throne, it was without Ricimer's support, and Anthemius had little choice but to have him executed.

Whatever the truth, unsurprisingly the death of his close friend Romanus angered and frightened Ricimer, and drove a wedge between him and Anthemius. Gathering 6,000 troops together, Ricimer now determined to overthrow Anthemius and led his troops north, establishing his headquarters at Milan.[53] It is possible that in part his decision to move to the Po Valley was determined by the fact that his action would divide Italy geographically: the north, worried about events in Gaul, would naturally follow Ricimer, who had a close alliance with the Burgundians; the south and Rome may have had more sympathy with Anthemius, as they were largely worried about attacks from Gaiseric and had less interest in 'northern' affairs. In this context, the most likely cause for Ricimer's withdrawal from Rome was that he wanted to gather support from the Burgundians prior to an attack upon Anthemius. Ricimer's choice would be further reinforced by the fact that in the fifth century 'resilient' cities were becoming 'centres of regional loyalties', a factor which was especially the case with ex-imperial residences such as Milan.[54] Milan would give its loyalties to anyone who promised to protect the city from attacks crossing the Alps.

The low number of 6,000 men following Ricimer is probably accurate. What is interesting to note is that in the last days of the Western Empire the major political figures could command troops numbering roughly the same as a single legion from the Early Empire, clearly demonstrating the military weakness of the Empire at this time. Furthermore, it is probable that this represents the remnants of the *praesental* army in Italy, based in the Po Valley to be ready to repel armies crossing the Alps or to move swiftly down the Roman roads to counter Vandal attacks.

The two men now called upon all of the assistance that they could muster. It is assumed that Anthemius was able to unite the conservative and anti-barbarian elements in Italy. On the other hand, it is usually accepted that Ricimer was allied to the various barbarian peoples with whom he had ties of blood or friendship: in other words, through sources of support that were traditional to the power of the *Generalissimos*.[55]

More recently, these assumptions have been challenged.[56] In reality, it is likely that support for both men was more fragmented than previously thought. Events were to show that Ricimer's support was the army, coupled with the Burgundians. There is no evidence that he was supported by any other barbarian troops, including the Goths, in the upcoming Civil War.[57]

His opponent, Anthemius, was likely able to secure the support of Conservative and anti-barbarian elements in Italy, but the extent of this support appears to have been overestimated. What little evidence we have suggests that Anthemius was not wholly accepted by the Senate and people of Rome, almost certainly due to his being from the East and therefore not being sensitive to the desires and hopes of the West. Moreover, and possibly of even more importance, early in his reign Anthemius had alienated the Church, who were prepared to support opposition to his rule.[58]

Ricimer had either been extremely lucky or had chosen his time well. In 470 affairs surrounding Leo and his *magister militum* Aspar had finally reached boiling point. Either late in 470 or early in 471 Aspar was executed, possibly at the instigation of Zeno the Isaurian.[59] Faced with political and military turmoil, and needing to keep a firm control of events, Leo was in no position to send military aid to his Western counterpart.[60] As war clouds gathered, and the attention of the West was focused on Italy, Euric was making his presence felt in Gaul.

Gaul

If not before, then by 470 at the latest Euric had appointed a man named Victorius as a military commander in Gaul, possibly with the title of *Dux Aquitaniae Primae* (Duke of Upper Aquitaine), in command of that part of the province now owned by the Goths.[61] Since the *Brittones* had fought against the Goths and had then retired on the Burgundians, supporters of Anthemius' regime, it was clear that a state of war existed between the Empire and the Goths. However the Empire was still struggling to recover from defeat in the Vandalic Campaign, with the concomitant loss of men and materiel, and especially of the finances used to fund the expedition. Knowing that Western resources were low, Euric was willing to take the risk of fighting, and Victorius was given orders to expand into the Auvergne.

In the campaign season of 470 Victorius led his troops east, capturing the territories of the Bituriges, Gabali, Lemovices, Cadurci, Ruteni, Albigenses and Vellavi.[62] At the same time Euric may have led a campaign further south against Roman territory to the west of the Rhone. It was now clear that Euric intended to seize as much territory as he could before affairs in Italy settled and the Empire could launch a counter-attack.

In the north of Gaul, Childeric and Adovacrius are attested as attacking the 'Alamanni'.[63] Unfortunately, there is no evidence that the Alamanni had any settlements so far north and west of their own territory. There is the possibility that Gregory has made a mistake and that the new allies attacked one of the Alan settlements in Gaul: it is even possible that Gregory is conflating this attack with the earlier attack by the Alans under Beorgor.[64] However, as mentioned earlier, there is evidence that the Alamanni had raided as far west as Troyes.[65] It is possible that the Alamanni recorded as being attacked are either a large raiding party or tribesmen intending to extend their territory by settling in lands farther west than previously recorded. Sadly, no firm conclusion is possible in this case.

471

The split between Anthemius and Ricimer at this time of Gothic aggression was unfortunate and, as already noted, in the confusion surrounding the fall of Aspar the Eastern Emperor Leo could not send direct military aid to Anthemius.[66] Despite his difficulties, he could send a clear message to Ricimer that Anthemius had Leo's full support and that a continuation of the conflict could eventually lead to military intervention from the East. In 471 a marriage was arranged between Anthemius' son Marcian and Leo's daughter Leontia. Leontia had been married to Patricius, a son of Aspar, but obviously the marriage had been annulled upon Aspar's overthrow.[67] The marriage to Marcian gave a whole new dimension to the civil war. In effect, Leo was giving his full backing to Anthemius, and he may have hoped that Ricimer would recognize this and come to terms. Ricimer now knew that ousting Anthemius would lead to the East withdrawing all support from the West.

Furthermore, pressure in Gaul was mounting. In 471 the Goths laid siege to Clermont.[68] At this point Ecdicius allegedly bypassed the Goths as they laid siege to Clermont and entered the city with only eighteen men.[69] Dismayed, the Goths appear to have lifted the siege. Ecdicius was the son of the Emperor Avitus and the brother-in-law of Sidonius.[70] After this feat he was to raise a small army at his own expense to resist the Goths and continue the struggle for several years.[71] In return for his bravery Anthemius promised him the title of *patricius*.[72]

Epiphanius[73]

The expansion of the Gothic kingdom into unprotected parts of Gaul did not go unnoticed by the provincials. Recognizing their danger, the 'nobles of Liguria' begged Ricimer to come to terms with Anthemius. Ricimer agreed to attempt to secure peace and secured the help of Epiphanius, Bishop of Pavia, to act as an emissary. Interestingly, Ennodius implies that Anthemius and Ricimer were of approximately equal status, although this relies on the use of only a few words, and most notably that the word *principes* (sing. *princeps*: 'leading man') was used for both men.[74] Nevertheless, Ricimer was not portrayed as a barbarian or as a rebellious general, but as the junior of two rulers.[75] Over the winter of 470 – 471 Epiphanius worked to affect a reconciliation between Anthemius and Ricimer.

Peace Talks

The description by Ennodius of the negotiations and of the 'dialogue' between Anthemius and Ricimer is one of the few representations of the personalities of these men and deserves attention. However, it should be noted that although the general tone may be accurate, the specific wording may not be as precise, relying on memory and being interpreted in a way that gives the most credit to Epiphanius, the subject of the story.[76]

It is clear from Ennodius' account that Ricimer had been unnerved by the royal marriage and was not convinced that he could win a civil war. If he had been he would not have acceded to the request of the Ligurians that he send an embassy to Anthemius. Despite his caution, Ennodius may give a slight indication of the problem between Ricimer and Anthemius when Ricimer allegedly describes Anthemius as *Galatam concitatum*.[77] Usually translated as 'excitable', probably due to this being the most common use of the word *concitatum*, there are several other possibilities, with 'enraged' or 'emotionally violent' almost certainly being better alternatives – especially when the next line reads: 'For, when begged a favour, he, who does not control his temper with natural moderation, always loses control.'[78]

It would appear that Anthemius was a man prone to losing his temper with his subordinates – and Ricimer was no exception in receiving this treatment. Yet in some respects this is understandable. Anthemius was used to working in the Eastern court, where strong rulers were once again in the process of imposing themselves upon their military commanders – in this case Aspar. Furthermore, Anthemius was privy to Leo's efforts to curtail the power of Aspar and will have felt that he could do the same in the West with Ricimer. Unfortunately, the political situation in the West was different to that in the East and Anthemius did not yet have the political and military backing with which to overawe Ricimer.

For his part Anthemius saw Ricimer as a 'skin-clad Goth' that had mistakenly been admitted to the imperial family by marriage to Anthemius' daughter.[79] Anthemius also later claimed that Ricimer was untrustworthy, and that 'neither the bonds of friendship nor of marriage have been able to hold him to his agreements'.[80] Obviously the allegation that Ricimer was a 'skin-clad Goth' is merely the reversion to a stereotypical image of the barbarian: as a long serving Roman commander Ricimer will have dressed and deported as a true 'Roman' in the presence of the Emperor. What is more interesting is the loss of trust between Anthemius and Ricimer: without trust the two most powerful men in the West would be unable to work together.

Despite the apparently insurmountable difficulties, in March 471 Epiphanius' work came to fruition and the two parties came to an agreement: civil war was averted.[81] Ricimer's decision to remain at peace was at least in part influenced by the news of the impending marriage between Marcian and Leontia. In the circumstances Ricimer was wise to come to terms with Anthemius.[82]

Valila

It is possible that as part of the agreement a man named 'Flavius Valila *qui et* Theodobius' (Flavius Theodovius Valila), who was most likely an Ostrogoth, was appointed as *comes et magister utriusque militiae*.[83] His name and position is only recorded in the *Carta* (*Charta*) *Cornutiana*, a document found in the *Liber Pontificalis*. On 17 April 471 he 'dictated, proofread, and subscribed to an extant *donatio* (deed of gift) that established a church at Tivoli'.[84] Furthermore, later he bequeathed a house on the Esquiline Hill in Rome to the Church.[85] His name also appears on a seat in the Flavian Amphitheatre dated to either 476 or 483, suggesting that he retained his title between at least 471 and 476 and that he was a supporter of Ricimer, not Anthemius: given later events, it is almost certain that he would have been removed from office by Ricimer. However, it should be noted that this hypothesis is not accepted by all.[86]

Anthemiolus and Euric

Once peace with Ricimer had been assured, Anthemius determined to punish Euric for his military campaigns in Gaul. A large part of Anthemius' Italian army was placed under the command of his son Anthemiolus. It is probable, though unattested, that some of Ricimer's 6,000 followers also joined the expedition. Since it is likely that at this time Anthemiolus was aged twenty at the most, he was accompanied by two otherwise unknown men, named Thorisarius and Everdingus, as well as by Hermianus, the *comes Stabuli* (Count of the Stables), sent to act as military advisors.[87] Anthemius gave Anthemiolus orders to march with his army to Arles to counter Euric's aggressive moves.[88]

Sadly for Anthemius, it would appear that Euric had spies in Italy that kept him fully informed of events. As Anthemiolus traversed the Alps, Euric crossed the River Rhône and moved to meet him. At an unknown place the two forces clashed. No description of the battle remains: all that is known is that the Goths were utterly victorious, killing all of the Roman commanders and many of their troops before laying waste to local Roman territory.[89]

It is possibly this major victory, along with the assumed weakness of the Empire, which gave Euric the idea of finally breaking with Rome. He knew that the laws being used in the Gothic Kingdom were wholly Roman and did not fully deal with all of the complexities that would arise were the Goths to fully disassociate from Rome. As a result, in 471 he gave orders for the drafting of a new Law Code.[90] The Code would deal with the problems of Romano-Gothic relations from the point of view of the Goths, rather than from that of the native 'Romans'.

Ricimer: the Civil War resumes

With the loss of the battle against the Goths and the death of his son, Anthemius' reputation reached a new low. The failure of the campaign was almost certainly the last straw for Ricimer. Frustrated by the Emperor, and possibly prompted by unrecorded arguments and divisions, and not least by the encouragement of supporters on both sides, in either late 471 or early 472 Ricimer finally lost his patience. The Vandal expedition had failed; the attempt by Anthemius to establish a northern alliance with the Burgundians and the *Brittones* had also been defeated. Now, to add insult to injury, the Goths had broken free of the imperial fetters and were in control of Northern Hispania, as well as expanding their influence in Gaul. The defeat and death of Anthemiolus was the final proof that the new regime was unfit to rule. It is likely that many of Anthemius' supporters also began to lose faith in their emperor. Discounting the alliance with the East, Ricimer prepared for war.

The East

Leo was still attempting to assert full control over affairs in the East: Aspar had been a major political and military power and thanks to the many repercussions of his fall, affairs in the East would take time to settle. As a result, it was not until the following year that Leo would attempt to end the civil war in the West, in a move that would lead to a surprising twist. In the meantime, Anthemius was on his own.

Africa

Little is known of affairs in Africa at this time, but it is likely that in 471 Gaiseric received some sad news. Eudocia, daughter of Valentinian III, wife of Huneric, and mother of Hilderic, had lived in Africa for sixteen years, ever since her abduction during the Sack of Rome in 455.[91] As Gaiseric's main link with the Theodosian House she had been a valuable political pawn. In 471 Eudocia was allowed to leave Carthage and travel to Jerusalem, where after only a few days' stay she died.[92]

There must have been compelling reasons for her being allowed to leave Africa, although none are given. This is especially the case given her political value to both Gaiseric and the Empire. However, the fact that she died shortly after reaching Jerusalem suggests a viable explanation: it is likely that shortly before being allowed to leave it was discovered that she was suffering from a terminal illness – she was only in her early forties when she died. In this context her travelling to Jerusalem is understandable. Gaiseric was allowing her to go on pilgrimage to the Holy Land before her death – in this imitating the example of Helena, Constantine I's mother – and he knew that her short life expectancy would ensure that she was not used politically against him by the East.

472

The chronology of events in 472 is extremely confused. Several sources give an account of proceedings but rarely give specific dates – and where they do they usually differ. What follows is an attempt to piece together the information to give a coherent account. Unfortunately, some of the details are conjectural and it should be remembered that it is possible to construct a different order of events.

As noted above, Ricimer had decided that civil war was the only option. In Gaul, Goar, the King of the Burgundians, was no longer the Imperial *magister militum per Gallias* (as opposed to Syagrius, the unofficial commander in Gaul). At some point prior to 472 – the actual date is unknown, but it is likely to have been when Ricimer and Anthemius were still on friendly terms – Goar's son Gundobad, who was also the nephew of Ricimer, had succeeded to his father's position, doubtless to ensure the continuation of the alliance with the Burgundians.[93] Since Gundobad was a relative of Ricimer, this can be seen as a major concession by Anthemius and may be linked to the negotiations masterminded by Epiphanius over the winter of 470–471.

Interestingly, Goar's eldest son, Chilperic, was not made *magister militum per Gallias*. This suggests that Goar may have been attempting to secure an Imperial career for Gundobad, who as a relative of Ricimer could be assured of favourable promotions with the Empire. It may also have been hoped that the promotion would remove Gundobad from the Burgundian succession when Goar died, as otherwise there would be four sons competing for the throne. Goar may have been taking steps to obtain alternative employment for his three younger sons.

For Ricimer the appointment was a major bonus: always aware of the fate of Stilicho and Aetius, Ricimer would now be certain that should Anthemius have him assassinated, Gundobad would attempt to avenge his uncle's death.[94]

Unfortunately for Anthemius, Gundobad was to remain loyal to his uncle. Early in 472 Ricimer summoned Gundobad and his forces to Italy to help in the civil war.[95] Hearing of Gundobad's decision to support his uncle, Anthemius sent envoys to Gaul with a letter that elevated a man named Bilimer, who is otherwise unknown, to the position of *Rector Galliarum* (Rector of Gaul) and summoned him to Rome.[96] The army he was to bring was small, and the most plausible theory concerning its origin is that it was the remnant of the army that had been defeated by Euric and had in the intervening period remained as garrisons in Gaul to restrict Euric's gains following his victory. It would not arrive for a long time, almost certainly delayed by a cautious approach to the Alps caused by the need to avoid forces in South Gaul and Northern Italy loyal to the Burgundians and Ricimer respectively.

Reinforced by the 'Gallic' army, Ricimer left Milan and marched his troops south. Finally, coming near to Rome, Ricimer set up his camp at the *pons Anicionis*.[97] Otherwise unknown by this name, several possibilities for the identity of the bridge have been put forward. The most obvious translation of the bridge would be 'bridge over the River Anio', but this is deemed as being too far away to effectively blockade the city.[98] As a result, historians have focused on those bridges close to Rome, usually the ones crossing the Tiber.[99]

Yet this theory fails to note Ricimer's possible motives for setting up camp at a slight distance from Rome. For example, he may have hoped that the losses of Anthemius' army in Gaul would have left the city largely defenceless. In that case, the threat of military action may have been enough to convince the Senate that resistance was futile and that Anthemius should be handed over. Therefore, by positioning his camp on the River Anio Ricimer was far enough away to remove any possibility of his men getting out of hand and attacking the city without orders but near enough to pose a threat. If these deductions are correct, then the most likely candidate for the position of Ricimer's camp would be the *Ponte Salario*, only 3km north of the city, or a lesser possibility would be the *Ponte Nomentano*, 3.9km outside the city. Wherever the camp was placed, included in the army it contained was a man named Odovacar, who was to take a major part in the events of 476.[100]

This, the second stage of the civil war, was to last for five months. Yet whilst the siege was ongoing, an envoy from the East would appear. His arrival would decisively affect the course of the war.[101]

Chapter Twelve

Olybrius

April/May 472–22 October/2 November 472

472

A lthough he felt unable to take effective military action with regard to Ricimer's rebellion, Leo did decide upon one measure which has since confused historians: he sent Olybrius, a member of the Roman Senate and the husband of Placidia, as an envoy.[1] Olybrius' wife, Placidia, and daughter, Anicia Juliana, remained in Constantinople.[2] Malalas outlines Olybrius' alleged objectives:[3]

> Meanwhile … Leo … sent to Rome Olybrius, a Roman patrician, after he and Rusticus had served in the consulate, so that, as a representative of the Roman senate, he might quell the hostilities that existed between Anthemius and his son-in-law Ricimer. In addition, Leo enjoined upon him in his directive that, after he had reconciled Anthemius and Ricimer, he should depart from Rome and go to the king of Africa, the Vandal Gaiseric, with whom Leo did not doubt that he had great influence because the sister of Olybrius' wife Placidia had married his son, and persuade him to reconcile himself with him [Leo].
>
> *Malalas 373–4.*

On the surface, the remit was sensible. Olybrius was a 'Westerner', a senator, and a member of the Anicii, a long-established senatorial family. His political and family connections could easily help to secure the support of the Senate for Anthemius. Perhaps most importantly of all, as a member of the Theodosian House he could hope to gain the full support of the army, so rendering Ricimer's military power obsolete. Furthermore, Olybrius had built a church in Constantinople dedicated to St. Euphemia:[4] given Anthemius' earlier conflict with the Pope, it may have been hoped that Olybrius would also ease tensions between the emperor and the Church.[5] In addition, on the political level Gaiseric would find it hard to continue his attacks on Italy, supposedly in support of Olybrius, if Olybrius himself asked that they be stopped. The move could clearly be seen as a political master stroke.

The cause of confusion amongst scholars is that John Malalas includes in his account the tale of a secret letter being sent from Leo to Anthemius:[6]

> The emperor Leo, however, suspected that Olybrius favoured Gaiseric and would secretly take his side. He therefore feared for his own sake, lest Olybrius, who had a tie of marriage with Gaiseric, would betray Constantinople to Gaiseric

if Gaiseric declared war upon him. Therefore, after Olybrius had departed for Rome, having left his daughter and his wife Placidia at Constantinople, the most sacred emperor Leo gave a message to a subordinate of the Master of Offices to be delivered to Anthemius, emperor of the Romans, in these words: 'I have removed', he said, 'Aspar and Ardaburius from this world, so that no one who might oppose me would survive. But you also must kill your son-in-law Ricimer, lest there be anyone who might betray you. Moreover, I also have sent the patrician Olybrius to you; I wish you to kill him, so that you might reign, ruling rather than serving others'.

Ricimer had placed at Portus [Ostia] and the individual ports of Rome a Gothic guard, nor was entry permitted to anyone before he had indicated to Ricimer what his mission was. Therefore, when Modestus the *magistrianus* [*Magister Officiorum*], who had been sent by Leo to Anthemius, came to Rome he was immediately searched and the letters of the emperor, sent from Leo to Anthemius, were taken from him and handed over to Ricimer, who showed them to Olybrius.

Malalas 374–5.

Obviously, the accuracy of this story has long been disputed.[7] There are three main theories which need to be analysed before a conclusion can be reached.

The first of these is that the whole story is a fabrication spread by Ricimer to justify Olybrius being given the throne. Ricimer needed a viable candidate to crown in opposition to Anthemius in order to give his opposition to Anthemius credibility, as well as to give both opponents and supporters of Anthemius an alternative behind whom they could unite. Fortunately for Ricimer, at this crucial juncture Olybrius arrived. Shown the fabricated letter, Olybrius was convinced that Leo and Anthemius were in league against him. At this point he needed little persuasion to accept the crown.

The second possibility is that the story given is not quite true, but an interpretation of events by later historians working in hindsight. In this hypothesis a letter was indeed sent by Leo to Anthemius and was captured by Ricimer. However, in this version the possibility that Leo would give Anthemius specific orders to kill Olybrius is dismissed. Instead, it is suggested that Anthemius obliquely informed Anthemius that if the need to assassinate Olybrius arose it would not cause a political breach between East and West, as Leo would see it simply as the removal of a potential threat. However this dismisses the concept that Malalas' sources had access to accurate documentation.[8] As a result, this version of events is probably best dismissed.

The third theory is that the story is fact. Before this can be accepted, Leo's motives need to be assessed.

The first piece of evidence is that shortly before Ricimer had rebelled for the second time Leo's daughter Leontia had been married to Anthemius' son Marcian.[9] It would appear that Leo was attempting to instigate a new dynastic house, based upon his own rule, in both East and West.

If this was the case, Leo will have seen Olybrius as a major threat.[10] As a member of the Theodosian House, even though only by marriage, Olybrius' candidacy for the Eastern throne was actually stronger than that of Leo. In this context the removal of Aspar in 471 could leave Olybrius open to temptation. If Aspar's supporters decided to overthrow Leo, they had a ready-made candidate for the throne in Olybrius. Furthermore, it would not matter whether Olybrius was party to a plot or not, as he could simply be nominated as a figurehead against his will and forced to accept the throne. To keep Olybrius alive in Constantinople was tempting fate: obviously, the best solution would be the death of Olybrius.

Yet Leo will have recognized that any attempt to assassinate Olybrius in the East would cause even more resentment and could easily lead to civil war. Olybrius needed to be sent away from the capital and quickly. As a result, Leo gave Olybrius a political task that would take him away and yet be a valid excuse for Olybrius' departure. If Olybrius was then killed by 'traitorous' elements in the West, and given the disturbed political situation in Rome it was probable that Olybrius would become politically involved in the various ongoing machinations and could easily be a casualty, Leo could not be blamed.[11] In addition, there had been major disturbances surrounding Aspar's execution. This meant that it would be understandable if Leo limited his response to Olybrius' death to a political statement of outrage rather than a physical attack on the West. In this way the new 'Leontine' House would remove all possible future opponents.

There is one further factor. When Olybrius and his party set out from Constantinople it is unlikely that Ricimer had yet declared open war on Anthemius, or, if he had, word had not yet reached Constantinople. Leo would not have known of the blockade around Rome. It would have been expected that the letter would have reached Anthemius without anybody else being aware of its contents. It is only the fact that Ricimer had moved quickly and established a blockade that resulted in his being able to intercept the letter. As a result of these deliberations it is likely that the story is in fact true and that Leo did in fact send a letter suggesting that Anthemius have Olybrius killed.

A New Emperor

Whether there was a letter or not is in one way immaterial: either in April, or at the latest in early May, Ricimer proclaimed Olybrius as the new emperor.[12] Ricimer's reasons for elevating Olybrius to the throne are obvious. Olybrius was a 'Westerner' (as opposed to the 'Easterner' Anthemius); a senator; a member of a long-established senatorial family; his political and family connections could easily help to secure the support of the Senate for himself; and his obvious piety would ensure the support of the Church. Furthermore, as a member of the Theodosian House Olybrius could tempt Anthemius' supporters to change sides. Although Ricimer could easily lose the loyalty of the army to the 'legitimate' emperor, it was a risk worth taking.

One further aspect needs to be remembered: throughout this period Gaiseric was free to roam the western Mediterranean, attacking the Empire at will. By fulfilling Gaiseric's ambition to have his son's father-in-law on the Western throne it is possible that Ricimer managed to finally halt Gaiseric's attacks, although this is nowhere mentioned.[13]

On the other hand, that Ricimer was hoping to secure an alliance with Gaiseric by installing Olybrius as the new emperor, or that this possibility had a major part to play in Olybrius' elevation, is unlikely: the two men appear to have harboured a 'mortal enmity'. Sidonius, the source for their antagonism, claims that this was because Ricimer had 'royal blood' whereas Gaiseric was illegitimate, and that there was also a long-standing enmity between the Vandals and the Goths caused by the Goths' attack on the Vandals in Hispania prior to their settlement in Gaul in 418/419.[14]

In addition, Gaiseric would have been totally unacceptable as Ricimer's ally to the citizens of Italy and there is no record of any formal agreement between the two men.[15] Nor is there any evidence that Olybrius would ever have been willing to accept Gaiseric as a political ally.[16] In fact, Priscus believably claims that Gaiseric saw Ricimer as a major obstacle to his own ambitions in the West.[17] Given the evidence, it is more likely that the situation was simply a happy coincidence rather than Ricimer attempting to secure Gaiseric's support.[18]

Death of Anthemius

Earlier, Ricimer had loosely blockaded the city, ensuring that supplies would be difficult to secure. Thanks to the blockade he had also managed to capture the incriminating letter from Leo to Anthemius. With Olybrius' arrival it was now possible for Ricimer to claim that he was acting on behalf of a legitimate emperor and further that Anthemius was a usurper who needed to be removed. Despite this, John of Antioch claims that support for Anthemius remained strong in Rome: 'both those in authority and the mob sided with Anthemius, but the host of his fellow barbarians were with Ricimer'.[19] Although doubtless John was following a traditional literary device in dividing 'Romans' from 'barbarians', it is likely that many in Rome would have wanted to support Ricimer but in the circumstances were afraid to do so: earlier, during the negotiations overseen by Epiphanius, Ricimer was not portrayed as a barbarian or as a rebellious general, but as the junior of two rulers.[20] Ricimer will have been hoping that the citizens of Rome would simply hand over Anthemius without bloodshed.

Eventually, Ricimer was forced to go on the offensive, as waiting too long could give Leo time to send military support for Anthemius. Positioning his forces, Ricimer forced his way into the city and 'succeeded in separating the port on the Tiber from the Palatine', where Anthemius was based. The emperor and his men began to suffer the effects of famine.[21]

The exact chronology of events is difficult to determine, but it would appear that shortly after this successful thrust into the heart of the city Anthemius' ally Bilimer arrived from Gaul. As Ricimer had only reached the Tiber at one point, Bilimer positioned his forces on the opposite side of the city, determined to prevent Ricimer from executing a pincer movement which would definitively cut Anthemius off from any external support. His efforts were in vain: in July Ricimer launched a second assault and again managed to breach the defences and reach the Tiber, entering the city via the Pons Aelius, next to the Castel Sant'Angelo (Mausoleum of Hadrian).[22] Bilimer died in the defence and his remaining troops defected to Ricimer.[23] Despite the two defeats, Anthemius was not yet ready to surrender, but fought on: 'Losing any hope of external help and pressed by the scarcity of food, Anthemius tried to rally, but his men were defeated and killed in great numbers.'[24]

Finally, Anthemius lost all hope. Disguised as a beggar he now sought sanctuary in a church, either Saint Peter's or 'Santa Maria in Trastavere' – the sources differ and the *Gallic Chronicle of 511* goes as far as to record both accounts.[25] It was Gundobad who found Anthemius and who, on 11 July 472, beheaded the emperor.[26] Although other accounts suggest that it was Ricimer who was the 'guilty party', this is likely to be a laying of blame for the deed, rather than being personally involved in the execution of Anthemius.[27] Having helped to win the war, Gundobad quickly returned to Gaul to oppose any advances made by Euric.[28] The dislike felt by Ricimer and his supporters for the dead emperor are highlighted by their treatment of Anthemius' body: 'Ricimer did not deem him [Anthemius] worthy of Royal burial.'[29]

With victory secured the city was now defenceless and suffered 'great destruction'.[30] Yet it should be noted that although it was Ricimer's men who are usually attested as being the culprits, in many cases this may not have been the case: Paul the Deacon notes that:

> Not only was Rome devastated by the hunger and disease which afflicted it in this time, but it was also gravely ravaged, except the two regions in which Ricimer was with his own men. All the rest of the city was devastated by the greed of the looters (*Praedatorum*).
>
> *Paulus Diaconis 15.4, trans. MacGeorge, 254.*

The fact that Paul claims that Ricimer maintained control of those troops in his own 'regions', and names the 'looters' as separate from Ricimer's troops suggests that a large part of the damage was caused by either troops who had escaped from Ricimer's control – possibly those brought from Gaul by Gundobad – or by Roman citizens intent on relieving their own misery by searching for food and so causing riots, or by political enemies of those who had supported Anthemius taking revenge on their opposites, or maybe a combination of the three. It would take some time before order was restored in the city.

The civil war of 472 culminated in the third sack of Rome in sixty-two years. Strangely, this whole episode is usually either ignored or downplayed by modern historians.[31] Yet the loss of manpower, equipment, and money, and the need to repair the damage after the sack, suggests that it had a devastating effect on the city and the Empire: in fact, Pope Gelasius (Pope 492–496) lists the sack alongside those of the Gauls in the fourth century BC and of Alaric in 410.[32] In this context the evident weakness of the West following the civil war is understandable and helps explain many of the events that were to happen later.

Analysis

When analysing the last days of the Western Empire it is common for Anthemius' reign to be held up as the last chance for Western survival. In many respects this is correct. The reign of Anthemius saw the last attempt to recover Africa. Yet this is not the whole story. Despite the alliance with the East, Anthemius failed to secure his reign in Italy. It would appear that in many ways he attempted to enforce an Eastern method of rule on the Western Empire. This was a mistake, alienating the church and dividing the Senate and people of Italy into camps for and against his rule. The net result was a division of resources and a focus on internal politics which culminated in the loss of large parts of Hispania and Gaul to Euric. These victories also encouraged Euric to break with tradition and attempt to conquer large areas of the West for his own rule, rather than under the aegis of the Empire. In effect, Euric had finally declared the Goths to be an independent kingdom along the lines of that established by the Vandals.[33] Furthermore, the reversion to civil war to settle differences resulted in the West squandering its last resources on futile internal squabbles when they were needed to protect its rapidly diminishing dominions.

Perhaps Anthemius' greatest failing was his inability to secure the loyalty of the army, despite the fact that earlier in his career he had successfully commanded in the East. This is odd, given the precedents set by Majorian's rule. It appears that, once in the West, Anthemius failed to assume personal command of any military campaign. For the war against the Vandals command was given to Basiliscus, Marcellinus, and, in the north, Ricimer; although Basiliscus was chosen by Leo to command in Africa, there is no reason why Anthemius could not have led the Roman troops in Italy and the surrounding islands rather than giving command to Marcellinus. Even for the war against the Goths Anthemius failed to take personal command. The net result was the death of his son Anthemiolus and the loss of a large proportion of the remaining Italian army. His failure to establish his rule encouraged the rebellion of Ricimer and the ensuing civil war. Overall, and despite the earlier promise, his reign must be seen as a failure.

Olybrius

After the victory Ricimer quickly 'established Olybrius as emperor at Rome, with the approval of the Senate'.[34] Sadly for Olybrius, Leo maintained his dynastic connection to Anthemius and refused to accept Olybrius' rule as legitimate. It is sometimes believed that Ricimer only raised Olybrius to the purple after the death of Anthemius, but this is an error: both the *Fasti vindobonenses priores* and Cassiodorus clearly state that Olybrius was crowned before Anthemius death.[35]

There is very little evidence for either Olybrius' personality or his policies. The only clue comes from his coinage. Breaking with tradition, Olybrius struck coins with the 'innovative legend *Salvs Mundi* ('Salvation of the World')'. It is almost certain that the legend demonstrates 'a reflection of his pious preoccupation with religious matters', as also evidenced by his earlier building of a church in Constantinople.[36]

Ricimer

Ricimer was to have little time to enjoy his triumph. Only thirty-forty days after his victory he died, seemingly of natural causes, although the fact that he passed away after 'vomiting much blood' is a little odd.[37] According to the *Fasti vindobonenses priores* he died on 18 August 472.[38] Surprisingly, given his tumultuous life, nowhere in any of the sources is there any mention of foul play. The only assumption must be that his victory over Anthemius had finally established him as the undisputed authority in the West and in this, the time of his greatest power, nobody was willing to attempt to oust him.

Analysis

As has already been noted, opinions concerning Ricimer's actions and motives underwent a sea change between the end of the nineteenth century and the middle of the twentieth. Earlier historians relied upon contemporary sources for the basis of their information. During the twentieth century historians attempted to evaluate Ricimer's personality, which would help them to gain an insight into the pivotal period during which he was *magister militum*. During this time Ricimer became anathematized as the duplicitous barbarian whose selfish actions brought about the Fall of the West. Furthermore, as part of the change in opinion Ricimer also became the puppeteer who, for the years between 457 and his death in 472, manipulated a series of weak emperors, callously eliminating those who attempted to gain independence. The culmination of these changes is that Ricimer is now held to be largely responsible for the collapse of Rome and the end of the Western Empire.

The analysis of events during his time as *magister* outlined in this and the preceding chapters suggests that maybe the historians of the nineteenth century were correct. As seen in the elimination of Avitus, Ricimer was not working alone but within the framework of Late Imperial politics. A similar interpretation is possible of the assassination of Majorian, as Ricimer was not the sole perpetrator of Majorian's death but was acting in conjunction with a large number of like-minded Italian nobles. Likewise, the death of Severus should not automatically lie at Ricimer's door: it is far more likely that Severus died a natural death.

In fact, the only emperor whose death may be attributable to Ricimer's personal feelings above all else is that of Anthemius. Yet even here a close look at the sources and associated events suggests that Ricimer was not alone in his feelings and may have received a large amount of support from the Italian aristocracy, as well as the army.

Yet despite the exoneration of blame for many of his alleged actions, it is obvious that Ricimer, once in position as *magister militum*, was determined, like his predecessor Aetius, not to lose his power. It was only the desperate political and military condition of the West that made Ricimer reliant upon the East, and made him willing to petition the East to nominate an emperor. Sadly for the West, and despite early indications, Anthemius was not up to the task. Instead, his failure to work within a Western framework, and the possibility that he attempted to change the Western system to mirror that of the East, ensured that many Western senators, nobles, and leading churchmen became opposed to his views and methods. In this context it is obvious that Anthemius would never have succeeded as emperor of the West without winning the allegiance of the army. When this was not forthcoming, it was obvious that conflict with Ricimer would occur and that Anthemius would lose without direct help from the East.

On the other hand, Ricimer should not be absolved of all blame. The fact that three times he was willing to wait for the East to nominate an emperor clinically demonstrates that he knew that the West could not continue without external support. The fact that despite this he could not find a *modus vivendi* with Anthemius clearly demonstrates that above all else he was determined to survive. In this he fell below the standards set by his predecessor Stilicho, who, rather than risking the safety of the state in Civil War, willingly gave himself up to the executioner's sword.

Finally, it has been suggested that throughout this period Ricimer was attempting to reach an agreement with the Eastern emperor which would allow Ricimer to rule in the West on behalf of the East. The main evidence given for this theory is the alleged protracted negotiations which took place during each of the *interregnae*. However, as has been seen all of these delays reflect, not Ricimer's desires, but major internal difficulties in the East. Without these difficulties it is possible that the Eastern emperors would have quickly chosen a candidate for the West, so solving the problem of who was to be Western emperor without the need for Civil War or for weak emperors who were unsuited to rule in such dire circumstances.

Overall, most of the negative hypotheses concerning Ricimer's time as *magister militum* need to be reassessed. Like most of his compatriots Ricimer was determined to put his own safety before the safety of the Empire. In this respect he deserves some of the vitriol which has been aimed at him. However, the number of powerful individuals throughout history who were actually willing to renounce their authority remains very small. Probably the only example of this is Stilicho. None of Stilicho's successors could live up to his high example.

Olybrius

With the death of Ricimer, Olybrius was forced to choose a new *magister militum*, hopefully one that would not be as domineering as Ricimer. Possibly attempting to ensure continued good relations with the Burgundians, now one of the few political entities in the West willing to pay lip service to the Empire, he chose Ricimer's nephew Gundobad.[39] At the same time Olybrius may have made changes to other posts, including the naming of a new *comes domesticorum* (Count of the Household), an otherwise unknown man named Glycerius.[40]

Whether the new pairing of emperor and *magister* would have been a success was never to be known: Olybrius survived Ricimer by only a short period, dying in the seventh month of his reign.[41] Two specific dates are given for his death: the *Fasti vindobonenses priores (no. 609)* claims 22 October, whereas the *Paschale Campanum* claims he died on 2 November. There is no way of knowing which, if either, of these two sources is correct. Again, as with the death of Ricimer, there is no indication in the sources of foul play, with Olybrius' death being attributed to dropsy (oedema).[42]

His death left the new *magister militum* Gundobad with a serious dilemma: he now needed to either elevate his own nominee as emperor, or to send envoys to Constantinople asking Leo to nominate yet another candidate. It is almost certain that he sent envoys to the East and that over the winter of 472–473 Gundobad awaited news. Finally, losing patience and needing at least a figurehead, if not an able emperor, he made a decision. Sadly, this would not go down well with Leo.

Part Three

DISSOLUTION OF THE EMPIRE

GUNDOBAD AND ORESTES

Chapter Thirteen

Glycerius

3 March 473–June 474

Over the winter of 472–3, and as had by now become traditional, there was an interregnum as Gundobad awaited news from the East, negotiated with the Senate, and pondered his next move. In late February he made his decision: the *comes domesticorum* (Count of the 'Domestics'; an elite unit of the 'Imperial Guard'), a man named Glycerius, was to be the new emperor. Glycerius does not appear to have welcomed his promotion and it was only concerted pressure from Gundobad that caused him to accept the throne.[1] However it should be noted that this may be the traditional *topos* of a 'reluctant' emperor. Finally, on 3 March 473 Glycerius was crowned as the new emperor in Ravenna 'with the support of the army'.[2]

It is usually accepted that Gundobad's decision to make Glycerius the new emperor was due simply to him following in his Uncle Ricimer's footsteps: after all, according to the now-traditional theory that Ricimer was a 'Kingmaker', it stands to reason that his successor would follow suit. However, it has been already shown that Ricimer's reputation may have been undeserved, and so Gundobad's actions need to be seen in context before any decision can be made.

The main factor in his choice may have been the reaction of the West to the last emperor imposed by the East. Anthemius had been seen as a 'Greekling', with Eastern attitudes as to how to rule, and especially Eastern prejudices with regards to religion. These two unwanted traits had combined to force a large proportion of the Western Senate, Church and army to regard Anthemius as unwanted. The same would most probably be true of any Eastern nominee.

Furthermore, the Western Senate had their status and privileges to uphold, and wanted above all else to secure the safety of Italy. Anthemius had waged unsuccessful wars against both the Goths and the Vandals, severely weakening the West. The Senate would not want a repetition of these events – which would appear likely given Leo's desire to punish the Vandals for their attacks – should the new man be an Eastern nominee.

Another factor in the decision was that the demands of the army needed to be met. By this stage of the Empire it would be extremely surprising if a 'Roman Citizen' Army of Italy – the command of the *magister militum praesentalis* (the 'Master of the Troops in the Presence of the Emperor') – still remained in existence. The wars against the Vandals and the Goths had wasted large numbers of men, lost huge amounts of equipment, and exhausted what little was left in the imperial treasury,

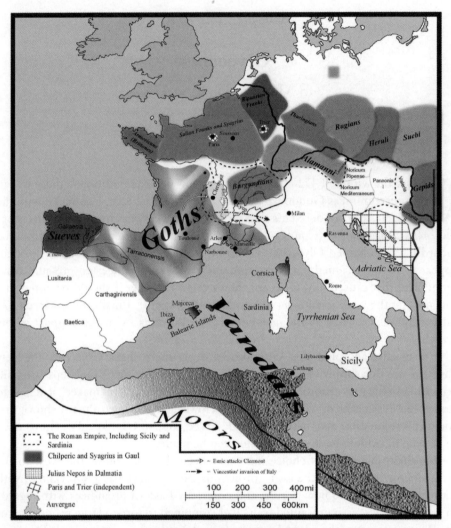

Map 18: The Reign of Glycerius.

meaning that the Empire was even less financially viable in its own right than ever before. The net result was that the West could not afford to train and equip new recruits. As a result, if there were troops still remaining in the West, with a few exceptions – such as the *Scholae*, the 'Imperial Guard' – these were the old *limitanei* on the northern frontiers, stubbornly defending their homes and awaiting news and pay from the emperor in Italy.

Instead, the *praesental* army in Italy was without doubt composed almost wholly of mercenaries serving the Empire – or in many cases serving the main military commanders of the Empire, men who had the personal resources to hire them. These troops were now aware that the West was in a very poor condition and that they were vital to the safety of the Empire, and especially to the survival of Gundobad. Accordingly, it is likely that they too wanted a Western emperor with whom they could bargain, rather than an Eastern nominee who could bring fresh troops from the East with which to oppose their influence.

In effect, Gundobad will have had little choice but to nominate a Western successor, and in the circumstances nominating Glycerius, who, in his position as *comes domesticorum*, almost certainly commanded the last true Roman units in Italy, was the most obvious solution.

The reasons behind Glycerius being crowned at Ravenna rather than Rome are unknown. However, throughout the early part of his reign he was to remain in Northern Italy, possibly so that he could be near to the frontier and so respond to news when it crossed the Alps from Gaul or Noricum.[3] In some ways this was to be a blessing.

The East

Unsurprisingly, Leo refused to acknowledge Glycerius as the new Western emperor. After the rebellion of Ricimer and the death of Anthemius, Leo appears to have lost patience with the West. However at this point he was more concerned with his failing health – born in 401, Leo was now 71 and understandably his age was a factor in his physical condition.

473

Shortly after his accession, on 11 March 473 Glycerius passed the only law that has survived from his reign. Concerned with *Simony* ('paying to receive religious favours, especially ordination to a position in the hierarchy of the church'), the law shows that Glycerius was intent upon controlling and securing the support of the Church, thereby ensuring that he did not follow in the footsteps of Anthemius in creating a major opponent in the West.[4] Although he appears to have understood the importance of Italian support, he may not have predicted the external threats he was about to face.

Victory

Not long after the coronation of Glycerius, the Gothic King Euric decided to drastically up the stakes:

> Vincentius … having been sent by King Euric like a Master of Soldiers ('*quasi magister militum*'), was killed in Italy by the counts Alla and Sindila.

Several items in this short passage deserve attention. The first is the fact that even in its poor state the West could still muster an army and was still capable of winning battles. Sadly, however, no description of the encounter survives so it is impossible to even guess at the number of troops who took part, or of the severity of the fighting. All that can be said is that it was a Roman victory.

Second is the 'terminological confusion that arose after the disappearance of Roman authority: Vincentius' position was *like* that of a Master of Soldiers, but not the genuine article.'[5] If Vincentius was simply a Gothic general, it is almost certain that he would have been named as such. Instead, it is possible to assert that Euric had claimed that the earlier right of Theoderic, to take away the title of *magister* from Nepotianus and give it to Arborius, still remained in place and that Glycerius was a usurper not to be obeyed.[6] As a result, and in conjunction with Euric's grandiose ambitions, as well as the Goths' assimilation of other Roman practices, it would appear that Vincentius had been given the title *magister militum*, which the author of the *Gallic Chronicle* has reported obliquely. Obviously, Vincentius could not be a 'true' *magister militum*, as otherwise he would not have been appointed by a barbarian king and would not have invaded Italy on behalf of a barbarian in Gaul.

A final point that deserves attention is the name of the two Roman commanders, Alla and Sindila. Both of these are Germanic in origin and may attest to the fact that in the mid-late fifth century the citizens of Rome were no longer being appointed to high military command. The reasons for this are easy to understand. Firstly, service in the armed forces was no longer necessary to political advancement and so was to be avoided. Secondly, few Romans at this time will have had the fluency in Germanic languages necessary to command the army in the field – in direct contrast to Aetius and Ricimer.

As a result, army commanders were now being appointed from within the ranks of the barbarian troops, in this case by Gundobad. It should be noted, however, that Alla may have been the same man named earlier as Valila. If so, he had been made *comes et magister utriusque militiae* prior to Gundobad's elevation by Glycerius, attesting to the fact that even in the 'new' Roman army precedence was given to 'dynastic' relationships.[7] Sadly, Sindila is otherwise unknown and so gives no support either for or against this hypothesis.

Defeat

Unfortunately for Glycerius, however, Euric was not content merely to order a large army to cross the Alps into Italy. At the same time, and possibly a move intended both to protect the invading army's supply lines as well as extending his own power, Euric led his troops into Southern Gaul.

As noted in the previous chapter, the majority of the troops in Southern Gaul had previously been withdrawn to support either Ricimer or Anthemius in the civil war, where a large number had been killed. Although Gundobad had quickly returned to Gaul, the death of his uncle had forced him to attend upon Olybrius in Italy in order to be given the title of *magister utriusque militiae*. It would appear that Gundobad had taken quite a large contingent of troops with him to Italy in order to protect himself, and it is possible that the presence of these troops in Italy had helped to turn the earlier battle against Vincentius in the Empire's favour. On the other hand, there were now not enough troops to successfully garrison all of the cities in Southern Gaul against Euric's drive into the region.

Facing little opposition, Euric was able to achieve a feat which had eluded his predecessors: in 473 the Goths finally captured Arles and Marseilles.[8] At the same time he attacked the city of Clermont. However in this case the city was ably defended, not least by the advice from its bishop, Sidonius Apollinaris, coupled with help from the Burgundians. However the Gothic attacks on the region had devastated the crops and the end result was famine. Ecidicius, son of the Emperor Avitus and hero of the siege of Clermont in 471, joined with Patiens, Bishop of Lyon, in supplying food from his own estates at his own expense for the relief of some 4,000 Burgundians.[9] The Roman position was continuing to weaken.

Despite the setback to Gothic arms in Italy, by this point, if not earlier, the weakness of the West had become apparent to all, and Euric was intent on taking advantage of the situation to the full. The capture of the two major ports in Gaul that remained to the West was a devastating blow. The loss of their taxes, both the normal citizen tax and the tax on trade, further weakened the imperial treasury. But possibly the worst damage of all was that done to the morale of the citizens of Italy. The Empire had shrunk to only the peninsula itself, a Sicily severely damaged by prolonged Vandal attacks, plus a small area of land on the far side of the Alps that was under constant threat from the Goths. It would have been apparent to many that the West was doomed.

The Ostrogoths

As if to add insult to injury, probably after the Gothic attack, the Empire was soon faced with yet another major invasion, this time from the Ostrogoths:

> The [Ostro-]Goths began to lack food and clothing … so … approached their king Thiudimer and … begged him to lead forth his army. He summoned his brother [Vidimer] and, after casting lots, bade him go into the country of Italy … saying that he himself as the mightier would go to the East.
>
> *Jordanes*, Getica 283.

Sadly for Vidimer he died shortly after entering Italy and was succeeded by his son, also confusingly named Vidimer.[10] Rather than fighting another battle, Glycerius determined to use money and politics to remove the new threat from Italy:

> The emperor Glycerius, after bestowing gifts and saying that Vidimer's relatives, the Visigoths, ruled there, transferred him from Italy to Gaul, which then was assailed on all sides by various peoples.
>
> *Jordanes*, Getica 284.

The gift was allegedly 2,000 golden *solidi*.[11] It is possible that Glycerius was hoping that the introduction of a new 'Gothic' dynasty into Gaul would undermine Euric and cause a civil war amongst the Goths. If so, he was to be disappointed: instead, the people of Vidimer stayed in Gaul and simply amalgamated with the people of

Euric. The Gothic army had now been reinforced to make up for the losses incurred during the invasion of Italy.

474

All of the above probably consumed Glycerius' attention during the year of 473, but late in the year he made a concerted attempt to secure Eastern support for his rule. East and West traditionally nominated one candidate each for the two posts of consul for each year. Glycerius decided to forego the privilege. As a result, the sole consul nominated for 1 January 474 was Leo, grandson of the Eastern emperor.[12] As Leo I was now an ill old man and his grandson had been made Caesar by his grandfather in October 473, Glycerius was attempting to win the support of both the Leo who was currently emperor and his nominated successor.

Sadly for Glycerius, events in the East now took a downward turn. On 18 January 474 the old Emperor Leo died of dysentery.[13] His grandson Leo II, son of Leo's daughter Ariadne and Zeno the Isaurian, became emperor, aged 7.

Zeno

Three weeks later Leo II 'nominated' his father Zeno as joint emperor.[14] Zeno had originally owed his promotion to his participation in the downfall of Aspar's son Ardabur in 466.[15] Made *comes domesticorum* as a reward for his efforts, shortly afterwards he was married to Ariadne, Leo I's daughter, before being promoted to *magister militum per Thracias* and receiving the consulship. He was then made *magister militum per Orientem*, at which time he probably participated in the events surrounding the downfall of Aspar.[16] As a military man, it was clear that should Zeno wish to accept Glycerius' appointment then support could easily follow. On the other hand, should he reject Glycerius, an invasion was likely.

Unfortunately for Glycerius, Zeno (as a minor Leo II was unlikely to have been a major player in the decision) took the latter view and quickly determined to send a replacement to Italy. His choice fell on Julius Nepos.[17] It should be noted, however, that Nepos may have already been chosen by Leo I before Leo's death and that Zeno was simply continuing his predecessor's policies.[18] Son of Nepotianus[19] and nephew of Marcellinus, Nepos was also married to the niece of the recently deceased Leo I, hence the agnomen *nepos* – 'nephew'.[20]

Nepos had succeeded to Marcellinus' rule of Dalmatia on his uncle's death in 468.[21] Either at that time or at an unknown later date, he was given the title of (or recognized as) *magister militum Dalmatiae* (Commander of the Troops in Dalmatia) and probably in 474 he was accorded the title *patricius* prior to his projected invasion of the West.[22]

Gundobad

In the meantime, in Italy Glycerius had to deal with the repercussions of Euric's capture of Arles and Marseille. Although the Gothic invasion of Italy had been defeated, much to the relief of the Senate, the loss of a large part of Gaul to the barbarians was a severe blow to the Empire. What action Glycerius took to rectify the situation – if any – is unknown. It is possible that he was focused upon affairs in the East and so determined simply upon the defence of the Alps prior to (hoped for) Eastern help.

Also unknown are the actions of Gundobad. It is usually assumed from later events that Gundobad quickly realized that the East was going to invade and so decided to return to the kingdom of the Burgundians in Gaul – a possibility reinforced by Malalas' laconic comment that he 'abruptly returned to Gaul'.[23] It is also assumed that, at the same time as Nepos prepared to invade, Gundobad's father Gundioc died and Gundobad made the decision to quit the Empire and claim his portion of the Kingdom.[24] These remain possibilities, but given his Uncle Ricimer's political ability to withstand incoming emperors they remain merely unproven hypotheses. Yet if Gundobad did not simply flee from Italy, viable alternatives need to be found.

The likelihood is that Gundobad did not flee and leave Glycerius to his fate. Instead, along with the vast majority of the few available forces left to the West, he had been ordered by Glycerius to oppose any further attempts by Euric to extend his kingdom in Gaul and, if possible, to attack Euric and force him to relinquish at least some of his newly won territory.[25] Furthermore, not only was an army desperately needed in Gaul to recapture Arles and Marseille, but the attacks of the previous year had caused a famine in Burgundian territory.[26] Gundobad may have been desperate to return and help his people in their time of need.

Although the possibility of an Eastern nominee for the throne attacking Italy remained, it may have been assumed that any attack on Italy from the East would land on the eastern coast of Italy, giving the army in Gaul time to return to Rome to protect the Emperor. Whatever the case, the absence of Gundobad and the army when Glycerius most needed them was to be a vital part in the downfall of the Western emperor.

With Gundobad in Gaul, Glycerius finally moved to Rome – remaining in Ravenna would leave him open to direct attack from the East – where he struck coins with the legend *Victoria Auggg*, the three 'Gs' of which attest to the existence of three emperors, who must be Glycerius, Leo II and Zeno.[27] Hoping that this sign of comradeship with the East would make Zeno willing to accept his rule, Glycerius could now only await developments.

Julius Nepos

These were not long in coming. In summer 474 Nepos set sail with an army from Dalmatia. It is possible that part of the Italian army had been posted on the east coast of Italy in case forces from the East attempted to land. If so, Nepos outwitted them. He sailed around the coast of Italy and in June 474 landed directly at Ostia, the port of Rome:[28]

The Caesar Glycerius, who held the imperial power at Rome, was deposed from power at the port of the city of Rome [Ostia] by Nepos, son of the sister of the former patrician Marcellinus.

Marcellinus comes, s.a. 474.2.

With no army to protect him, and taken completely by surprise, Glycerius meekly submitted to Nepos, who:

Took Rome, captured Glycerius without a fight and, having stripped him of royalty, appointed him bishop of Salona[29] ... Nepos was immediately appointed emperor and ruled Rome.

John of Antioch, fr. 209.2, *trans. Gordon, 122–3.*

It is possible that Nepos' lenient treatment of Glycerius was due to Glycerius' previous reluctance to accept the post of Emperor. This, plus the fact that there is no evidence from his reign of executions or other 'criminal' activity, suggests that Nepos quickly decided that a dead Glycerius could act as a martyr and a focus for opposition to his own reign and that therefore the best action was simply to remove Glycerius from temptation in Italy. Further, by sending Glycerius to Salona, in Nepos' own heartland of Dalmatia, it would be easy for him to be supervised and prevented from causing further trouble.

Whatever the cause of Nepos' leniency, the short reign of Glycerius, from 3 March 473 to June 474, was over. The brevity of his reign means that he is one of the less well known emperors. Some of the ancient sources feel that this is a just result for his reign:

After Anthemius had been killed at Rome, Zeno, through his client Domitianus, named as emperor at Ravenna Nepotianus' son Nepos, who had been joined in marriage to his niece. Nepos, having taken legal possession of the empire, deposed Glycerius, who had imposed himself upon the empire in a tyrannical manner, and made him bishop of Salona in Dalmatia.

Jordanes, Romana, 338–9.

Possibly in an attempt to excuse the Goths' continued expansion during Glycerius' reign at the expense of the Empire, Jordanes claims that Glycerius was a man 'who in a tyrannical manner imposed himself upon the empire': Jordanes was not even willing to accept Glycerius' reign as a fact. Furthermore, some Eastern accounts of Glycerius' reign tend to either dismiss him as irrelevant or to paint him in a poor light. For example, the historian Marcellinus claims that Glycerius had become emperor 'more by presumption than by constitutional selection'.[30]

Despite these comments, some contemporary writers were minded to praise Glycerius. For example, Ennodius states that:

After Olybrius, Glycerius ascended to the rule. With regard to whom I summarize, in my desire for brevity, the numerous things he did for the well being of many people. For, when the blessed man [bishop Epiphanius of Pavia] interceded, he pardoned the injury done to his mother by some men under his authority.

Ennodius, Vita Epiphanii, 79.

Glycerius appears to have had at least some habits associated with great men, and even in the East Glycerius is sometimes seen in a favourable light: 'Glykerios ... a man who was by no means worthless'.[31] It is possible that, given more time, or born during the early Empire, Glycerius could have become a major force in Western politics and that accordingly his name would be well remembered. Sadly for him, he was unable to convince the East to support his regime and he was quickly overthrown and removed from the limelight. It is suggested by Marcellinus *comes* that Glycerius died soon after his overthrow.[32] However, other evidence suggests that he continued to live in Dalmatia for some time after his deposition: it is even possible that he had one more act to play in the last days of the West.[33]

Chapter Fourteen

Julius Nepos

June 474–28 August 475

The New Emperor

Following the surrender of Glycerius the majority of the sources state that Nepos was made emperor at Rome in June 474, however Jordanes claims that: 'After Anthemius had been killed at Rome, Zeno, through his client Domitianus, named as emperor at Ravenna Nepotianus.'[1] Jordanes also states that Nepos was named Caesar, or 'junior', by Leo I, presumably in August 473.[2] This implies that only after he had landed in Italy was Nepos able to claim the title Augustus (Emperor). The theory is reinforced by the fact that some sources only allow a short reign to Glycerius – which could be considered accurate if Nepos is accepted as ruling after being acclaimed Caesar by Leo I in 473, rather than after his coronation in 474. The passage further suggests that Nepos was crowned at Ravenna before the removal of Glycerius. Although all of this is possible, in this case it is more likely that Jordanes is mistaken and that the more contemporary sources are correct about the location of the coronation.[3]

In theory the West now returned to a more viable regime as the addition of Illyricum to Italy and the remnants of Gaul gave the West added revenues and manpower, and Nepos being Zeno's nominee could result in Eastern military support if required. It was possibly with this in mind that Nepos' first action was an attempt to resist, if not reverse, the expansion of the Goths in Gaul.

Gaul

In Gaul events were now reaching towards a conclusion and Nepos needed to take swift action in order to repel the advances of the Goths.

Euric

Euric had been taking full advantage of the ongoing civil war in Italy. Following the capture of Arles and Marseilles in the previous year, in 474 he continued his campaign in Southern Gaul, now reinforced by the Ostrogothic followers of Vidimer:[4] some of these had been sent to the northern border along the Loire, but many had entered the royal retinue, serving alongside Euric.[5]

The course of this campaign is not recorded, but it is possible that a few disunited sources give some clue as to the train of events. Euric appears to have focused on two distinct areas. Following the capture of Arles and Marseilles he appears to have

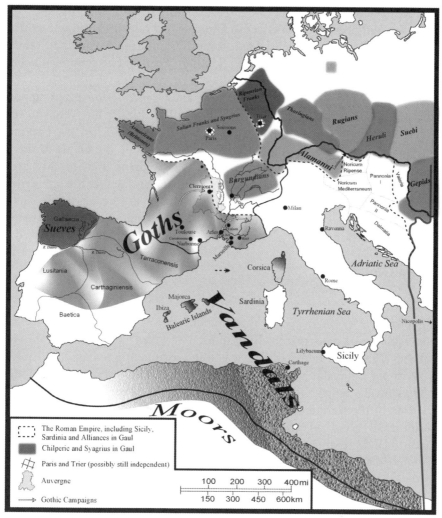

Map 19: The Reign of Julius Nepos and Gothic Expansion.

continued to campaign in Provence, intent upon annexing the whole of the region. Later events suggest that Euric succeeded in extending his conquests in this area.

Further north, in the Auvergne, in 473 Euric had been repulsed from the walls of Clermont by a defence led by Sidonius Apollinaris.[6] In 474 Euric appears to have made another concerted attempt to capture the city. Roman resistance to the Goths was still being organized partly by Sidonius, but in the New Year mainly by Ecdicius.

Ecdicius

Ecdicius was the son of the Emperor Avitus and the brother-in-law of Sidonius.[7] In 471 he had allegedly bypassed the Goths as they laid siege to Clermont, unexpectedly reinforcing the city, after which he had raised a small army to resist them.[8] Although he had been promised the title of *patricius* by Anthemius, Anthemius had died before the promise had been put into effect so Ecdicius had remained without a title.[9] In addition, in 473 he had supplied food to the Burgundians during their famine.[10] This was a man known and respected in Southern Gaul and he continued to be the focus for resistance to Gothic attacks.

On the other hand, Gundobad, the *patricius* and *magister militum*, had supported the regime of Glycerius and so it would be hard politically for Nepos to retain his services. What Nepos needed in Gaul was a man who had the backing of the people of Gaul, whose appointment would reconcile the Gauls to the new regime, who could work in tandem with the Burgundians, and who had proven military ability and could be relied on to drive back and defeat Euric.[11] Ecdicius seemed tailor-made for the appointment and late in 474 he was made *patricius* and *magister utriusque militiae praesentalis* ('patrician and master of all troops in the presence of the emperor').[12] In one respect Nepos' appointment worked: the later issuing of coins at Arles suggests that his regime was accepted in at least Southern Gaul.[13]

Gundobad

Simultaneously, it would appear that Gundobad was campaigning in the same region, as Sidonius states that the Burgundians were also fighting against the Goths in the Auvergne.[14] As noted earlier, it is often assumed that Gundobad realized that he would be unable to resist an invasion from the East and so left Italy, or that Gundobad's father Gundioc died and Gundobad quit the Empire to claim his portion of the Burgundian Kingdom. However it is more likely that before his deposition Glycerius had sent Gundobad to oppose Euric in Gaul and that before Gundobad could react to Nepos' invasion Glycerius had been overthrown.[15]

Gundobad's reaction to Ecdicius' appointment is not recorded. Yet given later events a tantalizing hypothesis presents itself. Gundobad was to maintain good relations with the East throughout his life, which may appear unlikely in the event of his opposing Nepos, the Eastern nominee for the throne. In this context it is possible to suggest that Gundobad recognized that in the circumstances he would not be able to continue as *magister militum utriusque militiae* as he had under Glycerius.

On the other hand, Nepos needed the continuing alliance with the Burgundians if he was to stand a chance of resisting the Goths. As a result, it is possible to suggest that there was a complex series of negotiations between Nepos and the Burgundians.

To some degree this convoluted series of discussions may be demonstrated by events depicted by Sidonius Apollinaris. According to Sidonius, in autumn 474 there was a plot by some Gallo-Romans within the Burgundian territory and that his uncle, Apollinaris, to whom this letter is addressed, was involved:[16]

There [at Vienne in the Burgundian region] I found ... Thaumastus ... [whose report claimed that] venomous tongues have been secretly at work, whispering in the ear of the ever-victorious Chilperic, our Master of the Soldiery, that your machinations are chiefly responsible for the attempt to win the town of Vaison for the new Emperor.

Sidonius Apollinaris, Epistle 5.6.

A second letter, to Apollinaris' brother, the Thaumastus mentioned in the first letter, gives more information:

At last we have discovered who the villains are who have accused your brother [Apollinaris] before our tetrarch for siding with the partisans of the new Emperor.

Sidonius Apollinaris, Epistle 5.7.1.

These two letters are the source of a great deal of confusion.[17] The first letter claims that Chilperic, Gundobad's elder brother, was now 'our Master of Soldiers', whilst the second attests that Chilperic is a 'tetrarch'.

The first question to be addressed is whether Chilperic was appointed *magister militum* by Rome or was self-designated. Apart from the possible exception of Euric discussed earlier there is no record of any loyal 'barbarian king' claiming a Roman title for which he is not recognized by Rome: indeed, to do so would likely diminish his standing as he would be seen as a fraud by his subjects. He was almost certainly appointed from Italy.

There then remains the question of who was responsible. One theory is that he was appointed during the brief reign of Glycerius and under the auspices of Gundobad. Yet there is no evidence for this, and nor is there any need for this to be the case: in fact, it is usually accepted that Gundobad left his post in Italy in order to compete with his brothers for the kingship of the Burgundians.[18] If this was so, and later events suggest that there may have been intense rivalry between the brothers, this would imply that there is little likelihood of Gundobad agreeing to his brother being elevated to an imperial rank. It is unlikely that Glycerius made the appointment.

The alternative is that Chilperic was created *magister militum* by Nepos, and that Gundobad chose not to interfere. The second letter may provide supporting evidence for this theory. It is usually assumed that when Sidonius talks of 'our tetrarch' he is referring to Chilperic as one of the four rulers of the Burgundians.[19] This assumes that by this time Gundobad had returned to rule as one of the Burgundian kings and had been accepted by his brothers. The assumption may be mistaken, although the alternative is quite complicated.

In late 474 Nepos appointed Ecdicius as *magister militum praesentalis*. It is also possible, as noted earlier, that Chilperic was appointed *magister militum* by Nepos to ensure Burgundian support for his rule. The appointment of Chilperic would make sense as far as Nepos was concerned, as it would ensure a division of Burgundian resources should Gundobad attempt to overthrow Nepos.

At the same time Gundobad appears to have remained one of the joint kings of the Burgundians and throughout this period continued to claim the title of *magister militum*. In this context it is possible to assume that, in order not to alienate a capable ally, Nepos asked Gundobad to carry on serving in Gaul as *magister militum*, possibly *per Gallias*, on the condition that he did not return to Italy or support another candidate for the throne. This would clarify the following confusing points: that Gundobad maintained good relations with the East – even going so far as to mint coins in the name of the Eastern emperor – despite his association with Glycerius;[20] that he did not invade Italy until after the death of Nepos; and that he retained the title of *patricius* and *magister militum* in the sources throughout his life, which may not have been the case had he been stripped of them by Nepos.

It would also mean that there were three *magistri* in Gaul: Ecdicius, Chilperic, and Gundobad. During the 'rule' of Ricimer the *magister* was seen as working alongside and as 'equal' to the emperor. This would add up to four men in joint command of the West, and explain Sidonius' use of the phrase 'tetrarch'. Although seemingly complex, the hypothesis would appear to be more convincing than that the arch-Roman Sidonius would use the Roman word 'tetrarch' to describe barbarian kings.

There then remains the question of who wanted to surrender the town of Vaison and who the 'new emperor' was. Given the context proposed above it is now feasible to propose that the new air of optimism surrounding the appointment of Ecdicius and the inclusion of Chilperic and Gundobad in the new regime led some unknown patriots in Vaison to assume that they could now leave the orbit of the Burgundians and return their allegiance to the Empire. If true, then the emperor in question was Nepos.[21] Sadly, there was no chance of the weakened Empire being able to enforce their decision.

Syagrius and the Franks

Earlier, Anthemius had made an alliance with the *Brittones* of Riothamus, before these had been defeated by the Goths.[22] Although he may have attempted a similar arrangement with Syagrius, for an unknown reason this appears to have failed: upon their defeat the *Brittones* had fled towards the Burgundians, not to the north, implying that there was no agreement with Syagrius.

On the other hand, a series of coins in the name of Nepos found in northern Gaul suggests that the expansion of the Goths was causing fear throughout the region and that when envoys from Nepos arrived at Syagrius' court, they were welcomed and an alliance was formed – helped no doubt by the removal of Ricimer's heir from his post alongside the emperor.[23] As a side effect, the alliance between Syagrius and Childeric appears to have resulted in the alliance being extended – the Franks in the area were to maintain their nominal allegiance to the Empire until 481.[24]

The Vandals and the East

Nepos wasn't the only emperor attempting to secure new political agreements. Zeno was anxious to remove the threat posed by the Vandals to eastern security. Accordingly he appointed a senator named Severus to act as an ambassador and, after making him a patrician, sent him to Africa.[25] Unfortunately, Gaiseric learned of the proposed embassy and launched a swift attack on the East, capturing the town of Nicopolis on the coast of Epirus.[26]

After prolonged discussions in either late 474 or early 475 Severus finally managed to negotiate a treaty with Gaiseric on behalf of Zeno:

> But at that time Gizeric [sic] was plundering the whole Roman domain just as much as before, if not more, circumventing his enemy by craft and driving them out of their possessions by force, as has been previously said, and he continued to do so until the emperor Zeno came to an agreement with him and an endless peace was established between them, by which it was provided that the Vandals should never in all time perform any hostile act against the Romans nor suffer such a thing at their hands. And this peace was preserved by Zeno himself and also by his successor in the empire, Anastasius. And it remained in force until the time of the emperor Justin.
>
> *Procopius 3.7.26.*

Although the treaty allowed the East to remove troops from coastal towns for other purposes, it came at a cost: Zeno may have believed that as the senior emperor the treaty with Gaiseric was also binding on the West, but Gaiseric does not appear to have agreed and was now able to use the treaty to his advantage when dealing with Nepos.

Defeat

In the meantime, Nepos' hopes for a successful campaign in Gaul were to be dashed. Instead, although he fought a long campaign against the Goths, Ecdicius was defeated by Euric:

> Euric … seized the city of Arverna [Clermont], where the Roman general Ecdicius was at that time in command. He was a senator of most renowned family and the son of Avitus … Ecdicius strove for a long time with the Visigoths, but had not the power to prevail. So he left the country and (what was more important) the city of Arverna to the enemy and betook himself to safer regions.
>
> *Jordanes*, Getica 240–1.

After several years of trying, Euric had finally managed to capture the elusive city of Sidonius.

It was probably at around this time that Nepos first began to have doubts about the ability of the West to survive without Eastern support. Although he now had an alliance with the Burgundians and (possibly) Syagrius, neither of these forces was capable of halting Gothic expansion and organizing a joint campaign would be extremely difficult, especially as the Goths now controlled most of

Provence and could easily threaten the flank and rear of any troops crossing the Alps. Furthermore, the continuing attacks on the coasts by the Vandals meant that Nepos was unable to send the whole of the *praesental* army in Italy into Gaul in order to help force a decision. The defeat of Ecdicius and the remnant of the imperial forces in Southern Gaul, not to mention the fact that the Burgundians seemed incapable of helping to any degree, may have forced Nepos to send envoys to Zeno to ask for military help.

474–475

As the campaign season closed it became clear to Nepos that he had to make a momentous decision: the West could not survive the ongoing wars alone. Envoys were almost certainly sent East but Zeno would be unable to send help thanks to two major setbacks. The first was that in November 474 the young Leo II died of an illness: the joint reign of Leo II and Zeno had lasted for only ten months. Time would have to be allowed for Zeno to bury his son. The second occurred in January 475, when a coup in the East forced Zeno to abandon Constantinople and flee to Isauria with his wife and mother, to some degree the hostility against Zeno possibly being caused by the treaty with the Vandals.

Ecdicius and Orestes

As he awaited news from the East, in late 474 Nepos sent Epiphanius, the man who had brokered the truce between Anthemius and Ricimer, to Euric to discuss peace. At the same time he recalled Ecdicius to the court in Italy. Once at court Ecdicius was relieved of his command.[27] Although the reasons for this decision are unclear, two major factors will have made the result inevitable. Firstly, if a peace treaty was to be agreed with Euric concessions would have to be made, almost certainly against the wishes of Ecdicius. To leave Ecdicius in command of an army in Gaul, no matter how small, would be foolish. Secondly, Ecdicius' father Avitus had been declared emperor at the instigation of Theoderic I in 455 and there remained the distinct possibility that the signing of an unfavourable treaty would encourage Ecdicius to follow in his father's footsteps, either with or without Gothic support. Nepos had little choice but to call Ecdicius to the court, remove him from command and then supervise his activities, at least for a short time.[28]

Ecdicius' replacement was a Pannonian named Orestes. Although some doubts have been raised about the identity of Orestes, it is likely that this was the same man who had been sent as *notarius* (secretary, senior civil servant) to Attila by Aetius in the 440s and who had acted as Attila's envoy to Constantinople in 449 and 452.[29]

If the connection between the Orestes of the 470s and that of the 440s is incorrect, then all that can be said is that we know nothing of the man before he became *magister militum*. If, on the other hand, the connection is accurate, it is likely that, after the death of Attila and the breakup of the Hunnic Empire, Orestes had returned to the Empire.[30] It is also possible that he had been a follower of Aetius and that after Aetius' death he had remained in the vicinity of Pannonia, serving first with Marcellinus and then with Nepos, although in that case the question of why he later turned upon Nepos remains unanswerable. Orestes was obviously a remarkable man: he had survived the political intrigues of Attila's court for several years and some twenty years later was in a position to rise to the post of *magister militum* and *patricius*.

Whatever his origin, he now found himself *magister militum praesentalis* and *patricius* in command of the army in Italy at a time of political and military crisis.[31] In theory he was a man perfectly suited to the needs of Nepos. As Orestes had been a follower of Aetius in his earlier years, Nepos may have hoped that Orestes would act as an intermediate between himself and the Senate, helping to secure senatorial support for his new regime.[32] In addition, having served under Attila he was well acquainted with the 'barbarian mind set', as he will have had experience of dealing not only with Huns but also with the large number of separate tribes living under the control of Attila's Empire. In his position with Attila he will have certainly learned the Hunnic language, and may have become at least understandable in several others, including Gothic. It may have been hoped that with him being able to communicate directly with the mercenaries who now made up the vast majority of the Roman army he could transfer their loyalty to Nepos, so ensuring the longevity of his reign.[33]

In the meantime, Epiphanius was negotiating with Euric. Why Euric was willing to open negotiations when he was in such a strong position is unclear, but the possibility of an imperial attack using Eastern reinforcements may have convinced Euric that diplomacy was the way forward.

Finally Epiphanius returned, the 'bonds of peace having been undertaken'.[34] Despite Ennodius' implication that peace was agreed, it was only a truce at this stage.[35] In the New Year a further embassy of four bishops was sent to discuss the terms of a full treaty. In Clermont, Sidonius was so impressed with the authority of the four bishops – Leontius of Arles, Faustus of Riez, Basilius of Aix, and Graecus of Marseilles – that in a letter to Graecus he wrote: 'Through you delegations come and go; to you, first of all, in the absence of the emperor, peace is not only reported when it has been negotiated, it is even entrusted to be negotiated.'[36] Only a short time later Sidonius' praise would turn to shock.

Early in the New Year news arrived from the East of Zeno's overthrow. This was a major setback for Nepos, as he had now lost the major support for his rule in the West, and obviously the removal of Zeno meant that the treaty with the Vandals was now void and that in the new campaign season Gaiseric would be free to unleash his men on both the East and the almost defenceless West. What Nepos needed most was time during which the remaining core of the West would be able to recover from the seemingly never-ending series of military and political disasters it had faced. Nepos was forced to make an unpalatable decision: in early 475 he felt he had no option but to come to terms with the Goths and the Vandals, whatever the cost.

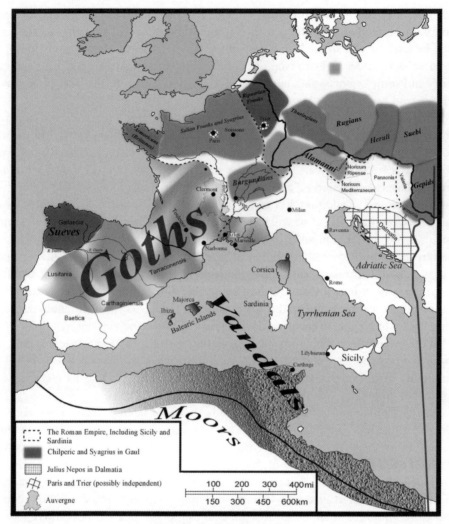

Map 20: The Empire in 475.

The Gothic Peace Treaty

Early in the New Year, although the exact date is unknown, Nepos agreed terms with Euric and the long war against the Goths was over. The terms were harsh and would severely damage Nepos' standing as emperor. Under pressure from the Senate in Italy, and especially those members who had land holdings in Southern Gaul, Nepos was forced to request the return of Provence, captured by Euric in the previous year's fighting. Euric agreed, but demanded a major concession: that the region of the Auvergne be handed to him. Despite the knowledge that such a treaty would severely undermine his position, Nepos had little choice but to accept.

It is sometimes claimed that Euric also demanded that the Goths now be accepted as totally independent from the Empire. This appears to be a misinterpretation of the terms of the treaty. Ennodius claims that as part of the treaty Nepos 'at least is willing to be called friend [*amicus*], who ought to be called master [*dominus*]'.[37] As a consequence, it is clear that the 'sovereignty of the Visigothic kingdom was not recognised de jure in 475': only de facto – which explains why Euric was now able to begin the process of consolidating his regime (see below).[38]

In Gaul, when news of the treaty arrived in Clermont Sidonius' response was bitter, and especially directed at the men whom he had so recently praised, specifically Graecus of Marseilles:

> And this is to be our reward for braving destitution, fire, sword, and pestilence, for fleshing our swords in the enemy's blood and going ourselves starved into battle. This, then, is the famous peace we dreamed of, when we tore the grass from the crannies in the walls to eat; when in our ignorance we often by mistake ate poisonous weeds, indiscriminately plucking them with livid hands of starvation, hardly less green than they. For all these proofs of our devotion, it would seem that we are to be made a sacrifice.
>
> If it be so, may you live to blush for a peace without either honour or advantage. For you are the channel through which negotiations are conducted. When the king is absent, you not only see the terms of peace, but new proposals are brought before you. I ask your pardon for telling you hard truths; my distress must take all colour of abuse from what I say. You think too little of the general good; when you meet in council, you are less concerned to relieve public perils than to advance private fortunes. By the long repetition of such acts you begin to be regarded as the last instead of the first among your fellow provincials.
>
> But how long are these feats of yours to last? Our ancestors will cease to glory in the name of Rome if they have no longer descendants to bear their memory. Oh, break this infamous peace at any cost; there are pretexts enough to your hand. We are ready, if needs must, to continue the struggle and to undergo more sieges and starvations. But if we are to be betrayed, we whom force failed to conquer, we shall know beyond a doubt that a barbarous and cowardly transaction was inspired by you.
>
> But it little avails to give the rein to passionate sorrow; you must make allowance for us in our affliction, nor too nicely weigh the language of despair. The other conquered regions have only servitude to expect; Auvergne must prepare for punishment. If you can hold out no help in our extremity, seek to obtain of Heaven by your unceasing prayers that though our liberty be doomed, our race at least may live. Provide land for the exile, prepare a ransom for the captive, make provision for the emigrant. If our own walls must offer an open breach to the enemy, let yours be never shut against your friends. Deign to hold me in remembrance, my Lord Bishop.
>
> *Sidonius Apollinaris*, Epistle *7.7.3–6.*

Much has been made of Sidonius' polemic, but it needs to be remembered that many Roman senators had extensive estates in the south of Gaul and so the decision to exchange Provence for the Auvergne made some sense politically, as it regained the lost estates for the Senate.

On the other hand, even the tacit acceptance of the Goths as a separate political entity was against Roman tradition and will have caused great anger in the West, and especially in Gaul. Although not specifically mentioned in the sources, it is clear that Euric was now the king of an autonomous kingdom, as he immediately began a 'persecution' of Christian bishops and for a short period many churches became vacant as bishops were either executed, or evicted, or died and were not replaced.[39] This included Sidonius, who was taken prisoner and confined in 'Fort Livia', near Carcassonne.[40]

What is usually overlooked is the question of why Euric agreed to such a treaty when he had already conquered large parts of both Provence and the Auvergne and the West had little chance of recovering either. The main reason must be one of validity: although by accepting the treaty he was forced to give up land, the obvious acknowledgement by the emperor that the Goths were now an autonomous kingdom far outweighed the loss of territory, especially with regards to the 'Roman' citizens now under his rule in Gaul.

Furthermore, his newfound autonomy meant that he now had a free hand in Iberia, where many of the inhabitants formally pledged their allegiance to Euric. On the other hand, many, especially in the south, still felt that he had no right to rule any of the peninsula and continued to fight for their freedom.

The Vandals

There remained the ever-present raids from Africa to be dealt with. As with Euric, Nepos was forced to the conclusion that victory was impossible and that the only means of saving the West was to reach an accommodation with Gaiseric similar to that made with Euric. Prolonged negotiations may have begun but it is unlikely that these came to a satisfactory conclusion before internal events intervened.[41]

Analysis

The treaty definitively signals the end of Roman rule in Gaul except for the territory of Provence. A side effect of the treaty was that the other barbarian 'kingdoms' were forced to realign their political compass, as by this time the Goths far surpassed the Empire in military and political power. As a by-product, the Burgundians also appear to have gained a new level of independence, if only because the emperor could no longer expect them to ask Rome for guidance and support in the face of their aggressive neighbours the Goths. Unfortunately, the recent defeats of the Empire, in which they had played a part and lost, had certainly weakened their military effectiveness, at least in the short term.[42]

Orestes

Unsurprisingly, the peace treaty made many in the West unhappy. Certainty is impossible due to the lack of detailed information, but it would appear that the Senate disagreed with Nepos' approach to the problems facing the West. As with Anthemius, Nepos was an outsider whose primary loyalty was seen as being to the East, rather than to the Senate and the West.[43] Even at this early stage in his rule it was clear that he was using Eastern exemplars in how to rule, including the promotion of several competing *magistri*. It would appear that in their dismay the Senate were supported by Orestes, the new *magister militum praesentalis*.

What follows is extremely confused, largely because the sources fail to include the details needed for a full description of events, but it would appear that, following the 'disgraceful' treaty and with the overthrow of Zeno in the East, which removed Nepos' Eastern support, Orestes agreed to lead the army in revolt against the new emperor:

> While Nepos was in the city, the Patrician Orestes was sent against him [Nepos] with the main force of the army. But because Nepos dared not undertake the business of resisting in such desperate conditions, he fled.[44]
>
> Auctuarii Hauniensis ordo prior *s.a. 475.*

The fact that Orestes was 'sent against' Nepos suggests that the Senate was involved in the decision to revolt against Nepos' rule. It has been suggested that 'the city' (*urbs*) referred to in this translation is in fact Ravenna, not Rome, but not only does this fail to take into account that the source could be heavily abbreviated, but additional information given by both Jordanes and the *Anonymous Valesianus* help to clarify the matter:[45]

> Orestes, having taken charge of the army and having departed from Rome against the enemy, arrived at Ravenna.
>
> *Jordanes*, Getica *241, trans. Mathisen 1998.*

> Soon Nepos arrived at Ravenna, pursued by the Patrician Orestes and his army.
>
> *Anonymous Valesianus 7.36, s.a. 474.*

It is clear that Nepos was first attacked whilst still resident in Rome and that he instantly sought the safety of Ravenna. At this point Orestes pursued 'the enemy', reaching Ravenna shortly after Nepos' arrival. Realizing that he had no hope of resisting Orestes and the Italian army, on 28 August 475 Nepos fled to Salona in Dalmatia and Orestes entered Ravenna.[46] Nepos' brief direct reign of just fourteen months was over. However, once back in the safety of Dalmatia he was to continue to claim the throne for a number of years to come.

Analysis

Although it has been claimed that Nepos was the last strong emperor who could have reversed the collapse of the West, it seems that this is based more on the belief that he was being supported by the East than on his ability and the military and political realities of the time. In the East the emperor still ruled supreme. In the West, real power lay with the army, and in many cases the army closely adhered to the guidance of the Senate.[47] Furthermore, Nepos arrived in the West with a preconception from the Eastern court of how an emperor should act and how his subjects should respond. Sadly, this was at odds with the Western template for a successful emperor. Although in arranging the treaty that ensured his downfall Nepos simply acknowledged the fact that without the East the West was unable to drive back its enemies, this was anathema to the Senate, still imbued with the superiority of Roman culture and of the Roman military machine. Needless to say, they rejected Nepos as soon as he ignored their traditions and 'humiliated' the once proud name of Rome. Although Nepos may have been a competent general, he lacked an army of the size needed to ensure victory, and, imbued with the ethos of the Eastern court, he failed to gain acceptance either with the Senate or with the troops. In these circumstances, his downfall was inevitable.

Although Nepos can be castigated as the author of the final disintegration of the West – the possession of Italy, and parts of Gaul and Sicily hardly classifies the West as an 'Empire' – a close analysis of events has clearly demonstrated that there was nothing else he could do: the Western army was no longer an efficient fighting force and was incapable of retaking the lost territory unaided, and the loss of his Eastern sponsor Zeno removed any hope he had of Eastern intervention. Nepos had no alternative than to accept the reality of the situation and make the best of a terrible state of affairs. At least that way the West remained a viable proposition and with luck at some point the East would come to its aid. Sadly, the Senate failed to accept their weakening position and Nepos was removed.

Chapter Fifteen

Romulus Augustulus

31 October 475–4 September 476

Interregnum

As noted in the previous chapter, Orestes, the new 'ruler' of Rome, has one of two histories. In the first, he is a complete unknown who may have owed his entire career thanks to his service either in Italy, the East, or in Dalmatia. If in Italy or the East it is surprising that no record exists of his rise to power: if in Dalmatia, and given the reception of Nepos, it is surprising that no Western source states that he was an Eastern usurper.

Orestes is most likely the same man that had served as *notarius* (secretary, senior civil servant) to Attila and had been Attila's envoy to Constantinople in 449 and 452.[1] Son of a man named Tatulus and with a brother named Paulus, Orestes had married the daughter of an important official named Romulus – a Western senator, not the son of Anthemius – who had acted as an envoy to Attila during the overlordship of Aetius.[2] The couple had a son, also named Romulus, born in the mid-late 460s.[3]

After the death of Attila, Orestes had returned to the Empire, but whether to the East or the West is not stated in the sources. If the West, the fact that he is nowhere stated as a political player during the tumultuous years between 454 and 476 is surprising. On the other hand, if he had returned to the East and then supported Nepos in his attempt on the throne, the speed with which he turned against his benefactor is extraordinary.[4] It has been claimed that his 'career' amongst the barbarians may have resulted in his being distrusted in Rome, but, given that for the previous twenty years the *magistri* had been full-blooded barbarians, the fact that Orestes was actually a Roman almost certainly outweighed any possible distrust.[5]

Sadly, the lack of information regarding Orestes' origin is mirrored by the lack of source material concerning his time in control of the Western Empire. On 28 August 475 Orestes found himself the new controller of the West. Not one of his actions from this point until the end of October is known, but it is probable that he sent messengers to Basiliscus in the East – Zeno was still in exile – informing him of events and asking for feedback, possibly in the form of recognition for a Western nominee for emperor.

The two-month interregnum whilst the messengers returned from Constantinople will have been used to arrange for envoys to go to the Goths and the Vandals, for new appointments by the new regime, and for the consolidation of Orestes' power. Throughout this time he appears to have remained in Ravenna, as this was the best place to send and receive messengers from the East.

The New Emperor

What response Orestes received from Basiliscus is unknown, but, with or without the blessing of the in situ Eastern emperor, on 31 October 475 Orestes crowned his teenage son Romulus as the new Roman emperor.[6] Needless to say, Orestes retained real power in his own hands.[7] On his accession Romulus took the traditional title of Augustus,[8] but his contemporaries soon began to refer to him as *Augustulus* (little Augustus) and it is by a combination of these names that he is known to posterity: Romulus Augustulus.[9]

The reasons behind Orestes' nomination of his son, rather than taking the diadem for himself, have long been debated with no consensus being reached. The idea that he was ineligible to become emperor, in this mirroring his predecessors Ricimer and Gundobad, does not hold water. As a native of Pannonia Orestes was a full Roman citizen and fully entitled to claim the throne.

Consequently, a different explanation needs to be reached. The fact that he may have been *notarius* to Attila in 449 suggests that he was born at the latest around 425. As a result, by the time of his accession to power Orestes was at least 50-years-old. Bearing this fact in mind, it is likely that Orestes decided that he needed to maintain close contact with the troops, allowing him to both control the Senate and deter any attempt at rebellion. By crowning his son it would allow Augustulus time to mature under his father's tutelage as well as meaning that when Orestes died there would be a smooth transition of power to the first member of a new dynasty.[10]

In accordance with his desire to create a new dynasty, Orestes may have promoted his brother Paulus to a position of power within the new regime, but unfortunately the sources fail to give any indication as to what post he might have occupied.[11]

476

There can be little doubt that over the winter of 375–6 messengers were travelling between Ravenna and Constantinople, although as usual there is no record of any diplomatic activity. The fact that on 1 January 476 the two consuls who were nominated both originated in the East, with one being the 'usurping' Emperor Basiliscus, can imply that Orestes relinquished the right to nominate a consul in the hope of ingratiating himself with the Eastern court and ensuring its support for his new regime. On the other hand, it is also possible that Basiliscus refused to recognize Romulus and ignored an unrecorded request to accept a Western nominee as consul. Unless some new information comes to light, the truth is unknowable.

Gaul

In Gaul the elimination of Nepos had one major political result. Traditionally, Germanic leaders had classed treaties as being with individuals, not with monolithic states. Accordingly, the ousting of Nepos and his replacement by Romulus meant that Euric's treaty with the 'Roman Empire' was void: in fact, in theory he could

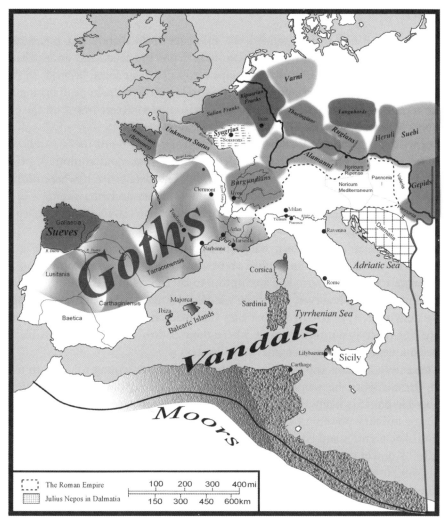

Map 21: The Empire after the Reign of Romulus Augustulus. Note that the region 'ruled' by Syagrius may have been little more than the city of Soissons itself.

now resume the offensive, but if necessary this time claim he was doing so in the name of Nepos. Obviously, should Nepos regain the throne Euric could expect further concessions from the Empire for the return of any conquered territory – if he returned it at all. Consequently, in 476 Euric attacked again.

As in 473 and 475 his target was Provence, and once again he took the cities of Arles and Marseille.[12] Although it is sometimes assumed that the earlier reference to the capture of the two cities is a doublet, merely confusing the date of the attack, this is almost certainly an error.[13] In 475 Euric had made a treaty with Nepos in which Provence was exchanged for the Auvergne; with Nepos removed, Euric saw the opportunity to gain new territory on a permanent basis and took it.[14]

Gaiseric

The fact that Euric again resumed the offensive immediately put pressure on Orestes. Knowing that he would get no help from the East, and aware that he needed to gather all of his available troops into one major force in order to repel the Goths, Orestes was forced to send envoys to Gaiseric in the hope of arranging a peace treaty.[15] If accomplished, the troops garrisoning strategic towns on the coast of Italy could travel north to reinforce Orestes' army.

Surprisingly, given the weakness of the West, at some point in 476 – allowing time for events to unfold, probably between mid summer and autumn – a treaty was concluded between Orestes and Gaiseric.[16] The details are nowhere outlined but the majority opinion – based both on contemporary and later events – is that Orestes recognized Gaiseric as being in full control of Africa, Sardinia, Corsica and the Balearic Islands.

In addition, at an unknown date during the previous decade Gaiseric had managed to gain a foothold in Sicily. Later events are confused and some historians have suggested that Gaiseric was attempting to lay claim to the whole of the island. What appears clear, however, is that the Vandals had managed to capture Lilybaeum and its environs. It is also likely that they had made major inroads into the rest of Sicily, but there is no indication of where their control ended. It is possible that these conquests were also recognized by Orestes.

There only remains the question of why Gaiseric was willing to come to terms with Orestes when he was in such a position of strength. As usual, certainty is impossible but it is likely that at this time he was attempting to reach terms with all major military powers in the Mediterranean. Born c. 390, Gaiseric was now in his mid-late eighties and later events suggest he may have been suffering from poor health.[17] Knowing that his end was near, he may have been determined to bequeath to his son Huneric a rich and viable realm free from war with any external powers. Given the pacific nature of Huneric's later rule, it is likely that Gaiseric knew that his son did not have his own political or military ability and decided that overriding peace was the only way the Vandal state could survive.

Crisis

In the meantime, Orestes continued his attempts to secure his position in Italy. A letter of the time clearly demonstrates that Orestes made at least some progress in this area, as he had some support amongst the nobility/clergy of Italy.[18] Furthermore, the production of coins for the new emperor in Rome, Ravenna and even at Arles prior to the Gothic takeover, suggests that the new regime was welcome in what remained of the Western Empire.[19]

Although politically Orestes was making headway, on the military front in Italy events would soon overtake him. Orestes had a long history of dealing with barbarians and it is probable that he could speak at least some of their languages, a factor which may have contributed to his rise to the position of *magister militum*. On the other hand, it is possible that his prolonged and close contact with the army, now composed (almost) entirely of barbarian mercenaries, led the troops to believe that he was sympathetic to them and would support them in what may have been a novel request.[20]

At some point in 476 the troops asked for lands in Italy on which they could settle, according to Procopius demanding a 'third part'.[21] Although the exact nature of their request has divided opinion, the most likely explanation is that they requested to be treated in the same manner as the barbarian troops who had served the Empire earlier in the century: namely, that they be settled as *hospites* (guests), given one third of the land of their 'hosts' and allowed to settle as farmers.[22] Furthermore, it is probable that they were interested in settling only in the northern regions of Italy, especially in the valley of the Po around garrison towns.[23] There is no evidence that they were expecting to acquire lands throughout the whole of the Italian peninsula.

Contrary to expectations, Orestes simply refused the request outright.[24] The reasons for his decision are not made clear by the sources, which has resulted in much modern debate. For example, it has been claimed that it was due to his 'attachment to Italian aristocratic tradition', a suggestion which has been dismissed with the assertion that he was 'not motivated by Roman tradition and pride'.[25]

In reality there may have been several reasons for his decision to refuse the troops' request. One is that earlier settlement of barbarians on these terms had been in Gaul, where the landowners had been more willing to accede to the demand as the troops so settled would help to defend their homes against external attack, which was a common occurrence.[26] Although the Goths had launched an attack across the Alps earlier in the decade, and the barbarians to the north were also now in a position to attack, Italy had remained relatively inviolate and there was doubtless outrage amongst the Italian senators at the proposal that they give up their land to barbarian troops. The concept of 'land distribution' was almost certainly opposed by the Senate.[27]

Secondly, although there is no evidence that Orestes was wedded to 'Italian aristocratic traditions', as a high-ranking Roman he may still have been unhappy with the idea of giving land that had been demanded in the home of the Empire to barbarians. Although unlikely to have been an overriding factor, such considerations may have contributed to his decision.

Finally, and perhaps crucially, Orestes was attempting to establish a new dynasty. Giving land to the barbarian troops would doubtless have alienated a large section of the Senate and the aristocracy, which would not have been an acceptable legacy for his son after his own death. In retrospect, there was very little chance of Orestes ever acceding to the demands from the troops and the obvious nature of his decision may have resulted in him underestimating the effect of his refusal on the troops.

Odovacer

Baulked in their attempt at acceptance, the mercenaries turned to one of their number in the hope of getting satisfaction. The man's name was Odovacer. Historians in the mid-twentieth century sometimes accepted that the first mention of Odovacer was by Gregory of Tours, who describes the action of a barbarian leader he names Adovacrius leading his men in Gaul against Syagrius and Childeric.[28] However, more recently this has been challenged and is no longer widely accepted. The most likely explanation is that the two men simply had similar names and, with so few facts surviving from the period, their similarity was conspicuous and so the link was made.[29]

In fact, Odovacer is first attested by Eugippius in the *Life of Saint Severinus*:

> Among such visitants was Odovacer, later king of Italy, then a tall youth, meanly clad. While he stood, stooping that his head might not touch the roof of the lowly cell, he learned from the man of God that he was to win renown. For as the young man bade him farewell, 'Go forth!' said Severinus, 'Go forth to Italy! Now clad in wretched hides, thou shalt soon distribute rich gifts to many.'
>
> *Eugippius*, Life of Saint Severinus 7.

After this episode Odovacer appears to have entered Italy, but the claim in Jordanes that he invaded Italy as 'king of the Torcilingi … [and] leader of the Sciri, the Heruls and allies of various races' appears to be mistaken.[30] Instead, by 472 Odovacer was part of the Roman military establishment, helping Ricimer in his war against Anthemius, possibly after becoming one of the Emperor's bodyguards.[31] The 'Torcilingi, Sciri, and Heruls' appear to have been the barbarian warriors who formed the backbone of the *praesental* army in Italy.

Approached by the troops, Odovacer promised to grant their request for land if they made him king. Accordingly, on 23 August 476 Odovacer was proclaimed *rex*, after which he mustered his forces before advancing against Orestes.

Death of Orestes

Unaware of Odovacer's decision, Orestes agreed to meet the *magister* at Ticinum. The location suggests that Odovacer's invitation was to discuss the problem of countering Euric's aggression, although this is not stated by Ennodius. Ennodius' description of what followed was based in many respects upon Roman literary traditions, as well as the Christian belief that Satan was behind the disaster:

> Secretly sowing the seeds of discord, he [Satan] raised up an army against the patrician Orestes. He roused in wicked hearts the desire to revolt and inspired in Odovacar the ambition to rule; in order to bring ruin to Ticinum, he invited Orestes to that city with a promise of protection … Within that city gathered vast hordes, inflamed with a mad lust for plunder. Everywhere grief, everywhere fear, everywhere death, under many guises![32] … The rude barbarians sought on earth treasures that had transferred to heaven's coffers … They burned both churches; the whole city glowed, as it were a funeral pyre.
>
> *Ennodius*, Vita Epiphanius 95–100.

Sadly, Ennodius does not state the details of what occurred, meaning that modern historians have either resorted to guesswork or ignored the problem completely.

Certainty is impossible, but the most likely scenario is that Odovacer and the 'army' were in Ticinum to guard the northern frontier against the attacks of Euric in Gaul – after all, one Gothic army had already crossed the Alps and been defeated in 473.[33] Odovacer requested that Orestes meet him in the city in order to discuss the nature of the upcoming campaign. Travelling north with his *bucellarii* (mercenary bodyguard), Orestes entered the city and his bodyguard, taken by surprise, clashed with the main army. In the resulting conflict the city was severely damaged, to such an extent that after the crisis was over Epiphanius was able to secure a remission of the city's taxes for five years.[34]

Losing the battle, Orestes withdrew and rallied his few remaining loyal troops. On 28 August 476 Odovacer led his troops against the *patricius* and near to Placentia (Piacenza) defeated him in battle.[35] The majority of Orestes' forces were either killed, captured, or driven off, while Orestes himself was captured and executed.[36] After regrouping his forces, Odovacer marched towards Ravenna.

The East

The confusion prevalent in the West was being mirrored in the East. Also in August 476, Zeno led an army to Constantinople and laid siege to the city. Shortly afterwards he entered the city and regained the throne, after which Basiliscus and his family were exiled to a fortress in Cappadocia, where they were incarcerated in a cistern and allowed to die from exposure.

Deposition of Romulus Augustulus

Having defeated and killed Orestes, Odovacer marched his troops across the north of Italy towards Ravenna. Outside the city the troops captured Paulus, brother of Orestes and uncle of Romulus Augustulus, who was quickly executed. Although the *Auctores Prosperi Hauniensis ordo posterior marginalia* gives the date of 31 August, the later date of 4 September, as given by the *Fasti Vindobonenses Priores*, is to be preferred due to the time needed to march across the north of Italy.[37]

Quickly entering the city, on the same day Odovacer authorized the deposition of the young Emperor Romulus. Fortunately for Romulus, according to the majority of the sources the young man was granted his life due to his 'youth and beauty', allowed to retire to live with relatives on an estate called Lucullanum in Campania, and granted a pension of 6,000 *solidi* per annum.[38] The only discordant notes are Marcellinus *comes* and Jordanes, who both state that Romulus was 'exiled', rather than retired, to the castle of Lucullus in Campania.[39] Whether there was a difference between 'retired' and 'exiled' is open to question.

The ancient historian Malchus declares that before his exile Romulus had one last act to perform: namely, that:

When Augustus, the son of Orestes, heard that Zeno had driven out Basiliscus and regained the sovereignty of the East, he compelled the Senate to send an embassy to Zeno proposing that there was no need of a divided rule and that one, shared emperor was sufficient for both territories. They said, moreover, that they had chosen Odovacar, a man of military and political experience, to safeguard their own affairs and that Zeno should confer upon him the rank of patrician and entrust him with the government of Italy.

Malchus, fr. 14, *trans. Blockley.*

Although dismissed as fictitious by some, it is possible that an embassy was sent to Zeno in the name of Romulus: after all, the young man had no option but to agree to any demands from Odovacer.[40] If true, it was the last act of his short reign.

His fate is unknown and the fact that the owner of the villa converted at least part of the building into a monastery at some time between 492 and 496 implies that Augustulus may not have lived at the villa until his death – although it is possible that he had previously been moved to a different residence.[41] On the other hand, Cassiodorus in his *Variae* includes a letter dated to either 507 or 511 to a man named Romulus who may have been the ex-emperor.[42] Sadly, certainty is impossible.

Analysis

The brief reign of Romulus Augustulus would be insignificant except for the fact that it is the last time that a Roman emperor accepted by the Senate was to rule in the West. It has often been claimed that Orestes 'had the confidence of the barbarians and that service with Attila made him acceptable to them'. Although this is now doubted, it is likely that at the start of his 'rule' the barbarians will have had high hopes that Orestes would give them the security they desired.[43] It was only when he failed to comply with their demands that they turned on him.

It has also been suggested that it is best to think of Romulus' removal, not as the 'End of Empire', but as a failed coup that ended with the mutiny of the army: after all at that point there were four emperors in existence; Romulus and Nepos in the West, Basiliscus and Zeno in the East.[44] This concept has some validity, but if so the label of 'failed coup' should also include the reigns of Petronius Maximus, Avitus, and Glycerius.

The legitimacy of the claim that the crowning of Romulus was simply a coup that failed is strong. In hindsight it is clear that Orestes couldn't win. He needed a strong army to resist the expansion of the barbarian kingdoms, yet the Senate resisted attempts at taxation and recruitment despite their insistence on using 'Roman' troops, meaning he had to rely on mercenaries. At the same time he could not afford politically to accede to the request of the barbarian troops to settle in Italy after their service, so alienating the army needed to protect his own position.[45]

Although Orestes was a man of the greatest discretion, his sense of loyalty to the Western Empire meant that he was doomed to failure, and the only surprise is that his son Romulus was allowed to live after his father's death.[46] Attention now turned to the newcomer Odovacer and whether he would accept Nepos' outstanding claim to be the true Western Emperor.

Part Four

THE END

ODOVACER, JULIUS NEPOS AND SYAGRIUS

Chapter Sixteen

Odovacer, Julius Nepos and Syagrius

The New Regime

With the removal of Romulus, Julius Nepos was once more the undisputed claimant to the Western throne. Yet his previous rule in Italy had alienated the Senate and it was clear to everybody that he would not be able to recover his throne without Eastern help.

Despite Nepos' weak position, Odovacer knew that he needed some form of accommodation with the East if he was to secure his position in Italy. As noted in the previous chapter, and according to Malchus, Romulus had agreed to send an embassy to Zeno abdicating in favour of having a single emperor for both East and West, and nominating Odovacer as the West's choice for Zeno's subordinate.[1]

Due to the fact that Zeno acknowledged Nepos as the legitimate emperor and saw Romulus as a usurper, the signature may have had little effect. On the other hand, the document clearly demonstrated that the Senate and People of Rome did not want Nepos to return. The 'abdication' of Romulus merely added weight to the conviction that Nepos was not wanted in the West.

Yet Zeno's problems concerning what to do about the West did not stop there:

On the same day [as Odovacer's envoys arrived] messengers from Nepos also came to congratulate Zeno on the recent events concerning his restoration, and at the same time to ask him zealously to help Nepos, a man who had suffered equal misfortunes, in the recovery of his empire. They asked that he grant money and an army for this purpose and that he co-operate in his restoration in any other ways that might be necessary. Nepos had sent the men to say these things.

Malchus fr. 10, trans. Gordon 127–8.

After long deliberation, eventually Zeno sent a reply to Odovacer:

Zeno gave the following answer to those arrivals and to the men from the Senate: the western Romans had received two men from the eastern Empire and had driven one out, Nepos, and killed the other, Anthemius. Now, he said, they knew what ought to be done. While their emperor was still alive, they should hold no other thought than to receive him back on his return. To the barbarians he replied that it would be well if Odovacer were to receive the patrician rank from the emperor Nepos and that he himself would grant it unless Nepos granted it first. He commended him in that he had displayed this initial instance of guarding good order, suitable to the Romans, and trusted for this reason that, if he truly wished to act with justice, he would quickly receive back the emperor [Nepos] who had given him his position of honour. He sent a royal epistle about what he desired to Odovacer and in this letter named him a patrician. Zeno gave this help to Nepos, pitying his sufferings because of his own, and holding to the principle that the common lot of fortune is to grieve with the unfortunate. At the same time Verina also joined in urging this, giving a helping hand to the wife of Nepos, her relative.

Malchus fr. 10, trans. Gordon, 127–8.

The reply is open to several different interpretations; the main difficulty posed being the fact that Zeno named Odovacer *patricius*. This has been interpreted as Zeno refusing to give Nepos his full backing, instead hoping that the wording of the order would allow Odovacer to maintain his position in the West without the need for Zeno to intervene militarily in order to restore Nepos. In some respects this makes sense: Zeno had only recently recovered the throne and he will not have wished to alienate his subjects by immediately embarking on yet another campaign to sit the East's claimant on the Western throne.

Yet on reflection this may not be the case. The letter twice tells the Romans to receive Nepos back as their emperor, and even goes so far as to state openly that Zeno 'gave this help to Nepos'.[2] Some modern historians appear to have forgotten to take into account the full context of Zeno's position. There would be very little chance of Zeno sending troops to the West to aid in Nepos' restoration. As just noted, Zeno had only just recovered the throne himself and needed all of the loyal troops he could muster to deal with the repercussions of his return to power. Furthermore, he was facing almost continuous war with one Ostrogothic faction or another (see below), and so could not spare troops to help Nepos. To send some of his troops away, as well as to interfere in the political developments of the West, would be likely to incite unrest by appearing to concentrate on affairs not central to the security of the East.

There was no chance of him interfering directly in Nepos' claim and in the circumstances he did the next best thing, stressing that the West should accept Nepos back. In this context, the granting of the title *patricius* to Odovacer can be seen as an attempt to bribe Odovacer into 'doing what was right', whilst at the same time not giving Odovacer any specific powers by the use of the title.[3] Further, in the circumstances Odovacer accepting the title would mean that he was openly accepting that Nepos had the right to be emperor of the West.[4] The fact that Odovacer never addressed himself as *patricius* demonstrates that Odovacer was aware of this: but from this point Zeno addressed him as such.

On the other hand, Odovacer was acutely aware of Zeno's weak position in the East and so adopted a politically astute policy of appeasement. He sent the imperial regalia to Constantinople, yet minted coins in the name of Nepos and outwardly accepted Nepos as the emperor – secure in the knowledge that after his previous escape from Rome Nepos would never dare to actually set foot in Italy without an Eastern army to protect him.[5] As a by-product, Odovacer was to continue to acknowledge the superiority of Zeno until events determined otherwise.

Instead of *patricius*, Odovacer usually called himself *Rex* (King) – but never on public inscriptions. Further, he is referred to as *Odovacro Italiae regi* (Odovacer, King of Italy) by Victor Vitensis.[6] On the other hand, and unlike the Goths and the Vandals, he continued to use the names of the consuls for the dating system in the traditional Roman manner, rather than dating events by the year of his 'reign'.[7] The nebulous manner in which he is described in the ancient sources is evidence of the political manoeuvres adopted by Zeno to have Nepos reinstated and by Odovacer to avoid the same. The net result is that Odovacer's status, both at the time and in the present day, is unclear.

In the meantime, he allowed his men to settle – presumably in the Po Valley in Northern Italy – in the traditional Roman manner as *foederati* (allies), although whether they took land from Roman citizens or occupied vacant land owned by the Roman State is unclear. However, the fact that there is no mention of any problems arising from the settlement implies that the latter may have been the method in at least the majority of cases.[8]

It is possible that some land was taken from individuals, but Odovacer maintained the West's traditional offices and filled them with Roman officials, in this way maintaining cordial relations with the Senate.[9] Although these were, in effect, nominal appointments, as the majority of these positions no longer carried any real power, the Senate appeared to be happy with the recognition of its ancient dignity, however hollow in reality. However these appointments were not recognized in the East, as they did not emanate from Nepos' court.

Yet in one way Odovacer did make a change. It is usually accepted that it was with his takeover that the last regular Roman army units, the guard units of the *scholares* and the *domestici*, were pensioned off, with the position of *comes domesticorum* (Count of the Household) becoming a sinecure office used solely to confer honorary rank.[10] At the same time true military ranks, rather than those given as honorary positions, were reserved for Odovacer's barbarian supporters.

In one case, though, Odovacer made an exception: he created a new financial official, named either *vice dominus* (sub-king) or *comes patrimonii* (Count of the Inheritance), who was usually a Goth and whose task was to supply funds for the king's own personal use, especially with regards to donatives to the army. The money came from lands taxed specifically for this purpose.[11]

Yet, despite the precautions against an Eastern invasion, Odovacer knew that the only thing that would secure his position was to ensure that as many of his frontiers as possible were free from attack. In this respect his main military opponents were Euric in Gaul and Gaiseric in Carthage.

Euric

Over the winter of 476–477 the envoys which passed back and forth between East and West debating Odovacer's political status had another issue for which Odovacer wished imperial guidance. During his 'civil war' against Romulus, the Goths had taken advantage of Roman preoccupation by invading Provence and once more seizing Arles and Marseilles.[12] Odovacer wanted Zeno's guidance on the matter: he had only c. 15,000 men available, not enough to defeat the Goths and simultaneously man strategic defences in Italy.[13] Furthermore, Odovacer had many outstanding internal issues to address and needed the army to remain with him in Italy to ensure the inhabitants acceded to his wishes.

In the circumstances, Odovacer had no option but to enter negotiations with the Goths from a position of extreme weakness. Unable to counter Euric, Odovacer was forced to cede Provence.[14] Sadly, any other provisions in the treaty have been lost. Luckily for Odovacer, he had the full support of the army and so any protest by the Senate was likely to be muted and not result in overt political antagonism. In addition, Zeno responded by giving Imperial sanction to the Treaty.

Euric was now far and away the most powerful of the German kings, his only rival being Gaiseric in Carthage. Sidonius goes so far as to say that:

> Scant leisure has the King even for himself ... we see in his courts the blue-eyed Saxon, ... [the] aged Sygambrian warrior, ... the Herulian, ... the Burgundian, ... the Ostrogoth, ... [the] Roman, [and] the Parthian Arsacid.
>
> *Sidonius Apollinaris 9.5.*

Although the rhetoric goes a little far, it is clear that Euric was now recognized as the dominant political figure in the West, a fact which may have been more than a little galling to the Senate in Rome. Although it is possible that as part of the treaty with Odovacer and Zeno Euric may have accepted that he was only in control of the conquered territories 'in agreement with' (and therefore technically subordinate to) Rome, the reality was obvious to all.

In the circumstances, and virtually abandoned by Rome, the Burgundians had little choice but to come to terms with Euric. On the other hand, further north the Franks and Syagrius retained their complete independence. If not earlier, Euric would cement alliances with the Heruli, the Warni, and the Thuringians – tribes on the far side of the Franks – helping protect the Goths from the Frankish threat by simultaneously threatening the Frankish rear.[15] Yet at this point Euric was far more concerned with cementing his rule in the south of Gaul and in Hispania.[16] For example, and possibly only in frontier regions, in order to forestall rebellion he put in place roadblocks in order to question messengers about their business.[17]

By contrast, at the time of his death in 484 the whole of the northern Iberian Peninsula, except the Suevian kingdom in the north-west, and possibly the Vascones, were entirely under his dominion. Yet even prior to his death slowly the power of the Franks continued to grow and before long Euric was being forced into a more defensive policy, helping to protect his neighbours, including the Burgundians, against the expanding Franks.[18]

Gaiseric

Alongside the treaty with Euric, Odovacer most desired a treaty with the man who had been the bane of the West since 435: Gaiseric. It would appear that immediately upon his accession Odovacer sent envoys to Gaiseric in the hope of securing peace for his own regime, as the treaty Gaiseric had made with Orestes was now invalid. Since Odovacer became the ruler of Italy in August 476 and the sailing season ended in November it quickly becomes clear that Odovacer was an astute politician with a grip on the realities of his situation: before the end of the year a deal was struck between Odovacer and Gaiseric.[19]

The details of the Treaty are unknown, the only 'specific' information being the testimony of Victor of Vita:

> Sicily, he [Gaiseric] later conceded to Odovacer, the King of Italy, by tributary right. At fixed times Odovacer paid tribute to the Vandals as to his lords; nevertheless, they kept back some part of the island for themselves.
> *Victor Vitensis*, Historia Persecutionis Africanae *1.14.*

As usual, the ambiguity of the phrasing has confused historians. It is sometimes claimed that prior to the treaty the Vandals had claimed the whole of the island for themselves and that in order to regain the lost territory Odovacer was forced to pay tribute.

On the other hand, it must be remembered that Victor was writing in the context of Vandal Africa and so it is likely that he is repeating the propaganda as presented by Gaiseric and Huneric. It is far more likely that earlier Gaiseric had captured the city of Lilybaeum but little else, and this is the territory retained by the Vandals.

In this context the treaty would fit into the context of fifth-century Romano-barbarian politics, specifically with relation to the political arch-master Gaiseric: Gaiseric was demanding and receiving recognition of his conquests and extracting 'tribute' in order to halt his attacks on the West – specifically Italy. This would allow Gaiseric to consolidate his Empire in preparation for his expected death: after all, he was now in his mid-late eighties.[20] The timing was perfect for both Odovacer and Gaiseric: on January 25, 477, Gaiseric, the Vandal who had for so long tormented the Empire, died. His son Huneric inherited his kingdom and the Roman Empire breathed a huge sigh of relief.

477

Despite his apparent superiority in Italy, Odovacer was not to have everything his own way without opposition. On 11 July 477:[21]

> At the very outset of his reign [he] slew Count Brachila at Ravenna that he might inspire fear of himself among the Romans.
> *Jordanes*, Getica *243.*

Since Brachila was obviously a 'barbarian', the suggestion that he was killed 'to inspire fear among the Romans' is odd, and is contradicted to some degree by other sources who give the name as Bravila and suggest that he may have been in 'revolt' against Odovacer.[22] These disagreements are confusing, but a compromise solution has been suggested: Brachila may have been closer to the Senate than Odovacer, and so the Senate may have supported him in opposition to Odovacer.[23] If true, this would explain how Brachila's death would inspire fear of Odovacer among the Romans. Whatever the truth, it is clear that Odovacer did not have the full support of the Senate and of the barbarian troops at this early stage.

478

This hypothesis is supported by events in the following year. In 478 a *vir nobilis* (noble man; a sign of rank) named Adaric also rebelled against Odovacer's rule. He was quickly defeated and executed, along with his mother and brother, on 19 November 478.[24] Although both 'rebellions' were quickly quashed, Odovacer was facing opposition to his rule. Having said that, from this point on there is no indication in the sources that there were any further rebellions, so it is likely that the speed with which he disposed of Brachila and Adaric encouraged other potential rebels to think twice before raising the standard of revolt.

Politically, external events also favoured Odovacer. It quickly became clear that Huneric did not have the political or military ability of his father Gaiseric, and, possibly thanks to his marriage to Eudocia (daughter of Emperor Valentinian III), his reign began with a policy of appeasement. Soon after his accession he entered negotiations with the East and the legacy of Olybrius' ties to the Vandals surfaced when, in 478:

> Ambassadors came to Byzantium from Carthage, under the leadership of Alexander, the guardian of Olybrius' wife [Placidia]. He formerly had been sent there by Zeno with the agreement of Placidia herself. The ambassadors said that Huneric had honestly set himself up as a friend of the emperor, and so loved all things Roman that he renounced everything that he had formerly claimed from the public revenues and also the other moneys that Leo had earlier seized from his wife [Eudocia]… He gave thanks that the emperor had honoured the wife of Olybrius…
>
> *Malchus, fr. 13.*

In effect Huneric withdrew the last Vandal claims over the patrimony of Valentinian III (see Chapter Eight) and, despite his Arianism, accepted the appointment of a Catholic archbishop in Carthage.[25] In addition, he also allowed some of the property appropriated by Gaiseric to be returned to the original owners.[26] Although the religious policies would soon be reversed, he would become increasingly involved with internal politics rather than attempting to emulate his father in the persecution of the Empire.

In contrast to this pacific policy, it has been claimed that with Gaiseric's death the treaty was declared void and the Vandals under Huneric resumed their raids.[27] Yet Victor's statement that 'at fixed times Odovacer paid tribute to the Vandals' implies that Huneric recognized the continuation of the terms agreed with his father.

With the signing of the two treaties with Euric and Huneric, Odovacer managed to bring a little stability to the West. The treaties had given to Euric and Gaiseric vast areas of the Western Empire, meaning that at this point the West only consisted of Italy, (Dalmatia), most of Sicily, and 'what remained of Raetia and Noricum'.[28] At least part of Noricum Ripenses remained outside of Odovacer's control, as shortly after his takeover a man named Primenius, who had associated himself with Orestes, fled there for safety, and the fact that the barbarian leaders in the area were now making treaties with local towns, not the Empire, indicates that Roman control of the area was over.[29] The Goths were cementing their grip on Northern Hispania and Southern Gaul, whilst the rest of Gaul was held by the Burgundians, the Franks, with an enclave of 'Roman' rule in Soissons, and the Vandals had large parts of North Africa and the western Mediterranean Islands. Britain had long since passed from Roman control. These areas never returned to Imperial control, although, acting theoretically as an appointee of the East, King Theoderic I of Italy (who succeeded Odovacer – see below) did later manage to retrieve the province of Provence from the Goths in Gaul and joined it to his kingdom in Italy.

480

Between 478 and 480 the uproar surrounding Odovacer's installation in power in Italy appears to have died down and nothing is recorded in 479. However on 25 April or 9 May 480, at his villa near Salona in Dalmatia, Julius Nepos was murdered by his *comes* Ovida and a man named Viator.[30] According to Malchus the former Emperor Glycerius, now serving as the Bishop of Salona, was also involved in Nepos' murder.[31] Although this is possible, several alternate sources mention Nepos' death but none record any involvement by Glycerius. Yet based on Malchus' claim it has been suggested that, as a reward for his part in the assassination, Glycerius was appointed Bishop of Milan by Odovacer. Sadly, the evidence for this is insecure and so this must be seen as possible but unlikely.[32]

Upon Nepos' death Ovida, who was possibly a Goth, seized Dalmatia for himself, almost certainly hoping to succeed to the position owned by Marcellinus, and Nepos before his elevation to Emperor: there would be little chance of him succeeding Nepos as titular emperor of the West as he was a barbarian and Zeno would not have supported him after his murder of Nepos.[33]

From later evidence it would appear that Zeno did not mourn for his nominal Western colleague and there is no indication from the sources that he took steps to avenge Nepos. On the other hand, Odovacer saw Nepos' death as a chance to extend his realm. Despite the fact that Nepos had not dared to set foot in Italy during Odovacer's supremacy, Odovacer had paid lip service to Nepos as the Western emperor and now acted to punish the men who had killed him.

481

Gathering his forces, in the following year Odovacer invaded Dalmatia.[34] Ovida also mustered his forces and opposed Odovacer, but to little avail: he was defeated and captured by Odovacer, before being executed on either 27 November or 9 December 481.[35] The territory of Dalmatia was added to the Royal *Patrimonium*, greatly enhancing Odovacer's financial strength and enabling him to reward his warriors for their work.[36] Furthermore, the conquest of Dalmatia enhanced Odovacer's prestige and may even have encouraged the Senate in Rome to think that it was still possible to resurrect the frontiers of the old Empire.

It was not to be. Probably at the same time as they heard of Nepos' death:

> The Gauls of the West revolted against Odovacer, [and] both they and Odovacer sent an embassy to Zeno. He preferred to support Odovacer.
>
> *Candidus, fr. 1.*

Sadly, who these 'Gauls of the West' are is not reported, and so it is necessary to resort to speculation. Although it is possible that Euric was playing political games in the hope of having Odovacer removed and of taking his place, the fact that Candidus mentions 'Romans' implies that this is not the case. The same implication holds for possible envoys from both the Franks and the Burgundians. Therefore the most likely source of the envoys is from Syagrius, the son of the last 'correctly instated' *magister militum per Gallias*. Syagrius may have suggested to Zeno that his own installation as *patricius* in Italy, if not as emperor, would bring parts of Gaul back under direct imperial control, as well as bringing allies in the form of the Franks to hold Euric in check.

Tempting as the offer may have been, Zeno was unable at the time to send direct military aid to either Odovacer or 'the Gauls' as he was in conflict with a man named Illus (see below). Further, any overthrow of Odovacer would negate the treaties with the Goths and the Vandals, with the possible resumption of barbarian attacks. In addition, if Huneric was to follow the example of his father Zeno could expect raids on the Eastern, as well as the Western, Empire. This was, to say the least, undesirable.

As a consequence, Zeno accepted Odovacer's regime in Italy, and from this point onwards Odovacer continued to appoint Romans to the traditional imperial posts, including those of the patriciate and the consulate.[37] The latter, whilst not officially recognized in the East, 'by a gentleman's agreement' were to receive the codicils from Zeno and so were entered in the *fasti*, the official lists of the consuls.[38] On the other hand, effective military posts remained in the hands of the barbarians. In return, Odovacer issued coins with the image of Zeno and displayed Zeno's portrait in Rome.[39]

Later Years

With Odovacer in effective control of the rump of the Western Empire, and with the Goths and Vandals holding to their agreements, for the next few years the sources become quiet on events in Italy. Yet there are a few events recorded elsewhere in what had once been the Roman Empire.

484

In 484 in the city of Arles the Gothic King Euric died of natural causes and on 29 December 484 was succeeded by his son Alaric (II).[40] The succession of a young, unproven king could be seen as being a major problem, but fortunately for the Goths in 481 Childeric, King of the Franks, had also died, leaving his 15-year-old son Clovis as his heir.[41] For the next twenty-three years the two kings would be in conflict in their desire to control Gaul, with Alaric heading a coalition aimed at keeping the Franks in check.

The Revolt of Illus[42]

Meanwhile, away from the West, events in the East were conspiring against Odovacer. One of Zeno's most powerful officials was a man named Illus. Made *patricius* in 477, almost immediately relations with the imperial family soured when, after a failed attempt on his life, he learned that Verina, Zeno's mother-in-law, was behind the plot. Zeno recalled Illus to the capital, but Illus refused to attend the emperor unless Verina was given into his custody. Arrangements made, he returned to Constantinople and attended trials in the city before, in 480, he defended the city against a group of Ostrogoths led by a man named Theoderic Strabo (not to be confused with Theoderic the Amal – see below).

In late 481 Illus was appointed *magister militum per Orientem* (Master of the Troops in the East). This was after he had quarrelled with the Empress Ariadne, who had demanded the release of her mother, Verina, and so may have been an appointment simply to remove him from court. Leaving for the East, relations between Illus and Zeno continued their downhill trend until in 484 Illus openly rebelled, sending envoys to potential allies such as the Persians and the Armenians. Unfortunately for Odovacer, he was a recipient of one of these envoys. Despite Odovacer refusing to help Illus, once Zeno heard of the exchanges he lost confidence in Odovacer and began to plot his downfall.[43] Furthermore, he refused to accept Odovacer's nominations for the post of Western Consul for both 486 and 487, reinforcing the suggestion that Zeno was doubtful of Odovacer's loyalty.[44]

486 Clovis and Syagrius

Whilst relations between Ravenna and Constantinople were deteriorating, in Gaul the Kingdom of the Franks was beginning its rise. In 486 Clovis, now around 20 years of age, launched an attack on Syagrius in Soissons. Gregory of Tours describes events surrounding the Battle of Soissons:

> After these events Childeric died and Clovis his son reigned in his stead. In the fifth year of his reign Syagrius, king of the Romans, son of Aegidius, had his seat in the city of Soissons which Aegidius, who has been mentioned before, once held. And Clovis came against him with Ragnachar, his kinsman,

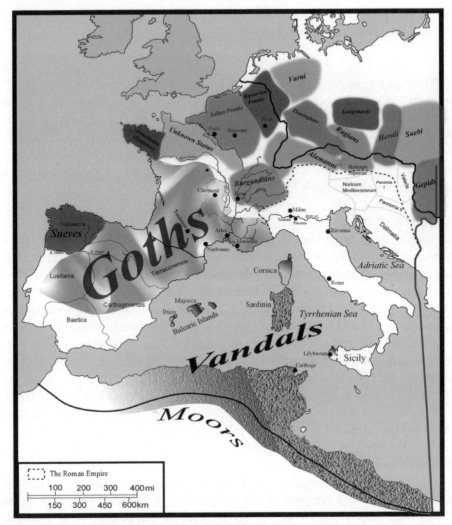

Map 22: Odovacer's Empire at its greatest extent (c. 486)

because he used to possess the kingdom, and demanded that they make ready a battlefield. And Syagrius did not delay nor was he afraid to resist. And so they fought against each other and Syagrius, seeing his army crushed, turned his back and fled swiftly to king Alaric at Toulouse.

Gregory Turensis 1.27.

Ragnachar was the leader of one of the Frankish tribes based around Cambrai. There are two possible reasons for the claim that he had once held Soissons. One is that his predecessor had controlled the city for a short period, but the fact that Aegidius had taken control of the region from an early date suggests that this is unlikely. The other is that this is a spurious claim made by Clovis to justify his attack, hoping that the claim would deter other tribes – and especially the Goths – from supporting Syagrius. On reflection, the second of these is more likely.

Also involved in the battle was a Frankish leader named Chararic:

> When he [Clovis] ... fought with Syagrius this Chararic had been summoned to help Clovis, but stood at a distance, aiding neither side, but awaiting the outcome, in order to form a league of friendship with him to whom victory came.
>
> *Gregory Turensis 2.41.*

After the Battle of Vouillé in 507 Clovis would depose Chararic for this action.[45]

Clovis now took control of territory down to the River Seine and took up residence at Soissons. This would make sense: after all, Soissons was an Imperial city and had not suffered too much in the years of warfare prior to the battle, so it is likely that much of its Roman infrastructure remained intact. In addition, the remaining buildings may have struck awe into many of the envoys that would arrive from the barbarian hinterland.

Although the evidence for these events is sparse, and contrary to common thought, it is possible that he did not conquer the land bordering the River Seine for several more years. With Syagrius' removal the last part of Gaul ruled by a general with true Roman pedigree was conquered by the barbarians.

Concerning Syagrius, Gregory also states:

> And Clovis sent to Alaric to send him back, otherwise he was to know that Clovis would make war on him for his refusal. And Alaric was afraid that he would incur the anger of the Franks on account of Syagrius, seeing it is the fashion of the Goths to be terrified, and he surrendered him in chains to Clovis' envoys. And Clovis took him and gave orders to put him under guard, and when he had got his kingdom he directed that he be executed secretly.
>
> *Gregory Turensis 1.27.*

The story that Syagrius was quickly surrendered to the Franks by Alaric II is generally accepted as fact, yet, as at least one historian has noted, the claim is dubious in several respects.[46] The first is that there is no evidence that Clovis took control of the territory up to the River Loire at this date, and so any threat of war would be at once removed. Another is that the tale 'in no way reflected the actual balance of power': Clovis was still merely the leader of a part of the Frankish tribes and it would only be later in the fifth century that he would be able to command enough men to defeat the Goths.

As a result, it is possibly better to see Syagrius living in exile at the Gothic court for many years. Only after the Franks had conquered the area bordering the Loire, and Theoderic the Amal had conquered Italy from Odovacer – shortly afterwards marrying the sister of Clovis in an attempt to establish friendly relations with the Franks – was he handed over.[47] This was probably after 493, when the demands from Clovis mentioned above arrived. By this time Theoderic and Clovis were related by marriage and Alaric would have been hoping to forestall a Frank-Ostrogothic alliance against him.

487–488

In Italy, when Odovacer had overthrown Romulus in 476 he appears to have had some support from the tribe of the Rugi. These peoples had earlier settled to the north of the Danube but at some point in the mid-fifth century their power had crossed the river and was then felt in Noricum.[48] It seems that Zeno's newfound distrust for Odovacer led him to seek alliances, and the Rugi were one of the tribes targeted. Their king was named Feletheus, but Feletheus' nephew, a man named Ferderuchus, was a supporter of Odovacer and when he heard of the proposed alliance he opposed it. As a result, Feletheus had Ferderuchus executed.

Learning of Ferderuchus' death and of the Rugians' plans to take up arms against him, Odovacer decided upon a pre-emptive invasion. He gathered all of his forces and late in the campaign season of 487 he launched a major attack on the Rugi. Forewarned, Feletheus gathered his own forces and the two joined battle beyond the Danube. In mid-December the two armies met in a close-fought engagement, and eventually Odovacer's troops won the day: Feletheus was captured and taken back to Ravenna, where he was later executed.[49] His son Fredericus escaped. Over winter Odovacer conducted 'mopping-up' operations in the region before taking the booty and a large number of captives to Italy, the captives being settled in the south of the peninsula. Odovacer sent some of the spoils to Zeno, probably to prove to Zeno that he was innocent of all suspicions, and in the hope of averting further conflict.[50] The arrival of the spoils, probably in mid-488, appears to have restored Zeno's belief that Odovacer was loyal once more, as in 489 he accepted Odovacer's nominee as Western Consul.[51]

The Destruction of the Rugi

Yet this was not the end of the Rugian problem. At some time early in 488 Odovacer learned that Fredericus, the son of Feletheus, had returned to claim his father's throne: 'At once he dispatched a great army, under his brother Onoulfus; before whom Fredericus fled again.'[52] Once again, the lands of the Rugi were devastated, and it would appear that the remnants of the people followed Fredericus, who travelled to Moesia and joined Theodoric the Amal.[53] Not long after the Langobards (Lombards) would move into the vacuum that had been created.

At this point Odovacer realized that defending Noricum was stretching his manpower beyond reason: 'Onoulfus, however, at his brother's command ordered all the Romans to migrate to Italy' – in this venture being aided by Pierius, *comes domesticorum* – whereat 'all the provincials ... abandoned the towns on the banks of the Danube and were allotted the various abodes of their exile through the different districts of Italy'.[54] The Empire had resumed its territorial decline.

Theoderic the Amal

Furthermore, at some point in 488 events in the East had occurred that would again have severe repercussions in the West in 489, but this time of a far more serious

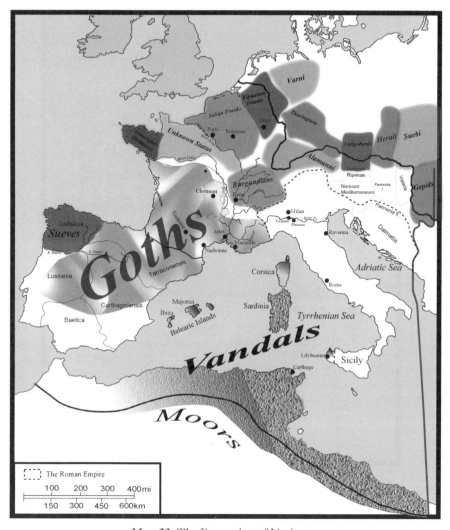

Map 23: The Evacuation of Noricum.

nature. To understand these it is necessary to analyse the history of the East in a little more depth, a course that will also help in understanding Zeno's reluctance to become involved in Western politics.

The story revolves around three men: the Emperor Zeno; Theoderic the Amal (of the Amal 'dynasty'); and Theoderic Strabo ('the Squinter'), the two latter being leaders of separate Ostrogothic forces in the Balkans.*

Born c. 454, in 461/2 Theoderic was sent as a hostage to Constantinople. For the next ten years he received a Roman (probably Greek) education and was released in

---

* For the sake of simplicity from here onwards the name 'Theoderic' will be used for Theoderic the Amal and 'Strabo' for Theoderic Strabo.

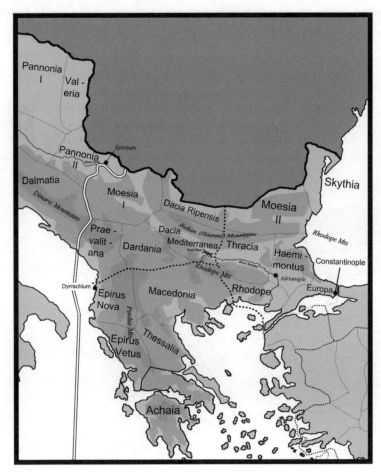

Map 24: The East.

471/2.[55] Shortly after, aged 18, without his father's knowledge he led an army of less than 6,000 men across the Danube and defeated the Sarmatians, before capturing the city of Singidunum (Belgrade) – which he refused to return to the Empire.[56]

Despite these victories, the Goths were struggling to survive in Pannonia:

> The [Ostro-] Goths began to lack food and clothing ... so ... approached their king Thiudimer and ... begged him to lead forth his army. He summoned his brother [Vidimer] and, after casting lots, bade him go into the country of Italy ... saying that he himself as the mightier would go to the East.
>
> *Jordanes*, Getica *283*.

As noted in Chapter Fourteen, Vidimer led his men towards Italy, himself dying on the way. Theodemer, along with Theoderic, moved East, where the emperor granted them seven towns in Macedonia to settle. Then, in 474 Theodemer died and Theoderic, aged 20, succeeded to the kingdom.[57] At some time before 476 Theoderic had led his people to Moesia Secunda.[58]

Theoderic's counterpart, Strabo, was much older and had been on friendly terms with Constantinople since 459, but in 471 had attacked Constantinople from his base in Thrace to avenge the death of the *magister militum* Aspar at the hands of Emperor Leo.[59] Fortunately for the East, in 473 peace was agreed under the terms of which Strabo had received a 'subsidy', recognition as leader of his people, and was made *magister militum*.[60]

On the accession of Zeno in 474, Strabo again revolted and lost his post as *magister militum*. When Basiliscus made his bid for the throne Strabo used his men to support the usurper and when Zeno fled in January 475 Strabo regained his post as *magister militum*.[61] Sadly for Strabo, almost immediately Basiliscus removed him again and appointed his own nephew, Armutus, as *magister militum*. At this point Strabo threw his support behind Zeno, who returned to power in August 476. However, this was not the only support Zeno received at this time: Theoderic also helped Zeno in his recovery of the throne.[62] As a reward, Theoderic was made *patricius*, *magister militum*, and may also have undergone a 'form of adoption' by Zeno.[63]

Naturally, this was displeasing to Strabo and in 478, after extended negotiations with Zeno, he again revolted.[64] Theoderic was sent against Strabo, the plan being that when he reached the Haemus Mountains – now known as the Balkan Mountains – the (unnamed) *magister militum per Illyricum* would join him with 2,000 cavalry and 10,000 infantry, and after crossing the mountains he would be joined by another 20,000 infantry and 6,000 cavalry in the region of Adrianople. When he arrived at the foot of Mount Sondis, which is otherwise unknown by this name, none of the reinforcements appeared. At this point his troops forced him to ally with Strabo against Zeno.[65] Naturally, he lost his position as *magister militum*.[66] Theoderic now led his troops against Rhodope, however Strabo quickly reached an agreement with Zeno, and took Theoderic's old title of *magister militum*.[67]

479

In the following year Theoderic attacked Greece, after which he also entered into negotiations with Zeno, but these had not come to fruition before Theoderic seized Dyrrachium.[68] In the meantime, Strabo had supported two men, Procopius Anthemius and Marcianus, in their rebellion against Zeno. Naturally, when this failed he was removed from his post and escaped from Constantinople, after which he joined Theoderic and attacked Thrace.[69]

The Death of Strabo

Nothing is known of events in 480, but in 481 Strabo launched an attack on Constantinople, and when this failed he attempted to cross the sea to Bithynia, a plan which also failed. He fell back and regrouped his forces before attacking Greece, during the course of which he was killed in a bizarre accident, falling off his horse onto a spear.[70] He was succeeded by two of his brothers, who are sadly not named, and by his son Recitach in a three-way rule. However Recitach soon had his two uncles killed and thereafter ruled alone.[71]

Theoderic and Italy

The death of Strabo did not affect Theoderic's relations with Zeno, and in 482 he plundered Macedonia and Thessaly.[72] This appeared to be the last straw for Zeno and in the following year a deal was struck whereby Theoderic regained the post of *magister militum*, and was also announced as consul for 484.[73] As part of the agreement it is possible that Zeno induced Theoderic to kill his cousin Recitach, who was murdered in Bonophatianae, a suburb of Constantinople.[74] However in some ways this may be unlikely: the death of Recitach allowed Theoderic to absorb at least some of Recitach's followers into his own army, and Zeno would have known that this would be the likely outcome. Zeno would not have wanted to replace two warring Gothic factions with an enlarged army led by an aggressive and capable leader. It is far more likely that Theoderic simply saw the opportunity of removing a rival and took it.

As consul, it is possible that Theoderic fought against the rebel Illus, although the sources disagree on this.[75] Yet as usual the agreement between Theoderic and Zeno was not to last: in 486 Theoderic again rebelled, and again ravaged Thrace.[76] In 487 Theoderic led his forces against Constantinople and, although he failed to capture the city the pressure paid off and negotiations with Zeno were resumed. It was probably after his return from this campaign that he was joined by Fredericus, the heir to the Rugian 'throne', after Fredericus' defeat by Odovacer's brother Onoulphus.

The Treaty of 488 that resulted has confused scholars ever since. This is largely because there are at least two distinct traditions in the sources. It is agreed that as part of the deal Theoderic was to lead his troops to Italy and attempt to remove Odovacer from his position of power. What is not agreed is which of the two men the instigator was. For example, the *Anonymous Valesiani* and Procopius claim that the initiative belonged to Zeno, who desired to rid himself of Odovacer.[77] On the other hand, writers such as Ennodius in his panegyric to Theoderic and Jordanes in his *Getica* (History of the Goths) claim that the plan belonged to Theoderic.[78]

The fact that earlier that year Odovacer had sent some of the spoils taken in his war against the Rugi to Zeno and had been granted the consulship for 489 in return can, when taken in context, be used for both arguments.[79] Yet without doubt early in the year Zeno had – for the moment – resolved his differences with Odovacer in order to focus his attention on Theoderic, who remained the main threat in the Balkans. Therefore Zeno may not have been the instigator.

If the idea is not attributed to Zeno, then it must have been Theoderic's. His motive may be found in the notice in Ennodius' *Vita Epiphania* that, following Fredericus' arrival, Theoderic was determined to avenge the execution of the Rugian King Feletheus and his wife by Odovacer.[80] What is even more likely is that the claim was used simply as a pretext by Theoderic to justify to Zeno his desire to invade Italy: continuously short of provisions in the Balkans, and needing supplies

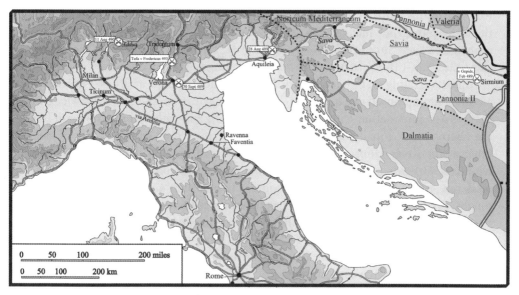

Map 25: Theoderic's invasion of Italy.

from the Empire whenever possible, Italy would appeal to Theoderic as a place where he would be safer from Zeno's political machinations, and the peninsula would easily supply his followers with all of their needs.

As a result of these deliberations it is best to assume that the plan was Theoderic's and that Zeno agreed to it. It was a win–win situation: he would rid himself of the Ostrogothic nuisance that had plagued his reign since it began; he would remove at least one barbarian leader he couldn't trust; and it was certain that the forces of both Odovacer and Theoderic would be greatly weakened by the war.[81]

The Invasion of Italy

In mid 488 Theoderic began the preparations for his attack on Italy, gathering what supplies were available, before late in 488 beginning the march.[82] Not all of the Ostrogothic people joined the attack, but included in Theoderic's forces were the remnant of the Rugians led by Fredericus, and it is likely that there were Huns and Romans, as well as small groups of other peoples, who joined the move.[83]

489

In Italy, and probably as reward for his long and loyal service, on 18 March 489 Odovacer gave estates worth 690 *solidi* per annum to Pierius, the *comes domesticorum*, details of which are contained in a papyrus document purported to be the first document from a 'king' of Italy that has survived.[84] Pierius was not long to survive the gift.

In the meantime, Theoderic was advancing along the Danube to Sirmium, after which the Ostrogoths entered the territory of the Gepids, who opposed their move.[85] At the River Ulca (Vulca) in February 489 a battle was fought and the Ostrogoths were victorious, with Trapstila, King of the Gepids, being killed.[86] Thankfully for the Ostrogoths, they managed to capture the Gepids' storehouses and in this way replenished their supplies.[87] Shortly afterwards, Theoderic gained another victory, this time against the Sarmatians, before continuing towards Italy.[88]

Almost certainly on or before 1 April 489 Odovacer became aware of Theoderic's advance: he appointed a man named Tufa to be *magister militum* (so acknowledging that his accommodation with the East had ended), and gathered his troops to face the Ostrogoths.[89] Finally, on 28 August 489 the two armies came in sight of each other at the River Izonso, where Odovacer suffered his first defeat.[90] He quickly withdrew to Verona, and on 27 September made a fortified camp on a plain of moderate extent before the city. Theodoric pursued him and a second battle was fought, probably on 30 September. The outcome was the same and Odovacer fled to Ravenna.[91] Theoderic declined to follow Odovacer, instead entering Milan.

At this point large numbers of Odovacer's troops surrendered to Theoderic, including the *magister militum* Tufa.[92] Shortly after, Tufa was ordered to take a large force towards Ravenna, laying siege to Faventia (Faenza). However he now disavowed his allegiance to Theoderic and declared his re-allegiance to Odovacer.[93]

In 490 Theoderic moved to Ticinum and it was here that Odovacer, probably reinforced by Tufa, caught Theoderic and laid siege to the town. However, in the intervening period Theoderic had not been idle and had arranged a treaty of support with Alaric II, King of the Goths in Gaul. A Gothic force arrived outside the city and Odovacer was forced to raise the siege. Theoderic pursued Odovacer and near to the River Addua, on 11 August 490, defeated Odovacer in a third battle, during the course of which Pierius, Odovacer's *comes domesticorum*, was killed.[94] After the battle Odovacer retreated to Ravenna and Theoderic returned to Ticinum before gathering his troops and advancing to Ravenna, where he was to lay siege to Odovacer for the next three years.[95] Tufa remained at large in the north of Italy, where he appears to have become independent, striking an agreement and working with Fredericus, King of the Rugi.[96]

Whilst the siege was ongoing, on 9 April 491 the Emperor Zeno died, probably of either dysentery or epilepsy – although the legend survived that he was instead buried alive and his wife refused to allow anyone to open the sarcophagus.[97] His nominal replacement was his brother, Longinus, but Zeno's widow supported a man named Anastasius, who thus became the next Eastern emperor.

At an unspecified point during the siege Odovacer announced that his son Thela was now Caesar.[98] Analysis of this event usually concentrates upon the interpretation that Odovacer was aiming to 'secure his power by reinforcing his support for Roman Imperial institutions', and that by using the post of Caesar, Odovacer was hoping to avoid alienating his supporters in Italy by straying too far from tradition.[99]

Although a possibility, the concept that the Roman Senate would accept the nomination of a barbarian to a rank formerly reserved solely for Romans is slightly odd. It would seem safer to assume that in this case either Odovacer or John of Antioch have used the term Caesar, earlier used to signify the heir to the imperial throne, solely to signify that Odovacer's son Thela was the heir to Odovacer.[100]

Later, Ennodius' Panegyric to Theoderic was to claim that if Odovacer was attempting to gain Senatorial support in this way, it failed, as Theoderic was by then seen as acting on behalf of Zeno and thus of being supported by senators conforming to 'constitutional legitimacy'.[101] Furthermore, it is claimed that Thela's promotion as Caesar was seen as proof that Odovacer was simply a tyrant, not a representative of Zeno.[102] Unfortunately, although almost certainly correct, the argument is inconclusive as Ennodius was following the propaganda of Theoderic, who obviously posed as the legitimate ruler of Italy and as being supported in his attack by Zeno.

In the meantime, the siege continued. Finally, in 493 events in the north of Italy may have marked the end of Odovacer's resistance. Tufa, Odovacer's *magister militum*, had been free to conduct attacks throughout Northern Italy, in the company of the Rugian King Fredericus. However at this point Tufa and Fredericus quarrelled. The source of the argument is unknown, but, given the location of what happened next it is possibly related to Theoderic's siege of Odovacer. A battle was fought between Tridentum (Trento) and Verona, during the course of which Tufa was killed.[103] Odovacer appointed a man named Livila, who is otherwise unknown, to take Tufa's place.[104]

Although speculation, it is possible that Tufa was Odovacer's last hope for the raising of the siege. Whether true or not, Theoderic and Odovacer finally opened negotiations and an agreement was reached whereby the two men would share the rule of Italy. As proof of his trustworthiness, Odovacer gave Theoderic his son Thela as a hostage.[105] However, and possibly at a banquet organized to celebrate the peace, Theoderic killed Odoacer with his own hands.[106] John of Antioch claims instead that ten days after the agreement Odovacer was at Theoderic's headquarters, when:

> Two of [Theoderic's] henchmen came forward as though suppliants and grasped Odovacer's hands. Therewith those hidden in ambush in the rooms on either side rushed out with their swords. They were panic-stricken at the sight of their victim, and when they did not attack Odovacer, Theoderic himself rushed forward and struck him with a sword on the collarbone. When he [Odovacer] asked 'Where is God?' Theoderic answered, 'This is what you did to my friends.' The fatal blow pierced Odovacer's body as far as the hip, and they say Theoderic exclaimed, 'There certainly wasn't a bone in this wretched fellow.' Sending the body outside … he buried it in a stone coffin.
>
> *John of Antioch*, fr. 214a, *trans. Gordon 182–3.*

Thela was not executed, but exiled to Gaul. He later escaped and returned to Italy – possibly hoping to secure support to overthrow Theoderic – but was captured and this time killed.[107] Odovacer's brother Onoulphus was also executed.[108] Theoderic killed any of Odovacer's federates who had remained hostile and gave their land to his own followers.[109] As with the rest of the West, Italy was now under the control of a barbarian with no previous service in, and therefore owing no loyalty to, the Western Empire.

Analysis

The date of 476 and Odovacer's removal of Romulus Augustus from power is cited as the date for the end of the Western Empire by the vast majority of modern works, wherein Odovacer is the break with Roman tradition. This is largely due to the fact that Odovacer did not place his own nominee on the throne, instead paying hollow homage to Nepos in Dalmatia, on condition – or in the knowledge that – Nepos would not set foot in Italy. To emphasize the point that Nepos was not wanted Odovacer refused to use the title of *patricius*, simply calling himself *rex*.[110]

Furthermore, the disbanding of the Roman troops and the fact that Odovacer's barbarian followers now had loyalty only to their king marks another significant break with the past. Odovacer was their leader solely because of his title of *rex*, not, as in previous years, on his having the title of *patricius*.[111] The 'reign' of Odovacer marks the last time that the master of the West was a Western citizen, or had served in Western armies prior to the assumption of the role of *patricius*. The fact that Odovacer was promoted by his own barbarian troops, combined with the fact that there is no evidence that he owed direct allegiance to the Senate, other than promoting its members to sinecures which held little or no power, has most commonly resulted in his time as commander being seen as the ultimate break with the 'imperial' past. Therefore the date of 476, and the deposition of Romulus, is usually interpreted as being the end of the Roman Empire in the West.

Clearly his rule marked a fundamental change in the West, but the ensuing confusion surrounding his ambiguous constitutional position remains a burning question to modern historians, a factor not helped by contradictory traditions. The Western *Excerpta Valesiana* gives Odovacer a reign of 'between thirteen and fourteen years'. Sadly, this number can be used to fulfil two different assumptions: that his reign began either in 476 and ended with Theoderic's invasion of 490, or began in 480 and ended with his death in 493.[112] Both of these are valid assumptions, but their implications are widely divergent.

In the East, an often overlooked passage in Theophanes makes a clearer statement:

> For next Odoacer, a Goth by race but brought up in Italy, subdued the Empire with a barbarian army. He, assuming for himself the title of 'Rex' and filling every office according to the ancestral law of the Romans, held power for ten years.
>
> *Theophanes AM 5965.*

A reign of ten years is mirrored by Procopius, clearly showing that as far as the East was concerned Nepos remained ruler until 480, with Odovacer acting merely as *patricius* between 476 and 480. The East did not recognize Odovacer as the official regent, but gave de facto recognition and maintained diplomatic relations with Ravenna, even if only with the hope that at some point Nepos would return to Italy and resume the throne.[113]

Odovacer was only recognized as in independent control between 480 and 489, at which time Theoderic was 'sent' to replace him, but even then his position was clearly as a barbarian subordinate, along the same lines as the other barbarian leaders such as Theoderic and Strabo.[114] In theory, after 480 or at the latest 493, Zeno was accepted by both East and West as the sole ruler of a reunited Empire.

The fact that Odovacer was able to survive politically, rather than militarily, is often overlooked. Theoretically, the Senate could easily have replaced him by bribing his officers and undermining his men's loyalty with large financial donatives. But, unlike previous 'barbarian' leaders, Odovacer was able to build a personal fortune based upon lands held first in Sicily and then Dalmatia, territory that had been removed from Senatorial control by the Vandals in Sicily, and by Marcellinus and Nepos in Dalmatia.[115] In this way he made himself independent of the Senate, without alienating its members by large land confiscations, and was thus no longer reliant on senatorial support for his regime, although it is almost certain that to some degree the approval of the Senate would remain a factor in his decision making.

Finally, the fact that Odovacer was an Arian is often overlooked. However, if negative evidence is permitted then it is noteworthy that both Ennodius, in his *Vita Epifanius* and his biography of Pope Felix, and the entries in the *Liber Pontificalis*, fail to castigate Odovacer for his oppression of Catholics. That Odovacer ruled for fourteen years (476–490) without any criticism of his rule by church historians suggests that, at least in Italy, his regime was accepted. However, the swift defection of his troops and the rapid transferral of the loyalty of the remaining power bases in Italy from Odovacer to Theoderic imply that, although he managed to rule peacefully and successfully, he never managed to gain the undisputed loyalty of the troops and the citizens to the same degree as had the earlier Aetius or Ricimer. His reign remains one of success, but not unqualified success.

Chapter Seventeen

Conclusion

The Kingmakers

The emperors who ruled during the last three decades are almost wholly shadowy figures hidden by the dominating figures of the Patricians, and, due to his longevity, with only two imperial exceptions that dominating figure is Ricimer. Also thanks to his extended period as *magister militum*, it is almost universally accepted that Ricimer is the man most responsible for the Fall of the West. This is largely due to his presentation as a power-hungry barbarian willing to let the Empire fall into ruin as long as he could install the puppet emperor of his choosing upon the imperial throne in Italy.

Hopefully, the preceding chapters have demonstrated that this impression is based largely upon preconceptions and a superficial analysis of the little evidence that remains. The fact that Ricimer 'ruled' Italy with little in the way of opposition for sixteen years is usually ascribed to the fact that Ricimer had the support of the army, who in turn terrorized the Senate into acquiescence. On the other hand, the same evidence can be used to suggest that Ricimer worked within the politics of the Italian Senate, who were intent more upon preserving their lifestyles in Italy than the preservation of the Empire.

On their own, it is impossible to choose between the two opposed theories of 'dominating warlord' and 'senatorial participant', as both can be used to explain the collapse of the West. Yet there is one further factor that needs to be considered. Over the centuries during which the Empire was in existence it appears to have become a standard belief that any group of people or tribes that acknowledged Roman superiority, whether by force or by negotiation, became subservient to the Empire and were, in effect, part of the *Imperium*. As a result, it becomes clear that the defeats of almost all of the barbarian tribes living 'inside' the Empire throughout the fifth century resulted in the 'restoration' of the territory in which they lived to the Empire. In this way it is possible to declare that as far as the (self-deluding) Senate of Rome was concerned, the only territory lost during the period when Ricimer 'ruled', between 456 and 472, was a small part of Hispania to the Sueves. The 'rebellions' of both Aegidius and Marcellinus would be seen as temporary and having little effect on the Empire overall.

In this context it is possible to see Ricimer as being as successful as Aetius. Neither had control of Africa, yet, like Aetius, and even with a tax base further reduced as territory was granted to outsiders, Ricimer was able to maintain the 'integrity' of the Empire. He managed this even without the safety net of a dynastic emperor to fall back on, relying instead upon the support of the Army and the cooperation of the Senate in his decisions.

In this new environment it is possible to understand Gundobad being unwilling to start a civil war when Nepos invaded. Despite his elevation of Glycerius, Gundobad did not have Ricimer's relationship with either the Army or the Senate, and so could not count on the wholehearted support of the 'West' against the East's nominee. His acceptance of 'exile' in Gaul as the price for peace is understandable, and may also demonstrate that Gundobad, who had not been brought up in the Senatorial tradition, was aware that the Empire was no longer worth fighting for. On the other hand, his pride in the use of his imperial titles attests to the continuing power of the symbolism of Rome.

The reasons behind Orestes' decision to assume power are easily understandable: although appointed by Nepos, Orestes had no loyalty to the Easterner and at the first opportunity rid himself of the unwanted Easterner. The question then remains as to why Orestes did not assume the throne himself. Doubtless he was worried that this would take him away from the army, the real source of power in Italy, and so allow another individual to take control of the troops. As a result, he remained in control of the army and instead elevated his son Romulus. Not only would this mean continued command of the troops, it could also bring into being a new dynasty. Sadly, his refusal to grant the troops land in Italy resulted in them rebelling and his own overthrow. It was now that the West lost its last chance of survival in any meaningful form.

Majorian and Anthemius

There were two emperors who ruled when Ricimer was Patrician who were free from the domination of both the Senate and Ricimer: Majorian and Anthemius.

Majorian was the major exception in Western emperors. Firstly, he was a Westerner himself and had first achieved prominence during the period when Aetius 'ruled' the West. Further, he was of such standing that he could be endorsed as a suitable individual for marriage into the Imperial family. The fact that he was in 'retirement' when Aetius was assassinated and so obviously not involved in the plot resulted in him maintaining the loyalty of the army, with the result that he was an ideal candidate for the throne.

Once upon the throne, and aware of the weaknesses of the Empire, Majorian took steps to rectify the situation. Had these measures been successful, the future of the Empire in some form would have been assured. Sadly, his attempt to reconquer Africa failed and the cost of failure was his execution at the hands of Ricimer.

The case of Anthemius is different in its most important aspects. Although a successful military commander, Anthemius was imposed upon the West by the Eastern emperor. As a consequence, Anthemius brought to the West his Eastern preconceptions concerning how Emperors should be treated, how the Empire should be run, and how the army should be organized. All of these things caused conflict with the Senate, but were not the immediate cause of his downfall.

The rebellion against his rule was the result of two interconnected factors. One was his failure to gain the support of the army. The other was his quarrel with Ricimer, who had the support of both the army and, due to Anthemius' actions, the majority of the Senate. Only when both Ricimer and the Senate had been pushed beyond endurance did the civil war occur.

It is interesting to note that both Majorian and Anthemius were deposed after the failure of their respective campaigns against the Vandals. Although the defeat of their campaigns may have had a bearing on their regimes, it should be remembered that, although Majorian's death came shortly after his expensive failure to retake Africa, Anthemius' campaign was financed largely by the East and it was largely Eastern troops that bore the brunt of the defeat. This accounts for Anthemius continuing to reign for four years after the campaign had failed. It was his domestic (Senate) and personal (Ricimer) policies rather than military incompetence that were the cause of his overthrow. When Anthemius was killed the West lost the support of the East and so lost its last chance of survival in any recognizable form.

The Fall of the West

Many explanations have been put forward by modern authors for the Fall of the Western Roman Empire. In 1984 a list of 210 of these reasons was published, with the author wanting to demonstrate the sheer variety of causes under consideration, from the obvious to the ridiculous.[1]

Abolition of gods	Abolition of rights	Absence of character
Absolutism	Agrarian question	Agrarian slavery
Anarchy	Anti-Germanism	Apathy
Aristocracy	Asceticism	Attack of the Germans
Attack of the Huns	Attack of riding nomads	Backwardness in science
Bankruptcy	Barbarization	Bastardization
Blockage of land by large landholders	Blood poisoning	Bolshevization
Bread and circuses	Bureaucracy	Byzantinism
Capillarite sociale	Capitalism	Capitals, change of
Caste system	Celibacy	Centralization
Childlessness	Christianity	Citizenship, granting of
Civil war	Climatic deterioration	Communism
Complacency	Concatenation of misfortunes	Conservatism
Corruption	Cosmopolitanism	Crisis of legitimacy
Culinary excess	Cultural neurosis	Decentralization

Decline of Nordic character

Decline of the cities

Decline of the Italian population

Deforestation

Degeneration

Degeneration of the intellect

Demoralization

Depletion of mineral resources

Despotism

Destruction of environment

Destruction of peasantry

Destruction of political process

Destruction of Roman influence

Devastation

Differences in wealth

Disarmament

Disillusion with stated

Division of Empire

Division of labour

Earthquakes

Egoism

Egoism of the state

Emancipation of slaves

Enervation

Epidemics

Equal rights, granting of

Eradication of the best

Escapism

Ethnic dissolution

Excessive aging of population

Excessive civilization

Excessive culture

Excessive foreign infiltration

Excessive freedom

Excessive urbanization

Expansion

Exploitation

Fear of life

Female emancipation

Feudalization

Fiscalism

Gladiatorial system

Gluttony

Gout

Hedonism

Hellenization

Heresy

Homosexuality

Hothouse culture

Hubris

Hypothermia

Immoderate greatness

Imperialism

Impotence

Impoverishment

Imprudent policy toward buffer states

Inadequate educational system

Indifference

Individualism

Indoctrination

Inertia

Inflation

Intellectualism

Integration, weakness of

Irrationality

Jewish influence

Lack of leadership

Lack of male dignity

Lack of military recruits

Lack of orderly imperial succession

Lack of qualified workers

Lack of rainfall

Lack of religiousness

Lack of seriousness

Large landed properties

Lead poisoning

Lethargy

Levelling, cultural

Levelling, social

Loss of army discipline

Loss of authority

Loss of energy

Loss of instincts

Loss of population

Luxury

Malaria

Marriages of convenience

Mercenary system

Mercury damage

Militarism

Monetary economy

Monetary greed

Money, shortage of

Moral decline

Moral idealism

Moral materialism

Mystery religions

Nationalism of Rome's subjects

Negative selection

Orientalization

Outflow of gold

Over refinement

Pacifism

Paralysis of will

Paralyzation

Parasitism

Particularism

Pauperism

Plagues

Pleasure seeking

Plutocracy

Polytheism

Population pressure

Precociousness

Professional army

Proletarization

Prosperity

Prostitution

Psychoses

Public baths

Racial degeneration

Racial discrimination

Racial suicide

Rationalism

Refusal of military service

Religious struggles and schisms

Rentier mentality

Resignation

Restriction to profession

Restriction to the land

Rhetoric

Rise of uneducated masses

Romantic attitudes to peace

Ruin of middle class

Rule of the world

Semieducation

Sensuality

Servility

Sexuality

Shamelessness

Shifting of trade routes

Slavery

Slavic attacks

Socialism (of the state)

Soil erosion

Soil exhaustion

Spiritual barbarism

Stagnation

Stoicism

Stress

Structural weakness

Superstition

Taxation, pressure of

Terrorism

Tiredness of life

Totalitarianism

Treason

Tristesse

Two-front war

Underdevelopment

Useless eaters

Usurpation of all powers by the state

Vaingloriousness

Villa economy

Vulgarization

Obviously, some of these have more to do with the agendas of the original authors than with the realities of the fifth century. However, it is also obvious that many of these are valid: for example, the large number of plagues that occurred in the fifth century; the refusal of great landowners to allow their workers to be taken for military service; and the pressure of taxation causing many citizens to abandon their loyalty to the Empire and transfer it to either local bishops or barbarian leaders, all weakened the Empire in one way or another.

Yet the two major factors, and the ones which the majority of modern historians debate, is whether the major cause was the large number of 'Germanic' invasions or the disintegration of the political core of the Empire as barbarian *magistri* and imperial aristocrats squabbled over who was to be the major power behind the puppet emperors that they installed. Both arguments are compelling and deserving of analysis.

Barbarian Invasion and the Army

The following quote summarizes the overall stance of 'Barbarian Invasion' historians:

> Gothic groups demand (and succeed in establishing) less subservient diplomatic relationships … any substantial change in the strategic balance of power was prompted by the growing strength and cohesion of Germanic groups, not the enfeeblement of the Roman Empire. … Individually, the new Germanic powers were still no match for the Roman state in the fourth century …. The most important effect of the Huns, therefore, was to make sufficient numbers of these new Germanic powers, which were not themselves politically united, act in a sufficiently similar way at broadly the same time. The Huns, however, induced too many of these more substantial groups to cross the frontier in too short a space of time for the Roman state to be able to deal with them effectively … By creating an accidental unity of purpose among Rome's neighbours, the Huns shattered frontier security, and set in motion processes which generated – out of unprecedented combinations of outside military power and existing local Roman elites – a new political order in Western Europe.
>
> *Heather, 1999, 41.*

The most valuable observations in the passage are the 'catalytic' effect of the Huns and the 'accidental unity of purpose' provoked along the Roman borders. However, similar crises had occurred in the third century and despite large parts of the Empire breaking away and massive barbarian incursions, the Empire had eventually recovered without the loss of territory, although in the process the imperial system itself was forced to change from the Principate to the Dominate.

Furthermore, apart from the Goths in 376 the number of barbarian invaders appears to have been small, especially in comparison to the number of Roman troops theoretically available: in practice, the Romans should have been able to eliminate the enemy in short order. So the claim that Rome was simply overrun by large conglomerations of barbarians does not fully explain the Fall: although the theory is valid to a point, without internal weakness the Empire should have survived.

Internal Collapse

As with the previous argument, the case of those promoting internal weakness can be summarized by a quote:

The Roman Empire continued for a very long time. Successive blows knocked away sections of it, as attackers uncovered its weaknesses. Yet at times the empire could still be formidable and did not simply collapse. Perhaps we should imagine the Late Roman Empire as a retired athlete, whose body has declined from neglect and an unhealthy lifestyle. At times the muscles will still function well and with the memory of former skill and training. Yet, as the neglect continues, the body becomes less and less capable of resisting disease or recovering from injury. Over the years the person would grow weaker and weaker, and in the end could easily succumb to disease. Long decline was the fate of the Roman Empire. In the end, it may have been 'murdered' by barbarian invaders, but these struck at a body made vulnerable by long decay.

Goldsworthy, 2009, 414–15.

The arguments for internal disintegration are also very strong. It has been noted that after 454 there was a 'vicious circle ... with too many groups squabbling for a shrinking financial base', the net result being that there were always groups unhappy with their share of the dwindling resources.[2] Furthermore, financially the loss of Africa to the Vandals destroyed the economic viability of the West, a problem exacerbated by the fact that rapid regime changes meant that there was the need to give 'gifts' both to supporters and the army in an attempt to gain support, further weakening the Empire financially.[3]

There were only two ways to break the circle: either reduce the number of groups or expand the financial base of the West. This simple factor helps to explain much of the political methods of both Majorian and Anthemius, in that they attempted to subdue the barbarians in the north and reduce them to their previous status as *foederatae*, and they were also determined to re-establish a firm financial foundation with the reconquest of Africa.[4] The fact that they failed to conquer Africa remains the foundation for the failure of their respective regimes.

The loss of revenue from Africa has led to the suggestion that by the time of Ricimer and his successors the army was composed almost entirely of 'East German tribes' – namely Heruls, Rugi and Sciri – employed as mercenaries.[5] Yet this wasn't entirely the case. There were small numbers of Imperial troops in Italy, Gaul and Illyricum, providing the cores around which the Imperial armies were formed. In addition, there may have been some troops surviving either along the frontiers or as personal bodyguards to the emperor, but the number and nature of these troops are unknown.[6]

Yet to finance these armies financial cutbacks had to be implemented, meaning that the number of troops in Hispania and Roman Africa west of the Vandal kingdom had had to be reduced – if not removed. This theory accounts for how the Sueves and Vandals managed to expand after 443 despite imperial opposition: in strict manpower terms the strongest barbarian kingdoms of Vandal Africa, Gothic Gaul and Suevic Hispania could either match or overpower the Empire in local areas.

Whenever the Empire brought overwhelming force to bear the barbarian kings could easily submit, safe in the knowledge that the troops were too valuable to be risked in battle and would soon be removed for service elsewhere in the Empire. At that point it would be possible to revert to an aggressive policy. At many key points this also explains why the barbarian kingdoms were allowed to continue, and also how they managed to pursue policies inimical to the survival of the Empire without being destroyed by Rome.

The removal of the army from areas of barbarian pressure was especially the case whenever the Empire descended into Civil War, especially between 406 and 412, and in the 430s when the Vandals took advantage of Roman infighting to take control of Africa. As will be described below, the Goths were also to take advantage of Roman internal division to expand their sphere of influence. Obviously, if the Empire had remained free from internal troubles the barbarian invasions could not have succeeded. Yet without the barbarian invasions the Empire should have survived for a long time, as internal divisions at the core had little immediate effect on those parts of the Empire free from 'external' attack.

As a result of these observations, it is obvious that the argument between 'barbarian attack' and 'internal weakness' is circular: without the one, the other would not have succeeded – at least to the same devastating end result.

Outside Italy

Yet there is more to the disintegration than simply a rotten centre. The growth of parochialism is another factor in the Fall.

> The core of Ausonius' hometown loyalty lay in an emerging late Roman conception of urban identity that was still developing even in the later writings of Sidonius. Both Ausonius and Sidonius conceived of the cities of Gaul as distinct peoples. They traced their ancestry through cities. And in troubled times the natal city inspired genuine patriotism. Sidonius consistently envisioned the people of Clermont-Ferrand as the sharers of a common fate. He wrote with great pride of how the townspeople of Clermont-Ferrand had withstood adversity, and in a letter in which he offers up the tradition that his fellow citizens were 'brothers to Latium ... a people sprung from Latin blood', he describes the stubborn heroism of his people under siege, when they had resorted to eating grass from cracks in the wall.
>
> *Frye, 2003, 194–5.*

Many people outside Italy lost faith in the Empire to protect them, a fact which was especially galling to individuals struggling to pay their taxes. This explains why in many cases there is little evidence of opposition to barbarian expansion, as the local barbarian overlord would at least attempt to defend his territory in return for the taxes that had once travelled to Italy.

Furthermore, those inhabitants of the Empire who did not have this sense of belonging, such as over-taxed peasants and slaves, appear to have joined the armies of the barbarian kings in the hope of gaining a better life. In this way the small numbers of barbarian invaders who crossed the frontiers were rapidly reinforced by local recruits, so enabling them to face down the Imperial armies successfully. Finally, the strength of the barbarian armies reached a level that they at least equalled – if not outnumbered – the Imperial forces ranged against them, and at this point even patriots such as Sidonius bowed to the inevitable and accepted service with barbarian kings.

Barbarian Identity

The above serves notice that from their intrusion into the Empire in the early fifth century the application of ethnic labels such as 'Goth', 'Vandal', or even 'Frank' hides the fact that settled barbarian tribes were actually composed of many different people from a wide variety of origins, including men from other tribes, runaway slaves, Roman peasants, and even more affluent Romans who believed that they stood a far greater chance of improving their status serving newly-landed barbarians rather than an imperial court that was remote and seemingly not interested in affairs outside Italy. In these circumstances, with the growth of 'barbarian identities' incorporating even previously Roman citizens, it is obvious that the Empire was doomed.[7]

Ancient Responses to the Fall of the West

Yet the lack of appreciation of what was happening outside Italy extends to the indigenous peoples of the whole Empire. After 476 contemporaries did not see the removal of Romulus as momentous, as there was little difference between the current interregnum and those previous: a barbarian warlord was in power and would decide with Eastern guidance who would be the next emperor.[8]

Consequently, contemporary Christians did not believe that the West would fall. For example, in 456 Sidonius – in a Gaul contracting under pressure from the Franks and Goths – expected the Empire to last for centuries, and even as late as 474 wrote that he expected a continuation of the Empire for generations.[9] One exception to this trend is Augustine in his *de Civitate Dei*, written after the Gothic Sack of Rome in 410, yet even here the assumption is based more on his analysis of religious ideas than on specific contemporary events.[10] Another is the *Liber Genealogus* analysed in Chapter 3, concerned with the death of Valentinian III.

Composed c. 518, Marcellinus' *comes* is the earliest secure surviving reference to the 'End of the Western Empire', ascribing it to the removal of Augustulus.[11] There is also the work of John Rufus, *Plerophories*, which suggests that Timothy Aelurus, who died in 477, was the first to develop the idea of the Fall. But *Pleropheries* is dated to the early sixth century and so may be a later interpretation imposed on an earlier date.[12]

The fact that contemporaries could not see that Rome had fallen is unsurprising. The Empire had been in existence for over twenty generations: the concept that something so permanent could end was inconceivable to many at the time, and helps to explain the continued fascination the Fall exercises today.

Conclusion

In hindsight, it is obvious that the period when the Patricians ruled Rome was always doomed to be the last days of the Western Roman Empire. Nor is this a simplistic question of barbarian invasion or internal collapse. Many factors contributed to the Fall of Rome.

One of these is that the loss of the Imperial dynasty, coupled with a combined fear of and respect for the East, led to many interregnums which were damaging to Roman prestige. Furthermore, after waiting for a decision and not getting one, when the West imposed their own nominee, more often than not the East refused to accept the individual, leading to 'civil war' and the focus remaining solely upon Italy. In this respect, the division of the Empire helped to accelerate the Fall of the West.

Another, and one that interacts with the previous factor, is that the growth in power of the Senate of Rome and the aristocracy of Italy meant that the overriding priority was the defence of Italy and those areas of Southern Gaul where the Senate had estates. The net result was a loss of faith in the Empire in many other areas of the West, and the ensuing growth in readiness of provincial elites to either rebel or ally with local barbarian warlords. Yet this should not be overplayed, as one of the main legacies of Rome was that many people still wanted a connection to the Empire – even barbarian kings, who valued the titles given by the 'emperor'. Yet there remains the fact that emperors who concentrated any significant resources outside Italy, such as Avitus, Majorian and Anthemius, quickly lost the affiliation of Italy and thus their rule and their lives, encouraging the alienation of non-Italians to the emperor and their change of allegiance to powerful men – usually barbarian kings – who would fulfil the role of protector once provided by the legions.

A further characteristic is that the loss of Africa and hence of financial viability meant the loss of a Roman army and the switch to the use of mercenaries. Although in theory there should have been little difference in fighting capabilities, there was a change in loyalty from either the emperor or concept of Empire, to single military leaders, usually the *magister militum*. When coupled with the focus on Italy, this meant that there was little support for areas outside Italy or Southern Gaul, a theory reinforced by the secession of the Auvergne to Euric in return for the restoration of Provence. The latter was an integral part of the senators' landed domains and therefore seen as far more important than any other region in Gaul.

A final factor, and one not usually commented upon by modern authors, is that at this vital time the quality of the two major opponents faced by the West was exceptionally high. In Gaiseric the emperor had a political and military genius as an opponent. Gaiseric was able to successfully conquer large parts of the Western Mediterranean and repel two major Roman invasions, whilst at the same time continuing a political policy of divide and conquer that enabled him to make peace with East and West separately whilst continuing attacks on the other.

Furthermore, in Euric the Goths found a political and military commander who was superior to the Roman combination of *magister militum* and Senate. Although the timing of his campaigns was immaculate, hitting the Empire when it was unable to react, his political acumen could easily be ignored. For example, his willingness to return Provence to the Empire, in exchange for the Auvergne and the recognition of his release from Roman domination, even when it was obvious that the Empire was unable to strike back, is overlooked. Yet in real terms the treaty enabled him to deal with both Gallic and Hispanic subjects in a new way, as from this point on they were dealing with an imperially recognized king, not an over-powerful servant of the emperor. There was now no hiding the fact that the Gothic kingdom was an autonomous entity, and acceding to Euric was a clear abandonment of the Empire, a factor which accounts for the resistance Euric encountered in southern Hispania.

It is sometimes claimed that if Aetius had not been assassinated by Valentinian III in 454 he might have been able to reverse the decline of the West and give the Empire a new lease of life. It is clear that the financial, political, and social ills that plagued the West were too much for one man to counter, and that although he might have been able to prolong the Empire's life for a few years at the most; the end of Imperial rule was irreversible. Whatever happened, the Empire was doomed to fall.

Outline Chronology

425   Coronation of Valentinian III
451   Battle of the Catalaunian Plains: defeat of Attila
452   Attila invades Italy
453   Death of Attila
454   Battle of the Nedao, collapse of the Hunnic Empire
       21/22 September, Assassination of Aetius; secession of Marcellinus in Dalmatia
455   16 March, assassination of Valentinian III
       17 March – 22/31 May, reign of Petronius Maximus
       Vandals sack Rome: Valentinian's widow Eudoxia and daughters Placidia and Eudocia taken to Carthage: Marcellinus expands power in Illyricum
       Sueves raid Hispania
       9 July 455, Proclamation of Eparchius Avitus with Gothic support
456   Gaiseric allies with Moors, expands into North Africa: Eastern Emperor Marcian prepares for war
       Ricimer made *comes* in Sicily: defeats Vandal attack at the Battle of Agrigentum
       Unrest in Rome: Vandals attack Italy, defeated by Majorian in Corsica
       5 October, Goths defeat Sueves at Battle of the River Urbicus
       17 October, Battle of Piacenza, defeat of Avitus by Ricimer
       October 456/February 457, Death of Eparchius Avitus
       Interregnum
457   26 January 457, death of Eastern Emperor Marcian: East's campaign against Vandals cancelled
       27 March 457, Ricimer and Majorian acknowledged as joint *magistri*
       Late March, 900 Alamanni invade Italy: defeated by Burco
       1 April 457, Majorian crowned Emperor
       Aegidius appointed *magister militum per Gallias*: gains alliance of Salian Franks
       Ricimer defeats Vandals in Italy: Gaiseric begins annexation of North Africa and Mediterranean Islands
       Theoderic invades Hispania
       Franks capture Cologne and Trier
       Eastern Emperor Leo accepts Majorian as imperial colleague
458   Majorian raises taxes and begins recruitment of a large army and navy to recapture Africa from Vandals

Nepotianus appointed *magister militum*
Marcellinus accepts Majorian's rule and Dalmatia rejoins Empire
Sueves resume attacks in Hispania
Theoderic attacks Narbonne, forced to retreat
Theoderic lays siege to Aegidius in Arles
Majorian crosses Alps with army, sends Nepotianus with troops to relieve Arles: Battle of Arles, Roman victory and new treaty agreed
East accepts Ricimer's nomination as *Consul*

459   Suevic civil war
Ostrogoths under Valamir invade Dalmatia: Marcellinus on the defensive

460   Marcellinus, now *magister militum Dalmatae*, leads his army from Dalmatia to Sicily
May, Majorian crosses Pyrenees
Nepotianus and Suniericus sent to quell the Sueves
Roman fleet sent to Elche
Gaiseric gathers ships to oppose Roman navy
Battle of Elche: defeat of Roman fleet
Treaty with Gaiseric: West agrees to loss of North Africa and those Western Mediterranean islands occupied by Vandals
Betrayal of Roman army in Hispania, retreat of Roman forces

461   Majorian disbands invasion army
Near Dertona, Majorian captured by Ricimer and executed
Marcellinus and Aegidius refuse to acknowledge Ricimer and set up opposition regimes in Dalmatia and Gaul respectively
Aegidius enters alliance with Franks, separate from Rome
Nepotianus in Spain also refuses to acknowledge Ricimer, turning to Theoderic for support
Interregnum
Theoderic the Amal sent to Constantinople as hostage
Vandals ravage Sicily and parts of Southern Italy
19 November 461, Severus crowned

462   Agrippinus appointed *magister militum per Gallias* and organizes treaty with Theoderic: Narbonne ceded to Goths: Theoderic given permission to appoint a new *magister militum per Hispaniae*
Leo I of East comes to agreement with Gaiseric: gives Gaiseric the *Patrimony of Valentinian* to administer on behalf of Eudocia, Eudoxia and Pulcheria sent to Constantinople

463   Vandals renew attacks on West
Gundioc, King of the Burgundians appointed *magister militum per Gallias* to replace Agrippinus
Gaiseric annexes Sardinia, Corsica, and part of Sicily
Aegidius fights Frederic at the Battle of Orleans: Aegidius victorious and Frederic killed
Sueves pillage widely in Hispania

464   Beorgor King of Alans attacks Italy: defeated by Ricimer at Battle of Bergamum

Childeric captures Paris

Frumarius, King of Sueves, dies: Suevic attacks cease

465   Franks recapture Cologne

Death of Aegidius in Trier: succession of Syagrius: Childeric assumes primary role in North Gaul

Goths probe Syagrius' defences: Saxons around Angers assert independence

Sueves resume attacks in Hispania

Marcellinus lands in Sicily to defend island from Vandal attack

15 August 465, death of Severus

Interregnum

Sueves attack Senona: Theoderic sends embassy to Sueves, but is ignored

466   Rising tension between Leo and Aspar, the *magister militum* in the East: Leo fails to make a decision about a new Western emperor

Vandals switch attacks to East, especially Illyricum, the Peleponnesus, and Greece

Death of Theoderic, accession of Euric: Euric spends rest of 466 and 467 establishing regime

Seuves continue raids in Hispania

467   Spring 467, Anthemius sent from East to be new Western Emperor, accompanied by army led by Marcellinus

12 April 467, Anthemius crowned

Marriage of Ricimer to Anthemius' daughter Alypia

Leo sends envoys to Gaiseric demanding peace: Gaiseric refuses: citizens of Alexandria panic, expecting Vandal attack

Summer, Ricimer defeats Ostrogothic invasion of Noricum: Marcellinus sent to Sicily

Gaiseric attacks area around Rhodes

Bad weather cancels prospective invasion of North Africa from Sicily by Marcellinus

Sueves halt attacks in Hispania

468   Marcellinus seizes Sardinia

Heraclius invades Tripolitana from Egypt, defeats Vandals at Battle of Tripolis; advances on Carthage

Basliscus invades Africa, landing at Mercurium (Cap Bon): Gaiseric delays further action by the dispatch of envoys to Basiliscus

Battle of Cap Bon: Roman fleet defeated by Gaiseric; Heraclius retreats to Tripolitana

Assassination of Marcellinus

Trier and Paris maintain some form of autonomy

Arvandus, Praetorian Prefect of Gaul, sends letter to Euric urging him to make war on Anthemius

Euric launches invasion of Lusitania and overthrows Tarraconensis

Anthemius organizes alliance of Burgundians and Brittones against Euric: Franks and Syagrius refuse to join alliance

Brittones attacked and defeated by Goths at Battle of Bourg-de Déols: in turn, Count Paul defeats Goths, Paul later killed

469   Julius Nepos takes control of Dalmatia

Childeric and Syagrius expand their sphere of control in North Gaul: Saxons driven out of Angers and settlements on islands in Loire destroyed

Alamanni expand into Noricum

470   Gaiseric resumes attacks on Sicily and Italy: Ricimer assumes responsibility for defence

Romanus executed: Ricimer rebels and takes 6,000 men to Milan

Gothic commander Victorius attacks Auvergne, Euric attacks Roman territory further south

471   Epiphanius arranges reconciliation of Anthemius and Ricimer

Anthemiolus, son of Anthemius, sent to Gaul to attack Euric, but defeated and killed

Ricimer resumes rebellion: Gundobad appointed *magister militum per Gallias* to replace his father: Ricimer begins Siege of Rome

Eudocia leaves Carthage and travels to Jerusalem, where she dies

Theoderic the Amal returns home after acting as hostage for ten years: Theoderic Strabo attacks Constantinople

472   Leo sends Olybrius to West in hopes of ending Civil War

April/May 472, Olybrius crowned by Ricimer

Attempting to lift the Siege of Rome, Bilimer defeated by Ricimer

With the help of Gundobad, Ricimer captures Rome: 11 July 472, Anthemius executed and Rome sacked

18 August 472, death of Ricimer: Gundobad assumes role of *magister militum*

22 October/2 November 472, death of Olybrius

Interregnum

473   3 March 473, Glycerius crowned

Euric sends Vincentius to invade Italy: defeated by Imperial forces under Alla and Sindila

Euric captures Arles and Marseilles: Clermont successfully defended: famine in South Gaul: Gundobad ordered to Gaul to face Euric

Vidimer the Ostrogoth invades Italy: paid 2,000 *solidi* to go to Gaul, where he joins Euric

474   18 January 474, death of Leo: accession of Leo II in East

c. 8 February 474, Zeno becomes co-emperor; determines to replace Glycerius with Julius Nepos

Theoderic Strabo rebels and later supports Basiliscus

Summer 474 Nepos invades Italy: Glycerius deposed and made Bishop of Salona

June 474, Julius Nepos crowned

Gundobad continues with title of *magister militum*, but Ecdicius and Chilperic also given title

Euric again attacks Auvergne and Clermont and takes control of the whole of Provence: Ecidicius organizes defence of Auvergne

Alliance Nepos, Syagrius and Childeric: Ecidicius defeated by Goths

November 474, death of Leo II

Late 474/early 475 Zeno signs treaty with Gaiseric

475 January 475, Zeno removed by coup of Basiliscus and forced to flee to the East

Ecdicius recalled and removed as *magister militum*: replaced by Orestes

Treaty Nepos and Euric: Clermont surrendered to Goths in return for restoration of Provence, including Arles and Marseilles, to Empire

Orestes leads army against Nepos: Nepos deposed and flees to Dalmatia, from where he continues to claim title of Emperor

Interregnum

31 October 475, Romulus Augustus (Augustulus) crowned

476 Euric attacks Provence, again capturing Arles and Marseilles

Autumn (probable) Treaty Orestes and Gaiseric: Vandal possession of North Africa, Balearic Islands, Sardinia, Corsica, and western Sicily accepted

Barbarian mercenaries in Roman army request land to settle in Italy: Orestes refuses

August/September 474, Zeno ousts Basiliscus and resumes Eastern throne with help of Theoderic Strabo and Theoderic the Amal: Theoderic the Amal appointed *magister militum*

23 August 476, mercenaries elect Odovacer as king

Battle of Ticinum, Odovacer victorious

28 August 476, Battle of Placentia: Orestes captured and executed

4 September 476, Augustulus deposed

Envoys from both Nepos and Odovacer arrive in Constantinople: Zeno unable to commit troops, verbally supports Nepos

Odovacer settles troops in Italy

Odovacer signs Treaty with Gaiseric: Sicily (except Lilybaeum) returned to Empire in return for tribute

477 25 January 477, death of Gaiseric: Huneric becomes King of the Vandals: Huneric signs Treaty with Zeno in which Vandals renounce rights to 'Patrimony of Valentinian III' and accept a Catholic Bishop of Carthage

Odovacer signs Treaty with Euric, who is confirmed in possession of Provence

11 July 477, execution of Brachila after brief revolt

478 Rebellion of Adaric: his defeat and execution

Theoderic Strabo rebels: Theoderic the Amal sent to attack Strabo but under pressure from his own men the two become allies: Strabo negotiates with Zeno and accepts post of *magister militum*

479   Theoderic the Amal attacks Greece and seizes Dyrrachium: Strabo supports a rebellion and loses post of *magister militum*: Strabo joins Theoderic the Amal

480   25 April/9 May 480, assassination of Julius Nepos: Ovida seizes Dalmatia

481   Odovacer invades Dalmatia: defeat and death of Ovida: Dalmatia added to West

Embassy from both Odovacer and the 'Gauls of the West' to Zeno: Zeno accepts Odovacer's regime in Italy

Illus appointed *magister militum per Orientem* in East

Strabo attacks Constantinople and Greece: Death of Strabo

482   Theoderic plunders Macedonia and Thessaly

483   Treaty between Theoderic and Zeno: Theoderic made *magister militum* and *Consul* for 484

484   Death of Euric: 29 December 484, accession of Alaric II

Rebellion of Illus against Zeno

(485)

486   Clovis, King of the Franks, defeats Syagrius at the Battle of Soissons: Syagrius flees to Toulouse

Theoderic the Amal rebels

487   Odovacer learns of the Rugian plan to attack: late 487 launches a pre-emptive strike, and defeats and kills Feletheus, King of the Rugi

488   Odovacer launches second attack and destroys Rugi: remnants flee to join Ostrogoths: Odovacer orders abandonment of Noricum; refugees settled in South Italy

Agreement between Theoderic the Amal and Zeno: mid-488 Theoderic begins invasion of Italy

489   February 489, Battle of River Ulca between Theoderic and the Gepids; Gepids defeated

Theoderic defeats Sarmatians

Odovacer appoints Tufa as *magister militum*

28 August 489, Theoderic defeats Odovacer at Battle of River Izonso

30 September, Theoderic defeats Odovacer at Battle of Verona

490   Odovacer lays siege to Theoderic in Ticinum: siege raised by Goths under Alaric II

11 August 490, Theoderic defeats Odovacer at Battle of the River Addua: Theoderic begins siege of Ravenna

9 April 491, death of Emperor Zeno: Anastasius eventually becomes new emperor

Odovacer declares his son Thela *Caesar*

(491–492)

493   Battle of Tridentum/Verona, Fredericus defeats Tufa, Tufa killed

Negotiations between Theoderic and Odovacer: peace agreed: Theoderic executes Odovacer

493–4   Alaric II hands Syagrius to Clovis: Syagrius executed

Notes and References

Introduction
1. See Hughes, (2012) 116f.
2. R W Burgess, *Bryn Mawr Classical Review 2003.09.44*.

Chapter One – The Roman Empire, 395–455
1. Many of the conclusions and references around which this chapter is based can be found in Hughes, (2012) passim. To avoid repetition, only the most important points have been referenced specifically.
2. Mitchell, (2007) p. 2.
3. See Map 2. On the *bacaudic* revolts, see below.
4. Hughes, (2012) p. 105; 209.
5. For a more detailed analysis, see Hughes, (2012) pp. 151–153.
6. See Map 1.
7. MacGeorge, (2002) pp. 306–11, '*Appendix: Naval Power in the Fifth Century*'.
8. *Nov. Val.* 6.3.1 (July, 444).
9. For a more detailed analysis of these problems, see Hughes, (2010) esp. Chapters 6 and 12.
10. Hughes, (2010) Chapter 12.
11. Cass. *Variae*, 11.1.9: Jord. *Rom.* 329.
12. Pol. Silv. 257: see Map 1.
13. MacGeorge, (2002) pp. 35–6.
14. MacGeorge, (2002) p. 35.
15. Sid. Ap. *Carm.* 2, 468–9.
16. Heather, (1995) p. 30.
17. Hanson, (1972), p. 279.
18. For example, Pope Leo I and his intervention with Gaiseric during the Sack of Rome in 455 (see Chapter 3) or Sidonius coordinating the defence of Clermont in the 470s. However note that the commonly accepted idea that Leo intervened with Attila the Hun in Italy in 452 is mistaken: Hughes, (2012) pp. 182–3.
19. Heather, (1995) p. 31.
20. See Chapter 14, where Nepos gave the Auvergne to the Goths in return for their returning Provence, in which region many of the Roman Senate held extensive estates.
21. Brown, (2012) p. 4.
22. For more on the problems of recruitment and tax see Hughes, (2010) esp. p. 51, 221.
23. *Eparchius Avitus* – see Chapter 4.
24. This section focuses on the three main Christian groups: the Nicene (Orthodox) Christian, the Arians and the Donatists. There were several other 'heretical' groups during this period, such as the Pelagians of Britain, Africa and Palestine.
25. For more on these debates see for example Brown, (2012) and dal Santo, (2012).
26. For more on these views, see Hughes, (2012) pp. 189–190.

Chapter Two – The Roman Army, 455
1. For example, Elton, (1996); Heather, (1995).
2. Salmon, (2010) 305f. For a greater analysis of the *Leges Porciae*, see SP Oakley, *A Commentary on Livy, Books VI-X : Volume IV: Book X: Volume IV:, Books 6–10* 130f.

3. Duncan-Jones, (1990) pp. 105–17; Elton, (1996) p. 89; Goldsworthy, (2003) p. 206; and Mattingly, (2006) p. 239.
4. For example, Holder, (2003); Coello, (1996).
5. There appears to be some confusion over the use of *riparienses/ripenses* and *limitanei*: see Nicasie, (1998) pp. 19–22 and Southern and Dixon, (1996) p.36 for clarification. For the sake of simplicity the traditional separation into river- and land-frontier forces respectively has been used.
6. Elton, (2004) 204f.
7. For example, the Balkan campaigns of Valentinian I against the Alamanni, Southern and Dixon, (1996) p. 41.
8. *palatina*: from *palatium*, 'palace'.
9. See Southern and Dixon, (1996) p. 57.
10. Southern and Dixon, (1996) p. 47.
11. Southern and Dixon, (1996) p. 47: *Not. Dig. Or.* XI. 6. 10; *Oc.* X1. 7.
12. *Not. Dig. Oc.* XLII. 46–70.
13. Elton, (2004) p. 131.
14. Southern and Dixon, (1996) p. 48; Liebeschuetz, (1991) p. 9.
15. Elton, (2004) p. 135.
16. Olymp. *fr.*7.4.
17. For more on these appointments, see Hughes, (2012) passim.
18. Christie, (2007) p. 569.
19. Elton, (2004) p. 129.
20. Liebeschuetz, (1991) p. 20.
21. See Southern and Dixon, (1996) p. 69.
22. Elton, (2004) p. 129.
23. *Cod. Th.* 15.1.13.
24. Zos. 4.23.2–4.
25. Tomlin, (1990) p. 117.
26. Southern and Dixon, (1996) pp. 62–3: Burns, (2003) p. 183.
27. Burns, (2003) p. 184: *Cod. Th.* 7.4.28.
28. Most of the information for this section is taken from Hughes, (2012) passim.
29. On the small number of the barbarian invaders crossing the Rhine in 406 see Hughes, (2010) p. 179.
30. Hyd. 49. For a more detailed reconstruction of these events, including the hypothesis that Gerontius invited the barbarians into Hispania, see Hughes, (2010) pp. 213–214; Hughes, (2012) p. 15.
31. Hyd. *s.a.* 411.
32. Hughes, (2012) p. 15.
33. Hyd. *s.a.* 420
34. Hyd. *s.a.* 422: Prosp. *s.a.* 422/423.
35. Hughes, (2012) 59f.
36. CAH 136.
37. Hyd. *s.a.* 430.
38. Emerita, Hyd. *s.a.* 439; Martylis, PLRE 2, *Censorius*, 280.
39. Hyd. *s.a.* 441, 443.
40. Hyd. *s.a.* 446: Halsall, (2007) p. 250.
41. See Hughes, (2012) 69f. for a discussion of the problems in Hispania.
42. *Narratio de imperatoribus domus Valentinianae et Theodosiae* 6.9, written between 423 and 452.
43. Hyd. *s.a.* 449.
44. The exact date of the attack is unknown: Hydatius simply dates events to '453–454'.
45. Prisc. *fr.* 24.

46. See Chapter Sixteen.
47. Attacks, e.g. 431 (Hyd. *s.a.* 431); successful campaign e.g. 437 (Hyd. *s.a.* 437: Jord. *Get.* 34 [176]).
48. Hyd. *s.a.* 452–453.
49. For more details on events, see Hughes, (2010) 177f. for the invasion of Gaul; Hughes, (2012) 106f. for the invasion of Africa.
50. Hughes, (2012) p. 24f.
51. Prosp. *s.a.* 427.
52. Hughes, (2012) p. 81f.
53. Hughes, (2012) p. 85.
54. For a more detailed analysis of these events see Hughes, (2012) 24f.
55. *Addit. Ad. Prosp. Haun. s.a.* 453.
56. For more details on the interpretation, see Hughes, (2012) pp. 185–186.
57. Sid Ap. *Ep.* 7. 12.3.
58. Siege, *Chron. Gall. 511*, no. 621: failure to break siege, Sid Ap. *Ep.* 7. 12.3.
59. *Chron. Gall. 511*, no. 621: Sid Ap. *Ep.* 7. 12.3.
60. Greg. Tur. 2.7.
61. On the problem of Illyricum and the 'treaty' of 437 see, e.g. Wozniack, (1981) 353f.
62. MacGeorge, (2002) p. 18.
63. Hyd. *s.a.* 431. See Hughes, (2012) pp. 82–3.
64. MacGeorge, (2002) p. 171.
65. See Chapter 1.
66. Cass. *Variae* XI, 1.9: Jord. *Rom.* 329: c.f Wozniak, (1981).
67. Proc. 3.6.7–8.
68. See for example MacGeorge, (2002) p. 35f plus references.
69. Prisc. *fr.* 21, 23; c.f. Prisc. *fr.* 11.1. for further analysis, see Hughes, (2012) pp. 134–135.
70. Wozniack, (1981) p. 354.
71. Prisc. *fr.* 9.3.
72. The concept that a later request from Julius Nepos to the Eastern emperor for a judicial decision confirms that Dalmatia was part of the East is not valid: the response was given in 473, when the East refused to accept the Western emperor and when Nepos, the successor to Marcellinus, was in open opposition to the West. In these circumstances, the Eastern Emperor was the only viable option for a decision. *Cod. Iust.* 6.61.5.
73. Prosper, *s.a.* 452.
74. Wozniack, (1981) p. 356.
75. Jord. *Get.* 264–265.
76. Wozniak, (1981) pp. 351–352.
77. MacGeorge, (2002) p. 19.
78. Marc. com. *s.a.* 468: Christian symbols, c.f. MacGeorge, (2002) p. 29 and associated bibliography.
79. For more on the controversy concerning the relationship between Marcellinus and Aetius, see MacGeorge, (2002) p. 66: *comes rei militaris*, PLRE II, *Marcellinus 2*, 707–708: *patricius*, Marc. com. *s.a.* 467.
80. For a more detailed appraisal, see, MacGeorge, (2002) p. 41f.
81. *Suda*, II, 473: on Marcellinus' use of Hunnic mercenaries, see Chapter Ten.
82. For a more in-depth examination of the issue, see MacGeorge, (2002) p. 35f.
83. Elton, (1996) p. 89.
84. For more information concerning the reluctance of the senate to participate in the defence of Rome, see Hughes, (2010) and (2012).
85. No serious manpower shortages, Elton, (1996) p. 154.
86. See Hughes, (2012) p. 103.

Chapter Three – Petronius Maximus

1. Joh. Ant. *fr.* 201.6: 'paymaster', Sid. Ap. *Carm.* 5. 116–125, 266–268; Oost, (1964) p. 25; Rousseau, (2000) p. 255: Egyptian origin, Halsall, (2007) p. 262.
2. For more detail on these, see Hughes, (2012) 188f.
3. Sid. App. *Carmina*, 5.290–300.
4. Prosp. *s.a.* 454.
5. The background information on Maximus is derived from PLRE II, *Maximus 22*, 749–751, supported by Mathisen, (2007).
6. Proc. 3.4.16; Nic. Call. 15.11; Cedr. 1.605; Theoph. AM 5947: c.f Mathisen, 2007. Re-establish, Mommaerts, (2002) p. 118.
7. Drinkwater and Elton, (2002) p. 118.
8. Mathisen, (2007).
9. PLRE 2, *Maximus 22*, 749–751.
10. Prisc. *fr.* 30 = Joh. Ant. *fr.* 201. c.f Prosp. *s.a.* 454.
11. Prosp. *s.a.* 454: c.f. Evag. 2.7 (54).
12. 21 Sept. = *Addit. Ad Prosp. Haun. s.a.* 454: 22 Sept. = *Ann. Rav. s.a.* 454.
13. Both quotes, Joh, Ant. *fr.* 200–201.
14. Hyd. *s.a.* 454.
15. Proc. 3.6.7.
16. Ores mined, MacGeorge, (2002) p. 17.
17. Wozniak, (1981) p. 359.
18. MacGeorge, (2002) pp. 19–21.
19. Oost, (1964) p. 25.
20. Sid. Ap. *Carmina*, 5.306–308: Joh. Ant. *fr.* 201, 4–5.
21. Hyd. *s.a.* 453–4.
22. Prisc. *fr.* 30 = Joh. Ant. *fr.* 201.
23. Joh. Ant. *fr.* 200–201: trans. Gordon, pp.51–52; *Addit ad Prosp. Haun. s.a.* 455.
24. C.f Joh. Mal. 360; *Addit ad Prosp. Haun. s.a.* 455; Marc. *com. s.a.* 455; Jord. *Rom.* 334; Greg. Tur. 2.8; plot, Vict. Tonn. *s.a.* 455.
25. Mathisen, (1997).
26. Proc. 3.4.36.
27. C.f Vict. Tonn. *s.a.* 455.
28. cf. Oost, (1964) p. 24.
29. cf. Mathisen, (1998).
30. Mal. *Chron.* 366: see Chapter 4.
31. Brother-in-law, Drinkwater and Elton, (2002) p. 119; c.f. Mathisen, (1997).
32. For more detail on Avitus during this period, see Hughes, (2012) passim.
33. Prosp. *s.a.* 455: c.f Reynolds, (2011) p. 176.
34. For a detailed analysis of this claim, see Hughes, (2012) pp. 148–149.
35. cf. Hyd. Proc. Marc. com.
36. For acceptance, see e.g. Gibbon, ii, 384; Contra, Oost, *Galla Placidia Augusta; a Biographical Essay* (Chicago, 1968) p. 305, as referenced in Reynolds, (2011) p. 177. Hyd. *s.a.* 455.
37. Clover, (1966) p. 147; 156–61.
38. Clover, (1966) p. 147.
39. Heather, (1995) p. 32.
40. Prosp. a. 455.
41. Prisc. *fr. 30* = John of Antioch *fr.* 201.
42. The Latin phrase '*cum imperium deserere vellet*' (Hyd. a. 455) has been translated by Mathisen (1997) as 'desired to abdicate', although Murray's translation (2000) reads 'attempting to abandon Imperial rule'. Either of these translations is a possibility, although given the circumstances 'abdicating' would not have solved Maximus' problems, and may therefore be the less likely of the two.
43. Jord. *Getica* 235: Sid. *Carm.* 7.742–743.

Chapter Four – Eparchius Avitus

1. C.f. Prosp. a. 455: 'Gaiseric obtained the city devoid of all protection'.
2. Hughes, (2012) pp. 182–183.
3. Gaiseric in the palace, Proc. 3.5.1.
4. It should be noted that it was at the time of writing the Chronicle that Placidia was the wife of Olybrius, not at the time of the Sack.
5. Hyd. a. 455.
6. Mal. *Chron*. 366: c.f. Clover, (1966) 180f.
7. Prosp. a. 455.
8. Reynolds, (2011) p. 178.
9. PLRE 2, *Hildericus*, 564–5: according to Procopius (3.9.10) and Corripus (*Ioh*. 3. 263) he was an old man in 530, meaning that his birth dates to some time in the 450s.
10. Hyd. a. 455.
11. cf. Brown, (2012) p. 392, on Paulinus of Pella, *Eucharisticus*, 500–2.
12. Heather, (2002) pp. 89–91.
13. Brown, (2012) p. 393.
14. Heather, (2002) p. 85.
15. See Chapter 2.
16. Heather, (2002) p. 85; Sid. Ap. *Carm*. 7.392ff.
17. Clermont, Greg. Tur. 2.11; Sid. Ap. *Carm*. 7.149, 153–4; c.f. Hyd. *s.a.* 455: Senatorial family, Greg. Tur. 2.11.
18. Law, Sid. Ap. *Carm*. 7.207.
19. Sid. Ap. *Carm*. 7.220.6, 481–3; 495–9.
20. Campaigns, Sid. Ap. *Carm*. 233–4; c.f. Hyd. 93, 95, *s.a.* 430, 431: *MVM* and the siege of Narbo, Sid. Ap. *Carm*. 244–71, 278–94; c.f. Prosp. *s.a.* 437; Sid. Ap. *Carm*. 475–80.
21. PP in Gaul, Sid. Ap. *Carm*. 7. 295–8, 312–15, 462–3; treaty, Sid. Ap. *Carm*. 297–31; Hyd. *s.a.* 439.
22. Sid. Ap. *Carm*. 7.318–20, 346–52, 547–9.
23. Sid. Ap. *Carm*. 7.378–81.
24. Sid. Ap. *Carm*. 7.430–6.
25. Sid. Ap. *Carm*. 7.517.
26. 9 July and Viernum, Sid. Ap. *Carm*. 7 508–9, 520–1, 571–80: 10 July, *Fast. Vind. Prior*, *s.a.* 456. Also, Hyd 163 (*s.a.* 455); Vict Tonn. *s.a.* 455.
27. Sid. Ap. 7.571–9.
28. cf. *Fast. Vind. Prior*. *s.a.* 456; Theoph. AM 5948.
29. Mathisen, (1979) p. 617. It should be noted, however, that this is 'informed speculation' and is not directly supported by the sources.
30. Consentius, PLRE 2, *Consentius* 2, 308–9; Sid. Ap. *Carm*. 23. 428–32: Mathisen, (2002) p. 232.
31. Mathisen, (2002) p. 236.
32. Mathisen, (2002) p. 236.
33. Sid. Ap. *Ep*. 1.6.1.
34. *Auct. Prosp. Haun. s.a.* 455.
35. *Fast. Vind. Prior*. n. 575; Cassiod. 1264.
36. Avitus' embassy to Vandals, Prisc. *fr*. 31; Hyd. 166. An embassy to Marcian would be obligatory and is implied by Marcian's repeated envoys to the Vandals; Prisc. *fr*. 31.
37. Prisc. fr. 24.
38. Hyd. *s.a.* 456.
39. Prisc. *fr*. 31.
40. Hyd. *s.a.* 456–7.
41. Hyd. *s.a.* 456–7: Gothic autonomy, Halsall, (2007) p. 259.
42. Date, *Auct, Prosp*. no. 7: Sid. Ap. *Ep*. 1.6.1.

43. On the context, see Mathisen, (1997).
44. Sid. Ap. *Carm.* 7.589–690.
45. On the debate, see Mathisen, (1997).
46. Sid.Ap. *Carm.* 7.233; see also Chapter 2.
47. Sid. Ap. *Carm.* 7: analysis, Harries, (2002) p. 304.
48. Although Hydatius claims that the two halves of Empire worked together, it would appear that this was by coincidence rather than design: Hyd. 166.
49. cf. Clover, (1966) pp. 171–2.
50. Proc. 3.5.22: *Fast. Vind. Prior. s.a.* 455.
51. Prisc. *fr.* 31.
52. Theod. Lect. 1.7: Clover, (1966) pp. 172–3.
53. Vict. Vit. 1.13.
54. Hyd. 456–7 (169 [176]), *s.a.* 456–7: Prisc. *fr.* 31.
55. Hyd. *s.a.* 456; Prisc. *fr.* 31; Sid. Ap. *Carm* 2. 367.
56. Gillett, (1995) pp. 380–3.
57. Gillett, (1995) p. 382.
58. *ILS* 1294: *Fl(avius) Ricimer v(ir) i(nlustris) magister utriusque militiae patricius et ex cons(ule) ord(inario) pro voto suo adornavitI.* The inscription was located in the apse, which sadly collapsed in 1589.
59. Sidonius, *Carm.* 5, 266–268
60. Sid. Ap. *Carm.* 2. 367.
61. Sid. Ap. *Carm.* 2.367. c.f. Hyd. 456–7 (176–7); 'At this time it was announced to king Theoderic [of the Visigoths] that through Avitus a great multitude of Vandals, which had set out from Carthage for Gaul and Italy with sixty ships, was destroyed after being trapped by Count Ricimer': c.f. Joh. Ant. fr.202.
62. Hyd. *s.a.* 456–7.
63. Relationship, Jord. *Get.* 229, 231.
64. Hyd. *s.a.* 456–7 (168, 170, 172, 173).
65. For a discussion of the problems surrounding the chronology of Avitus' fall, see Mathisen, (1985) esp. p. 327 n.4 and 331; Burgess, (1987) esp. p. 339.
66. *ILS* 1294.
67. Sivan, (1989) pp. 88–9.
68. Sivan, (1989) pp. 89–90.
69. cf. the famine in Rome during the 'rebellion' of Gildo in Africa in 396; Hughes, (2010) p. 105.
70. Joh. Ant. *fr.* 202.
71. Prisc. *fr.* 32: Joh. Ant. *fr.* 202.
72. *Fast. Vind. Prior. s.a.* 456: *Auct. ad. Prosp. Haun. s.a.* 456: after defeat of Vandals, PLRE 2, *Ricimer 2*, 944.
73. Greg. Tur. 2.11: Joh. Ant. *fr.* 202.
74. MacGeorge, (2002) p. 191.
75. The sack of Capua is mentioned in numerous online articles, most notably by the Encyclopaedia Britannica (http://www.britannica.com/EBchecked/topic/94379/Capua), and in some it is dated to March of that year, but sadly no reference is given to the ancient sources. However, it is mentioned by Landolfus Sagax (15.19f.) as happening at the same time as Gaiseric's sack of Rome. On the widespread nature of the attacks, Prisc. *fr.*24: Vict. Vit. 1.23.
76. 'When as in the time of the cruel Vandals, that part of Italy which is called Campania was overrun and sacked, and many were from thence carried captive into Africa: then the servant of God, Paulinus, bestowed all the wealth of his Bishopric upon prisoners and poor people.': Gregory of Rome, *Dialogue* 3.1.
77. Hyd. *Chron.* 176–177.

78. See below: Burgess, (1987).
79. For a full discussion, see, MacGeorge, (2002) p. 186 and Bibliography.
80. The embassy sent to Theoderic is described by Hydatius (*s.a.* 456 (176[177]). The interpretation that Avitus was informing Theoderic of his intention to move to Arles eliminates many of the problems from the chronology.
81. Date, *Auct. Prosp. Haun. s.a.* 456; *Fast. Vind. Prior. s.a.* 456: c.f. Theoph. AM 5948.
82. This is claimed in several internet sites, but the origin is undisclosed.
83. Burgess, (1987) p. 339, recognizes that the accepted chronology is at fault.
84. MacGeorge, (2002) p. 191.
85. Drinkwater, (2007) pp. 261–2.
86. See Chapter 2; Prisc. *fr.* 24: 'Roman leaders', Halsall, (2007) pp. 259–60.
87. Hyd. 164; Halsall, (2007) pp. 259–60.
88. Hyd. *s.a.* 456–7.
89. The claim that Avitus was either the 'dupe' or a 'traitor' in allowing the Goths to 'legally invade Hispania' is unwarranted and is based largely on hindsight: at the time of the Gothic attack on the Sueves it was not known that the Goths would eventually conquer Hispania and incorporate it into their own kingdom: for the claim, see Burgess, (2002) p. 22.
90. Jord. *Get.* 44.231.
91. Hyd. *s.a.* 456–7.
92. See above.
93. Rechiarius, *Auct. Prosp. Haun. s.a.* 457: Aioulfus, Jord. *Get.* 233.
94. Hyd. *s.a.* 456–7.
95. Burgess, (1987) p. 339.
96. Agrippinus is only attested as *MM* in 456–457, however the PLRE *II* (*Agrippinus*, 37–38) suggests that he could have been appointed as early as 451. Given the political manoeuvres outlined above it has been assumed that he was appointed after the death of Remistus by Avitus.
97. This description also takes into account the discrepant dates for the so-called 'Battle of Piacenza': 17 Oct., *Fast. Vind. Prior. s.a.* 456; 18 Oct. *Auct. Prosp. Haun. s.a.* 456: c.f. *Chron. Gall. 511* no. 6281; Theoph. AM 5948.
98. Greg. Tur. 2.11: Joh. Ant. fr. 202.
99. Eusebius of Milan, Vict. Tonn. *s.a.* 455; c.f *Auct. Prosp. Haun. s.a.* 456; *Fast. Vind. Prior. s.a.* 456; Theoph. AM 5948; Jord. *Get.* 240; Vict. Tonn. *s.a.* 456; Joh. Ant. *fr.* 202; Mar. Av. *s.a.* 456.
100. Majorian only appears in the narratives/chronicles at this point: Mar. Avit. 2.232.
101. The details surrounding Avitus' death are contradictory and have been the subject of extremely different interpretations. The one used here appears to be the most logical in the context surrounding political manoeuvres of the time. For more details on the problems and controversies, see Mathisen, (1985) p. 327, n.4.
102. Max, (1979) p. 225.
103. Mathisen, (1985) p. 335.
104. The claim that the death of Avitus was linked to the *coniuratio Marcelliniana* are unconvincing, again according to the chronology, the speed of transmission of news, and the distances involved: for a more detailed analysis of both sides, see e.g. Max, (1979) passim, and Mathisen, (2007) plus attendant bibliographies.
105. Sid. Ap. *Ep.* 3.3.9.
106. '*Inpartius Avitus ann. I mens. III./post ipsum mensibus XV reguum vacavit*': *Cont. Prosp. ad a 462.*
107. Dates: early = Burgess, (1987) p. 341; late = Mathisen, (1985) p. 332.
108. *Gall. Chron. 511*, No. 628: '*et Avitus occisus est a Maioriano comite domesticorum Placentiae*'.
109. *CIL XIII* 863; Allmer and Dissard, (1892) pp. 27–8: see also e.g. Halsall, (2007) p. 262.
110. Greg. Tur. *Glory of the Confessors* 62.

111. Sid. Ap. *Ep.* 1.11.6,
112. On the differing interpretation of the *coniuratio*, see Max, (1979) passim, and Mathisen, (2007).
113. Mathisen, (2007).
114. Mathisen, (1985) p. 333.

Chapter Five – Majorian

1. For example Olybrius, later husband of Placidia, daughter of Valentinian II, and emperor in his own right in 472 (see below): Clover, (1966) pp. 174–182, 192–195.
2. 'Gaping interregnum', Sid. Ap. *Ep.* 1.11.6.
3. Max, (1979) p. 225.
4. Sid. Ap. *Carm.* 5. 266f: 'moreover, there is linked with him in bonds of affection one who is armed with the great spirit of a royal grandfather (Ricimer's grandfather was Wallia, the King of the Goths who had died in 418)'.
5. 'This year the Burgundians occupied the lands of Gaul they had divided with French senators', (*Eo anno Burgundiones partem Galliac occupaverunt terrasque cum Gallis senatoribus diviserunt*), Mar. Av. *s.a.* 456.
6. *Lib. Hist. Franc.* 8: on the dating, Halsall, (2007) p. 263, and related notes.
7. The fact that messengers were immediately sent East is supported by the speed of response made by Leo; c.f. MacGeorge, (2002) p. 196: see below. On Marcian's proposed campaign, see Theod. Lect. 1.7: Clover, (1966) pp. 172–3 and Chapter 4.
8. Mathisen, (1998). This is a tempting theory and the fact that Marcian had been prepared to respond would help to explain the interregnum that followed as the East went about nominating Leo I as their own emperor. However, it should be noted that it is based upon a single reference from Malalas: 'Furthermore, Marcian gave to Anthemius in marriage his daughter from an earlier marriage, and he made him emperor in Rome. From her Anthemius had a daughter, whom he placed with the Master of Soldiers Ricimer... While Leo was ruling, Anthemius reigned at Rome, whom Marcian had raised to the imperial power' (*Chron.* 368–369).
9. Date, *Fasti. Vind. Prior. s.a.* 457. The concept that the rank of patrician now assumed an independent status is almost certainly erroneous – see, MacGeorge, (2002) p. 197.
10. Claim that Ricimer wanted to act as regent, e.g. MacGeorge, (2002) n.84.
11. See above.
12. Sid. Ap. 5.385–440. This was whilst Majorian was still a *magister* but before his acclamation as emperor by the troops – see below.
13. '*Burcomem dirigis illo exigua comitante manu*', Sid. Ap. *Carm.* 5.378–9.
14. Sid. Ap. *Carm.* 5.373–383: Thompson, (1963) p. 234.
15. AM 17.2.
16. Date, *Fast. Vind. Prior.* 583: unwilling, Sid. Ap. *Carm.* 5.9–12: 'at the little columns', Mathisen, (1998). The main difficulty when assessing events at this point is that there are two dates in the ancient sources for Majorian's accession to the throne. As just noted, the *Fasti Vindobonenses Priores* give the date as 1 April 457: on the other hand, the *Auctarium Prosperi Hauniensis* (*s.a.* 458) gives the date of his coronation as 28 December 457. Many attempts have been made to reconcile the different dates, some more successful than others. It is now generally accepted that he was first acclaimed by the troops in April but only crowned in Ravenna in December when Leo had agreed.
17. C.f Max, (1979) 234f; referencing esp. O. Seeck, *Geschichte des Untergangs der antiken welt*, (Berlin and Stuttgart, 1913–1920) p. 339.
18. Hyd, 179; Halsall, (2007) p. 264.
19. Hyd. *s.a.* 457.
20. Hyd. 181 [188], *s.a.* 457.
21. Hyd. 181 [188], *s.a.* 457.

22. Returned to Gaul, Hyd. *s.a.* 457: division; '*Eo anno Burgundiones partem Galliac occupaverunt terrasque cum Gallis senatoribus diviserunt*', Mar. Av. *s.a.* 456; also, Auct. Prosp. Haun. *s.a.* 457.
23. Mathisen, (1979) pp. 170–171.
24. Hyd, 179 [186], *s.a.* 457.
25. MacGeorge, (2002) p. 170.
26. Bury, (1923) I, p. 334.
27. E.g. Majorian became emperor at the bidding of 'Marcian', Jord. *Get.* 236, although Jordanes names the wrong Eastern emperor.
28. Date, *Auct. Prosp. Haun. s.a.* 458.
29. *Cons. Const. s.a.* 458.
30. E.g. O'Flynn, (1983) p. 107.
31. E.g. Mathisen, (1979) pp. 12–13; MacGeorge, (2002) p. 200.
32. cf. MacGeorge, (2002) p. 201.
33. O'Flynn, (1983) p. 109.
34. *Nov. Maj.* 2 (11 March, 458, Ravenna).
35. *Nov. Maj.* 5 (4 September 458, Ravenna): *Nov. Maj.* 7 (unknown).
36. *Nov. Maj.* 3 (8 May 458, Ravenna): *Nov. Maj.* 6 (26 October 458, Ravenna): *Nov. Maj.* 9 (17 April 459, Arles): *Nov. Maj.* 10 (Unknown): *Nov. Maj.* 11 (28 March 460, Arles).
37. *Nov. Maj.* 4 (11 July 458, Ravenna)
38. cf. MacGeorge, (2002) pp. 167–8.

Chapter Six – Majorian: Apotheosis

1. See Chapter 4.
2. Served alongside Majorian, Prisc. *fr.* 30: On his support for Majorian, see below: appointment, Greg. Tur. 2.1.
3. MacGeorge, (2002) pp. 154–5, gives a more detailed analysis and bibliography than here.
4. *Lib. Hist. Franc.* 8: on the dating, Halsall, (2007) p. 263, and related notes.
5. Greg. Tur. 2.12; *Lib. Hist. Fran.* 7; Fred. *Chron.* 3.11. Greg Tur. *HF* 2.12 states that Aegidius took Childeric's place for eight years. As Aegidius died in 365, he must have become 'king' of the Franks in either late 556 or early 457. For discussion, Halsall, (2007) p. 263.
6. For more on Childeric and his attempts to regain his lost throne, Greg. Tur. 2.2: Fred. 3.11; c.f. Ian Wood, *The Merovingian Kingdoms* (London, 1994).
7. Halsall, (2007) p. 263.
8. Mathisen, (1993) pp. 608–9 suggests that the Franks would have been useful as a counter to the Goths, but the capture of Cologne and Trier by the Ripuarians would neutralize any threat to the Goths from the Salians.
9. cf. PLRE 2, *Aegidius*, 12.
10. Accusation, V. *Lupicini*, 11: Lyon, Mar. Av. *s.a.* 456.
11. *V. Lupicini*. 11.
12. cf. PLRE 2, Agrippinus, p.38.
13. See Chapter 8.
14. *Nov. Maj.* 2, (11 March 458, Ravenna).
15. *Nov. Maj.* 2.4, (11 March 458, Ravenna).
16. cf. Mathisen, (1993) p. 20.
17. Thompson, (1963) p. 235.
18. See below.
19. cf. MacGeorge, (2002) p. 205.
20. Mathisen, (2007).
21. Agreement with Majorian, (Jones, 1986) p. 241: Marcellinus either taking independent action or by order of Leo to put pressure on Geiseric, McGeorge, (2002) pp. 46–48; c.f. Thompson, (1963) p. 237.
22. Prisc. *fr.* 28: Thompson, (1963) p. 235.

23. Hyd. 192 (*s.a.* 458): Isid. *Hist. Goth.* 33: Fred. 2.55.

24. Hyd. 185 [192], *s.a.* 458.

25. Hyd. 182 [189], *s.a.* 458.

26. Hyd. 183 [190], *s.a.* 458.

27. Hyd. 186 [192], *s.a.* 458.

28. Julius Nepos son of Nepotianus, Jord. *Rom.* 338: Julius Nepos nephew of Marcellinus, Marc. *com. s.a.* 474; Jord. *Get.* 239: but see Burgess, (2002) p. 25 for the opposite view.

29. O'Flynn, (1983) p 110, 207: Sid. Ap. 5.553f.

30. Sid. Ap. *Carm.* 22. *ep.* 1, 23; 59–75: Chronology of attack, Mathisen, (1993) p. 627.

31. Priscus, *frs.* 36–37.

32. CIL XIII 863; ET. ME / M OR S / U L P I C / R O S I C / I A E D F: Allmer and Dissard, (1892) pp. 27–8; Mathisen, (2007) see Chapter 4.

33. Mathisen (1993) p. 609.

34. Prisc. *fr.* 27; Sid. *Carm.* 5.364.

35. Mathisen, (1993) p. 609; tax, Sid. Ap. *Carm.* 5.446–8: hostages, Sid. Ap. *Carm.* 5.572..

36. Mathisen, (1993) pp. 618–9.

37. See Chapter 4.

38. Halsall, (2007) p. 263.

39. Mathisen, (1979) p. 602.

40. Paulinus Petricord (Paulinus of Perigueux), *Vita San Martini*, 6.111f: Greg. Tur, (*Vita Mart.*) 1.2.

41. *Nov. Maj.* 7 (6 November, 458, Ravenna).

42. Date, *Nov. Maj.* 7 (6 November, 458, Ravenna).

43. On this episode, Sid. Ap. *Carm.* 5. 483–510.

44. Sid. Ap. *Carm.* 5. 500–505. The claim in PLRE 2, *Tuldila*, 1131, that the affair took place near the Danube has been discounted: c.f. MacGeorge, (2002) p. 206, n.138.

45. cf. MacGeorge, (2002) p. 206.

46. Mathisen, (1979) p. 620.

47. Greg. Tur. *Vita Mart.* 1.2: trans. Van Dam, (2006) p. 202.

48. *Hydatius Chron.* no. 197, 197, *s.a.* 459: c.f. Paul. Pet. *Vit. Mart.* 6.111–142; Greg. Tur. *Vit. Mart.* 1.2.

49. Heather, (2002) p. 85.

50. *Carmina 5*; Lyons, *Carm.* 5. 574–6.

51. Sid. Ap. *Carm.* 5.446–8.

52. Sid. Ap. *Carm.* 5.255–6.

53. Sid. Ap. *Carm.* 5. 353–60.

54. Halsall, (2007) pp. 263–4.

55. Sid. Ap. *Ep.* 1. 11. 13.

56. Sid. Ap. *Carm.* 5 .574–585.

57. Heather, (2002) p. 91.

58. Mathisen, (2002) p. 236.

59. Halsall, (2007) p. 264.

60. Hyd. 192 (*s.a.* 458); 193 (*s.a.* 459).

61. Hyd. 189 [194], *s.a.* 459; c.f. Hyd. 164 [171], *s.a.* 456: under Theoderic, Halsall, (2007) p. 265.

62. Hyd. 188 [193], *s.a.* 459

63. Hyd. 190–1 [195–6], *s.a.* 459.

64. Hyd. 192 [197], *s.a.* 459.

65. Prisc. *fr.* 28: Thompson, (1963) p. 235; Heather, (2005) p. 368.

66. Hughes, (2012) p. 165.

67. Thompson, (1963) p. 235: Prisc. *fr.* 37, 00 Sud. 3.325.23. p. 133. See also, Zintzen, *Damascii vitae Isidori reliquae* 158.

68.

Chapter Seven – Majorian: The Fall

1. Hyd. 192 [197], *s.a.* 459: Halsall, (2007) p. 265. This is implied rather than clearly stated, since Hydatius refers to Suniericus and Nepotianus sending envoys to the Sueves telling them of the renewed alliance between the Goths and the Romans.
2. Hyd. 190 [195], *s.a.* 459.
3. Hyd. 193 [198], *s.a.* 460.
4. Hyd. 194 [199], *s.a.* 460.
5. Hyd. 192 [197], *s.a.* 459: Prisc. *fr.* 38. Common threat, Wozniak, (1981) p. 359: there is no evidence for his having a fleet of his own: *contra* Wozniak, (1981) p. 359.
6. PLRE, *Marcellinus* 6, 709.
7. Appointment, Wozniak, (1981) p. 359: pressure, Thompson, (1963) p. 236.
8. Hyd. 223 [227]. Unfortunately this entry in Hydatius is brief and has almost certainly been misplaced by a careless copyist, as otherwise Hydatius dates the episode to either 364 or 365. Historians have assumed that this could not be true, as by the later dates Marcellinus was in opposition to Ricimer and the new Emperor Severus and had placed himself under the command of Leo, who would not have agreed to the attack as it was against the terms of the treaty – see Chapter 8.
9. *Nov. Maj.* 11 (28 March 460, Arles).
10. Hyd. 195 [200], *s.a.* 460.
11. Hyd. 196 [201], *s.a.* 460.
12. For more on Frumarius' control of this territory, Hyd. 198 [203], *s.a.* 460.
13. Hyd. 201 [206], *s.a.* 460.
14. O'Flynn, (1983) p. 110, mentions this possibility, but it seems unlikely.
15. Much of this section is based upon MacGeorge, (2002) pp. 306–11.
16. For a major exception, see MacGeorge, (2002) pp. 306–11.
17. *Vict. Vit.* 3.20.
18. Sid. Ap. *Carm.* 5, 441–442.
19. cf. MacGeorge, (2002) p. 206.
20. Prisc. *fr.* 36. 1: Clover, (1966) p. 177.
21. Prisc. *fr.* 36. 1.
22. '*His diebus Maioranus imp. Caesaraugustam venit*', *Chron Caes. s.a. 460.*
23. *Chron.Gall. a 511*, 634; Mar. Avent. *s.a.* 460; Hyd.195 [200] *s.a.* 460.
24. Hyd. 195 [200], *s.a.* 460.
25. Traitors, Hyd. 195 [200], *s.a.* 460.
26. *Chron.Gall. a 511*, 634; Mar. Avent. *s.a.* 460; Hyd.195 [200] *s.a.* 460.
27. Hyd. 195 [200], *s.a.* 460.
28. *Chron. Gall. a 511*, 3.
29. Mathisen, (1998).
30. Hyd. 204 [209], *s.a.* 460.
31. Prisc. *fr.* 35.2.
32. Treaty of 442, Hughes, (2012) p. 122: These women were returned to the East in 462: Hyd. 211 [216], *s.a.* 462.
33. Hughes, (2012) pp. 188–9: Hyd. *s.a.* 456; Prisc. *fr.* 24; Sid. Ap. *Carm.* 2.367.
34. *Chron. Gall. a 511*, 635.
35. Hyd. 196 [201], *s.a.* 460.
36. Hyd. 196 [201], *s.a.* 460.
37. Hyd. 197 [202], *s.a.* 460.
38. Sueves fighting each other, Hyd. 198 [203], *s.a.* 460: eace with the Gallaecians, Hyd. 199 [204], *s.a.* 460.
39. Hyd. 201 [206], *s.a.* 460.
40. Mathisen, (1998).

41. Interestingly, Priscus claims that in 462 Aegidius 'projected hostilities against 'the Italians', suggesting that Majorian's assassination had been at least supported by a faction of the Senate in Rome.
42. On his way to Rome, Hyd. 205 [210], *s.a.* 461; Prisc. *fr.* 36.2: 'Arranging business essential for the empire and prestige of Rome', Hyd. 205 [210], *s.a.* 461.
43. Date, *Fast. Vind. Prior.* 588, *s.a.* 461: c.f. Marc. *com. s.a.* 461; Theoph. AM 5955.
44. Prisc. *fr.* 36.2.
45. *Fast. Vind. Prior.* 588, *s.a.* 461.
46. Proc. 3.7.14.
47. Proc. 7.14–15; Mathisen, (1979) p. 13: Vict. Ton. *s.a.* 463.
48. Jord. *Get.* 236.
49. Ennod. *Epig.* 135: inter Sirmond. Opera, tom. i. p. 1903; ref. Gibbon, *The Decline and Fall of the Roman Empire*, Vol. 1, Chapter 36: http://www.ccel.org/g/gibbon/decline/volume1/chap36.htm, n. 055.
50. Mathisen, (1998).
51. O'Flynn, (1983) p. 110.
52. O'Flynn, (1983) p. 111; Bury, (1923) I, p. 332.
53. Grubbs, J E, (2002) p. 110.
54. The greatest example of the 'never-say-die' attitude was during the Punic Wars in the third and second centuries BC, a low point against which military disasters could be compared.
55. cf. Drinkwater, (2007) pp. 265–6.

Chapter Eight – Libius Severus

1. Prisc. *fr.* 38 (1): dating, MacGeorge, (2003) p. 47.
2. Prisc. *fr.* 30.
3. MacGeorge, (2003) pp. 154–5.
4. Murray, (2000) p. 190.
5. Drinkwater, (2007) p. 271: contra, MacGeorge, (2003) pp. 103–6. The main evidence against the identity is that the earliest certain record of Odovacer relates to Saint Severinus in Noricum (Eug. *Vita S. Sev.* 6). Had Odovacer been in Gaul, an advance through Noricum would have been extremely unusual.
6. Greg. Tur. 2.18, trans. Thorpe, (1982) p. 132.
7. See Chapter 15.
8. Gothic navy, Sid. *Ep.* 8.6.13–15. Allied to Goths, Drinkwater, (2007) p. 271.
9. No date is given for Childeric's return in any of the sources. Assessing all of the available information, the secession of Aegidius and the preparations for war in the south give the most likely date for the event. Childeric was definitely back prior to 463, when he is attested as supporting Aegidius – see below.
10. MacGeorge, (2002) p. 296.
11. The fact that Theodosius was the one who removed Nepotianus from office and not Ricimer implies that Nepotianus was no longer following Ricimer's orders: see below.
12. In 467 Sidonius Apollinaris wrote a panegyric in which he stated that only Noricum, Gaul and Sicily were part of the Western Empire alongside Italy: Sid Ap. *Pan.* 2, 468–9.
13. Heather, (1995) p. 30.
14. Levy in 443, *Nov. Val.* 6.2.
15. Noricum, *Vit. Sev.* 4. 1–4; 20.1: Gaul, Proc. 5.12.16ff: Heather, (1995) p. 30, n.4.
16. Jord. *Get.* 199.
17. Jord. *Get.* 268.
18. Jord. *Get.* 270–1; Prisc. *fr.* 28; Sid. Ap. *Carm.* 2. 223–6.
19. Clover, (1966) p. 188.
20. cf. Theodosius I v Eugenius and Arbogast in 394, and Theodosius II v John and Castinus in 425.

21. Prisc. *fr*. 38.
22. Prisc. *fr*. 38: 'Although many embassies were sent to him at various times, Gaiseric did not free the women until he had betrothed Valentinian's elder daughter, whose name was Eudocia, to his son Huneric'.
23. Date, *Fast. Vind. Prior. s.a.* 461; c.f. Cass. *Chron. s.a.* 361; Marc. *com. s.a.* 461; Mar. Avent. *s.a.* 461; Paul. Diac. *Rom.* 15. 1. 48; *Chron. Gall 511*, no 363; Vict. Tonn. *s.a.* 461 (dated 7 July); Theoph. AM 5955 (also dated 7 July).
24. Hyd. 211.
25. Oost, (1970) p. 228.
26. Not recognized, Jord. *Rom.* 335.
27. *Chron. Gall. 511*, 363; Cass. *Chron. s.a.* 461.
28. *Laterc. Imp. Ad Iust.*
29. *Chron. Pasch. s.a.* 462: Theoph. AM 5955.
30. Corrupt text, PLRE 2, *Libius Severus 8*, 1004–5.
31. *Chron. Pasch. s.a.* 462.
32. cf. the much earlier Cicero, whose name comes from the Latin for 'chickpea' or 'vetch' because one of his ancestors had either a cleft or wart on the tip of his nose resembling a chickpea, or because his family had prospered through the farming of chickpeas: see Trollope, A, The Life of Cicero, Vol. 1, 42: http://www.gutenberg.org/files/8945-h/8945-h.htm#CHAPTER_II.
33. Oost, (1970) p. 237.
34. ILS 813 = CIL X 8072.
35. Oost, (1970) p. 237.
36. Woods, (2002) passim.
37. Oost, (1970) pp. 233–4.
38. cf. O'Flynn, (1983) p. 111.
39. Prisc. *fr*. 39. 8f.
40. *CJ* 6.61.5a. For further discussions on Marcellinus as *magister militum Dalmatiae* see e.g. Wozniak, (1981) p. 360.
41. Marc. *com. s.a.* 645; Jord. *Rom.* 336.
42. See Chapter 6.
43. Mathisen, (1989) p. 218.
44. Hyd. 212 [217] *s.a.* 462: c.f. Elton, (1992) p. 172.
45. Hyd. 213, *s.a.* 461.
46. Hyd. 222, *s.a.* 465.
47. Hilarus, *Ep.* 9, dated 10 October 463.
48. Joh. Mal. 374–5; Joh. Ant. *fr.* 209.
49. Drinkwater, (2007) pp. 268–9.
50. That Theoderic now saw himself as equal to Ricimer can be inferred from the fact that Vincentius, Arborius' replacement, was sent by Theoderic to invade Italy. For more details, see Chapter 13.
51. Prisc. *fr*. 30.
52. The *Liber Historium Francorum* (8) claims that at some point a Frankish group drove Aegidius' allies from Cologne. As Cologne had earlier been lost to the Ripuarians, this implies that some of the Ripuarians had allied with Aegidius: see below.
53. Prisc. *fr*. 39.6f.
54. E.g. in 453; *Addit. ad. Prosp. Haun. s.a.* 453.
55. cf. MacGeorge, (2002) p. 230.
56. Prisc. *fr*. 38. 8–10: 39. 8f. Although it is feasible that Phylarchus could have arrived in 461, 462 is far more likely as after Majorian's death envoys would need to first travel to Constantinople, triggering the envoys from Leo to Marcellinus and Gaiseric. The embassy

to Marcellinus would take time and it is unlikely that these would all have been accomplished in 461.

57. Prisc. *fr*. 38. 8–10.
58. Prisc. *fr*. 38. 11f.
59. Prisc. *fr*. 38. 15–16.
60. Eudoxia ransomed, *Chron. Pasch. s.a.* 455.
61. Hyd. 211 [216], *s.a.* 462.
62. Prisc. *fr*. 38. 1–2.
63. Pris. *fr*. 39. 16f.
64. Oost, (1970) p. 238.
65. Prisc. *fr*. 39. 6f.
66. Sid. *Carm*. 7.431f: Heather, (2002) p. 88.
67. Greg. Tur. HF. 2. 18; Fred. 3.12; *Lib. Hist. Franc*. 8.
68. *Chron. Gall. 511*, no. 638; Hyd. 214 [218], a. 463; Mar. Av. *s.a.* 463.
69. *LHF* 8.
70. Hyd. 215 [219], *s.a.* 463.
71. Hyd. 216 [220], *s.a.* 463.
72. Prisc. *fr*. 39. 25f.
73. Date e.g. *Anon. Cusp. s.a.* 464: see note 61.
74. For a more detailed discussion on their origin, see MacGeorge, (2002) 230f.
75. Gordon, (1960) p. 120.
76. *Fast. Vind. Prior. s.a.* 464; Cass. *Chron. s.a.* 464; Marc. *com. s.a.* 464; Paul Diac. *Hist. Rom.* 15.1; Jordanes, *Getica* 236, places the battle in the reign of Anthemius.
77. *Vit. S. Gen.* 6.25; 7.34: Butler, (1956) pp. 28–9: c.f. Drinkwater, (2007) p. 270.
78. *LHF* 8: see below.
79. Hyd. 219 [223] *s.a.* 464–5; Jord. *Get*. 234.
80. Hyd. 222 [226] *s.a.* 464–5.
81. *Nov. Sev.* 2 (unknown, 25 September 465).
82. Oost, (1970) p. 238.
83. Hyd. 220 [224] *s.a.* 464–5.
84. See below.
85. Hyd. 224 [228] *s.a.* 464–5.
86. Hyd. 214 [218] *s.a.* 463.
87. Paul, Pertric. 6. 111–12.
88. See below: contra, see Drinkwater, (2007) p. 270.
89. This information is to be found in a multitude of places on the internet, never with any supporting reference.
90. For example, 'Count Paul': see below.
91. Hyd. 224 (228) *s.a.* 465.
92. Greg. Tur. 2.18.
93. Hyd. 225 [229] *s.a.* 464–5.
94. Hyd. 226 [230] *s.a.* 464–5: news, Hyd. 227 [231] *s.a.* 465–6.
95. Contra, MacGeorge, (2003) p. 50. Interestingly, MacGeorge later claims (p. 54) that Marcellinus would have not had a fleet, discounting her own suggestion that he landed in Sicily on his own initiative.
96. Hyd. 227 [231] *s.a.* 465–6.
97. On the interpretation of these events, see Clover, (1966) 192f.
98. *Pasch. Camp. s.a.* 465; Jord. *Rom*. 336; Jord. *Get*. 236. Given the date of Severus' second *novella* the date of 15 August given by the *Fasti Vindobonenses Priores* (*s.a.* 465) is probably a mistake.
99. Sid. Ap. *Carm*. 2. 317–318.
100. Cass. *Chron. s.a.* 464.

101. See e.g. O'Flynn, (1983) 111f; O'Flynn, (1991) p. 124; Oost, (1970) passim; *contra*, MacGeorge, (2003) pp. 232–3.
102. E.g. O'Flynn, (1983) 111f.

Chapter Nine – Anthemius: Hope Renewed

1. Prisc. *fr.* 38. 1–2: see Chapter Eight.
2. O'Flynn, (1983) p. 115.
3. The discussions in earlier chapters suggest that this is unlikely.
4. Hyd. 228 [232] *s.a.* 465–6.
5. Hyd. 229 [233] *s.a.* 465–6.
6. Goth, Jord. *Get.* 239, Damascius, *Epitome Photiana*, 69 = Photius *Bbl.* 242; Alan, *Candidus* = Photius *Bibl.* 79.
7. Prisc. *fr.* 35.
8. *Dan. Styl.* 55.
9. *V. Dan. Styl.* 55. On the variants of this name, see PLRE 2, Fl. Zenon 7, 1200.
10. See Chapter 13f.
11. Prisc. *fr.* 39.
12. On Marcellinus and Sicily, see Chapter 8.
13. The sources concerned are brief and open to both different dating schemes and alternative interpretations, but the sequence of events that follows allows all of the different sources to be used without any internal conflicts. Explanations concerning individual decisions concerning the sources are explained at the appropriate place.
14. On the dating of these attacks, see Clover, (1966) 193f; c.f. Gordon, (1960) p. 120.
15. Proc. 3.5.22–6.
16. Envoys, Hyd. 233 (a. 466): Salla, Isid. Sev. 33: Euric's assassination of Theoderic, *Chron. Gall. 511*, 10, *s.a.* 466: Mar. Av. a. 467:
17. See Chapter 8: Sid. *Carm.* 7.431f.
18. Hyd. 324 [238] *s.a.* 466–7.
19. Hydatius claims that the envoys were sent to the 'emperor', but he dates the coronation of Anthemius to 465–466, which is clearly a mistake.
20. Hyd. 234 [238] *s.a.* 466–7.
21. Hyd. 235 [239] *s.a.* 466–7.
22. Cass. *Var.* 3.3.3.
23. Mathisen, (1998), analysing Malalas, *Chron.* 368–369: see Chapter 5.
24. Sid. Ap. *Carm.* 2. 67.
25. Sid. Ap. *Carm.* 2.194–7; Jord. *Rom.* 336; Evag. 2. 16; Joh. Mal. 368: PLRE 2, *Aelia Marcia Euphemia 6*, 423–4; O'Flynn, (1983) p. 115.
26. PLRE 2, *Aelia Marcia Euphemia 6*, 423–4.
27. E.g. Damascius, *Vita Isidori*, 108: c.f. MacGeorge, (2003) p. 53.
28. O'Meara, (2003) p. 21.
29. PLRE 2, *Anthemius 3*, 96–8.
30. PLRE 2, *Anthemius 3*, 96–8.
31. Proc. 3.6.5: c.f. MacGeorge, (2003) p. 234.
32. Transported, e.g. Wozniak, (1981) p. 361; contra, MacGeorge, (2002) 53f.
33. Marc. *com. s.a.* 468: Jord. *Get.* 239.
34. Hyd. 230 [234] *s.a.* 465–6.
35. Date, *Fast. Vind. Prior.* no.597, *s.a.* 467: c.f. Marc. *com. Chron. s.a.* 467. Cassiodorus (*Chron.* 1283 *s.a.* 467) claims this was at a place called Brontotas, three miles from the city, whereas Hydatius (231 [235] *s.a.* 465–6) claims it was eight miles from Rome. cf. Mar. Avench. *a.* 467.
36. This claim is to be found throughout the internet.

37. Gillet, 'Rome, Ravenna and the Last Western Emperors', *Papers of the British School at Rome*, Vol. 69, Centenary Volume (2001) pp. 131–67, p.132.
38. Sid. *Ep*. 1.5.10–11.
39. Sid. *Ep*. 1, esp. 5.10 and 9.1: c.f. MacGeorge, (2002) p. 236.
40. MacGeorge, (2003) p. 235.
41. Despite earlier conjecture, it is now becoming accepted that it was possible to have more than one *patricius* at any one time: see MacGeorge, (2003) pp. 55–6, plus attendant bibliography.
42. cf. MacGeorge, (2003) p. 235.
43. Sid. *Ep*. 1.5.10–11.
44. Enn. Vit. Epiph. 51: c.f Theoph. AM 5947; Marc. com. *s.a.* 464.
45. Prisc. *fr*. 35. See above.
46. On context and dating, MacGeorge, (2002) p. 230.
47. Joh. Ant. *fr*. 206.
48. Sid. *Ep*. 1.5.1.
49. Help, Sid. *Ep*. 1.9.5–6: Panegyric, *Carm*. 1.
50. Sid. *Eps*. 1.9.6: 9.16.3: c.f. Greg. Tur. 2.21. cf. MacGeorge, (2002) p. 236.
51. O'Flynn, (1983) p. 118.
52. MacGeorge, (2002) p. 234.
53. MacGeorge, (2002) pp. 23–5.
54. O'Flynn, (1983) p. 118.
55. O'Flynn, (1983) 118f; contra, MacGeorge, (2002) p. 242.
56. Marc. *com. s.a.* 467.
57. Famines, Theoph. AM 5964; Sid. *Ep*. 1.10.2: Pestilence, Gelasius, col. 113; Celestial Phenomena, Hyd. 238 [244] *s.a.* 467; Cattle disease, *Fast. Vind. Prior. s.a.* 467.
58. Prisc. *fr*. 40.
59. See Chapter 4.
60. *Vit. S. Dan. Styl*. 56.
61. Clover, (1966) p. 194.
62. Proc. 3.5.22–6: c.f. Vict. Vit. 1.51: Rhodes, Nest. *Baz. Her*. p. 379: Clover, (1996) p. 193, esp. n.4.
63. For more on Hydatius, especially on his dating of events outside Hispania, see the Introduction.
64. Hyd. 223 [227] *s.a.* 465.
65. See Chapter 8.
66. Hyd. 232 [236] *s.a.* 466–7
67. Hyd. 232 [236] *s.a.* 466–7.
68. Hyd. 241 [247] *s.a.* 468.
69. Hyd. 236 [240] *s.a.* 466–7.
70. Hyd. 236 [240] *s.a.* 466–7.
71. Hyd. 237 [241] *s.a.* 466–7.

Chapter Ten – The African Campaign

1. Proc. 3.6.8f.
2. Proc. 3.6.1–2.
3. Proc. 3.6.8: '*[Leo] bade [Marcellinus] go to the island of Sardinia, which was then subject to the Vandals.*'
4. MacGeorge, (2002) p. 58; *Liber. Pont*. 48.
5. Hyd. 241 (247) *s.a.* 468; c.f. MacGeorge, (2002) p. 57.
6. Proc. 3.6.9: Marsus, Theoph. AM 5963.
7. Prisc. *fr*. 41: PLRE 2, *Heraclius 4*, 541–2.
8. Brother of Verina, Prisc. *fr*. 53.1; *Vit. Dan. Styl*. 69; Marc. *com. s.a.*475; Jord. *Rom*. 337; Zach. *HE* 5.1; Proc. 3.6.2 etc. On his competence, see below.

9. Prisc. *fr.* 43.
10. Prisc. *fr.* 53.1: PLRE 2, *Basiliscus 2*, 212–14.
11. Consulship. CIL V 5685; Prisc. *fr.* 53.3.
12. Patr. Const. 3. 26, 124 – dated 168: c.f. Joh. Mal. 372; Beshevliev n. 206 (quoted in PLRE 2, *Basiliscus 2*, 212).
13. PLRE 2, *Basiliscus 2*, 213.
14. Four years, Friell and Williams, (1998) p. 175.
15. Gordon, (1960) p. 205, n.11: Cedrenus p.613 (however this appears to be '1115' in the *Migne Patrologia Graeca*; p.667, see Bibliography).
16. Theod. Lect. 1.25.
17. E.g. MacGeorge, (2002) p. 57, has the translation 'marines'.
18. See below.
19. Proc. 3.6.8.
20. Theoph. AM 5963.
21. Theoph. AM 5963.
22. Hughes, (2012) 83f.
23. Prisc. *fr.* 53.1. There is a *lacuna* in the text which is sometimes amended to a specific number.
24. Proc. 3.6.10.
25. Hughes, (2009) 79f.
26. In contrast, after landing in Sicily Belisarius was to be informed that Gelimer was in the interior and so unaware of his approach, meaning that the coasts were clear and Belisarius was free to land: Hughes, (2009) pp. 79–80.
27. Theod. Lect. 1.25.
28. AM 31.12.13f: Hughes, (2013) pp. 191–2.
29. For more details on these campaigns, see Hughes, (2012) esp. 79f. and Chapter 10, '*The Treaty of 442*'.
30. cf. Theoph. AM 5961.
31. Friell and Williams, (1998) pp. 174–5.
32. Traitors, Hyd. 195 [200], *s.a.* 460.
33. Proc. 3.6.16.
34. Joh. Mal. 14.44. c.f. Prisc. *fr.* 53; Phot. *Bibl.* 79; Theod. Lect. *Epit.* 399; Zon. 14.1.24–6.
35. Theoph. AM 5963.
36. Proc. 3.6.26; Nic. Call. *HE.* 15.27.
37. Bury, (1923) p. 337.
38. See Chapters 14 and 15.
39. Withdrew, Proc. 3.6.25; Theoph. AM 5963: Helped Leo v. Aspar, Theoph. AM 5963.
40. Date, *Fast. Vind. Prior. s.a.* 468; Quote, Proc. 3.6.25: c.f. *Pasch. Camp. s.a.* 468; Cass. *Chron. s.a.* 468; Marc. *com. s.a.* 468; *Cons. Ital. s.a.* 468.
41. Marc. *com. s.a.* 468.
42. E.g. O'Flynn, (1983) pp. 117–8 and associated footnotes; Wozniak, (1981) p. 361: contra, MacGeorge, (2003) pp. 59–60.
43. Hodgkin, (1892) p. 450; see also Bury, (1923) pp. 336–7.
44. Damascius, 69d.
45. E.g. MacGeorge, (2003) p. 59, esp. n. 109.
46. Prisc, *fr.* 67: discussed in MacGeorge, (2003) 59, n. 109. The fragment itself reads: '*Oaths were given as mutual; sureties not only for themselves but also for those who had come from the Roman court to reconcile the men*', (*Suda* A 1660). Blockley suggests that an 'attempt by the Roman authorities to mediate a dispute between quarrelling barbarians in Roman service', Blockley, (1983) p. 400, n. 204.
47. O'Flynn, (1983) pp. 117–8.
48. O'Flynn, (1983) p. 118.
49. Proc. 3.6.25.

50. MacGeorge, (2003) p. 60.
51. MacGeorge, (2003) pp. 59–60.

Chapter Eleven – Anthemius: Disintegration And Civil War
1. O'Flynn, (1991) p. 123.
2. Sid. *Ep.* 1.7.5.
3. Ennod. *Vit. Epiph.* 54.
4. Gelasius, *Ep.* 13, '*Ad Episcopos Dardaneia*'.
5. Sid. *Ep.* 1.7.11.
6. Cass. *Chron.* 1287, *s.a.* 469.
7. Mathisen, (1998).
8. Cass. *Chron. s.a.* 469: Paul. Diac. *Hist. Rom.* 15.2.
9. '*Pellitus Geta*', Ennod. *Vit. Epiph.* 67: '*Galata concitatus*', Ennod. *Vit. Epiph.* 53.
10. *Auct. Haun. ordo prior. s.a.* 476; *s.a.* 486: *ordo post. s.a.* 487: Ennod. *Vit. Epiph.* 80 (= p.351): Cass. *Var.* 3.3.3; 5.39.13: Jord. *Get.* 244: Greg. Tur. 2.20; 25.
11. See Fanning, (2002) p. 288*f* (esp. 294) and associated Bibliography for discussions on the meaning of *Rex*.
12. Marc. *com. s.a.* 464: '*Beorgor rex Alanorum a Ricimere rege occiditur*' ('Beorgor, king of the Alans, was killed by king Ricimer').
13. Hyd. 238 (*s.a.* 467).
14. Isid. Sev. *Hist.* 34: date, Hyd. 238 [242] *s.a.* 468.
15. Isid. Sev. *Hist.* 34.
16. Isid. Sev. *Hist.* 34: c.f. *Gall. Chron. 511* 651–2.
17. Van Dam, (2006) p. 53.
18. Isid. Sev. *Hist.* 34.
19. See e.g. Fear, Fernández Urbiña, and Marcos, (2013) 245f.
20. Greg. Tur. 2.27. It should be noted that not all authorities accept this tradition.
21. Proc. 5.12.9; 5.12.13–19: c.f. Drinkwater, (2007) p. 271.
22. Trier, Sid. *Ep.* 4.17; *Austrasian Letters*, pp. 110–153; Paris, *Vit. S. Gen.* 3.10.
23. PLRE 2, *Riothamus*, 945.
24. 12,000 men, Jord. *Get.* 237.
25. Sid. *Ep.* 3.9.
26. See below.
27. Hughes, (2012) pp. 144–5.
28. Greg. Tur. 2.18; Drinkwater, (2007) p. 271, 277, suggests an alternative date of 470–1.
29. Jord. *Get.* 238: '*Euric, king of the Visigoths, came against them with an innumerable army, and after a long fight he routed Riotimus, king of the Brittones, before the Romans could join him*'.
30. PLRE 2, *Victorius 4*, 1162–64. Although Jordanes (*Get.* 237) claims that Euric led the troops, his chronological distance from events suggests that he has combined Riothamus' defeat with the later Gothic expansion under Euric in person.
31. Greg. Tur. 2.18; c.f. Jord. *Get.* 238.
32. Jord. *Get.* 237–8.
33. Drinkwater, (2007) p. 270.
34. E.g. Bury, (1928) p. 226.
35. Greg. Tur. 2.18.
36. MacGeorge, (2003) p. 60.
37. Title, *CJ* 6.61.6ᵃ (1 June 473).
38. See below.
39. Joh. Ant. *fr.* 209: Jord. *Get.* 277f.
40. Nixon, (2002) p. 74: on the Law Code, see below.
41. Heather, (2002) p. 93.
42. cf. Heather, (2002) p. 91.

43. Greg. Tur. 2.18–19.
44. Sid. *Carm.* 7.369–75, dated 1 January 456; Drinkwater, (2007) 327f.
45. Mierow, (1915) p. 179.
46. Eug. *Vit. Sev.* 9.
47. Eug. *Vit. Sev,* 27.3; 31.4.
48. *Life of Lupus of Troyes* 10; Drinkwater, p. 271.
49. Joh. Ant. *fr.* 207, Paul. Diac. 15.2: O'Flynn, (1983) p. 119; contra, Clover, (1966) p. 201.
50. Joh. Ant. *fr.* 207.
51. See also: Cass. *Chron.* 1289 *s.a.* 470 where Romanus was killed for a 'capital crime against the State'; Paul. Diac. 15.2, where he was found guilty of treason.
52. '*His conss. Romanus patricius affectans imperium capitaliter est punitas*'; Cass. Chron. 1289; c.f. Joh. Ant. *fr.* 207.
53. Joh. Ant. *fr.* 207. Note that Clover, (1966) p. 201 n.1, claimed that this is a mistake and that it was Anthemius who went north to Milan.
54. cf. MacGeorge, (2002) p. 253, esp. n.163.
55. O'Flynn, (1983) p. 118.
56. MacGeorge, (2002); see also 'Valila' below.
57. Nearer to the Burgundians, O'Flynn, (1983) p. 119, O'Flynn also claims Gothic support for Ricimer but there is no evidence for this.
58. See above.
59. O'Flynn, (1983) p. 120: Zeno the Isaurian, Jord. *Rom.* 338.
60. There is no evidence that any military campaign by Leo to support Anthemius would have resulted in an alliance between Ricimer and Gaiseric: see O'Flynn, (1983) p. 120.
61. PLRE 2, *Victorius 4*, 1162–4.
62. The date is secure thanks to Sidonius noting that Gabali was still a Roman city in 469: Sid. *Ep.* 5.13.2: c.f. PLRE 2, *Victorius 4*, 1163. These territories were either to the west of, south-west of, or within the region of the Auvergne: see Map 17.
63. Greg. Tur. 2.19.
64. See Chapter 8.
65. *Life of Lupus of Troyes* 10; Drinkwater, p. 271: see above.
66. See above.
67. *V. S. Marcelli*, 34; Marc. *com. s.a.* 471; Jord. *Get.* 239; Joh. Mal. *fr.* 31: PLRE 2, *Leontia 1*, 667.
68. Date, PLRE 2, *Ecidicius 3*, 383–4.
69. Sid. *Ep.* 3. 3. 3–6: Greg. Tur. 2. 24: PLRE 2, *Ecdicius 3*, 383–4.
70. Father, Jord. *Get.* 240: brother-in-law of Sidonius, Sid. *Ep.* 5. 16. 1. 3; *Carm.* 20: c.f. Greg. Tur. 2. 24.
71. Sid. *Ep.* 3. 3. 7–8.
72. Sid. *Ep.* 5. 16. 1–2.
73. This section relies heavily upon the account given by Ennodius in his 'Life of Epiphanius', especially 51f. As a hagiography many of the details are suspect but as little other information is available there is little choice but to use it.
74. For a more detailed analysis and bibliography, MacGeorge, (2002) p. 248.
75. MacGeorge, (2002) pp. 252–3.
76. MacGeorge, (2002) p. 247.
77. Ennod. *Vit. Epiph.* 54.
78. Ennod. *Vit. Epiph.* 54.
79. Ennod. *Vit. Epiph.* 67–8.
80. Ennod. *Vit. Epiph.* 70.
81. O'Flynn, (1983) p. 119; Ennod. *Vit. Epiph.* 51–74.
82. The claim by MacGeorge (2002) pp. 251–2 that Epiphanius' mission was a failure deserves some attention, however the fact that Epiphanius did not return to Milan after his mission to Anthemius may have been due to factors that are not contained in Ennodius' account.

83. On the origins and status of Valila, see esp. Abosso, (2006).
84. Mathisen, (2006) pp. 1034–5: See Martindale, PLRE 2, *Fl. Valila qui et Theodovius*, 1147; Helmut Castritius, 'Zur Sozialgeschichte der Heermeister des Westreichs nach der Mitte des 5. Jh. : Flavius Valila qui et Theodovius', *Ancient Society* 3 (1972) pp. 233–243.
85. *Liber pontificalis* 49: Duchesne, 250: dated to before 483, PLRE 2, *Fl. Valila qui et Theodobius*, 1147.
86. Amphitheatre seat, CIL VI 32169: dates, PLRE 2, *Fl. Valila qui et Theodobius*, 1147: contra, Abosso, (2006).
87. PLRE 2, *Anthemiolus*, 93.
88. *Chron. Gall. 511*, 13.
89. *Chron. Gall. 511*, 649, *s.a.* 471.
90. Nixon, (2002) p. 74.
91. Vict. Vit. 3.19: Vict. Tonn. *s.a.* 523: 'Sixteen Years', Theoph AM 5964: Zon. 8.25.29.
92. Theoph AM 5964: Zon. 8.25.30: Nic. Call. 15.12.
93. It is possible that Gundobad was appointed in either 471 or 472 by Ricimer alone, but if that had been the case Anthemius would have appointed Bilimer as *magister militum per Gallias* in opposition to Gundobad, rather than simply as *Galliarum rector*, see below. Securing alliance, MacGeorge, (2002) p. 244.
94. cf. O'Flynn, (1983) p. 127.
95. Malalas, 375, claims that he arrived later and that with his extra troops Ricimer stormed Rome. However it should be noted that Malalas has a very confused chronology: for example, he has Majorian crowned by Ricimer after the death of Anthemius.
96. Paul. Diac. 15.4.
97. Paul. Diac. 15.4.
98. MacGeorge, (2002) p. 254, n.16.
99. For options and bibliography, MacGeorge, (2002) p. 254.
100. Joh. Ant. *fr.* 209 (1).
101. Joh. Ant. *fr.* 209 (1). The first stage of the civil war probably lasted from June 470 to March 471 when Epiphanius succeeded in reconciling Anthemius and Ricimer – see above. The second stage, the Siege of Rome, may have lasted for five months: March – July 472. For a full discussion, MacGeorge, (2002) p. 253; Gordon, (1960) p. 122 and 205, n.14.

Chapter Twelve – Olybrius

1. Joh. Mal. 373–4: *Chron. Pasch. s.a.* 464: Theoph. AM 5964: Paul. Diac. 15.3.
2. Joh. Mal. 374. on Juliana, Marc. *com. fr.*16, trans. Gordon, (1960) p. 167.
3. Mathisen, (1998), 'Olybrius': Mathisen's translation of Malalas.
4. *Chron. Pasch. s.a.* 464.
5. O'Flynn, (1983) pp. 120–1.
6. Mathisen, (1998), 'Olybrius': Mathisen's translation of Malalas.
7. For an in-depth analysis and related references, e.g. O'Flynn, (1983) p. 121.
8. See below.
9. See above.
10. cf. O'Flynn, (1983) p. 121.
11. cf. O'Flynn, (1983) p. 121.
12. For the dating, see Mathisen, (1998), 'Olybrius'.
13. cf. PLRE 2, *Anicius Olybrius 6*, 796–8.
14. Sid. *Carm.* 2. 357–65.
15. Clover, (1966) pp. 205–6, n.1.
16. O'Flynn, (1983) p. 122.
17. Prisc. 29, 30: c.f. Joh. Ant. *fr.* 204: further analysis, O'Flynn, (1983) p. 124.
18. Contra, O'Flynn, (1983) p. 120: PLRE 2, *Anicius Olybrius 6*, 796–8.
19. Joh. Ant. *fr.* 209 (1).

20. MacGeorge, (2002) pp. 252–3; see Chapter 11.

21. Joh. Ant. *fr*. 209.1–2; trans. Gordon, (1960) pp. 122–3.

22. Paul Diac. 15. 4: date, Mathisen, (1998), 'Anthemius'.

23. Defection, Paul Diac. 15. 4: c.f. MacGeorge, (2002) p. 255.

24. Joh. Ant. *fr*. 209.1–2; trans. Gordon, (1960) 122f.

25. *Chron. Gall. 511* n. 650 (*s.a.* 472): Mathisen, (1998), 'Anthemius': St. Peter's, e.g. Malal. 375: Santa Maria in Trastevere; Anthemius 'went among the suppliants of the martyr Chrysogonus', beggar, Joh. Ant. *fr*. 209.1–2: trans. Gordon, (1960) pp. 122–123, reference and discussion, Mathisen, (1998), Anthemius: Gundobad returned to Gaul, Malal. 375.

26. Joh. Ant. *fr*. 209.1–2, trans. Gordon, (1960) 122f: Malal. 37: Date, *Fast. Vind. Prior*. 606, *s.a.* 472 – '*his cons. bellum civile gestum est Romae inter Anthemius imperatorem et Ricimere patricio, et levatus est imp. Olybrius Romae, et occisus est imp. Anthemius V idus Iulias*'.

27. E.g. Cass. 1293; Marc. *com. s.a.* 472; Proc. 3. 7.1–3; *Chron. Gall. 511*, 15; *Pseud. Zach. Rhet.* 3.12.

28. Returned to Gaul, Malal. 375.

29. Joh. Ant. *fr*. 29 (2), trans. Gordon, (1960) p. 123: however, MacGeorge, (2002) p. 260 and n.194, claims that the same passage states that Ricimer gave Anthemius a royal burial.

30. Cass. *Chron*. 1293, *s.a.* 472.

31. MacGeorge, (2002) p. 255.

32. Gelasius, *Adversus Andromachum*, col. 115: c.f. MacGeorge, (2002) p. 255.

33. cf. Sid. *Ep*. 7.6.4 (AD 472–3): 6.6.1 (AD 472).

34. Malal. 373–375.

35. *Fast. Vind. Prior*. no.606. *s.a.* 472 – 'During this consulate a civil war occurred at Rome between the emperor Anthemius, and the emperor Olybrius was proclaimed at Rome, and the emperor Anthemius was killed on 11 July': Cass. 1293, *s.a.* 472: 'During this consulate, the patrician Ricimer, having made Olybrius emperor at Rome, after a short battle in the city killed Anthemius'. Trans. Mathisen, (1998), 'Olybrius'.

36. For full discussion and bibliography, see Mathisen, (1998), 'Olybrius'.

37. Thirty days and 'vomiting much blood', Joh. Ant. *fr*. 209.2, trans. Gordon, (1960) pp. 122–123: forty days Cass. 1293, *s.a.* 472.

38. *Fast. Vind. Prior*. 607.

39. *Fast. Vind. Prior*.608: Paul. Diac. 15.5

40. Joh. Ant. *fr*. 209.2.

41. Thirteen days after Ricimer, Joh. Ant. *fr*. 209. 2: seventh month, Cass. *Chron*. 1293: cf. Enn. *Vit. Epiph*. 350.

42. Joh. Ant. *fr*. 209. 2, trans. Gordon, (1960) pp. 122–123.

Chapter Thirteen – Glycerius

1. Cass. *Chron. s.a.* 473: Joh. Ant. *fr*. 209.2.

2. Date, *Pasch. Camp. s.a.* 473, but c.f. *Fast. Vind. Prior. s.a.* 473, which gives the date as 5 March. Ravenna and support of the army, Paul. Diac. 15.5. See also: Jord. *Get*. 239; Ennod. *Vit. Epiph*. 79 = pp. 350–1; Evag. 2.16; Marc. *com. s.a.* 473; Joh. Ant. *fr*. 209.2; Mar. Avench. *s.a.* 473.

3. Mathisen, *Glycerius*, (1998), notes Glycerius' lack of movement but gives no reason.

4. Haenel, '*Corpus Legum…*' p. 260.

5. Mathisen, *Glycerius*, (1998).

6. See Chapter 8.

7. PLRE 2, *Alla*, 60–1.

8. *Chron. Caes. (The Chronicle of Saragossa) s.a.* 473: c.f. Isid. Sev. *Hist*. 34, but see Chapter 15.

9. Consequence of Gothic attacks, Sid. *Ep*. 6. 12: relief measures, Greg. Tur. 2. 24.

10. Jord. *Get*. 284.

11. Grierson and Mays, (1992) p. 263.

12. *Auct. Haun. ordo. post. s.a.* 474; Joh. Mal. 375; Theoph. AM 5967.

13. *Auct. Haun. ordo. post. s.a.* 474; Theoph. AM 5966; *V. Dan. Styl.* 67: dysentery, Joh. Mal. 376; Cedr. 1. 614–15; Mich. Syr. 9. 4.

14. For details and sources concerning Zeno, see PLRE 2, *Fl. Zenon 7*, 1200–1202.

15. *V. Dan. Styl.* 55: see Chapter 9.

16. See Chapter 11.

17. At the order of Zeno, not Leo, Anon. Val. 7. 36 (*s.a.* 474).

18. cf. Joh. Ant. *fr.* 209.2, but see previous note.

19. It should be noted, however, that not all authorities accept the relationship between Nepos and Nepotianus: Burgess in Drinkwater and Elton, (2002) pp. 24–5.

20. Mathisen, *Julius Nepos*, (1998).

21. Son of Nepotianus, Jord. *Rom.* 338: Nephew of Marcellinus, Marc. *com. s.a.* 474; Jord. *Get.* 239.

22. *Magister militum*, *CJ* 6. 61. 5ᵃ: *patricius*, Anon. *Val.* 7. 36; *Auct. Haun. ordo. post. s.a.* 474.

23. Mal. 374–5: c.f. PLRE 2, *Gundobadus 1*, 524–5.

24. E.g. PLRE 2, *Gundobadus 1*, 524–5.

25. The claim that he had 'returned to Gaul to recruit additional forces' appears a little odd, given that region's ongoing war with Euric; Mathisen, (1998), *Glycerius*.

26. See above.

27. Mathisen, (1998), *Glycerius*.

28. June, Mathisen, (1998), *Glycerius*.

29. cf. Marc. *com. s.a.* 474.2

30. Marc. *com. s.a.* 473

31. Theoph. AM 5965.

32. Marc. com. *s.a.* 474.

33. See below, Chapter 16.

Chapter Fourteen – Julius Nepos

1. Rome, John of Antioch, *fr.* 209. 2; Marc. *com. s.a.* 474.2. 19 June 474, *Auct. Haun. ordo. post. s.a.* 474: 24 June 474, *Fast. Vind. Prior.* 613–4. Ravenna, Jord. *Rom.* 338–339.

2. Jord. *Rom.* 338–339: '*occisoque Romae Anthemio Nepotem filium Nepotiani copulata nepte sua in matrimonio apud Ravennam per Domitianum clientem suum Caesarem ordinavit [sc.Zeno]. qui Nepos regno potitus legitimo Glycerium, qui sibi tyrannico more regnum inposuisset, ab imperio expellens in Salona Dalmatia episcopum fecit*'. On the short reign of Glycerius and his possible acclamation as Caesar in August 473, see MacGeorge, (2002) p. 273, n. 16.

3. For a recreation of events using this hypothesis, but with the amendment that Nepos was made Caesar in Ravenna prior to Glycerius' overthrow, see Mathisen, *Julius Nepos* (1998). Sadly, most of the sources simply state that 'Nepos was made emperor': Anon. Val. 7.36;

4. See previous chapter.

5. Royal retinue, Sid. Ap. *Ep.* 8.9.5; Loire, Wolfram, (1990) p. 476 n. 530 and Bibliography, citing Villa Toponyms in the region.

6. See previous chapter.

7. Father, Jord. *Get.* 240: brother-in-law of Sidonius, Sid. *Ep.* 5. 16. 1. 3; *Carm.* 20: c.f. Greg. Tur. 2. 24: see also Chapter 11.

8. Sid. Ap. *Ep.* 3. 3. 3–8: Greg. Tur. 2. 24: PLRE 2, *Ecdicius 3*, 383–4.

9. Sid. Ap. *Ep.* 5. 16. 1–2.

10. See Chapter 11.

11. Reconcile, O'Flynn, (1983) p. 133.

12. Sid. Ap. *Ep.* 5. 16. 1; 3.7.2: c.f. Jord. *Get.* 241.

13. Mathisen, *Julius Nepos*, (1998).

14. Sid. Ap. *Ep.* 3. 7. 1: c.f. MacGeorge, (2002) p. 273, n.19.

15. See Chapter 13.

16. Date, MacGeorge, (2002) p. 274.
17. cf. MacGeorge, (2002) p. 274 and associated notes and Bibliography.
18. Contra, MacGeorge, (2002) p. 274.
19. E.g. MacGoerge, (2002) 274f.
20. MacGeorge, (2002) p. 273.
21. Anderson (trans.), (1936) p. 185, n.5: c.f. Mathisen, *Julius Nepos*, (1998); contra, MacGeorge, (2002) p. 274.
22. See Chapter 11.
23. cf. Bury, (1923) p. 346.
24. Gordon, (1960) pp. 123–4: see below, Chapter 16.
25. Malchus, *fr*. 3, trans. Gordon, (1960) p. 124.
26. Malchus, *fr*. 3, trans. Gordon, (1960) p. 124.
27. Jord. *Get*. 241.
28. cf. O'Flynn, (1983) p. 133, who also believes that Nepos was simply acting in the presumptuous fashion of the Eastern emperors without acknowledging the differences in the West.
29. Prisc. *frs*. 11 (2) and 15 (2): accepted as same man, e.g. O'Flynn, (1983) pp. 133–4: doubts, see MacGeorge, (2002) 276f. For a more detailed account of his origins, see Chapter 15.
30. MacGeorge, (2002) 277f.
31. Jord. *Get*. 241: *Patricius*, e.g. *Fast. Vind. Prior. s.a.* 475, 476.
32. Mathisen, *Julius Nepos*, (1998).
33. cf. O'Flynn, (1983) p. 134; contra, MacGeorge, (2002) p. 281.
34. Ennod. *Vit. Epiph*. 91.
35. Sid. *Ep*. 5.12, dated to 474, refers to a truce, not a treaty.
36. Sid. Ap. *Epist*. 7.7.4.
37. Ennod. *Vit. Epiph*. 79–91, trans. Cook, G. M, in Ferrari, (1952) p. 324.
38. Wolfram, (1990) p. 459, n.258: c.f. 186–7.
39. Sid. Ap. *Ep*. 6.7.6: Greg. Tur. 25.
40. Bury, (1923) p. 343.
41. Mathisen, *Julius Nepos*, (1998), claims that Nepos recognized the Vandals' possession of Africa, Sardinia, Corsica, the Balearics, and part of Sicily in a treaty. Unfortunately, he provides no source for the assertion and it is probable that the treaty actually belongs to the reign of Romulus Augustulus – see Chapter 15.
42. cf. Gordon, (1960) p. 123.
43. O'Flynn, (1983) p. 194, n. 15.
44. cf. *Auct Haun ordo post. s.a.* 475, '*Nepos cum ab Oreste patricio cum exercitu persequeretur, fugiens ad Dalmatias usque navigavit*).
45. cf. e.g. Mathisen, (1998).
46. Date, *Fast. Vind. Prior.* 615, *s.a.* 475: *Salona, Anon. Val.* 7.36, *s.a.* 474: cf. *Auct. Haun. ord. prior. s.a.* 475; Jord. *Get*. 241.
47. cf. O'Flynn, (1983) pp. 132–3.

Chapter Fifteen – Romulus Augustulus

1. Prisc. *frs*. 7, 8, 11 (2), 12, and 15 (2): Anon. Val. 8.38: accepted as same man, e.g. O'Flynn, (1983) pp. 133–4: doubts, see MacGeorge, (2002) 276f.
2. Father and wife, Prisc. *fr*. 8, c.f. *fr*. 11 (2): brother, Anon. Val. 8.37; *Fast. Vind. Prior. s.a.* 476: *Auct. Haun. ordo prior. s.a.* 476: *Auct. Haun. ordo post. s.a.* 476: *Auct. Haun. ordo post. marg. s.a.* 476: Cass. *Chron. s.a.* 476.
3. He is described by Anonymous Valesianus as *infantiae* ('youthful'), implying that in 476 he was at the most in his mid-teens: Anon. Val. 8. 38.
4. MacGeorge, (2002) p. 278, prefers a career in the East/Dalmatia.
5. Distrust, MacGeorge, (2002) p. 276.

6. Anon.Val. 8.37; 7.36: *Fast. Vind. Prior. s.a.* 475: *Auct. Haun. ordo prior. s.a.* 475: *Auct. Haun. ordo post. s.a.* 475: *Auct. Haun. ordo post. marg. s.a.* 475: Jord. *Get.* 241; *Rom.* 344: Marc. *com. s.a.* 475: Proc. BG. 1.1.2: Evag. 2.16: Theoph. AM 5965.

7. *Auct. Haun. ordo prior. s.a.* 475: Proc. 1. 1. 2.

8. As shown on coins; PLRE 2, *Romulus 3*, 959–50: Proc. 5.1.2.

9. Anon.Val. 8.37; 7.36: *Fast. Vind. Prior. s.a.* 475: *Auct. Haun. ordo prior. s.a.* 475: *Auct. Haun. ordo post. s.a.* 475: *Auct. Haun. ordo post. marg. s.a.* 475: Jord. *Get.* 241; *Rom.* 344: Marc. *com. s.a.* 475: Proc. BG. 1.1.27: Evag. 2.16.

10. cf. O'Flynn's claim that Orestes was attempting to install a new dynasty, (1983) p. 134.

11. This is implied by the events surrounding the death of Paulus; see below.

12. *Auct. Haun. ordo. prior. s.a.* 476, 486.

13. *Chron. Caes. (The Chronicle of Saragossa) s.a.* 473. cf. Isid. Sev. *Hist.* 34, however this entry could be dated to either event. See Chapter 13.

14. *Auct. Haun. ordo prior. s.a.* 476.

15. It is possible that he simply continued negotiations opened by Nepos prior to his expulsion.

16. Paul Diac. 15.7, stating that it was the year after the accession of Augustulus. See Clover, (1966), for a more detailed analysis of the historiography of the treaty.

17. See below.

18. Eugip. *Ep. Ad Pasc*: cf. MacGeorge, (2002) p. 280.

19. O'Flynn, (1983) p. 135.

20. There may have been demands for land before this point, but if so they have gone unrecorded and were always refused.

21. Proc. 5.1.5.

22. Thompson, (1982) p. 64.

23. MacGeorge, (2002) p. 282.

24. Proc. 5.1.3–8.

25. 'Italian aristocratic tradition', O'Flynn, (1983) p. 135: 'not motivated by Roman tradition and pride', MacGeorge, (2002) p. 282.

26. Thompson, (1982) pp. 64–5.

27. Thompson, (1982) pp. 64–5.

28. Greg. Tur. 2.18: trans. Thorpe, (1982) p. 132, see Chapter 11.

29. For, e.g. Reynolds and Lopez, (1946); Against, e.g. Macbain, (1983).

30. Jord. *Get.* 242.

31. Joh. Ant. *fr.* 209: bodyguard, Proc. 5.1.6.

32. Taken from Virgil, *Aeneid*, 2.368–369; Ferrari (Ed), Cook (Trans), (1952) p. 326, n.13.

33. See Chapter 13.

34. Ennod. *V. Epiph.* 358.

35. Ennod. *V. Epiph.* 95–100: Anon.Val. 8.37: Eugipp. *Ep. Ad Pasc.* 8: Jord. *Get.* 242: Proc. 1.1.5: *Fast. Vind. Prior. s.a.* 476: *Auct. Haun. ordo prior. s.a.* 476: *Auct. Haun. ordo post. s.a.* 476: *Auct. Haun. ordo post. marg. s.a.* 476: Cass. *Chron. s.a.* 476: Marcell. *com. s.a.* 476.

36. Mathisen, (1997).

37. 31 August 476, *Auct. Haun. ordo post. marg. s.a.* 476: 4 September, *Fast. Vind. Prior. s.a.* 476: Anon. Val. 8.37: *Auct. Haun. ordo prior. s.a.* 476: *Auct. Haun. ordo post. s.a.* 476: Cass. *Chron. s.a.* 476.

38. Anon. Val. 8.38; 10.45: Jord. *Get.* 241–2; *Rom.* 344: Proc. 1. 1. 7: Theoph. Am 5965: Marc. *com. s.a.* 476.

39. Marc. *com. s.a.*476: Jordanes *Get,* 242.

40. No embassy from Romulus to Zeno, e.g. Thompson, (1982) p. 275, n. 14.

41. Thompson, (1982) p. 64.

42. Cass. *Var.* 3. 35 (a. 507/11).

43. Doubt, MacGeorge, (2002) p. 281.

44. MacGeorge, (2002) p. 281, states that there were three emperors, dismissing the existence of Basiliscus.
45. O'Flynn, (1983) p. 135.
46. 'Greatest discretion', Proc. 5.1.2.

Chapter Sixteen – Odovacer, Julius Nepos, and Syagrius
1. Malchus, *fr.* 10.
2. cf. Blockley, Vol 2, (1983) p. 458, n.21.
3. Jones, (1962) p. 127.
4. C.f Thompson, (1982) pp. 66–7.
5. Coins, Thompson, (1982) p. 67 and associated Bibliography: PLRE 2, Odovacer, Addenda, p. xxxix.
6. Vict. Vit. 1. 14.
7. Thompson, (1982) p. 68.
8. cf. Thompson, (1982) p. 69.
9. Watts, (2011) p. 98.
10. Jones, (1966) p. 98.
11. Jones, (1966) p. 98.
12. *Auct. Haun. ordo. prior. s.a.* 476, 486.
13. Estimate of 15,000 men, O'Flynn, (1983) p. 199, n. 64, referencing Stein, *Histoire du Bas-Empire: De la disparition de l'Empire d'Occident à la mort de Justinian (476–565 AD.)* Vol. 2, (1959) p. 41.
14. Bury, (1923) p. 343, claims that Zeno acceded to the claim. However an analysis of his sources suggests this may be an error: Procopius (5.12.20) claims that it was Odovacer who relinquished the claim to Provence, whereas Candidus (*fr.* 1) notes only that the 'Gauls of the West revolted'.
15. Sid. Ap. *Ep.* 8.9.5: c.f Cass. *Var.* 3.3.3. See Chapter 9.
16. Sid. Ap. *Ep.* 8.3.3.
17. Sid. Ap. *Ep.* 9.3.2; Wolfram, (1990) p. 189.
18. Cass. *Var.* 3. 3
19. Odovacer takes power in August, *Auct. Haun. ordo post.* and *marg. s.a.* 476: sea closed to navigation, Veg. *Epit. Rei Mil.* 4.39; Clover, (1999) p. 237.
20. Born c. 390, died 477.
21. On the date, see note 18.
22. *Auct. Haun. ordo prior, ordo post*, and *marg. s.a.* 477; *Fast. Vind. Prior. s.a.* 477 (11 July), Marc. *com. s.a.* 477.
23. cf. MacGeorge, (2002) p. 283, n. 1186.
24. *Auct. Haun. ordo prior, ordo post* (date), and *marg.* (date, mother and brother also killed), *s.a.* 478.
25. Malchus, *fr.* 17: Vict. Vit. 2.2–6: discussion, Merrill and Miles, (2010) p. 124.
26. Property returned, Malchus, *fr.* 13.
27. E.g. Clover, (1999) p. 239.
28. Jones, (1966) p. 92.
29. Primenius, Eug. *Vit. Sev. praef.* 8: treaties with towns, Eug. *Vit. Sev.* passim; Thompson, (1982) p. 119.
30. Marc. *com. s.a.* 480 (names and place killed); *Fasti Vind. Prior.* s,a. 480 (9 May); *Auct Haun. ordo prior. s.a.* 480; cf. *Auct Haun. ordo post.* and *marg. s.a.* 480.
31. Malchus, *fr.* 1.
32. cf. Mathisen, *Glycerius*, (1998).
33. Ovida a Goth, Jord. *Get.* 113.
34. *Auct. Haun. ordo prior. s.a.* 482.

35. 27 November, *Fast. Vind. Prior. s.a.* 482; 9 December, *Auct Haun. ordo prior. s.a.* 482; cf. *Auct Haun. ordo post. s.a.* 482. The date given in the *Fasti Vindobonenses Priori* (*s.a.* 481) of 9 October appears to be in error: see PLRE 2, *Ovida*, 815.

36. *Cons. Ital. s.a.* 481–2; Cass. *s.a.* 481.

37. cf. O'Flynn, (1983) p. 142.

38. Jones, (1966) p. 97.

39. Coin, Watts, (2011) p. 98; Portrait, *Anon. Val.* 9.44.

40. *Auct. Haun. ordo prior. s.a.* 486; *Chron. Gall.* 666.

41. Gregory of Tours states that the Battle of Tolbiac (AD 496) took place in the 'fifteenth year of Clovis' reign, suggesting that the date of his accession was c. 491: Greg, Tur. 2.30.

42. For events and sources for this section, see PLRE 2, *Illus 1*, 586–590.

43. Joh. Ant. *fr.* 214.2.

44. cf. O'Flynn, (1983) p. 144.

45. Greg. Tur. 2.41: after Vouillé, noting that Chararic was tonsured and therefore Clovis was by this time Christian; Wood, (1994) p. 49.

46. Wolfram, (1990) p. 191.

47. Wolfram, (1990) p. 191.

48. Paul. Diac. *De Gest. Lang.* 1.19.

49. Date and battle, *Auct. Haun. ordo prior. s.a.* 487; Prisoner in Italy, *Auct. Haun. ordo post. s.a.* 487.2; Feletheus killed, Paul. Diac. *De Gest. Lang.* 1. 19

50. Joh. Ant. *fr.* 214.2.

51. O'Flynn, (1983) p. 144.

52. Eug. *Vit. Sev.* 44: cf. *Exc. Val.* 48.

53. Eug. *Vit. Sev.* 44.

54. Eug. *Vit. Sev.* 44: cf. Joh. Ant. *fr.* 214.7; *Anon. Val.* 48; *Cons. Ital. s.a.* 487; Cass. *Chron.* 1316.

55. Cass. *Var.* 8.5: Jord. *Get.* 269ff: Theoph. AM 5977.

56. Jord. *Get.* 281–2.

57. Jord. *Get.* 283f; *Rom.* 347.

58. *Anon. Val.* 42.

59. Jord. *Get.* 270: Malch. *fr.* 2; Theoph. AM 5964.

60. Malch. *fr.* 2.

61. Malch. *fr.* 11: Theoph. AM 5970.

62. *Anon. Val.* 9.42: Ennod. *Pan.* 12.

63. Malch. *fr.* 18: adoption, Jord. *Get.* 289.

64. Malch. *fr.* 11.

65. Malch, *fr.*2.12ff.

66. Malch. *fr.* 15.

67. Malch. *fr.* 17: Joh. Ant. *fr.* 211.4.

68. Marc. *com. s.a.* 479: Malch. *fr.* 18: Joh. Ant. *fr.* 211.4: *Pasch. Camp. s.a.* 478.

69. Joh. Ant. *fr.* 211.3–4: Malch. *fr.* 19.

70. Marc. *com. s.a.* 481: Jord. *Rom.* 346: Evag. *HE.* 3.25: Theoph. AM 5970: Joh. Ant. *fr.* 211.5.

71. Joh. Ant. *fr.* 211.5.

72. Marc. *com. s.a.* 482: Joh. Ant. *fr.* 213: Mich. Syr. 9.6.

73. Marc. *com. s.a.* 483.

74. Joh. Ant. *fr.* 214.3.

75. Fighting against Illus, e.g. Evag. *HE.* 27, but cf. e.g. Joh. Ant. *fr.* 214.4.6.

76. Joh. Ant. *fr.* 214.7: Zach. 6.6.

77. *Anon. Val.* 49: Proc. BG 1.1.10: cf. Theoph. AM 5977.

78. Ennod. Pan. 25: Jord. *Get.* 289: cf. Marc. *com. s.a.* 489; Joh. Nik. 115.

79. O'Flynn, (1983) p. 144.

80. Ennod. *Pan.* 25: *Vit. Epif.* 109.

81. O'Flynn, (1983) p. 147; but see, e.g. Moorhead, (1997) pp. 17–19 for the opposite view.

82. cf. Ennodius' comment concerning the harshness of winter, *Pan.* 27; Moorhead, (1997) p. 19, n. 58.
83. Moorhead, (1997) p. 20.
84. Some authorities suggest that the document should be dated to 488. I have followed the example of PLRE 2, *Pierius* 5. 885.
85. Jord. *Get*, 292 but c.f. Proc. *BG.* 1.1.13.
86. Ennod. *Pan.* 28–34: date, Moorhead, (1997) 21, n. 67: death of Trapstila, Paul. Diac. 15.15.
87. Ennod. *Pan.* 34.
88. Ennod. *Pan.* 35.
89. *Anon. Val.* 11.51.
90. *Fast. Vind. Prior. s.a.* 490.
91. Date, *Anon. Val.* 11.50: Fast. Vind. Prior. *s.a.* 490; Cass. *Chron. s.a.* 489; Ennod. *Pan.* 39ff.
92. *Anon. Val.* 11.50–1.
93. *Anon. Val.* 11.51–2: Ennod. *V. Epif.* 111.
94. Pierius killed, *Anon. Val.* 11.53; *Auct. Prosp. Haun. s.a.* 491: Cass. *Chron. s.a.* 490; Jord. *Get.* 292ff; Ennod. *Vit. Epif.* 109–11, 127; Ennod. *Pan.* 36–47.
95. *Auct. Prosp. Haun. s.a.* 491: *Fast. Vind. Prior. s.a.* 491: Siege, Jord. *Get.* 293; *Anon. Val.* 11.53–6; Proc. *BG.* 1.1.14–15, 24: Marc. *com. s.a.* 489.
96. *Fast. Vind. Prior. s.a.* 493: *Auct. Prosp. Haun. s.a.* 493: Ennod. *Pan Theod.* 55.
97. Dysentery, Evag, Schol. 3.29; Malalas, 391.1–4: Epilepsy, Theoph. AM 4983: Buried alive, Cedrenus, 1; Zon. 14.2.31–35.
98. Joh. Ant. *fr.* 214*a*.
99. E.g. Watts, (2011) p. 98; O'Flynn, (1983) p. 145, 200, n. 25.
100. The practice of having an Augustus and a Caesar to inherit became relatively common after the period of the 'Tetrarchy'. cf. O'Flynn, (1983) p. 145.
101. Ennod. *Pan.* 30.
102. O'Flynn, (1983) p. 145.
103. *Fast. Vind. Prior. s.a.* 493: *Auct. Prosp. Haun. s.a.* 493: Ennod. *Pan Theod.* 55.
104. Thompson, (1982) p. 71.
105. *Anon. Val.* 11.54.
106. *Anon. Val.* 11.55; *Fast. Vind. Prior. s.a.* 493; *Auct. Prosp. Haun. s.a.* 493; Cass. *Chron. s.a.* 493; Proc. *BG.* 1.25; Joh. Ant. *fr.* 214*a*.
107. Joh. Ant. *fr.* 214*a*.
108. Joh. Ant. *fr.* 214*a*: *Chron. Gall.* 511, no. 670.
109. Jones, (1966) p. 99.
110. O'Flynn, (1983) p. 140.
111. O'Flynn, (1983) p. 141.
112. *Exc. Val.* 48.
113. Jones, (1966) p. 97.
114. cf. O'Flynn, (1983) pp. 145–6.
115. cf. O'Flynn, (1983) p. 143.

Chapter Seventeen – Conclusion

1. A, Demandt, *Der Fall Roms* (1984) p. 695. The list is given in full here so that readers who have not had access before can assess it for themselves.
2. Heather, (1995) p. 33.
3. Heather, (1995) pp. 33–4.
4. Heather, (1995) p. 34.
5. Gordon, (1960) p. 126.
6. Compare the evidence found in the *vita Severinus* for the survival of border units in Noricum.
7. On the shift in loyalties and the emergence of new identities within the borders of the old Empire, see especially Pohl and Heydemann, (2013) passim.

8. Mathisen and Shanza, (2011) p. 99.
9. Sid. Ap. *Ep*. 5.16.2.
10. Hanson, (1972) p. 276.
11. Marc. *com. s.a.* 476.2; cf. Damasius, *Vita Isidori, fr.* 51a; Zos. 4.59.
12. John Rufus, *Plerophories* 89 (150.11 – 151.1); Mathisen and Shanza, (2011) pp. 100–2.

Bibliography

Primary Sources

Additamenta ad Chronicon Prosperi Hauniensis, Chronica Minora, Vol. 1. The Copenhagen Continuation of Prosper: A Translation, Muhlberger, S, *Florilegium*, Vol. 6 (1984) pp. 71–95.

Anonymus Cuspiani, Now known as the Chronica Minora

Anonymus Valesiani, see Chronica Minora, Vol. 1

Auctarium Prosperi Hauniensis ordo Priori, Chronica Minora, Vol. 1

Auctarium Prosperi Hauniensis ordo Posterior, Chronica Minora, Vol. 1

Auctarium Prosperi Hauniensis ordo Posterior Marginialia, Chronica Minora, Vol. 1

Austrasian Letters, see, *Epistulae Austrasicae*

Bischoff, B and Koehler, W, Annals of Ravenna, 'Eine Illustrierte Ausgabe Der Spätantiken Ravennater Annalen', in Koehler, W R W, *Medieval Studies in Memory of A. Kingsley Porter*, Vol. 1, (New York, 1969) pp. 125–138.

Candidus, *Anonyma E Suda*, in Blockley, R C, *The Fragmentary Classicising Historians of the Later Roman Empire*, Vol. 2, (Liverpool, 1983) pp. 463–473.

Carta Cornutiana, in Duchesne, L, *Le Liber pontificalis : texte, introduction et commentaire*, Vol I, p.cxlvii. https://archive.org/stream/duchesne01/duchesne1#page/n161/mode/2up

Cassiodorus, *Chronica*. http://ia311003.us.archive.org/0/items/chronicaminorasa11momm/chronicaminorasa11momm.pdf

Cassiodorus, *Variae*, Trans. Barnish, S J B, (Liverpool, 1992).

Chronica Caesaraugusta, Chronica Minora, Vol 2.

Chronica Gallica 452, Burgess, R, in Mathisen, RW and Schanzer, D (eds.), *Society and Culture in Late Antique Gaul. Revisiting the Source* (Aldershot, 2001) pp. 52–84.

Chronica Gallica 511, Trans. Murray, A C, From Roman to Merovingian Gaul: a Reader (Ontario, 2000).

Chronica Gallica 511, Burgess, R, in Mathisen, RW and Schanzer, D (eds.), *Society and Culture in Late Antique Gaul. Revisiting the Source* (Aldershot, 2001) pp. 85–99.

Chronica Minora, Vol. 1. http://www.dmgh.de/de/fs1/object/display/bsb00000798_meta:titlePage.html?sortIndex=010:010:0009:010:00:00

Chronica Minora, Vol. 2. http://www.dmgh.de/de/fs1/object/display/bsb00000823_meta:titlePage.html?sortIndex=010:010:0011:010:00:00

Chronica Minora, Vol. 3. http://www.dmgh.de/de/fs1/object/display/bsb00000825_meta:titlePage.html?sortIndex=010:010:0013:010:00:00

Chronicon Paschale, 284–628AD, Trans. Whitby, M and Whitby, M, (Liverpool, 1989).

Codex Justinianus, The Code of Justinian, Trans. Blume, F H. http://uwacadweb.uwyo.edu/blume&justinian/default.asp

Collectio Avellana. http://www.archive.org/stream/corpusscriptoru02wiengoog#page/n9/mode/2up

Corpus Legum ab Imperatoribus Romanis ante Iustinianum Latarum, Haenel, (Lipsiae, 1857). http://books.google.co.uk/books?id=scYLAAAAYAAJ&printsec=frontcover&dq=haenel+corpus+legum&hl=en&sa=X&ei=skuDUriSI-fm7AakiYGACg&redir_esc=y#v=onepage&q=haenel%20corpus%20legum&f=false

Consularia Italica, Chronica Minora, Vol. 1.

Corpus Inscriptionum Latinarum. http://cil.bbaw.de/cil_en/dateien/datenbank_eng.php

Corpus Scriptorum Ecclesiasticorum Latinorum (CSEL). http://www.archive.org/

Corpus Scriptorum Ecclesiasticorum Latinorum (CSEL). http://books.logos.com/books/5553#content=/books/5553

Ennodius. http://archive.org/stream/monumentagermani07geseuoft#page/n7/mode/2up

Ennodius,*Panegyricto Theoderic.*http://www.dmgh.de/de/fs1/object/goToPage/bsb00000796.html?pageNo=203&sortIndex=010%3A010%3A0007%3A010%3A00%3A00&sort=score&order=desc&context=chronica+minora&hl=false&fulltext=chronica+minora

Epistulae Austrasicae (Austrasian Letters). http://www.dmgh.de/de/fs1/object/display/bsb00000534_00117.html?zoom=0.75&sortIndex=040:010:0003:010:00:00

especially. http://www.dmgh.de/de/fs1/object/display/bsb00000534_00142.html?sortIndex=040%3A010%3A0003%3A010%3A00%3A00&zoom=0.75

Eugippius, *Epistle ad Paschasius.* http://www.tertullian.org/fathers/severinus_02_text.htm#LETTER%20OF%20EUGIPPIUS%20TO%20PASCHASIUS

Eugippius, *Vita Severinus.* http://www.tertullian.org/fathers/severinus_02_text.htm#C18 http://www.tertullian.org/fathers/severinus_02_text.htm

Eunapius, *Testimonia*, in Blockley, R C, *The Fragmentary Classicising Historians of the Later Roman Empire*, Vol. 2, (Liverpool, 1983) pp. 2–150.

Eutropius, *Breviarium historiae Romanae (Abridgement of Roman History)*, Trans. Watson, J. S. http://www.forumromanum.org/literature/eutropius/index.html (February 2010).

Evagrius Scholasticus, *Ecclesiastical History*, Trans. Walford, E. http://www.tertullian.org/fathers/index.htm#Evagrius_Scholasticus

Evagrius Scholasticus, *The Ecclesiastical History of Evagrius Scholasticus*, Trans. Whitby, M., (Liverpool, 2000).

Fasti Vindobonenses Priori, Chron. Min., Vol. I.

Gelasius Cyzicenus. https://play.google.com/books/reader?id=ZZLYAAAAMAAJ&printsec=frontcover&output=reader&authuser=0&hl=en&pg=GBS.PT282 (Greek with Latin translation)

Georgius Cedrenus, *Compendium Historiarum.* http://www.documentacatholicaomnia.eu/20vs/103_migne_gm/1100-1200,_Georgius_Cedrenus,_Compendium_Historiarum_%28MPG_121_0023_1166%29,_GM.pdf (Greek text with Latin translation)

Gregory of Rome, *Dialogues*/ http://www.tertullian.org/fathers/index.htm#Gregory_Dialogues

Hilary, Pope, Letters of, *Epistolae Romanorum pontificum genuinae et quae ad eos scriptae sunt A.S. Hilaro usque ad Pelagium II.: A.S. Hilaro ad S. Hormisdam, ann. 461–523* Tom. 1, A Thiel, (Brunsberg, 1868). http://archive.org/details/epistolaeromano00thiegoog http://archive.org/stream/epistolaeromano00thiegoog#page/n8/mode/2up

Hydatius, *The Chronicle of Hydatius and the Consularia Constantinopolitana*, Trans. Burgess, R W, (Oxford, 1993).

Isidore of Seville, *Chronicon*, Trans. Wolf, K B. http://www.ccel.org/ccel/pearse/morefathers/files/isidore_chronicon_01_trans.htm

Isidore of Seville, *Historia de Regibus Gothorum, Wandalorum et Suevorum.* http://e-spania.revues.org/15552#tocto1n5 http://www.thelatinlibrary.com/isidore/historia.shtml

John of Antioch (excerpts), *The Age of Attila*, Trans. Gordon, C D, (Michigan, 1960).

John Malalas, *The Chronicle of John Malalas*, Trans. Jeffreys, E, Jeffreys, M, and Scott, R., (Melbourne, 1986).

Jordanes, *Getica (The Origins and Deeds of the Goths)*, Trans. Mierow, C C. http://www.northvegr.org/lore/jgoth/index.php (February 2010) http://people.ucalgary.ca/~vandersp/Courses/texts/jordgeti.html (February 2010)

Jordanes, *Romana (De summa temporum vel origine actibusque gentis Romanorum)*, selected text and translation http://www.harbornet.com/folks/theedrich/Goths/Romana.htm http://www.thelatinlibrary.com/iordanes.html

Landolfus Sagax (Landolfi Sagacis) *Historia Romana* http://books.google.co.uk/books/about/Historia_miscella.html?id=yGA_AQAAIAAJ&redir_esc=y

Liber Historiae Francorum. http://archive.org/stream/monumentagerman02hann#page/n5/mode/2up

Liber Pontificalis, https://archive.org/stream/bookofpopesliber00loom#page/n13/mode/2up

Malchus, in Blockley, R C, *The Fragmentary Classicising Historians of the Later Roman Empire*, Vol. 2, (Liverpool, 1983) pp. 401–462.

Marius Aventicensis, *Chronica Minora, Vol 2*

Nestorius, *The Bazaar of Heracleides* http://www.tertullian.org/fathers/index.htm#Bazaar_of_Heracleides

Olympiodorus, in Blockley, R C, *The Fragmentary Classicising Historians of the Later Roman Empire* Vol. 2, (Liverpool, 1983) pp. 151–221.

Paulus Diaconus (Paul the Deacon), *Historia Romana (Roman History)*. http://www.thelatinlibrary.com/pauldeacon.html

Paulinus of Pella, *Eucharisticus*

Paulinus Petricord, *Vita san Martini*. http://archive.org/stream/corpusscriptorum16stuoft#page/16/mode/2up

Paulus Diaconis (Paul the Deacon), *History of the Lombards*. http://www.google.co.uk/url?sa=t&rct=j&q=&esrc=s&source=web&cd=3&cad=rja&uact=8&ved=0CDsQFjAC&url=http%3A%2F%2Fwww.thule-Italia.org%2FNordica%2FPaul%2520the%2520Deacon%2520-%2520History%2520of%2520the%2520Lombards%2520%281907%29%2520[EN].pdf&ei=Dg57U62WO-Om0AXdyYGAAQ&usg=AFQjCNHZ5QxqeGSZ3X24as50XvdttK0e_A&bvm=bv.67229260,d.d2kitalia.org%2FNordica%2FPaul%2520the%2520Deacon%2520-%2520History%2520of%2520the%2520Lombards%2520%281907%29%2520[EN].pdf&ei=Dg57U62WO-Om0AXdyYGAAQ&usg=AFQjCNHZ5QxqeGSZ3X24as50XvdttK0e_A&bvm=bv.67229260,d.d2k

Philostorgius, *Church History*, Trans. Amidon, P R, Society of Biblical Literature (2007).

Philostorgius, *Epitome of the Ecclesiastical History of Philostorgius*, Trans. Walford, E. http://www.tertullian.org/fathers/philostorgius.htm

Possidius, *Vita Augustini*. http://www.tertullian.org/fathers/possidius_life_of_augustine_02_text.htm

Priscus, in Blockley, R C, *The Fragmentary Classicising Historians of the Later Roman Empire*, Vol. 2, (Liverpool, 1983), pp. 222–379.

Priscus, *Testimonia*, in Blockley, R C, *The Fragmentary Classicising Historians of the Later Roman Empire*, Vol. 2, (Liverpool, 1983), pp. 222–400.

Prosper Tiro, *Chronicum*. http://www.documentacatholicaomnia.eu/02m/0390-0463,_

Prosper Tiro, *Chronicum*, From Roman to Merovingian Gaul: a Reader, Trans. Murray, A C (Ontario, 2000).

Prosperus_Aquitanus,_Chronicum_Integrum_In_Dua_Partes_Distributum,_MLT.pdf

Sidonius Apollinaris, *Carmina*. http://www.documentacatholicaomnia.eu/02m/0430-0489,_Sidonius_Apollinaris_Episcopus,_Carmina,_MLT.pdf

Sidonius Apollinaris, *Letters*. http://www.tertullian.org/fathers/#sidonius_apollinaris

Sidonius Apollinaris, *Poems and Letters (2 vols.)*, Trans. Anderson, W B, (Harvard, 1936/1965).

Suda, *Suida*. http://www.stoa.org/sol/

Theodorus Lector, *Historia Tripartita*. http://books.google.com/books?id=QF02EF4y4_4C&pg=RA1-PA395&lpg=RA37-PA394&dq=%22patrol.+gr.+LXXX#v=onepage&q&f=false

Theodorus Lector, http://books.google.co.uk/books?id=QF02EF4y4_4C&pg=RA1-PA395&lpg=RA37-PA394&dq=%22patrol.+gr.+LXXX&redir_esc=y#v=onepage&q&f=false (In Greek and Latin)

Theophanes, *The Chronicle of Theophanes Confessor: Byzantine and Near Eastern History AD 284–813*, Mango, C and Scott, R, Trans. (Oxford, 1997).

Theophanes, *Chronographia*, Trans. Niebuhr, B G, (Bonn, 1849). http://www.veritatis-societas. org/203_CSHB/0700-0800,_Theophanes_Abbas_Confessor,_Chronographia_%28CSHB_ Classeni_Recensio%29,_GR.pdf (April 2010)

Victor of Vita, *History of the Vandal Persecution*, Trans. Moorhead, J, (Liverpool, 1992).

Victor Vitensis, *Commentarius Historicus De Persecutione Vandalica*. http://www.documen tacatholicaomnia.eu/04z/z_0430-0484__Victor_Vitensis__Commentarius_Historicus_De_ Persecutione_Vandalica_%5BTh_Ruinarti%5D__MLT.pdf.html

Vita Aniani Episcopi Aurelianensishttp://www.dmgh.de/de/fs1/object/display/bsb00000750 _00112.html?sortIndex=010%3A020%3A0003%3A010%3A00%3A00&zoom=1.00

Vita Daniel Stylites, Three Byzantine Saints: Contemporary Biographies of St. Daniel the Stylite, St. Theodore of Sykeon and St. John the Almsgiver, Trans. Dawes, E, (St. Vladimir's Seminary Press, 1977). http://www.fordham.edu/halsall/basis/dan-stylite.asp

Vita Genofevae Virginis Parisiensis, Monumenta Germaniae historica inde ab anno Christi quingentesimo usque ad annum millesimum et quingentesimum. Scriptorum rerum MerovingicarumVol. 1, 1885, Berlin. http://www.dmgh.de/de/fs1/object/display/bsb00000 750_00005.html?sortIndex=010%3A020%3A0003%3A010%3A00%3A00

http://archive.org/stream/monumentagerman03hann#page/204/mode/2up

Zonaras, *Epitome Historiarum*. http://www.documentacatholicaomnia.eu/30_20_1050-1150-_ Ioannes_Zonaras.html (Greek)

Zosimus, *New History*, Trans. Ridley, R T, (Canberra, 1982).

Secondary Sources

Abosso, D H, 'Flavius Valila qui et Theodobius and the *Charta Cornutiana*', International Congress on Medieval Studies, courtesy of the author (2006).

Allmer, A and Dissard, P, *Inscriptions Antiques Tome IV, Lyons*, (Musee de Lyons, 1892).

Anderson, W B, 'Notes on the Carmina of Apollinaris Sidonius', *The Classical Quarterly*, Vol. 28, No. 1 (Jan, 1934) pp. 17–23.

Baynes, N H, 'The Vita S. Danielis Stylitae', *The English Historical Review*, Vol. 40, No. 159 (Jul, 1925) pp. 397–402.

Bishop, MC, and Coulston, JCN, *Roman Military Equipment From the Punic Wars to the Fall of Rome, 2nd ed.* (Oxford, 2006).

Blockley, R C, *The Fragmentary Classicising Historians of the Later Roman Empire*, Vol. 2 (Liverpool, 1983).

Brown, P, *The Making of Late Antiquity* (Cambridge, 1993).

Brown, P, *Through the Eye of a Needle: Wealth, the Fall of Rome, and the Making of Christianity in the West, 350–550 AD* (Princeton, 2012).

Burgess, R W, 'The Third Regnal Year of Eparchius Avitus: A Reply', *Classical Philology*, Vol. 82, No. 4 (Oct, 1987), pp. 335–345.

Burgess, R W, 'A New Reading for Hydatius "Chronicle" 177 and the Defeat of the Huns in Italy', *Phoenix*, Vol. 42, No. 4 (Winter, 1988), pp. 357–363.

Burgess, R W, 'Bryn Mawr Classical Review 2003.09.44', review of: MacGeorge, P, *Late Roman Warlords* (Oxford, 2003).

Burns, T S, *Rome and the Barbarians, 100 BC–AD 400* (Baltimore, 2003).

Bury, J B, 'A History of the Later Roman Empire, London, 2 Vols. (1923). http://penelope. uchicago.edu/Thayer/E/Roman/Texts/secondary/BURLAT/

Bury, J B, 'The End of Roman Rule in North Gaul', *Cambridge Historical Journal*, Vol. 1, No. 2 (1924) pp. 197–201.

Bury, J B, *The Invasion of Europe by the Barbarians* (London, 1928). http://rbedrosian.com/ Ref/Bury/iebtoc.html

Butler, A, Butler's Lives of the Saints, (Rev. and Supp. Thurston, S J H, and Attwater, D,) 4 Vols. (Aberdeen, 1956).

Castritius, H, 'Zur Sozialgeschichte der Heermeister des Westreichs nach der Mitte des 5. Jh.: Flavius Valila qui et Theodovius', *Ancient Society 3* (1972) pp. 233–243.

Christie, N, *The Fall of the Western Roman Empire: An Archaeological and Historical Perspective* (Bloomsbury, 2007).

Clover, F M, *Gaiseric the Statesman: a Study of Vandal Foreign Policy* University of Chicago, PhD Dissertation (1966).

Clover, F M, 'The Family and Early Career of Anicius Olybrius', *Historia: Zeitschrift für Alte Geschichte*, Vol. 27, No. 1 (1st Qtr., 1978) pp. 169–196.

Clover, F M, 'Relations between North Africa and Italy, A.D. 476–500 : some numismatic evidence', *Revue numismatique, 6e série* Vol. 33 (1991) pp. 112–133.

Clover, F M, 'A Game of Bluff: The Fate Of Sicily After A.D. 476', *Historia: Zeitschrift für Alte Geschichte*, Bd. 48, H.2 (2nd Qtr., 1999) pp. 235–44.

Coello, T, *Unit Sizes in the late Roman Army* (Oxford, 1996).

Collins, R, *Visigothic Spain 409 – 711* (Blackwell, 2004).

Dawes, E, and Baynes, N H, *Three Byzantine Saints: Contemporary Biographies of St. Daniel the Stylite, St. Theodore of Sykeon and St. John the Almsgiver* (London, 1977).

Drinkwater, J F, *The Alamanni and Rome 213–496 (Caracalla to Clovis)* (Oxford, 2007).

Drinkwater, J, and Elton, H, *Fifth-Century Gaul: A Crisis of Identity?* (Cambridge, 2002).

Duncan-Jones, R, *Structure and Scale in the Roman Economy* (Cambridge, 1990).

Elton, H, *Warfare in Roman Europe, AD 350–425* (Oxford, 1996).

Elton, H, 'Warfare and the Military' in Lenski, N, *The Cambridge Companion to the Age of Constantine* (Cambridge, 2006).

Fanning, S, 'Emperors and empires in fifth-century Gaul', in Drinkwater and Elton, *Fifth-century Gaul: A Crisis of Identity* (Cambridge, 2002) pp. 288–297.

Fear, A, Fernández Urbiña, J, and Marcos, M, *The Role of the Bishop in Late Antiquity: Conflict and Compromise* (London, 2013).

Ferrari, R J (Ed.), *Fathers of the Church: Early Christian Biographies Volume 15* (Washington DC, 1952).

Flomen, M, *The Original Godfather: Ricimer and the Fall of Rome* (2008). https://secureweb.mcgill.ca/classics/sites/mcgill.ca.classics/files/2008-9-03.pdf

Friell, G, and Williams, S, *The Rome that Did Not Fall: The Survival of the East in the Fifth Century: The Phoenix in the East* (Routledge, 1998).

Frye, D, 'Aristocratic Responses to Late Roman Urban Change: The Examples of Ausonius and Sidonius in Gaul, *The Classical World*, Vol. 96, No. 2 (Winter, 2003) pp. 185–196.

Gibbon, E, *The Decline and Fall of the Roman Empire*, 4 Volumes (Liverpool, 1861).

Gillett, A, 'The Birth of Ricimer', *Historia: Zeitschrift für Alte Geschichte*, Vol. 44, No. 3 (3rd Qtr., 1995) pp. 380–384.

Gillett, A, 'Rome, Ravenna and the Last Western Emperors', *Papers of the British School at Rome*, Vol. 69, Centenary Volume (2001) pp. 131–67.

Goldsworthy, A, *Roman Warfare* (Phoenix, 2000).

Goldsworthy, A, *The Complete Roman Army* (2003).

Grierson, P and Melinda Mays, M, *Catalogue of Late Roman Coins in the Dumbarton Oaks Collection and in the Whittemore Collection, from Arcadius and Honorius to the Accession of Anastasius (Dumbarton Oaks Catalogues)* (Harvard, 1992).

Grubbs, J E, *Women and the Law in the Roman Empire: A Sourcebook on Marriage, Divorce and Widowhood* (Routledge, 2002).

Halsall, G, 'Review Article: Movers and Shakers: the barbarians and the Fall of Rome', *Early Medieval Europe* 8 (1) (1999) pp. 131–145.

Halsall, G, *Barbarian Migrations and the Roman West, 376–568* (Cambridge, 2007).

Hanson, R P C, 'The Reaction of the Church to the Collapse of the Western Roman Empire in the Fifth Century', *Vigiliae Christianae*, Vol. 26, No. 4 (December 1972) pp. 272–287.

Hassall, M, *The Army*, in *The Cambridge Ancient History (2nd Ed): Vol. XI (The High Empire)* (Cambridge, 2000). pp. 70–192.

Heather, P, 'The Huns and the End of the Roman Empire in Western Europe', *English Historical Review CX* (1995) pp. 4–41.

Heather, P, *The Fall of the Roman Empire* (2005).

Heather, P, 'Goths in the Roman Balkans ca. 350–500', *Proceedings of the British Academy* 141 (2007) pp. 163–190.

Heather, P, 'The Huns and the End of the Roman Empire in Western Europe', *The English Historical Review*, Vol. 110, No. 435 (Feb, 1995) pp. 4–41.

Heather, P, (Ed), *The Visigoths From the Migration Period to the Seventh Century: An Ethnographic Perspective* (Woodbridge, 1999).

Heather, P, 'The emergence of the Visigothic kingdom', in Drinkwater and Elton (2002) pp. 84–94.

Hodgkin, T, *Italy and her Invaders: Volume 2: Book 2 The Hunnish Invasions; Book 3 The Vandal Invasion and the Herulian Mutiny* (Oxford, 1892).

Holder, P, 'Auxiliary Deployment in the Reign of Hadrian', *Bulletin of the Institute of Classical Studies, Supplement 81*, Vol. 46, (2003) pp. 101–145.

Hughes, I, *Stilicho: The Vandal Who Saved Rome* (Barnsley, 2010).

Hughes, I, *Aetius: Attila's Nemesis* (Barnsley, 2012).

Jones, A E, *Social Mobility in Late Antique Gaul: Strategies and Opportunities for the Non-Elite* (Cambridge, 2009).

Jones, A H M, 'The Constitutional Position of Odovacer and Theoderic', *The Journal of Roman Studies*, Vol. 52, Parts 1 and 2 (1962) pp. 126–130.

Jones, A H M, *The Later Roman Empire, 284–602: A Social Economic and Administrative Survey*, 2 Volumes (Baltimore, 1966/1986).

Jones, A H M, *The Decline of the Ancient World* (Harlow, 1968).

Kelly, C, *Ruling the Later Roman Empire* (Cambridge, 2006).

Liebeschuetz, J H W G, *Barbarians and Bishops: Army, Church, and State in the Age of Arcadius and Chrysostom* (Clarendon Press, 1992).

Macbain, B, 'Odovacer the Hun?', *Classical Philology*, Vol. 78, No. 4 (Oct., 1983) pp. 323–327.

MacGeorge, P, *Late Roman Warlords* (Oxford, 2002).

Martindale, J R, *The Prosopography of the Later Roman Empire, Volume II, AD 395–527* (Cambridge, 2006).

Mathisen, R W, 'Sidonius on the Reign of Avitus: A Study in Political Prudence', *Transactions of the American Philological Association* (1974–), Vol. 109 (1979) pp. 165–171.

Mathisen, R W, 'Resistance and Reconciliation; Majorian and the Gallic Aristocracy After the Fall of Avitus', *Francia* 7 (1979) pp. 597–627. http://francia.digitale-sammlungen.de/Blatt_bsb00016282,00613.html

Mathisen, R W, 'Emigrants, Exiles, and Survivors: Aristocratic Options in Visigothic Aquitania', *Phoenix*, Vol. 38, No. 2 (Summer, 1984) pp. 159–170.

Mathisen, R W, 'The Third Regnal Year of Eparchius Avitus', *Classical Philology*, Vol. 80, No. 4 (Oct, 1985) pp. 326–335.

Mathisen, R W, 'Ten Office Holders: A few Addenda and Corrigenda to P.L.R.E.', *Historia: Zeitschrift für Alte Geschicht*, Bd. 35, H. 1 (1st Qtr., 1986) pp. 125–7.

Mathisen, R W, *Ecclesiastical Factionalism and Religious Controversy in Fifth-Century Gaul* (Washington, 1989).

Mathisen, R W, *Roman Aristocrats in Barbarian Gaul: Strategies for Survival in an Age of Transition* (Austin, 1993).

Mathisen, R W, *De Imperatoribus Romanis: Libius Severus* (1997). http://www.luc.edu/roman-emperors/libius.htm

Mathisen, R W, *De Imperatoribus Romanis: Petronius Maximus* (1997). http://www.roman-emperors.org/petmax.htm

Mathisen, R W, *De Imperatoribus Romanis: Romulus Augustulus* (1997). http://www.luc.edu/roman-emperors/auggiero.htm

Mathisen, R W, *De Imperatoribus Romanis: Anthemius (12 April 467 – 11 July 472 A.D.)* (1998). http://www.roman-emperors.org/anthemiu.htm

Mathisen, R W, *De Imperatoribus Romanis: Avitus* (1998). http://www.luc.edu/roman-emperors/avitus.htm

Mathisen, R W, *De Imperatoribus Romanis: Glycerius* (1998). http://www.luc.edu/roman-emperors/glyceriu.htm

Mathisen, R W, *De Imperatoribus Romanis: Julius Valerius Maiorianus* (1998). http://www.luc.edu/roman-emperors/major.htm

Mathisen, R W, *De Imperatoribus Romanis: Julius Nepos* (1999). http://www.luc.edu/roman-emperors/nepos.htm

Mathisen, R W, *De Imperatoribus Romanis: Valentinian III* (1999). http://www.luc.edu/roman-emperors/valenIII.htm

Mathisen, R W, 'Fifth-century visitors to Italy: business or pleasure', in Drinkwater and Elton (2002) pp. 228–238.

Mathisen, R W, 'Peregrini, Barbari, and Cives Romani : Concepts of Citizenship and the Legal Identity of Barbarians in the Later Roman Empire', *The American Historical Review*, Vol. 111, No. 4 (October, 2006) pp. 1011–1040.

Mathisen, R W, 'Ricimer's Church in Rome: How an Arian Barbarian Prospered in a Nicene World', in Lenski, N, and Cain, A (Eds.), *The Power of Religion in Late Antiquity* (Ashgate Press, 2009) pp. 307–326. Retrieved from academia.edu: https://www.academia.edu/3624056/_Ricimers_Church_in_Rome_How_an_Arian_Barbarian_Prospered_in_a_Nicene_World_

Mathisen, R W, and Shanza, D, *Romans, Barbarians, and the Transformation of the Roman World* (Farnham, 2011).

Mattingly, D, *An Imperial Possession. Britain in the Roman Empire* (London, 2006).

Max, G E, 'Political Intrigue during the Reigns of the Western Roman Emperors Avitus and Majorian', *Historia: Zeitschrift für Alte Geschichte*, Bd. 28, H. 2 (2nd Qtr., 1979) pp. 225–237.

Max, G E, 'Procopius' Portrait of the Emperor Majorian: History and Historiography', *Byzantinische Zeitschrift*, Volume 74, Issue 1, 3–6, 49, No. 2 (2nd Qtr., 2000) pp. 251–257.

Andy Merrills, A, and Miles, R, *The Vandals* (Malden, 2010).

Mierow, C C, 'Eugippius and the Closing Years of the Province of Noricum Ripense', *Classical Philology*, Vol. 10, No. 2 (Apr., 1915) pp. 166–187.

Mitchell, S, *A History of the Later Roman Empire, AD 284–641: The Transformation of the Ancient World* (Wiley-Blackwell, 2007).

Mommaerts, T S, and Kelley, D H, 'The Anicii of Gaul and Rome', in Drinkwater and Elton (2002) pp. 111–121.

Moorhead, J, *Theoderic in Italy* (Oxford, 1997).

Murray, A C, *From Roman to Merovingian Gaul: a Reader* (Ontario, 2000).

Nixon, C E V, 'Relations between Visigoths and Romans in fifth-century Gaul', in Drinkwater and Elton (2002) pp. 64–74.

Nicasie, M, *Twilight of Empire, the Roman Army from the Reign of Diocletian until the Battle of Adrianople* (Amsterdam, 1998).

O'Flynn, J M, 'A Greek on The Roman Throne: The Fate of Anthemius', *Historia: Zeitschrift für Alte Geschichte*, Bd. 40, H. 1, (1991) pp. 122–128.

O'Meara, D, *Platonopolis: Platonic Political Philosophy in Late Antiquity* (Oxford, 2003).

O'Meara, D J, *Platonopolis: Platonic Political Philosophy in Late Antiquity* (Oxford, 2005). http://www.scribd.com/doc/60370888/Platonopolis-Platonic-Political-Philosophy-in-Late-Antiquity#

Oost, S I, 'Aëtius and Majorian', *Classical Philology*, Vol. 59, No. 1 (Jan, 1964) pp. 23–29.

Oost, S I, *Galla Placidia Augusta. A Biographical Essay* (London, 1968).

Oost, S I, 'D. N. Libivs Severvs P. F. AVG', *Classical Philology*, Vol. 65, No. 4 (Oct, 1970) pp. 28–240.

Reynolds, R L and Lopez, R S, 'Odoacer: German or Hun', *The American Historical Review*, Vol. 52, No. 1 (Oct, 1946) pp. 36–53.

Rousseau, P, 'In Search of Sidonius the Bishop', *Historia: Zeitschrift für Alte Geschichte*, Bd. 25, H. 3 (3rd Qtr., 1976) pp. 356–377.

Rousseau, P, 'Sidonius and Majorian: The Censure in "Carmen" V', *Historia: Zeitschrift für Alte Geschichte*, Bd. 49, No. 2 (2nd Qtr., 2000) pp. 251 – 257.

Sabin, P, van Wees, H, and Whitby, LM (eds), *The Cambridge History of Greek and Roman Warfare Vol. 2: Rome from the Late Republic to the Late Empire* (Cambridge, 2007).

Salmon, ET, *Samnium and the Samnites* (Cambridge, 2010).

dal Santo, M, *Debating the Saints' Cults in the Age of Gregory the Great* (Oxford, 2012).

Shackleton Bailey, D R, 'Critical and Interpretative, on the Poems of Sidonius Apollinaris', *Phoenix*, Vol. 30, No. 3 (Autumn, 1976) pp. 242–251.

Sivan, H S, 'Sidonius Apollinaris, Theodoric II, and Gothic-Roman Politics from Avitus to Anthemius', *Hermes*, 117. Bd., H. 1 (1989) pp. 85–94.

Southern, P, and Dixon, K R, *The Late Roman Army* (Batsford, 1996).

Thompson, E A, 'Peasant Revolts in Late Roman Gaul and Spain', *Past & Present*, No. 2 (Nov, 1952) pp. 11–23.

Thompson, E A, 'The Visigoths from Fritigern to Euric', *Historia: Zeitschrift für Alte Geschichte*, Bd. 12, H.1, (Jan, 1963) pp. 105–126.

Thompson, E A, *Romans and Barbarians: The Decline of the Western Empire* (University of Wisconsin Press, 1952).

Thompson, E A, *Romans and Barbarians: The Decline of the Western Empire* Wisconsin Greg. Tur. 2.18: trans. Thorpe (1982) p. 132. See Chapter 11.

Tomlin, 'The Army of the Late Empire', in Wacher, J, *The Roman World*, Vol. 1 (London, 1990) pp.107–120.

Van Dam, R, *Saints and Their Miracles in Late Antique Gaul* [Paperback] (Princeton, 2006).

Watts, E, 'John Rufus, Timothy Aelurus, and the Fall of the Western Empire', in Mathisen and Shanza, *Romans, Barbarians, and the Transformation of the Roman World* (2011) pp. 97–106.

Whitby, M, 'The Late Roman Army and the Defence of the Balkans', *Proceedings of the British Academy*, 141 (2007) pp. 135–161.

Wolfram, H, *History of the Goths* (California, 1990).

Wood, I, 'The Fall of the Western Empire and the End of Roman Britain', *Britannia*, Vol. 18 (1987) pp. 251–262.

Wood, I, *The Merovingian Kingdoms: 450–751* (Harlow, 1994).

Woods, D, 'A Misunderstood Monogram: Ricimer or Severus', *Hermathena* No. 172 (Summer 2002) pp. 5–21.

Wozniak, F E, 'East Rome, Ravenna and Western Illyricum: 454–536 AD', *Historia: Zeitschrift für Alte Geschichte*, Bd. 30, H. 3 (3rd Qtr., 1981) pp. 351–382.

Zintzen, C, *Damascii vitae Isidori reliquiae* (Hildesheim, 1967).

Index

Ad Columellas, (at the little columns), 68
Addua River, Battle of, 214
Adovacrius, 97–8, 114, 145, 148, 192
Adrianople, 211
Adrianople, Battle of, 3, 19, 29, 132
Adriatic, 31, 33, 42, 76, 84, 86–7
Aegidius, 73–5, 77–81, 97–100, 103–104,
106–107
    death, 109–14, 141–3, 205–206, 218
Aelia Marcia Euphemia *see* Euphemia
Aetius, xiii, xix, 4–6, 9, 12–14, 17–18, 20–1,
23–9, 31–6, 39–46, 48–53, 55, 57, 59–60, 71,
73, 76, 85, 95, 107–108, 121, 142–3, 153, 161,
168, 180–1, 187, 217–19, 228
    death, 42
Africa, xiii, xv–xvi, xix, 4–7, 10–11, 13–14, 20,
23, 25–8, 31, 34–5, 46–7, 50–1, 55–6, 58, 76,
82–3, 85, 87–95, 100–101, 107, 110, 123–34,
136–8, 152, 154, 159, 179, 184, 190, 201, 203,
218–20, 224–5, 227
African Campaign, Anthemius, 125–37
African Campaign, Majorian, 87–94
Africa Proconsularis, 27
Agatha, Saint, Church of, 56–7
Agricola, 62
Agrigentum, Battle of, 57
Agrippinus, 58, 61, 73–4, 104–105
Aioulfus, 61, 65, 68
Ajax, 117
Alamanni, 67–8, 70, 146, 148
    invasion of Italy, 67–70
Alans, 4, 6, 12, 22, 24, 28–9, 36, 42, 76, 94, 106,
109–10, 148
Alaric, 3–4, 31, 49, 59, 158
Alaric II, 205–208, 214
Albigenses, 148
Alexandria, 120, 123
Alicante, Bay of, 90
Alla, 167–8
Alypia, 120–1, 137
Amiens, 100
Anastasius, 179, 214
Angers, 98, 114, 145
Anicia Juliana, 154
Anicii, 40, 44, 154
Anthemiolus, 120, 151, 159

Anthemius, xix, 67, 116–58, 159–61, 165, 167–8,
172, 174, 176, 178, 180, 185, 187, 192, 197,
211, 219–20, 224, 227
    marriage, 120
    nominated Augustus by Leo, 120
    proclaimed emperor, 121
    authorizes attempted invasion of 465, 123–4
    African campaign, 125–37
    civil war, 140–57
    death, 157–8
Aquae Flaviae *see* Chaves
Aquileia, 39
    Siege of, 28, 39
Aquitaine, 4, 6, 11, 23, 45, 119, 148
Arab, 129
Arbogast, fourth-century magister militum, 3
Arbogast of Trier, 142
Arborius, 105, 114, 168
Ardabur, 118, 155, 170
Argenton, 100
Ariadne, 170, 205
Arian(ism), 11, 56, 117, 130, 202, 217
Arles, 53, 59, 61, 78–82, 87, 93, 95, 151, 169–71,
174, 176, 181, 189–90, 200, 205
    Siege of, 29
Armorica, 9, 143
Armutus, 211
Arvandus, 138–40
Arverna *see* Clermont
Ascanius, 93
Asdings, 23
Aspar, 26–7, 55, 67, 101, 114–18, 120, 130,
135–6, 148–51, 155–6, 170, 211
Asturica, 60, 69
Astyrius, 23
Attila, xiii, 5–6, 25, 28–9, 31–2, 36, 39, 46, 49,
53, 84, 101, 120, 180–1, 187–8, 194
Aunona, 117, 119
Aurem tironicum, 119
Autun, 100
Auvergne, 121, 148, 175–6, 182–4, 189, 227–8
Auxilia Palatina, 15–16
Avitus, Eparchius, 45, 47, 49–64, 65–6, 68, 73,
78, 80–3, 95, 99–100, 105, 116, 149, 160, 169,
175, 179–80, 194, 227
Azestus, 47

Bacaudae/Bacaudic, 5–6, 9, 12, 24–5, 29, 60
Baetica, 22–5, 77, 83
Balearic Islands, xv, 23, 70, 90, 190
Balkan Mountains *see* Haemus Mountains
Balkans, 3, 30, 32, 76, 97, 107, 209, 212
Basiliscus, 127, 159, 187–8, 193–4, 211
    African Campaign, 129–37
Basilius, 24
Basilius, Bishop of Aix, 181
Bastarni, 75
Batavis, 146
Beorgor, 110, 148
Bergamum, 110
Bilimer, 153, 157–8
Bituriges, 142, 148
Bleda, 5, 56
Boethius, 42
Bolia River, Battle of, 144
Bon, Cap *see* Cap Bon
Boniface/Bonifatius, 5, 23, 25–7, 29, 130
Bonophatianae, 212
Bourg-de-Déols, 143–4
Bourges, 143–4
Bracara, 23, 60
Brachila *see* Bravila
Bravila, 202
Bretons *see* Brittones
Brioude, 62
Britain, xix, 14, 20, 142–3, 203
Brittany, 143
Brittones, 122, 142–4, 148, 151, 178
Brontotas, 121
Bucellarii, 17, 28, 35, 42–4, 73, 94, 193
Burco, 67–8, 70
Burgundians, xv, 5–7, 10, 12, 29, 54, 60, 63, 65,
    68, 74, 76, 78–9, 87, 105, 138, 140, 142–3,
    147–8, 151–3, 161, 169, 171, 176–180, 184,
    200, 203–204

Cadurci, 148
Caesaraugusta, 24, 87, 90, 93
Cambrai, 206
Campania, 69, 122, 193
Cap Bon, 131, 133
Cap Bon, Battle of, 133–5
Cappadocia, 193
Capua, sack of, 59
Carcassonne, 184
Cartagena, 23, 85, 90
Carthage, xiii, 5–6, 27–8, 47, 50–1, 69, 88–90,
    92–3, 107–108, 123, 125, 127, 129, 131–4,
    136, 152, 199–200, 202
Carthaginiensis, 24, 51, 87, 90
Carthago Spartaria *see* Cartagena
Castinus, 23, 25,
Castra, Martis, 32
Catalaunian Plains, Battle of, 5, 25, 29, 32, 36,
    39, 52–3

Catholic, 10–11, 117, 202, 217
Cemandri, 32
Chararic, 207
Chaves, 93
Childeric, 73, 98, 109–11, 113–14, 141–6, 148,
    178, 192, 205
Chilperic, Burgundian King, 60
Chilperic, son of Goar, 152, 176–8
Christianity, xviii, 10–11, 138, 220
Classis, 59
Claustra Alpium Iuliarum, 31
Clermont, 52, 62, 149, 169, 175, 179, 181, 183,
    225
Clovis, 205–207
Cologne, 66, 73, 106, 110–12
Comes (rei militaris), 18, 25, 27, 33, 54, 56, 114,
    127, 142, 203
Comes Africae, 27, 130
Comes domesticorum, 42, 55, 57, 71, 81, 161,
    165, 167, 170, 199, 208, 213–14
Comes domesticorum et Africae, 26
Comes et magister utriusque militiae, 150, 168
Comes Hispaniae, 23, 25
Comes Patrimonii, 199
Comes rei militaris Dalmatiae, 33
Comes rei militaris per Thracias, 120
Comes sacriarum largitionum, 40
Comes spectabilis, 82
Comes Stabuli, 151
Comes Tingitaniae, 27
Comitatenses, 15–16, 19, 21–2, 34
Conimbrica, 114, 124
Coniuratio Marcelliniana, 63, 80
Consentius, 53
Constantine III, 20, 22, 28
Constantinople, 3–4, 6, 30, 34, 42, 44, 50–1, 104,
    108, 118, 120, 122, 125–6, 129, 144, 154–6,
    160, 162, 180, 187–8, 193, 198, 205, 209,
    211–12
Constantius III, 4, 13, 28, 39
Corsica, xv, 59, 61, 69–70, 89, 108, 190
    trees for Vandal ships, 88
Council of the Seven Gauls, 9, 52–3, 82
Cyrila, 77, 83

Dalmatia, xv, 8, 30–3, 42, 51–2, 76–7, 86, 97,
    99–101, 104, 106, 144, 170–3, 185, 187,
    203–204, 216–17
Danube River, 52, 75, 120, 208, 210, 213
Dediticii, 16–17
Dertona *see* Tortona
Dictynius, 93
Diocletian, 10, 16, 33, 99
Donatistism, 10–11, 47, 138
Dromon, 89, 91
Duces, 18–19
Duero River, 77
Durius River *see* Duero River

Dux, 18, 83, 85, 148
Dyrrachium, 84, 211

Ecdicius, 62, 149, 175–80
Egypt, 16, 39, 123, 125, 127, 129
Elche, 90
Elche, Battle of, 90–1, 93–4, 96, 108
Emerita, 24
Ennodius, xix, 94, 121, 138, 140, 149, 172–3,
    181, 183, 192, 212, 215, 217
Eparchius Avitus *see* Avitus, Eparchius
Epiphanius, Bishop, xix, 149–50, 152, 157, 173,
    180–1, 192–3
Epirus, 8, 179
Eudocia, 39, 44, 46, 50–1, 90, 93, 107–108, 152,
    202
Eudoxia, 8, 31, 39, 43–7, 50, 93, 102, 107–108
    release from Africa, 108
Eugenius, 3, 67
Eugippius, xix, 146, 192
Euphemia, 120
Euphemia, St, 154
Euric, 119, 123, 138, 140–5, 148, 151, 153,
    158–9, 167–71, 175–7, 179–84, 188–90,
    192–3, 199–201, 203–205, 227–8
    Law Code of, 145, 151
Eusebius, Bishop, 61
Everdingus, 151

Fabricae, 22, 35, 100
Faenza, 214
Faustus, Bishop of Riez, 181
Favienta *see* Faenza
Feletheus, 208, 212
Felix, 23
Felix, Pope, 217
Ferderuchus, 208
Ferreolus, 29
Flavian Amphitheatre, 150
Foederati, 16–17, 199
Foedus, 32, 76
Fort Livia, 184
Framtane, 68, 77
Franks (*see also* Franks, Ripuarian and Salian),
    xv, 5–6, 20, 28–9, 54, 68, 73–5, 98, 106,
    109–10, 112–13, 122, 140, 142, 145–6, 178,
    200, 203–205, 207, 226
Franks, Ripuarian, 65, 73–5, 100, 106, 113
Franks, Salian, 73–5, 97, 122
Frederic, Gothic prince, 25, 29, 60, 109–10, 113,
    119
Fredericus, son of Feletheus, 208, 212–15
Frigidus, Battle of, 3
Fronto, 25, 54
Frumarius, 87, 93, 111

Gaiseric, 5, 39, 44–51, 54–6, 69–70, 77, 85, 88–
    93, 96, 101–102, 107–108, 110–12, 115–16,
118–19, 122–36, 141, 146–7, 152, 154, 156–7,
    179, 181, 184, 190, 199–203, 227
    Crossing to Africa, 5, 23, 26
    Defeat of Boniface, 5, 26
    Siege of Hippo, 26
    Sack of Hippo, 27
    Treaty of 435, 26–7
    Capture of Carthage, 27
    Treaty of 442, 27
    Sack of Rome, 46–9
    Defeats Majorian's invasion attempt, 87–93
    Returns imperial women, 107–108
    And the invasion of 468, 125–37
    Treaty with Orestes, 190
    Death, 201
Gallaecia, 22–3, 25, 60–1, 68, 77, 81, 83, 87, 93,
    110–11, 141
Galla Placidia, 31, 39
Gaudentius, 28, 40–1, 50, 107–108
Gaul, xiii, xv–xvi, xviii–xix, 4–9, 12, 14, 16,
    20–2, 24–5, 28–9, 31, 34–5, 45–6, 52–63,
    65–8, 71–5, 77–83, 85, 94–7, 99–101, 103–
    106, 109–14, 117, 119, 122, 124, 138, 141–5,
    147–9, 151–3, 157–9, 167–9, 171, 174, 176,
    178–80, 182–4, 186, 188, 191–3, 199–200,
    203–205, 207, 214–15, 219, 224–27
Genevieve, St, 111
Gentiles, 16–17
Georgius Cedrenus, 40
Gepids, 8, 65, 139, 213–14
Gerontius, 22
Gibuldus, 146
Gildo, 4
Glycerius, 161, 165–74, 176–8, 194, 203, 219
Goar, 152–3
Goths, xiii, xv–xvii, xix, 3–6, 8, 10–13, 17, 20,
    23, 25, 27–32, 36, 42, 45, 47, 49, 52–3, 55–6,
    58–9, 61, 65, 68, 77–81, 83–5, 87, 94–5,
    97–100, 103–106, 109–14, 117–19, 121–2,
    124, 127, 138, 140, 142–5, 147–9, 151, 157,
    159, 165, 168–9, 172, 174–6, 178–9, 181–2,
    184, 187, 190–1, 199–200, 203–205, 207, 214,
    223, 225–7
Graecus, Bishop of Marseilles, 181, 183
Gratian, 8, 29, 82
Greece, 3, 118, 123, 211
Gundioc, 60, 105, 142–3, 171, 176
Gundobad, xv, 152–3, 158, 161–2, 165–8, 170–1,
    176–8, 188, 219

Haemus Mountains, 211
Hebdomon, 122
Heraclea Sintica, 135
Heraclius, Eastern general, 127–9, 131, 135–6
Heraclius, Eunuch, 141–3
Hermeric, 56
Hermianus, 151
Heruli/Heruls, 60, 83, 119, 192, 200, 224

Hesychius, 61
Hilarus, Pope, xxi
Hilderic, 51, 93, 98, 109–11, 113–14, 141–6, 152, 178, 192, 205
Hippo Regius, 26–7
Hispalis, 23–4
Hispania, 4–6, 9, 13–14, 20–5, 27–9, 31, 34, 51–2, 57, 59–63, 65, 68, 77, 83, 85, 87–8, 90–4, 99–100, 103–106, 110–11, 113–15, 117–19, 122–4, 131, 141–5, 151, 157, 159, 200, 203, 218, 224, 228
Honoria, 5, 45–6
Honorius, 3–4, 13, 23, 25, 39, 82, 120–1
Huneric, 39, 44, 46, 48, 50–1, 88–90, 93, 96, 107–108, 152, 190, 201–204
Huns, 4–5, 8, 12, 27, 29, 31–3, 39, 46, 49, 53, 80–1, 97, 100–101, 118, 120, 127, 142–3, 181, 213, 220, 223
Hydatius, xvii, xxi, 22, 46–7, 50, 58, 60, 81, 83, 90–1, 93, 96, 105, 108, 111, 113, 115, 117, 119, 123, 125

Iberia, xv, 4, 25, 85, 93, 99, 184, 200
Iberians (Caucasus), 127
Ibiza, 90–1
Ilerda, 25
Illus, 204–205, 212
Illyricum, 3–4, 8, 29–34, 42, 51–2, 54–5, 76, 83, 97, 100–101, 103–104, 118, 120, 123, 144, 174, 211, 224
Interregnum, 62–3, 65, 67, 82, 101, 103, 115–16, 165, 187, 226–7
Ira River, 94
Isauria, 127, 148, 170, 180
Italy, xiii, xv–xvii, 4–6, 8–9, 14, 17, 23, 25–30, 32, 34–5, 39–40, 42, 45–9, 51–7, 59–63, 65, 67–72, 76–8, 80–1, 83, 85, 87–9, 92, 94, 96–7, 99–106, 108–10, 114, 116–23, 125, 136–8, 144–8, 151, 153–4, 157, 159, 165–205, 207–208, 210, 212–19, 224–7
Iuthungi, 28, 53, 55
Izonso River, Battle of, 214

John, Usurper, 4, 23, 25, 27, 67
John, Eastern commander, 134
Julian Alps, 31, 55
Julian, Emperor, 53, 68
Julian, St, Church of, 62
Julius Nepos see Nepos
Justin, 179

Laeti, 16–17
Lauriacum, 146
Law Code of Euric see Euric, Law Code of
Lazi, 127
Leges Porcia see Porcian Laws
Lemovices, 148

Leo, consiliarius, 145
Leo I, Eastern Emperor, 63, 67–8, 70, 75–6, 82–3, 86, 94, 101–102, 104, 107–108, 110, 114–23, 125, 127–31, 135–6, 144–5, 148–51, 154–7, 159–62, 165, 167, 170, 174, 202, 211
Leo II, Eastern Emperor, 170–1, 180
Leontia, 149–50, 155
Leontius, Bishop of Arles, 181
Leo, Pope, 49
Libius Severus see Severus
Licinia Eudoxia see Eudoxia
Liguria, 149
Lilybaeum, 190, 201
Limitanei, 15–16, 19, 21, 33, 73, 166
Lisbon, 68
Litorius, 35
Livila, 215
Loire River, 29, 54, 138, 142, 144–6, 174, 207
Longinus, 214
Lucania, 102
Lucullanum, 193
Lucus, 85, 87, 93
Lusitania, 23–4, 61, 68, 83, 124, 141
Lyon, 63, 65, 68, 74–5, 78–80, 82, 105, 169

Macedonia, 8, 138, 210, 212
Macon, 100
Magister militum (praesentalis), xiii, xv, 3–5, 13, 17–18, 22–5, 29, 39, 45, 53, 55, 58, 61–2, 67, 70, 77, 81, 85, 94, 96, 99, 101, 105–106, 115, 118–19, 125, 127, 142–3, 146, 148, 160–2, 165, 167–8, 170, 176–8, 180–1, 185, 190, 205, 211–12, 214–15, 218, 227
Magister militum Dalmatiae, 86, 104, 144, 170
Magister militum Hispaniae, 105–106, 114–15
Magister militum per Gallias, 4, 53, 58, 61, 73, 97, 104–105, 152, 204
Magister militum per Illyricum, 120, 211
Magister militum per Thracias, 127, 170
Magister officiorum, 17, 80, 146, 155
Magnus Maximus, 3, 40
Magnus of Narbonne, 79–80
Majorca, 90
Majorian, 43, 57–97, 99–103, 105, 107, 109, 113, 115–16, 120, 122, 131, 133, 135–6, 159–60, 219–20, 224, 227
    Possible marriage to Pulcheria/Eudoxia, 39–40, 44
    Retirement, 40, 42
    Comes domesticorum, 42, 55
    Defeats Vandals in Corsica, 59
    Death of Avitus, 62
    Magister equitum, 67
    Crowned emperor, 68–71
    negotiations with Marcellinus, 76, 85–6
    Retakes Gaul, 78–83
    Campaign in Hispania, 83, 87

Campaign against the Vandals, 88–93
Death, 94
Maldras, 61, 68, 77, 83, 85, 87
Mansuetus, 25
Marcelliniana, Coniuriato *see* Coniuriato
  Marcelliniana
Marcellinus, 32–5, 42, 51–2, 55, 76–7, 83–5, 97,
  99–101, 103–107, 114–15, 118, 120–1, 123–5,
  128–9, 131, 134, 136–7, 140, 144, 146, 159,
  170, 172, 181, 203, 217–18
Friendship with Aetius, 33
Declares independence, 42
Possible invasion of Africa, 123–4
In Sicily, 85–87
Refuses to acknowledge Ricimer, 97
Ricimer bribes Huns in Sicily, 97
And the campaign of 86, 129, 131, 134, 136
death, 136–7, 140
Marcellus, 63
Marcian, Eastern Emperor, 5, 8, 32, 54–6, 66–7,
  101, 119–20, 149–50
Marcian(us), son of Anthemius, 120, 155, 211, 479
Maritsa River, 30
Marius of Avenches, 58
Marseilles, 169, 174, 200
Marsus, 127, 135
Martylis *see* Mertola
Mauretania, 22–3, 26, 70
Mauretania Sitifensis, 26
Mausoleum of Majorian, 94
Maximianus, 43
Maximus, Petronius, 39–53, 58, 194
Mediterranean, 6, 22, 56, 87, 89–90, 93,
  105–106, 108, 118, 124–5, 128, 146, 156, 190,
  203, 227
Mercurium *see* Cap Bon
Mertola, 24
Messianus, 53, 61
Messius Phoebus Severus, 120
Milan, 28, 39, 147, 153, 203, 214
Milan, Sack of, 28, 39
Misenum, 76, 88
Mithraism, 10
Modestus, 155
Moesia, 208
Moesia Secunda, 211
Moors, 55–6, 69, 101
Moselle River, 113

Narbonne, 53, 63, 75, 78, 80, 105–106, 112
  given to Goths, 105–106
Navy, Rome, 59, 76, 87, 89–91, 130
Navy, Vandal, 88–9, 91, 107
Nedao River, Battle of, 39, 80
Neoplatonic, 120
Nepos, Julius, 77, 104, 144, 170–2, 174, 176–89,
  194, 197–9, 203–204, 216–17, 219

invades Italy and becomes Emperor, 171–2,
  174
appoints Ecdicius, 177
appoints Orestes, 181
Treaty with Goths, 182
rebellion of Orestes and flight from Italy,
  185–6
envoys to Zeno, 197
death, 203
Nepotianus, 77, 81, 85, 87, 90, 93, 97, 99,
  104–105, 168, 172, 174
Nicephorus Callistus, 40
Nicopolis, 179
Nola, Sack of, 59
Nori, 28, 31, 53, 55
Noricum, xix, 8, 28–31, 100, 121, 123, 137, 146,
  167, 203, 208–209
Noricum Mediterraneum, 30, 146
Notitia Dignitatum, 14–16, 129
Numidia, 26

Odovacer, xiii, 144, 191–4, 197–205, 207–208,
  212–17
kills Orestes, 192–3
Rex or Patricius, 198–9
Treaty with Goths, 199–200
Treaty with Vandals, 200–201
revolts against, 201–202
invades Dalmatia, 204
problems with Zeno, 205, 207–208
Theoderic the Amal invades Italy, 212–15
death, 215
Olybrius, 44, 50–1, 93, 108, 116, 154–7, 159–62,
  168, 173, 202
and Placidia, 44, 108
Gaiseric support for, 122
sent to Italy, 154–6
emperor, 156–7
appoints Gundobad, 161
death, 162
Ostia, 88, 155, 171–2
Ostrogoths, xii, xvi, 32, 84, 101, 107, 121, 141,
  144, 169–70, 205, 213–15
invasion of Italy, 212–15
Ovida, 203–204

Paeonius, 63, 79–80
Palatina/palatinae, 15–16
Palatine, 157
Palladius, 44, 46, 48, 51
Pamplona, 141
Pannonia, 54, 75–6, 83, 101, 144, 180–1, 188,
  210
Pannonia, Diocese of, 29, 31–2
Pannonia I, 8, 29, 31
Pannonia II, 8, 29, 31–2
Papianilla, 62

Paris, 110–11, 142
Patiens, 169
Patricius, 33, 40, 53, 61, 67, 70, 94, 96, 119–21, 127, 149, 170, 176, 178, 181, 193, 198–9, 204–205, 211, 216
Patricius, son of Aspar, 149
Patrimony, 107, 202
Paul, Count, 143–5
Paulinus of Nola, 59
Paulinus of Pella, 58
Paulus, brother of Orestes, 187–8, 193
Pavia, xix, 94, 149, 173
Pelagians, 138
Peloponnesus, 118
Persia/Persians, 52, 107, 127, 205
Petronius Maximus see Maximus, Petronius
Petrus, 78, 82
Phylarchus, 104, 107
Piacenza, 193
Piacenza, Battle of, 61
Pierius, 208, 213–14
Placentia see Piacenza
Placidia, 44, 50, 93, 96, 102, 116, 121, 154–5, 202
Po River, 42, 147, 199
Pollentia, Battle of, 4
Pons Anicionis, 153
Ponte Nomentano, 153
Ponte Salario, 153
Porcian Laws, 14
Portus Illicitanus, 90
Praefectus praetorio Italiae, 40
Praefectus Urbi Romae, 40
Praetor, 40
Primenius, 203
Priscus, xvi, 47–8, 78, 106–108, 127, 136, 157
Procopius Anthemius, 120, 211
Procopius, historian, xvi, 31, 40, 42, 51, 56, 94, 118, 120, 125, 128–33, 135, 137, 191, 212, 216
Procopius, Usurper, 120
Provence, 175, 180, 182, 184, 189, 200–201, 227–8
Pseudocomitatenses, 16
Pulcheria, release from Africa, 108
Pusaeus, 120

Quintanis, 146

Radagaisus, 4, 27
Raetia, 28, 67, 203
Ragnachar, 205–206
Ravenna, 42, 55, 58–9, 67–8, 70–1, 76, 82, 102, 122, 165, 167, 171–2, 174, 185, 187–8, 190, 193, 201, 208, 214, 216
Ravenna, Siege of, 214
Rechiarius, 60–1
Rechimundus, 77, 83, 93
Recitach, 212

Remismund, 111, 118–19, 124
Remistus, 53, 55, 58–9, 61
Rheims, 100
Rhodope, 211
Rhodope Mountains, 30
Rhone River, 148, 151
Ricimer, 56–65, 67–72, 77, 80–1, 83, 85, 87, 89, 94–107, 109–23, 127, 136, 140, 142–3, 146–61, 165, 167–8, 171, 178, 180, 188, 192, 217–20
    youth/early career, 56–7
    Battle of Agrigentum, 57
    deposes Avitus, 59–62
    Battle of Piacenza, 61
    defeats Vandal raid, 69–70
    crowning of Majorian, 70–2
    death of Majorian, 94–6
    bribes Huns of Marcellinus, 97, 100
    nominates Severus, 102
    Battle of Bergamum, 110
    Death of Severus, 115
    and Anthemius, 120
    marriage to Alypia, 121
    death of Marcellinus, 136–7
    trial of Romanus, 146–7
    rebels against Anthemius, 147–8
    betrothal of Anthemius and Leontia, 149
    truce with Anthemius, 149–50
    civil war resumes, 151
    and Olybrius, 154–7
    death of Anthemius, 157–8
    death, 160
Riothamus, 142–3, 178
Riparienses, 15–16
Romanus, 146–7
Rome, 4, 6–7, 9, 11–14, 20, 22, 24, 27, 36, 40, 42–7, 49–59, 62, 64–5, 67, 71, 74–8, 82–3, 85–9, 92–7, 101–109, 114–16, 118, 120–3, 133, 138, 141, 143, 145, 147–8, 151–60, 167–8, 171–2, 174, 177, 183–7, 190, 197–8, 200–201, 218–19, 222–3, 225–7
Rome, Gothic Sack of 410, 4
Rome, Sack of 472, 158
Rome, Vandal sack of 455, 49–53, 87
Romulus, Augustus/Augustulus, 187–94, 197, 200, 208, 216, 219, 226
    crowned Augustus, 188
    sends letter to Zeno, 193–4, 197
    deposed and exiled, 193
Romulus, father-in-law of Orestes, 187
Romulus, son of Anthemius, 120
Rugi, 75, 208, 212–15, 224
Ruteni, 148

Salian Franks see Franks
Salla, 119
Salona, 33, 42, 172, 185, 203
Saracen, 129

Sardinia, xv, 6, 70, 108, 125, 127, 129, 131–2, 136–7, 190
Sarmatians, 32, 210, 214
Sava River, 32–3
Savia, 8, 30
Saxons, 98, 114, 145
Scallabis, 87, 93
Scholae palatinae, 15–16, 166
Sciri, 118, 121, 144, 192, 224
Sebastian, son of Boniface, 5
Serdica, 120
Serena, 3
Serpentius *see* Severus
Severinus, St, xix, 146, 192
Severus, ambassador, 178–9
Severus Livius, Emperor, 97, 102–106, 108–10, 113, 115–17, 160
    nicknamed Serpentius, 102
    reappoints Agrippinus magister militum per Gallias, 105
    appoints Gundioc magister militum per Gallias, 105
    death, 115
Seville *see* Hispalis
Sicily, 6, 56–9, 67, 69, 85–7, 89–90, 97, 100–101, 108, 115, 118, 123–4, 131–2, 134, 136–7, 169, 186, 190, 201, 203, 217
Sidonius Apollinaris, 8, 46, 48, 53–5, 57, 62–3, 68–70, 75–6, 80–2, 89, 115, 121–2, 138–42, 145–6, 149, 169, 175–9, 181, 183–4, 200, 225–6
    supports father-in-law Avitus, 53–5
    made tribunus et notarius, 53
    pardoned by Majorian and gives panegyric, 82
    urban prefecture, 122
    resigns prefecture, 138
    dilemma over service with Goths, 145
    defends Clermont, 169, 175–6
    capture of Clermont, 179
    pleased with negotiations, 181
    dismayed by treaty with Goths, 183–4
    praises Euric, 200
Soissons, 100, 109, 142, 144, 203, 205–207
Soissons, Battle of, 203–204
Sondis, Mount, 211
Sophia, St, Church of, 135
Spain *see* Hispania
Spinio, 93
Split, 33
Stilicho, 3–4, 8, 13, 17, 29–30, 70–1, 121, 153, 161
Straits of Gibraltar, xv, 23, 27, 90, 96, 123
Succi Pass, 30
Sueves, 4–6, 21–5, 28, 42, 51, 54, 56–7, 60–1, 68, 77, 83, 85, 87, 90, 93–4, 99, 110–11, 114, 117–19, 122, 124, 140–1, 218, 224
Suniericus, 83, 85, 87, 93

Syagrius, 111, 119, 142–6, 152, 178–9, 192, 200, 204–207
    death, 207

Tarasicodissa *see* Zeno
Tarraco, 23
Tarraconensis, 9, 24–5, 60, 141
Tatulus, 187
Tetrarch, 177–8
Thaumastus, 176–7
Thebaid, 129
Thela, 214–15
Theoderic I, Gothic king, 53, 180
Theoderic II, Gothic king, 25, 29, 53–4, 57–8, 60–1, 63, 65, 68, 73, 75, 77–8, 80–3, 85, 87, 92, 99, 104–106, 109–15, 118–19, 168
    kills Thorismund, 29
    nominates Avitus, 53
    attacks Narbonne, 78
    attacks Arles, 80–1
    defeated in battle, 81
    becomes leading power in Spain, 99
    gains Narbonne, 105
    gains right to appoint magister in Spain, 105, 115, 168
    possible implication in Aegidius' death, 113
    death, 119
Theoderic, Strabo, 101, 205, 209, 211, 217
Theoderic the Amal (Theoderic I of Italy), xiii, xvii, 203, 205, 207–17
    hostage in Constantinople, 209
    becomes king, 210
    relations with East, 209–11
    invasion of Italy, 213
    wins Battle of the River Ulca, 213–14
    defeats the Sarmatians, 214
    wins Battle of the River Izonso, 214
    enters Milan besieged in Ticinum, 214
    wins Battle of the River Addua, 214
    lays siege to Ravenna, 214–15
    Treaty with and death of Odovacer, 215
Theodosius I, 3, 6, 8, 12, 46, 67, 93, 116, 120
Theodosius II, 4, 31, 67, 110–11
Theophanes, 40, 102, 135, 216
Thessaly, 212
Thiudimer, 169, 210
Thoringi *see* Thuringi
Thorisarius, 151
Thorismund, 29
Thrace, 31, 118, 120, 127, 135, 211–12
Thraustila, 43
Thuringi/ans, 73, 119, 146, 200
Tiber River, 48, 153, 157–8
Ticinum, 192–3, 214
Ticinum, Siege of, 214
Tingitana, 27
Tivoli, 150

Torcilingi, 192
Tortona, 94
Toulouse, 45, 52–3, 114, 119, 206
Trajan's Gate *see* Succi Pass
Trapstila, 214
Trento *see* Tridentum
Tribunus et notarius, 40, 53, 68
Tributarii, 16–17
Tridentum, 215
Trier, 66, 73, 100, 106, 111, 113, 142
Tripolis, 129, 131–2, 146
Tripolis, Battle of, 129
Tripolitana, 125, 127, 129, 136
Troyes, 146, 148
Tufa, 214–15
Tyrrhenian Sea, 59, 89

Ugernum *see* Viernum
Ulca River, 213
Ulixippona *see* Lisbon
Urbicus River, Battle of, 60

Valamer I, 84, 101, 104, 120
Valens, 3, 11, 122, 132, 138
Valentinian III, xiii, 4–8, 12–13, 29, 26–7, 31, 35,
    39–51, 56, 71, 82, 88, 93, 100, 102, 107–108,
    116, 121, 138, 152, 202, 226, 228
Valeria, 8, 30
Valila, 150, 168
Vandals, xiii, xv–xvii, xix, 4–6, 10–12, 14, 20,
    22–8, 31, 35, 39, 42, 44–6, 48–9, 51–2, 54–61,

66–7, 69–70, 72, 76–7, 85–91, 93, 97, 101,
    103, 108–11, 115, 118–21, 123–5, 127, 129–
    31, 133–5, 141, 146, 157, 159, 165, 178–81,
    184, 187, 190, 199, 201–204, 217, 220, 224–5
Vandals, Asding, 23
Vandals, Siling, 23
Vascones, 200
Vellavi, 148
Verina, 127, 130, 135, 198, 205
Verona, 204, 214–15
Verona, Battle of, 4
Vaison, 177–8
Viator, 203
Vice dominus, 199
Victorius, 143, 148
Viernum, 53
Vincentius, 167–8
Vitus, 24
Vouille, Battle of, 207
Vulca River *see* Ulca River

Wallia, 23, 56
Warni, 119, 200

Zaragoza, 141
Zeno (Tarasicodissa), 118, 135, 148, 170–1, 174,
    178–81, 185–7, 193–4, 197–200, 202–205,
    208–209, 211–15, 217